Murdering Miss Marple

ALSO EDITED BY JULIE H. KIM

*Race and Religion in the Postcolonial British
Detective Story: Ten Essays* (McFarland, 2005)

Murdering Miss Marple

*Essays on Gender and Sexuality
in the New Golden Age of
Women's Crime Fiction*

Edited by JULIE H. KIM

McFarland & Company, Inc., Publishers
Jefferson, North Carolina, and London

LIBRARY OF CONGRESS CATALOGUING-IN-PUBLICATION DATA

Murdering Miss Marple : essays on gender and sexuality in the new golden age of women's crime fiction / edited by Julie H. Kim.
    p.   cm.

Includes bibliographical references and index.

ISBN 978-0-7864-6331-2
softcover : acid free paper ∞

1. Detective and mystery stories, English — History and criticisim. 2. Women and literature — English-speaking countries. 3. Gender identity in literature. I. Kim, Julie H.
PR888.D4M88 2012
823'.0872099287 — dc23   2011053179

BRITISH LIBRARY CATALOGUING DATA ARE AVAILABLE

© 2012 Julie H. Kim. All rights reserved

No part of this book may be reproduced or transmitted in any form or by any means, electronic or mechanical, including photocopying or recording, or by any information storage and retrieval system, without permission in writing from the publisher.

Cover images © 2012 Shutterstock

Manufactured in the United States of America

McFarland & Company, Inc., Publishers
  Box 611, Jefferson, North Carolina 28640
  www.mcfarlandpub.com

For my family

Table of Contents

Introduction: Re-Imagining Gender and Sexuality in Women's Crime Fiction
  JULIE H. KIM 1

Nancy Drew vs. Nancy Clue: Girl Sleuths Discover Their Sexualities

1. Configuring Space and Sexuality: Nancy Drew Enters *The Bluebeard Room*
   MICHAEL G. CORNELIUS 13

2. Not-So-Nice, Indeed: Mabel Maney, Girl Detectives, and Sexual Awakenings
   JENNIFER MITCHELL 36

Long Ago, in Places Far Away: Gender Subversion in Detective Fiction Period Pieces

3. Repopulating the Margins: Rhys Bowen's Treatment of Gender, History, and Power
   KELLEY WEZNER 61

4. Assuming Identities: Strategies of Drag in Laurie R. King's Mary Russell Series
   MEGAN HOFFMAN 81

Genre vs. Gender, Sexuality, Race, and Class

5. Genre-Bending in Neely's Blanche White Series: Testing the Limits of Crime Fiction
   BETSY YOUNG 101

6. "W" Is for Woman: Deconstructing the Private Dick in Sue Grafton's Alphabet Series
   HEATH A. DIEHL 120

Language and Gender, Narrative and Sexuality: Rhetorics of Identity and Desire

7. Melancholia, Narrative Objectivity and the Eyewitness: The Role of the Narrator in Barbara Vine's *A Dark-Adapted Eye* and *The Minotaur*
   ANDREW HOCK SOON NG 143

8. Postfeminism(s) and Authority in Contemporary Glasgow Police Procedurals
   PETER CLANDFIELD 167

(De)constructed Body and Sexual Psychopathy: Serial Killing of Gender Binaries

9. Beyond Gender and Sexuality: The Serial Killers of Val McDermid
   NEIL MCCAW 191

10. Neither Victim nor Vixen: Reading the Female Detective's Receding Body and Textual Violence
    WINTER S. ELLIOTT   211

About the Contributors 231

Index 233

Introduction
Re-Imagining Gender and Sexuality in Women's Crime Fiction

JULIE H. KIM

As I re-read it for a recent course I taught on detective fiction, I was surprised to discover how much a favorite Miss Marple mystery (*A Murder Is Announced*) seemed to dig in its heels and declare — even at the moment of its publication in 1950 — its very old-fashioned-ness, as if self-conscious yet defiant about its status as already "classic" detective fiction. While Miss Marple in Agatha Christie's post–World War II mystery referenced the new "tough style" of hard-boiled American writer Dashiell Hammett, the rest of the spinster sleuth's generation seemed intent on calling attention to her datedness, with her contemporary Sir Henry Clithering repeatedly (and cringe-inducingly) proclaiming her an "old pussy," the "four-starred pussy. The super pussy of all old pussies."[1] Gill Plain in her 2001 study, *Twentieth Century Crime Fiction: Gender, Sexuality and the Body*, talks about the "death of the detective" brought about by the advent of the "monstrous" and "deviant" feminized other.[2] The essays in this collection deal not with the death of the *male* detective but with the murder of Miss Marple's image by a brave new generation of female crime fiction writers who reconsider and recast issues of gender and sexuality in ways probably inconceivable to those women who wrote during the first "Golden Age" of detective fiction.

During the interwar Golden Age of British detective fiction, notable women writers reigned sovereign in the field of mystery. Writers like Dorothy L. Sayers, Ngaio Marsh, and most significantly Agatha Christie introduced their now-famous sleuths to a mass audience which gobbled up one page-turning mystery after another. These writers meticulously plotted their mysteries and set them in cozy villages, loaded them with locked-room puzzles, psychological studies, and eccentric detectives. Sure, gender played an important role: Miss Marple is one of the earliest and still one of the most popular women detectives. And sex? Well, there were awkward scenes aplenty between Sayers' Lord Peter Wimsey and writer Harriet Vane or between Marsh's Inspector Alleyn and artist Agatha Troy. Any reader of Christie will also vouch for the fact that the Queen of Crime had a weakness for young lovers' dilemmas. But elements of sexuality and gender as we know it in today's crime fiction — soft porn, sexual psychopathy, or bisexual heroines— were hardly publishing imperatives in the classic mysteries of the 1930s.

So what happened? One could say half a century happened. While no such momentous change occurred between Wilkie Collins's or Sir Arthur Conan Doyle's works from the 1870s through the 1890s and those of the Golden Age writers some fifty years hence, crime fiction of the 1980s onward — the subject of this collection — treats gender and sexuality in radically different ways than they had been dealt with by writers on either side of the Atlantic, male or female, in the 1930s and '40s.[3] I do not mean to suggest that there was a singular cataclysmic shift in the treatment of gender and sexuality during the intervening decades. After all, the extraordinary longevity of Agatha Christie's popularity allowed her to publish novels featuring her "spinster" detective into the 1970s, thereby ensuring a measure of continuity and stability — dare I say stagnation?— to the genre. Yet it cannot be denied that by the 1980s, many popular women writers— the Americans Sara Paretsky and Sue Grafton, or the English P.D. James— reconceptualized what it meant to be a female detective.

Scholars of detective fiction suggest intriguing theories regarding the upsurge of interest in gender issues and the proliferation of women in mysteries, both as writers and detectives, in the last quarter of the twentieth century. Perhaps it was the publication of Betty Friedan's *The Feminine Mystique* in 1963 that later ushered in a new, more feminist, strain of interest — effectively staging "second wave" women's detective fiction. Conversely, maybe the recent rise in women's crime fiction is a response to the conservative backlash in the 1980s against feminist agendas set forth in the 1960s and '70s. Or did the death of Agatha Christie early in 1976 give birth to a new generation of women writers freed at last from the influence of the long-established mistress of classic mystery genre? Many agree that Marcia Muller's 1977 introduction of Sharon McCone in *Edwin of the Iron Shoes* gave the reading public its first real "hard-boiled" female detective. But perhaps P.D. James paved the way by creating in 1972 a "'countertraditional' professional female private investigator," Cordelia Gray in *An Unsuitable Job for a Woman*.[4] Even sharper differences can be identified in depictions of sexuality from the 1980s on — a period identified by *Publishers Weekly*, and recognized by most scholars, as a "New Golden Age of Mysteries"[5]— wherein readers are treated to the subtle psychosexual teasing in Barbara Vine (pen name of Ruth Rendell), confronted with the destructive and mutilating psychopathy in Val McDermid, and offered everything imaginable in between. Meanwhile, the almost strictly heterosexual detecting landscape has altered to accommodate gay, lesbian, bisexual, and transgendered characters not only in minor roles but showcased as lead detectives. While the questions of *why, how,* or *when* of the shifts are fascinating, this collection is ultimately not dealing with those issues.[6] That is, we are not looking at the topics of gender and sexuality as they transition between the 1930s and the 1980s. Instead, we jump into the 1980s and go beyond to examine the ways gender and sexuality have been reimagined by another, and quite different, Golden Age of women crime fiction writers.

Gender and Sexuality

No monolithic formula can be articulated for the last few decades of women's crime fiction. Since both liberal feminist protagonists *and* "post"-feminist detectives inhabit the same field, a study of gender and sexuality in contemporary crime fiction produces exciting and diverse interpretations, and the essays in this collection accordingly represent heterogeneous readings of this topic. So, the goal of this brief introduction is to clarify the general parameters of this study by staging the scene and identifying key concepts and questions to be treated more fully and specifically in the individual essays that follow.

When P. D. James's *Unsuitable Job for a Woman* introduced female private investigator Cordelia Gray in 1972, the reading public was already familiar with the authoritative male detective eminently *more* suitable for the job of criminal investigations—like James's own Adam Dalgliesh. Since then, titular spinoffs in critical analysis of women's crime fiction—for instance, "An Unsuitable Job for a Feminist?" by Kathleen Gregory Klein or "An Unsuitable Genre for a Woman?" by Sally Munt[7]—clearly indicate not only that women occupy an uncomfortable space in the traditionally conservative field of (especially hard-boiled) detective fiction but also that a lot of women still choose to crowd that space, and to write critically about encroaching upon that generically "masculine" territory. Perhaps we are all protesting too much though. Even taking social conservatism of male hard-boiled fiction as a given, women have hardly been underrepresented as author, detective, or reader in the field of detective fiction since at least the 1920s.[8] Winter S. Elliott presents some interesting statistics about the number of women reading and writing crime fiction, and she quotes Klein who describes a "woman-oriented trio of writer, detective/text, and reader."[9] But, of course, there *is* a marked difference in women's detective fiction of the last few decades.

In the introduction to her edited collection *Women Times Three: Writers, Detectives, Readers*, Kathleen Klein points out that women mystery writers today overwhelmingly choose to write about the "woman detective as protagonist"—unlike the majority of the Golden Age writers. Klein's essay, published in 1995, continues:

> Contemporary women-centered novels, even those not explicitly called feminist, are using the formula of traditional mystery fiction to trace a new investigation.... In these reworkings, readers can find what might be called archeological strata in layers of revisionist thinking about mystery fiction, women in society, authority, crime, and social justice.... The stereotype of the woman detective—the elderly spinster, the naïve young woman, the bored housewife—has never been easy to sustain. The contemporary crop of detecting women is not only a critique of those earlier stereotypes and a promise for women's roles in a more open future society but also a challenge to the limitations of women's current roles.[10]

This assessment encompasses past, present, and future: Klein suggests that women's detective fiction up to early 1990s is concerned with critiquing—and hopefully liberating female detective figures from—past stereotypes of spinster or housewife and promising better in a "more open *future* society" while offering a "challenge to the limitations" of women's present roles. In other words, aims are to depict more *realistic* and *aspirational* female detectives.

Tracing the history of liberal feminist contributions to detective fiction, Sally Munt appears to arrive at the same conclusion about the literature of the 1980s but with a slightly different appraisal for the 1990s. Munt suggests that

> the heyday for feminist crime novels was the 1980s. They are an expression of the decade of Thatcherism and Reaganism which reified an individualist, urban culture. The popularity of the sub-genre, by the beginning of the 1990s, began to decline. The historical moment is an important aspect in understanding the appearance of a literary form which has managed to be both comforting and challenging to readers. By offering women a fantasy of individualized power and control, ensconced within a consumer culture, readerly pleasures packaged within a "right-on" aesthetic became a passport to the more radical effects of these novels in producing an actual (if temporary) change of consciousness.[11]

In some ways, essays in our own collection—treating more works in the 1990s and beyond than those of the 1980s—support Munt's theories. Works published during the late 1990s or 2000s no longer package the "fantasy" of a superwoman—or appear to strain credibility, and invite criticism, when they do. Instead, many works—even mainstream popular series—do not content themselves with strenuously questioning previously accepted binaries of men-as-capable and women-as-unsuitable but proceed even further, as Peter Clandfield argues in Chapter 8, to challenge and guard "against simplistic assumptions that power for women is always and only a sovereign good."

Women's crime fiction of the 1980s on is balanced precariously between advancing a view of idealized can-do-everything female protagonist for women still yearning for equality and a later perspective which appears to critique crime-fiction-as-social-promotion — or at least recognizes that "equal opportunity" can carry different, and not always positive, meanings. Thus, one of the assumptions we can make about this collection is that we are scrutinizing gender (and sexuality) in women's crime novels which do not necessarily endorse a viewpoint that women are always victims, always oppressed, or even always right. Though liberatory empowering feminism is not exactly shunned (in works analyzed in several early chapters, for instance), many of the works studied in this collection (especially those considered in Chapters 8, 9, 10) nuance and complicate depictions of gender and sexuality in contemporary women's detective fiction.

Another assumption we can make about this collection is that gender and sexuality cannot be separated. Perhaps it is just barely possible that we can talk about gender without broaching sexuality, but it is nearly impossible to tackle issues of sexuality without recognizing concomitant gender issues. Essays in this collection are not treating gender *or* sexuality — and while individual essays might focus *more* on one than the other topic, it is rarely at the exclusion of the other. For instance, while essays on Rhys Bowen, Laurie R. King, and Barbara Neely might appear more explicitly to discuss gender identities, issues of sexual tension or desirability or (im)potency still intrude upon these works, even if not entirely overwhelming analyses of gender within the essays themselves.

Further, we might start with accepting, at the outset, Judith Butler's ideas not only about the cultural constructedness of gender but also its "performativity." Many essays in this collection — especially those that identify strategies of "drag" and those that treat homosexuality, bisexuality, and transgendered identity — owe much to Butler's studies. In *Gender Trouble,* she writes about how the triad of sex-gender-sexuality resists easy classification. She argues that despite cultural pressures towards a "false stabilization of gender," such a "construction of coherence conceals the gender discontinuities that run rampant within heterosexual, bisexual, and gay and lesbian contexts in which gender does not necessarily follow from sex, and desire, or sexuality generally, does not seem to follow from gender."[12] That is — at the risk of oversimplifying Butler — one's "natural sex" (also a vexed term) does not necessarily denote one's "gender" (as masculine/feminine), and one's "gender" does not determine one's "sexuality" (heterosexual, bisexual, gay, lesbian) —

no matter how much a patriarchal society wishes otherwise. In the genre of detective or crime fiction — widely perceived to be conservative in its original social agenda of restoration of status quo order — such issues of gender and sexuality (especially non-heteronormative kinds) can obviously create confusion and represent possibly irresolvable conflicts. Several essays in this collection tackle this thorny subject and do so by looking specifically at these sites of "gender discontinuities" within contemporary crime fiction.

About the Essays

At the most basic level, all essays in this collection treat some aspect of gender and/or sexuality in crime fiction written by British and American women (or a female front, in the case of Nancy Drew "author" Carolyn Keene) in the last few decades, with the earliest texts published in 1985 and 1986 and the most recent texts published in 2010 and 2011. They all are critically and theoretically informed, and they all present smart and interesting — and often quite novel — arguments about the texts under examination specifically and crime fiction more generally. Beyond these common denominators, the following essays are incredibly wide-ranging in subject matter, with the label "crime fiction" applying to works about girl sleuths, parodies and tributes, hard-boiled novels, police procedurals, psychological suspense, and recent serial killer series. Regardless of the varied subject matter, they are interrogating some or all of these important questions: What exactly is the relationship between "genre" and "gender"? Is it impossible to remain within the confines of a conservative genre like detective/crime fiction and still advocate for gender equality? To what extent is not only gender but even sexuality a "performance"? In what ways are these writers and their detectives participating in strategies of "drag"? Can we say that, especially in later works, we are leaving behind feminist ethos and entering into a field of "post-feminism"?

The order of these ten essays follow two basic guidelines: (1) they are roughly chronological according to the date of publication of the texts they treat; and (2) they are paired in such a way that we can look at the collection as offering five sets of studies on related sub-categories within the larger frame. The first two essays address some of our earliest works, published in 1985 and 1993; the next five cover the period between 1986 and 2005, with most of the works published in the 1990s; and the final three offer the most contemporary peeks at the issues of gender and sexuality in works published between 1995 and 2011. Chapters 1 and 2 are a natural fit: they study, respectively, a more sexually-aware Nancy Drew than had appeared in the earlier 76 volumes in the franchise and then an overtly sexualized and lesbian parody of Nancy Drew and other girl sleuths. Chapters 3 and 4 offer "period pieces" with the Molly Murphy series set in turn-of-the-century America and the Mary Russell series set in early twentieth-century England. Chapter 3's Evan Evans series and Chapter 4's Mary Russell series are also both set in Britain, with the Evans series set in a remote (though contemporary) Welsh village. Chapters 5 and 6 address the pressing critical question of whether the detective fiction convention can maintain its structural and thematic integrity and still pursue socially progressive goals in the area of ethnic and women's hard-boiled fiction. Chapters 7 and 8 offer some of the most theoretical readings of detective fiction in the ways these works deal with narrative, sexuality, and psychoanalysis (Chapter 7) and language, gender, and postfeminism (Chapter 8). Chapters 9 and 10 confront us with sexual psychopathy and the violence inflicted on bodies—both female and male—and these chapters, along with Chapter 8, more explicitly question the conventional binaries of women as weak and victimized and men as empowered victimizers.

Michael G. Cornelius starts off this collection with the declaration, "Until 1985, Nancy Drew was sexless." Thus begins a study of the first book in the long-running series that depicted a more sexually aware Nancy Drew, *The Bluebeard Room* (1985). Using aspects of space and feminist theory, the essay demonstrates that introducing sexuality into the girl-sleuth franchise quashes Nancy's identity as a detective. Based on her own fashioning, she cannot be both sexual and detective, because her detective authority derives from the lack of male figures that influence her life in any meaningful way. This is all played against the backdrop of the Bluebeard legend, a familiar fairy tale that—according to feminist critics—cautions about sexual curiosity and advocates for its containment. Cornelius argues that the Bluebeard legend and the sexual curiosity that accompanies it work to "contain" Nancy Drew herself in the book, and he points out that Nancy reverts to her "asexual" self two books later, restoring her prior authority.

Next, Jennifer Mitchell appears to enter into a dialogue with Michael Cornelius—or at least continue where he left off. Rather than allowing Nancy Drew to revert to her "asexual" self, Mabel Maney's lesbian parody/tribute pushes those traditional boundaries the sexually-curious Nancy started to encroach upon. Approaching Maney's *The Case of the Not-So-Nice Nurse* (1993) with Carolyn Keene's idyllic heroine in mind, Mitchell argues that Maney's project is a revision—and a "re-invention"—of the Nancy Drew brand. The essay argues that, through Nancy Clue, Maney is able to criticize and exploit conservative gender- and sexuality-based stereotypes by replacing them with significantly more controversial and political alternatives (like lesbianism, "butch" identity), though still presenting these alternatives simply as organic to the characters and the narratives of the girl-sleuth genre. Mitchell posits that reading Maney's text in light of contemporary theories of gender and sexuality enables us to "foster a reconsideration of the politics of innocence, discovery, heroics and friendship."

Kelley Wezner then compares two different series by Rhys Bowen to analyze the subversion of conventions represented by her protagonists to address both historical and current views of femininity. Wezner proposes that Evan Evans' success within the circumscribed sphere of (contemporary) Llanfair requires him to acquire knowledge and skills that the novels — and society at large — might code as feminine. By linking the acquisition of power and success to feminine norms, Bowen redefines and heightens the value of femininity. Similarly, Bowen uses Molly Murphy — an Irish immigrant operating on the margins of turn-of-century New York — to offer an alternative definition of female agency. While characters criticize and challenge her for deviating from contemporary gender expectations, the series not only refrains from subjecting her to disciplinary correction but also rewards her by tying those very deviations to her successful resolution of the crime. Wezner contends that Bowen's two series provide a palatable alternative to male/female and city/country binaries and suggests that the series' subversions of conventions is permitted, in part, by the restoration of order made possible by a wider range of available gender roles.

Megan Hoffman continues the thematic thread of gender subversion in her discussion of the ways Laurie R. King's Mary Russell novels use cross-dressing and other strategies of drag to subvert the masculine paradigms of Sir Arthur Conan Doyle's Sherlock Holmes stories. Though Sherlock Holmes is featured in this revisionist tribute series, he is upstaged by a young woman named Mary Russell. With the series, King creates the possibility of agency for a woman detective within the established framework of the conservative detective fiction genre through approaches like the appropriation and destabilizing of narrative control. Hoffman also analyzes how "drag" is employed in King's novels in order to question the original depiction of Holmes as masculine authority figure, revealing possibilities for multiplicity in his character that go beyond long-established interpretations. In the process, the Mary Russell novels question genre stereotypes by "undermining the assumptions that typically accompany the masculine detective figure and expose the potential for gender ambivalence already present in the Holmes stories."

Betsy Young's essay is one of several in this collection which contemplates the thorny intersection of genre (of detective fiction) and gender (of a female writer and protagonist). Barbara Neely's acclaimed Blanche White series of the 1990s added a new perspective to the evolving body of crime fiction by introducing an amateur detective who is an African American, staunchly feminist, domestic worker. That is, the genre butts heads not only with gender but also with race and class. While some critics have suggested that the traditionally conservative landscape of crime fiction constrained Neely's agenda, Young asserts that the opposite is true: it is precisely by putting Blanche and her tales into a "genre that's conservative in both ideology and form that Neely is able to showcase, by contrast, a black feminist voice and viewpoint." Blanche successfully exploits the tropes of African American literature and culture (including, for instance, references to hoodoo) to provide a platform and context for that voice. Young underscores the fact that Blanche's strong female identity is what gives power and urgency to her feminist voice, but also what ultimately leads her to a separatist stance and possibly, ironically, dilutes the power of that voice with the demise of the series.

Heath A. Diehl's contribution to this collection grapples with the recognized limitations of the detective fiction genre and, in doing so, perhaps might be responding to Kathleen Klein's concern that, when feminists attempt to write hard-boiled fiction, "either feminism or the formula is at risk."[13] On the flipside, as Maureen Reddy warns of in cases of merely superficial feminist approaches to detective fiction, "far too often, strong women detectives are found filling the (gum) shoes of strong male detectives, with only the gender changed."[14] Diehl lays out the terrain of scholarly study regarding women's hard-boiled fiction—concentrating on the critical reception to Sue Grafton's Kinsey Millhone "alphabet series"—and highlights a dilemma for feminist critics. Some critics view Grafton's Kinsey Millhone as a "gender traitor—a female P.I. who (figuratively) masquerades as a male" within the hard-boiled genre; others laud this same series as a "'radical' feminist intervention into a conventional, and oftentimes conventionally patriarchal, genre." Diehl's essay, planted firmly in the middle of this debate, maintains that Grafton's alphabet series centers on an ambivalence towards women's roles not only within the law enforcement profession but also within the traditionally conservative genre of hard-boiled detective fiction. Focusing specifically on Grafton's "*K" Is for Killer* (1994), Diehl concludes that Kinsey Millhone "occupies a conflicted position in relation to institutions of jurisprudence"—both as outsider (a female private investigator) and as insider (a former police officer).

Andrew Hock Soon Ng returns us to the British side of the Atlantic with his essay on two novels by Barbara Vine—*A Dark-Adapted Eye* (1986), Ruth Rendell's first novel under this pseudonym, and *The Minotaur* (2005). Ng's analysis of these two novels focuses on significant similarities in the ways both works represent women living in repressed environments and specifically the role of the female narrator in each novel who functions as the narrative's "detective." Seemingly neutral, and whose mission is merely to recount the events leading to the crime and to tie the threads of the plot together, the narrator is, nevertheless—according to Ng—the principal catalyst which exposes the fractured relationships between female family members. In fact, it is possible to read the narrator as the prime, if unwitting and even unaware, instigator of the crime. Deploying various relevant psychoanalytical frameworks, this essay explores the relationship between storytelling, sexuality, and the female criminal, with a particular focus on the family as a monstrous social unit. By looking at narrative tensions, gaps in memory, and the relationship between language and memory, Ng reveals an unconscious dynamic within narratives revolving around unacknowledged and unacknowledgeable desire.

Peter Clandfield continues this discussion about language and gender in contemporary crime fiction by concentrating on works by two female Scottish crime novelists, Denise Mina and Karen Campbell. He starts by referencing Gill Plain's belief that crime fiction "has become a literature of self-assertion, endlessly pressuring its boundaries to satisfy audience demand, and to prove its own strength."[15] Clandfield suggests that this observation points to the contemporary prominence of female protagonists who are "defined by self-assertiveness in several intersecting spheres: professional, sexual, rhetorical." Though of different backgrounds—suspect in a crime, journalist, police officers—characters studied in this essay are linked by the attention their novels focus on the pitfalls of female assertiveness, especially linguistic assertiveness in the appropriation of curse words, in the ways these women control dialogue, and in their general readiness to engage in verbal conflict. Clandfield argues that these novels "gain strength as detective fictions by challenging and guarding against simplistic assumptions that power for women is always and only a sovereign good," and his consideration of the concept of "postfeminism" in this collection complicates—in a significant, critical way—issues of gender and sexuality we are confronting in contemporary detective fiction.

The final two contributors to this collection bring us more serial killers and brutal mutilation of bodies than could have been imagined by all Golden Age classic detective fiction writers put together. Neil McCaw starts his essay by reviewing current depictions of sexual psychopaths—both in real crime and fictional crime — in popular media. McCaw explains that while the figure of the male psychopath looms large in the work of many writers who depict men as familiarly stereotypical perpetrators, the novels of Val McDermid take this characterization several complex steps further. McCaw argues that "the Psychopath" in McDermid's novels stands not simply as an ultimate (if freakish) aspect of masculinity — with women the perennial subjects and victims— but rather as a broader cross-gendered embodiment of the most intense forms of violent sexuality and marginal sub-cultural practice. The consequence of McDermid's portrayal of lives lived far beyond the margins is that the boundaries between male and female, masculine and feminine, heterosexual and homosexual, blur, transgressing any easy notion of women as victims and men as perpetrators. Thus, concepts of "gender and sexuality are ultimately deconstructed in these works, shifting away from signs of coherent identity towards a more fluid, dialectical understanding of what gender might mean and how it is constructed and played out."

In our final essay, Winter S. Elliott broadens the focus on sexual psychopathy to include in her essay works not only of Val McDermid but also of Chelsea Cain and Marcia Muller. Like McCaw, Elliott believes that the tried-and-true woman-in-peril formula no longer recurs with as much frequency in crime novels written by women. Instead, increasingly, such books feature *female* detectives or protagonists as well as endangered *men*. Works like McDermid's *Mermaids Singing* and Chelsea Cain's *Heartsick* feature violence inflicted upon male bodies, bodies open and exhibited to the reader. In contrast, the body of the female detective herself appears almost to be receding from the reader's perspective in works like Marcia Muller's *Locked In,* within which the main character Sharon McCone (the original female hard-boiled detective) is literally "locked in" her body, unable to move, for the duration of the book. Concentrating on the reader's perspective/gaze, Elliott argues that the reader is invited to take over space often vacated by frozen or "locked in" detectives. However, she concludes that while these works appear to question the status quo, they ultimately do not "undermine" the system but merely deconstruct the traditional male/perpetrator-female/victim binaries to create equal-opportunity victims.

Notes

1. Agatha Christie, *A Murder Is Announced* (1950; New York: Penguin Putnam, 2001), 74, 68.
2. Gill Plain, *Twentieth-Century Crime Fiction: Gender, Sexuality and the Body* (Edinburgh: Edinburgh University Press, 2001), 245–6.
3. Even works of male American hard-boiled writers with their "dames," Madonna/Whore complexes, and rampant misogyny did not feature overtly sexual scenes — and certainly not many culture-defying progressive women figures.
4. Priscilla L. Walton and Manina Jones, *Detective Agency: Women Rewriting the Hard-Boiled Tradition* (Berkeley: University of California Press, 1999), 16. For various discussions about this very productive period of women writing mysteries (1970s and especially the 1980s and beyond), one might also consult some of the following works: Kathleen Gregory Klein, *The Woman Detective: Gender and Genre* (Urbana: University of Illinois Press, 1988; second edition, 1995); Maureen T. Reddy, *Sisters in Crime: Feminism and the Crime Novel* (New York: Continuum, 1988); Sally R. Munt, *Murder by the Book? Feminism and the Crime Novel* (London: Routledge, 1994); Glenwood Irons, ed., *Feminism in Women's Detective Fiction* (Toronto: University of Toronto Press, 1995); Kimberly

J. Dilley, *Busybodies, Meddlers, and Snoops: The Female Hero in Contemporary Women's Mysteries* (Westport, Connecticut: Greenwood Press, 1998); Gill Plain, *Twentieth-Century Crime Fiction: Gender, Sexuality and the Body* (Edinburgh: Edinburgh University Press, 2001); Lee Horsley, *Twentieth-Century Crime Fiction* (Oxford: Oxford University Press, 2005).

    5. Walton and Jones, *Detective Agency*, 24.
    6. Again, consult the brief list in note 4 above.
    7. Klein's essay can be found in *The Woman Detective*, and Sally Munt's essay in *Murder by the Book?*
    8. See Walton and Jones, *Detective Agency*, "The Private Eye and the Public: Professional Women Detectives and the Business of Publishing."
    9. Kathleen Klein, "Women Times Women Times Women," in *Women Times Three: Writers, Detectives, Readers*, ed. Kathleen Klein (Bowling Green: Bowling Green State University Popular Press, 1995), 13.
    10. Klein, "Women Times Women Times Women," 11–12.
    11. Munt, *Murder by the Book?*, 201.
    12. Judith Butler, *Gender Trouble: Feminism and the Subversion of Identity* (New York: Routledge, 1990, 1999), 173.
    13. Klein, *The Woman Detective*, 202.
    14. Reddy, *Sisters in Crime*, 6. Gill Plain also wonders whether Sara Paretsky's "female appropriation of 'masculine' discourse" can offer more than "a crude inversion, proving only that women can perform roles of patriarchal dominance as successfully as men." *Twentieth-Century Crime Fiction*, 93.
    15. Plain, *Twentieth-Century Crime Fiction*, 245.

Works Cited

Butler, Judith. *Gender Trouble: Feminism and the Subversion of Identity*. New York: Routledge, 1990, second edition, 1999.
Christie, Agatha. *A Murder Is Announced*. 1950. New York: Penguin Putnam, 2001.
Dilley, Kimberly J. *Busybodies, Meddlers, and Snoops: The Female Hero in Contemporary Women's Mysteries*. Westport, Connecticut: Greenwood Press, 1998.
Horsley, Lee. *Twentieth-Century Crime Fiction*. Oxford: Oxford University Press, 2005.
Irons, Glenwood, ed. *Feminism in Women's Detective Fiction*. Toronto: University of Toronto Press, 1995.
Klein, Kathleen Gregory. *The Woman Detective: Gender and Genre*. Urbana: University of Illinois Press, 1988; second edition, 1995.
_____. "Women Times Women Times Women," in Kathleen Gregory Klein, ed., *Women Times Three: Writers, Detectives, Readers*. Bowling Green: Bowling Green State University Popular Press, 1995.
Munt, Sally R. *Murder by the Book? Feminism and the Crime Novel*. London: Routledge, 1994.
Plain, Gill. *Twentieth-Century Crime Fiction: Gender, Sexuality and the Body*. Edinburgh: Edinburgh University Press, 2001.
Reddy, Maureen T. *Sisters in Crime: Feminism and the Crime Novel*. New York: Continuum, 1988.
Walton, Priscilla L., and Manina Jones. *Detective Agency: Women Rewriting the Hard-Boiled Tradition*. Berkeley: University of California Press, 1999.

NANCY DREW VS. NANCY CLUE:
GIRL SLEUTHS DISCOVER THEIR SEXUALITIES

1. Configuring Space and Sexuality
Nancy Drew Enters The Bluebeard Room

MICHAEL G. CORNELIUS

Until 1985, Nancy Drew was sexless.

This is not to say that Nancy was without *gender*; indeed, "sex" in its more broadly-construed connotation played a key role in the development of America's premiere teen sleuth. Nancy Drew's entire characterization since her debut in 1930 is predicated on the simple notion that she is a *girl* sleuth, a figure perpetually on the cusp of womanhood who embodies the ideals of both girl-ness and woman-ness without taking on the inherent limitations, responsibilities, or burdens of either role. Nancy's identity, shaped by her incessant need to detect, to solve mysteries and to help others, is wrapped up almost entirely in notions of 1930s New Womanhood, proto-feminism, and an omnipresent woman-centeredness that, generally speaking, excluded any significant intrusion by males— all males— into her world.[1]

Of course, there are men in the Nancy Drew series: Nancy's father, stalwart and handsome criminal attorney Carson Drew; the River Heights police force, headed by Chief McGinnis; Ned Nickerson, who has been Nancy's dull but loving boyfriend since being first introduced in 1932's *The Clue in the Diary*; and perhaps most significantly of all, the many male criminals Nancy has diligently traced, tracked down, and brought to justice. More than her father, the official authorities, and her own boyfriend, it is these male criminals that most interest Nancy Drew, that most get her heart racing and her blood pumping; yet her ardor here is a passion for detection, and nothing more than that. Nancy swoons only for mystery, and for no man.

Many critics have pointed out the remarkable lack of central male figures in the Nancy Drew series. C. M. Gill writes, "[T]he inclusion of men in the [series] would likely disrupt the female-centric nature of the series; this, in turn, could create an eroto-romantic tension that could threaten Nancy's career."[2] Especially to 1930s-era Nancy, men represent a palpable threat: to her identity, to her mysteries, to her gender. Should Nancy decide someday to embrace romance (Ned) or male authority (her father, the police) she risks her own hegemony, the quality that not only makes her — well, that makes her Nancy Drew — but also makes her the authoritative, crime-solving machine that she is. For if Nancy accepts male authority, she is a girl, beholden to the designs and dictates of a patriarchal society; if she embraces the road of romance, she becomes a woman, and detection must sometimes take a backseat to dates, dances, and, eventually, marriage and child-rearing. If Nancy becomes a woman, she must then take on the responsibilities and rights of adulthood — none of which, sad to say, include solving mysteries, at least not in the carefree, identity-centric way Nancy Drew solves mysteries. Other sleuths of her day, including Ruth Fielding and Judy Bolton, married; Ruth Fielding had a child. They still solved mysteries, but they did so in between trips to the grocery store, or during their lunch break at work; they could not traipse off to Scotland, or France, or Africa at a moment's notice. They had obligations; their identities became at least partially subsumed by the men in their respective spheres. In short, they changed.

Becoming wholly a girl or a woman means accepting male hierarchy, a significant male presence in her life — father, boyfriend, husband — a presence that, by virtue of socially engendered values of male/female relations, must (at least at times) take precedence over Nancy's own needs and, more significantly, her desires. Remaining between the two roles of girl and woman means that Nancy Drew can remain without men. Thus for fifty-five years, Nancy Drew remained a model of consistency. No sex. No thoughts of sex. All talk of marriage was immediately forestalled. When two girlfriends are laughingly discussing their impending nuptials, Nancy assures them that her thoughts regarding men have not wavered as theirs have:

> Later, as Nancy, Helen, and Emily were talking, the two older girls suddenly stopped speaking on the subject of their forthcoming weddings. Helen said, "Goodness, Nancy, you must be tired of hearing us talk about steady partners when —"
> Nancy interrupted. Laughing gaily, she said, "Not at all. For the present, *my* steady partner is going to be mystery!"[3]

In suggesting that "for the present" — Nancy's own eternal present — that only mystery will be her "steady partner," Nancy really implies that her true steady partner is her*self*. Jungian scholar Betsy Caprio argues that Nancy Drew reflects a perpetual state of "psychological virginity [and] separateness.... Nancy Drew spurns togetherness so that she may have a union with herself.... She models one kind of relatedness, the inward kind."[4] Nancy reflects here a new type of girlhood, one made possible by the rise of New Womanhood and one that requires neither romantic partner, rigid parentalism/patriarchy, or even a grouping of like-minded peers in order to thrive; indeed, any of these types of relationship would weigh on Nancy, altering her individuality by causing her to enter into some form of dyadic partnership — with a beau, a parent, a peer — that would compel her primary form of relatedness to turn outward, to another, rather than inward, to herself. This constant inward gaze is reflected in Nancy's need to solve mysteries, to restore order, to aid others: at peace with herself, she wishes the world to be at peace as well.

This peace is shattered by the inclusion of sexuality in 1985s *The Bluebeard Room*.[5] The seventy-seventh Nancy Drew adventure, *The Bluebeard Room* introduces sexuality in Nancy Drew's world, a world that had existed in a sexless form for fifty-five years prior. The decision to do so was based simply on marketing: Simon & Schuster, the company who then owned the rights to the series, felt that "we need to breathe new life into [the series]. The characters are showing signs of age and need updating. Nancy, for example, doesn't reflect the reality of 1980s girlhood."[6] During the previous seventy-six books, Nancy and her boyfriend Ned never kissed once; yet in *The Bluebeard Room*, Nancy kisses two men, a rock star and a reporter, neither of which resembled stolid Ned Nickerson. Nancy also experiences a sexual desire she has never felt before, a longing that both confuses and excites her. Karen Plunkett-Powell notes that *The Bluebeard Room* alters the "basic structure" of the Nancy Drew book: "The adult chaperon ... is conspicuously missing," and the book shows "a more risqué side of Nancy Drew." The result of this newfound introduction to/of sexuality is a "challenge to Nancy's calm demeanor"; no longer able to placate or disregard desire, Nancy must now confront it.[7] Even more, Nancy embraces sexuality, exploring this new aspect of her subjectivity with the same thoughtfulness and fervor she usually employs in approaching a mystery. In doing so, however, she alters her subjectivity; by allowing men into her previously constricted "women-only" space, Nancy Drew, like Ruth Fielding and Judy Bolton, must change.

The fairy tale of "Bluebeard" is an excellent choice to serve as a backdrop for a Nancy Drew adventure since the story's construct features both a mystery (what is in the forbidden room?) and a female sleuth (Bluebeard's new bride). It seems incredibly revelatory that the introduction of sexuality into the Nancy Drew series coincided with a story that focused on the myth of the killer Bluebeard and a room that bore his name, for what happened in Bluebeard's infamous room — and what will happen to the character of Nancy Drew because of her encounter with that same metaphorical chamber — have been forever linked to the curiosities and dangers of women's sexuality. In this essay, I will explore the intersections of Nancy's newfound sexuality with Charles Perrault's original version of the "Bluebeard" legend. Using feminist readings of space, I will demonstrate that the tale of "Bluebeard" itself suggests that the original detective Nancy Drew and the sexualized Nancy Drew literally cannot inhabit the same space — both Nancy's body and the eponymous room of the book's title — and how the warning inherent to the text reflects on both the feminist and sexual modes of the Drew character herself. And yet, Nancy being Nancy, as much as *The Bluebeard Room* changes her, so does she, in turn, alter the nature of Bluebeard's room; in detecting a solution to the mystery of Penvellyn Castle, site of the eponymous room, Nancy brings her own unique brand of femininity/feminism into the masculine confines of the Bluebeard room itself. Nonetheless, this encounter leaves her shaken and bruised. The space of the Bluebeard room is a Pandora's box for Nancy; once it is open and the "evils" of sexuality are unleashed upon the girl, she becomes forever altered, or, is at least altered so long as romance, men, and sexuality compete with mystery in fashioning Nancy's subjectivity.

Constructing the Bluebeard Room

The legend of "Bluebeard" was first published by Charles Perrault in 1697, in his book *Histoire ou Contes du temps passé*, a collection of eight fairy tales that also included the first penned versions of "Little Red Riding Hood," "Sleeping Beauty," and "Cinderella." Perrault, of course, did not fabricate the tales, but based them on popular oral tradition of the time. "Bluebeard" tells the story of an aristocrat who was feared by the local women because, though married many times, the ultimate fate of his wives, who disappeared, remained unknown. He does finally persuade another young girl to marry him, and, immediately after the wedding, he tells her he must leave for urgent business. He gives her all the keys to his fantastic chateau, but warns her to stay out of a particular forbidden room. Curiosity finally gets the better of the bride, and she enters the room, only to discover, to her horror, that it is filled with the bloody remains of Bluebeard's previous wives. Almost immediately after this discovery, Bluebeard returns home, knowing what his wife has done. He draws his immense sword to behead her but she begs for fifteen minutes to say her prayers. He agrees to this, and just as the time is up, the bride's brothers appear and rescue her, killing Bluebeard and ending his wicked ways.

Perrault's tale of "Bluebeard" has commonly been interpreted via its two morals, both of which have been read as being directed towards women. As Maria Tatar correctly notes,

> Folklorists have shown a surprising interpretive confidence in reading Perrault's "Bluebeard" as a story about a woman's failure to respond to the trust invested in her. The homicidal history of the husband often takes a back seat to the disobedience of the wife. "Bloody key as a sign of disobedience"— this is

the motif that folklorists consistently single out as the defining moment of the tale. The bloodstained key points to a double transgression, one that is both moral and sexual. For one critic it becomes a sign of "marital infidelity"; for another it marks the heroine's "irreversible loss of her virginity"; for a third it stands as a sign of "defloration."[8]

Feminist scholars and critics have long contested this traditional interpretation of the tale. They rightly note that Bluebeard's "test" is not designed to judge his new wife's fidelity or obeisance; rather, the room and the temptation to peer within is more of a "setup. Bluebeard wanted his new wife to find the corpses of his former wives. He *wanted* the new bride to discover their mutilated corpses; he *wanted* her disobedience."[9] This desire for disobedience — Bluebeard lays the trap not to test his wife, but rather to ensnare her, since he knows she will "fail" his test — is suggestive of the sociopathic nature of both Bluebeard and his society. Bluebeard craves female transgression because of the punitive response it invokes; likewise, the society that created the "Bluebeard" legend demonstrates the violent consequences against those women who would indulge in such outrageous behavior as disobeying their husbands. If silence, obedience, and chastity are the desired feminine characteristics of Perrault's seventeenth-century world, then Bluebeard's wife repudiates her bond of obedience by opening the door to the forbidden room; likewise, as Tatar points out, scholars have long held that she also metaphorically breaks her bond of chastity, even if that bond is broken by entering into a secret chamber of her husband's own design. Though the new bride pleads with her husband for her life, he must imagine that, having already broken the vows of obedience and chastity, she will also break the bond of silence, and that only her doom will prevent his.

In his second moral to the tale, Perrault suggests, "No longer are husbands so terrible, / Demanding the impossible, / Acting unhappy and jealous. / They toe the line with their wives. / And no matter what color their beards, / It's not hard to tell who is in charge."[10] This moral accomplishes two purposes: first, while ostensibly lauding the fact that events such as these are relegated to the distant past (of course, sadly, this is not quite the case), Perrault implies almost a nostalgic remembrance of those "good-old-days gone by" when men did *not* "toe the line with their wives" and the punishments for wifely disobedience were indeed harsh, if not cruel.[11] Suggesting that men "toe the line with their wives" connotes a potential inversion of traditional male/female power dynamics, not a partnership, though it also implies that the lessons of the past might revisit an uppity woman at any time a man should deem it necessary (implying that the inverted form of power can swing back the opposite way). Of course, Perrault also directly intimates in his second lesson the reason that men "toe the line with their wives": the reference to "beards," coupled with the pronoun "their" that seems to directly refer back to the "men" but likewise indirectly nods to "women," suggests that women have gained some measure of control over their own bodies, at least enough to ensure their own domain regarding boundaries of sexual permission related to the self—meaning that female sexuality has become a continuing negotiation between man and wife, and not the expected right of the proprietary male. Men, Perrault contends, must "toe the line" in order to be sexually gratified, when, in Bluebeard's day, in a seemingly not-so-distant past, such niceties as "permission" were not generally considered or required.

At the heart of both the original Bluebeard myth and *The Bluebeard Room* is the figure of the girl sleuth—literally (the wife in Perrault's legend, Nancy Drew in her text) and metaphorically (the sexualization of the feminine body is at the heart of both tales). A woman's body is the first and last space she inhabits in her lifetime. Ruth Salvaggio considers this inhabitance "both figurative and historical."[12] Teresa de Lauretis believes that women's bodies have long served as the object of the male gaze, an object of representation in "the visual arts, the medical sciences, the capitalist media industry, and several related social practices from organized sports to individual jogging."[13] As an object, the body is both assailable and yet uncontrollable; women could not control the reception of their bodies in the patriarchal world, and yet despite all legislative and ecclesiastic efforts otherwise, men proved ultimately incapable of large-scale control over this individual female domain. As Jessica Benjamin explains, women's bodies "both form a boundary and open up into endless possibility."[14] Perrault, in suggesting that women have begun to exert individual control over this sphere (as Perrault writes in his second moral to the tale, "It's not hard to tell who is in charge"), intimates that women's influence now extends beyond it, a by-product of male desire and fears of cuckoldry and concerns over primogeniture and of women's own desire, which, "understood in these spatial terms, makes her body a kind of 'space-off' since she is at once separate from others and in between—at once 'here and elsewhere.'"[15] Because women "have never occupied a place in discourse other than as the object of representation," the effort of feminist spatial scholarship has been to "create new spaces of discourse, to rewrite cultural narratives, and to define the terms of another perspective—a view from 'elsewhere.'"[16] Perrault's joking reference to women's "beards" in his second moral to the tale commences this new space with the body itself, a concept that, while seemingly incongruent with traditional feminist beliefs, upholds Alice Jardine's notion of *gynesis*—of feminizing theory (or, in this case, text). Perrault's bawdy suggestion is actually a critique on feminist authority; the typically male "joke" regarding a woman's control of her own body and her own sexuality is, in fact, creating a feminist space, which, as Salvaggio points out, "signal[s] an important break with unified systems of theory."[17] Joking about women's bodies, especially in the grudging manner of Perrault, signifies a societal shift in the manner in which such forms are constructed, considered, and ordered. Men no longer control women's bodies, at least not wholly; Perrault's seemingly simple exchange of "repartee" actually demonstrates a male frustration at changing societal notions regarding women and the subjugation of their corporeal forms. In this instance, wit becomes a methodology to disguise vexation, a code for both men and women alike, seemingly benign to the latter while speaking volumes to the former. This sense of language is very important to the text. As Jardine writes,

> "Woman," as a new rhetorical space, is inseparable from the most radical moments of most contemporary disciplines.... "She" is created from close explorations of semantic chains whose elements have changed textual as well as conceptual positions, at least in terms of valorization; from time to space, the same to other, paranoia to hysteria, city to labyrinth, mastery to non-mastery, truth to fiction.[18]

In Perrault's moral, "woman" is configured as authoritative, maintaining mastery over her sexuality, much to the inherent "dismay" of the moralist himself.

Perrault's moral is thus in stark contrast to his tale (which Perrault himself points out) and its suggestion of punishment for sexual and moral transgressions committed by a wife against a husband. Daniela Hempen intimates that the myth of "Bluebeard" "offers one of the most graphic descriptions of the gruesome secrets which ... await new brides."[19] The suggested horror here is, of course, sexuality, discovered upon a bride's wedding night. The loss of virginity is sometimes equated with the loss of an individual identity. Caprio believes that the first main task in life is to "develop the ability to be separate."[20] This ability relates to what Marion Woodman calls "psychological virginity."[21] In describing the importance of virginity, Caprio relates the tale of Hera, wife of the chief Greek god Zeus, who "periodically bathed in the stream Canathos near Argos, so that she could regularly recover her (psychological) virginity, her one-in-herselfness. The ancients knew how essential was this quality of independence."[22]

In categorizing the myth of "Bluebeard," Tatar writes that Perrault's legend "frames the conflict between husband and wife as a conflict between the familiar and the strange."[23] The "strangeness" represented by Bluebeard the husband is the loss of virginity, which redefines the feminist space of the body into something less autonomous and, as Caprio indicates, something in need of spatial attention. Hera's ritual cleansing suggests both a physical and psychological restoration, a reconstruction of the self, necessary for her own sense of subjectivity. However, in the legend of "Bluebeard," the reconstruction is not done by the self, but by an other, a representative of the dominant patriarchy — in this case, Bluebeard himself. Thus what the wife faces in the tale on her wedding night is less a sense of reconstruction than simple construction, creating a new form — and new body — out of the material presented in the form of the virginized female body. For Bluebeard, however, this new form is less desirable than the former. When buildings are restored, their facades look resplendently new; the loss of virginity in "Bluebeard" seems to imply the degradation of the space of the female body, one that Bluebeard believes can only be restored by tearing down the old façade (i.e., destroying the body) and constructing a new one in its place (marrying another virgin bride). It is Bluebeard, and not his brides, who continually constructs and reconstructs the space of the female body in order that it may attain a façade that is (at least temporarily) more pleasing to him.

This constant (re)construction of the female form is manifested by the room in which Bluebeard houses his former wives. In Perrault's version of the tale, the room is located on a lower floor of the castle. Deserting her guests and racing down the backstairs, the bride pauses before the door of the forbidden room, reflecting on the punishment she may incur for not obeying her husband in this, his one, request. Still, "temptation was too strong for her to resist," and she opens the door.[24] The room itself receives little description in the tale. It is a dark room, but not windowless, though the windows are all "shuttered."[25] Bluebeard has previously described the room as "small," though it is large enough to house the corpses of several women, with apparently room for more.[26]

The size of the room is significant in considering how to approach it, and the text, systematically. The descriptor of the room as "small" suggests the nature of confinement that reflects the purpose of the room. Small quarters are cramped, constraining, and indicative of the loss of freedom. The size of the room as being large enough to hold all of Bluebeard's former wives, with room for more, however, reflects the continual process of (re)construction of the female form that Bluebeard and the patriarchy of Perrault's day are continually engaged in. This suggests a struggle that is never-ending, or at least one that can only be ended not by re-appropriating the purpose of the room, but by re-appropriating the purpose of the jailer. When configuring space, one can approach it from differing perspectives: "Space can be conceptualized in three ways: as *place*— the particular locale or setting; as *relational units* that organize ideas about places and implicitly or explicitly compare locations; or as *scale*, or the size of the units to be compared."[27] As *place*, Bluebeard's room is dark and confining, and "enclosed space and totalizing structures ... might well be regarded as 'masculine.'"[28] Doreen Massey would argue that a space such as Bluebeard's room might be designed as restrictive towards women: "The degree to which we [women] can move between countries, or walk about the streets at night, or venture out of hotels in foreign cities, is not just influenced by 'capital.' Survey after survey has shown how women's mobility ... is restricted — in a thousand different ways, from physical violence to being ogled at or made to feel quite simply 'out of place'— not by 'capital,' but by men."[29] Bluebeard's violence towards his wives does not end after their demise, but extends even beyond death, confining them to a lightless room, locked away from the world by a simple key, suggesting that rescue and aid are never far but also never coming. The shuttered windows add to the husband's cruelty, aiding his effort to assert his dominance over his wives; the room declares, quite simply, a husband's mastery over his wife in all things.

The *scale* of the room reinforces these notions, confirming what the *place* of the room has already suggested. Yet considering the *relational unit* of the room, concerned with the "ideas" that the room both confines and reveals, demonstrates the larger societal struggle in which Bluebeard has murderously inserted himself. As Perrault demonstrates, neither Bluebeard's actions nor his perspective are considered normative by the standards of his own society. An anachronism in both deed and thought, the room seeks to both hide this disturbing aspect of Bluebeard (and, by extension, the patriarchy itself) while also ultimately revealing it; the temptation to solve the mystery of the room is too great, and its secrets too troubling, to remain hidden forever. Truth will out, and society will progress; individuals like Bluebeard, who impede the work of both, will ultimately need to be destroyed if they cannot conform to larger societal will.

In many ways, Bluebeard's room is a violent incarnation of Michel Foucault's concept of heterotopia:

> There also exist, and this is probably true for all cultures and all civilizations, real and effective spaces which are outlined in the very institution of society, but which constitute a sort of counter-arrangement of effectively realized utopia, in which all the real arrangements, all the other real arrangements that can be found within society, are at one and the same time represented, challenged, and overturned: a sort of place that lies outside all places and yet is actually localizable.[30]

In his second moral to the tale, Perrault describes a utopian vision of a society where "no longer are husbands so terrible." The veracity of this statement can and should be called into question, along with Perrault's sincerity in uttering it; yet the propitious nature of the line, of the ideal of men and women living in a type of dualistic harmony, is no doubt referencing a form, if not function, of marital utopia. Foucault's heterotopia, then, becomes the antithesis to Perrault's vision of a married utopia; thus, just as a women's shelter would be a heterotopia to Perrault's moral (because it suggests not only a space where men do not "toe the line with their wives," but also evidence of the contrary), Bluebeard's room is a violently masculinized heterotopia where female hegemony is severely curtailed and the de-virginized female form acts as a threat to a highly patriarchal, domineering, and rapidly going-out-of-date system of male hegemony. The room is a bastion of old ideas, concepts that are not only no longer *au courant* but that have been so perverted that, to Bluebeard, the logical outcome of the culminating act of marriage — of the union between man and woman — has become death.

The room, however, is designed not only to contain female hegemony, but to lure it as well. In designing his test for his new bride, Bluebeard has assured that the slightest disobedience on her behalf (by seeking out the forbidden room) will be met with swift and terrible castigation. The room, then, becomes a test of female obeisance, and the desire of the patriarchy to contain any sort of feminist ideas of independence and sexual control. As Ann R. Tickamyer notes, "The natural and built environment, the design of space and place, shapes social relations."[31] Bluebeard's forbidden room defines marriage as an extremely patriarchal gesture, and suggests that only the virginal female form is sanctified enough to suit male hegemonical ideas of female virtue. Once the room has been breached, literally and metaphorically, the space of the female body must be reconstructed in order for patriarchy to be appeased. And it is into this world, into this type of space, that Nancy Drew is thrust in *The Bluebeard Room*.

Entering the Bluebeard Room

Ostensibly, eternally virginal Nancy Drew might be a woman who could navigate the sexual treachery and machinations of Bluebeard's forbidden room. Caprio suggests that Nancy's eternal virginity is representative of the Jungian archetype of the Virgin Goddess, and that Nancy's independence goes hand in hand with her virginal status. For Caprio, virginity equals "soloness," a state of being that precedes "togetherness" or intimacy: "Nancy Drew spurns togetherness so that she may have a union with herself."[32] As Ann Scott MacLeod notes: "The point about Nancy Drew's freedom is not just ... its completeness; it is its dignity. Nancy's independence is not a gift coaxed from dim or fond adults. Autonomy is her *right* ... and is never seriously questioned. The enviable ease with which she exercises her total independence of adult authority is as impressive as the independence itself."[33] In another piece on the girl detective, I suggest that Nancy's independence is directly connected to her rejection of the masculine and the overtly romantic:

Nancy's independence is not, strictly speaking, a freedom from the world of adults; indeed, who is more adult than Nancy, whose unselfish desire to exert authority and seek justice is a quality not traditionally associated with youth. Rather than freedom from adults, Nancy's autonomy is quite literally a freedom from *men*; she exists in a feminine sphere largely because she has constructed that space, *her* space, a "no man's land." Her boyfriend Ned Nickerson is no more than an effectual eunuch, useful for manual labor or punching out a bad guy, but never an [object] of sexual desire. Nancy realized early on in her career that making time out for romance would result in a reconstruction of her feminine sphere, creating a space around her over which she no longer exerted ultimate autonomy.[34]

This is often the case with girl sleuth figures; when a serious relationship alters the hegemony of the sleuth, the act of detection usually takes a backseat to other, more traditionally feminine pursuits, such as housekeeping and motherhood. Judy Bolton, as previously noted, marries during the course of her series, and the series itself is perceptibly altered: "Judy is torn between traditional and nontraditional roles, hoping for marriage and a family at the same time she wants independence and respect for her detective skills."[35] As Sally Parry observes, though, Judy does not receive the credit she is due: "Because the patriarchal system valorizes men in official positions, the credit she receives is mostly from friends and family."[36] Judy herself "sometimes ... [wishes she] were a boy.... A detective.... A great one who goes into all kinds of dangers."[37] Because Judy allows men (initially, her brother and male friends, and then especially her husband) to inhabit her feminine space, she must not only share the benefits of her sleuthing with them but must also bear witness to the male social privilege extended by patriarchy to its own members, leaving Judy wistful and conflicted.

Unlike Judy, Nancy never wavers in her conviction and single-minded belief in her self; this confidence results in a self-reliance that frees her from male social administration. In fact, Nancy's utter refusal to allow any male to inhabit her feminine space creates an aura of authority around her. This air of authority is part of what makes Nancy so successful as a sleuth. Ilana Nash writes that "Nancy's authoritative power contradicts ... our gendered expectations." She continues: "At no point is her behavior successfully constrained by others' definitions of her sex."[38] As a re-imagining of a gender paradigm, Nancy's rejection of the physical realm of sexuality likely reflects a measured decision on the part of her creators, who have crafted Nancy to reject all forms and manner of sexuality in favor of other, more individual pursuits. In *The Mystery of the Tolling Bell*, Ned Nickerson tries to ply Nancy with talk of their own (married) future, to which Nancy replies, "Ned, someday I'll promise to listen."[39] "Someday" had not yet arrived by the mystery of *The Witch Tree Symbol*; when Ned again hints at a married future, Nancy "pretended not to understand."[40] Nancy continually "puts off" thoughts of sexuality because she realizes that to embrace the sexual role would be to significantly alter her own feminine space, at the cost of her own feminine hegemony. Caprio notes that after the development of one's sense of "soloness" (i.e., a strong ego) comes "the capacity for some kind of intimacy with another or others ... and then to perform a life-long juggling act between these two complements of soloness and togetherness."[41] Nancy's rejection of intimacy reflects her approbation of soloness; rather than juggle traditional and nontraditional roles as Judy Bolton is forced to, Nancy accepts only that role which allows her to maintain her own feminine/feminist space: detective.

Notions of femininity and feminism are often viewed as being in conflict with one another, or creating a tension in the subject female. This is not the case in Nancy Drew, however, whose espousal of her society's views on femininity actually enables her proto-feminist tendencies. Bobbie Ann Mason hints at this concept when she notes, "The girl sleuth, it seems, was a comfortable fictional role that siphoned female energy away from more revolutionary ambitions."[42] By conforming to society's rules and expectations in all other aspects of their lives, girl sleuths are afforded a freedom from societal oversight necessary to detect. Manifesting aspects of girlhood in other facets of their lives allowed girls sleuths like Nancy to act in ways "unbecoming" to a girl of her day and thus exciting for those young women reading about the sleuth's daring and hardly "traditional" exploits. Nancy's feminist ontology should not be overlooked here. Parry considers Nancy Drew a "good feminist hero," a "protector" of the wronged and weak.[43] From this perspective, one might almost suspect that Nancy would take on the guise of the brothers in the tale and not of the hapless wife; she might represent the avenging figure who rides to save the damsel and bring the villain to justice. It is the duty of the detective figure to seek out injustice, right that which has been wronged, rescue the innocent from the clutches of evil, and punish those who continually transgress against the social order of the day. In imagining the familiar version of Nancy Drew cast into the tale of "Bluebeard," the audience would likely expect Nancy to reject any notion of marriage — especially to Bluebeard — as incomprehensible. Thus, relegating herself to the sidelines, she could abandon the cynosurial role of wife in favor of the role she has always chosen at the expense of her own sexuality: detective, the avenging eyes and arm of justice. This is the "moment in feminist history" that Carolyn Heilbrun ascribes to Nancy Drew; in rejecting the trappings and trap of female sexuality (but not, necessarily speaking, femininity itself), Nancy is free to pursue her own brand of womanhood. Diane Reynolds notes that "Nancy Drew [is] empowered ... because of her virginity."[44] Caprio likewise directly connects Nancy's "abilities as a detective" to the "psychological separation" that denotes her character.⁴⁵ Ultimately, Nancy is not defined by her rejection of sexuality, but that same rejection allows her to define *herself*, to construct her own feminine space sans the patriarchal influence that comes along with Caprio's "intimacy."

In finally embracing sexuality, then, Nancy's ability to define herself — to fashion her own unique subjectivity — becomes altered. Newly concerned with thoughts of romance and men, Nancy takes on a new role as lover and a new connectivity to men that requires her to abandon her "woman-centered" space in order to craft intimate bonds with members of the opposite sex. Sexuality displaces Nancy from the role of detective and avenging arm of justice — from the role of the brothers — and forces her to take on, instead, the guise of the wife herself. Though this new Nancy Drew may not be blunted in detective skills or curious instinct (as, indeed, the wife herself is driven by her own desire to seek the truth), the choice does drastically alter her "woman space" and, ultimately, Nancy herself.

The Bluebeard Room is set mostly in a castle in Cornwall, where Nancy Drew has gone to visit Lisa Penvellyn, an old friend. Nancy has gone to Cornwall at the behest of Lisa's mother, who tells Nancy of her daughter's odd behavior since her marriage and who believes that Lisa's husband Hugh may even be poisoning her. Thus, the initial mysterious act in the book is that of a marriage. Nancy's reluctance to become involved in the mystery ("[Nancy] felt deep misgivings about prying into Lisa's marriage. [N]one of her cases had ever involved her in problems between a husband and a wife") demonstrates that this is entirely new territory for the girl sleuth.⁴⁶ At this point in the text, Nancy may seem to inhabit the guise of Anne in the myth, a sisterly figure on hand near the wife (Lisa) and Bluebeard (Hugh), though Nancy will also, in time, inherit the mantle of the bride herself — though not, as one might surmise, that of the rescuing brothers later in the story.

Prior to Nancy's journey to England, she meets Lance Warrick, a "far-too attractive British rock star."⁴⁷ When told that Lance would like to dance with her, Nancy reasserts her feminine space: "No, thanks. Tell him I appreciate the honor, but I'd rather have another glass of punch" (19). Her independence does not last long, however. Watching Lance's band at a concert, Nancy finds herself under the singer's masculine, sexualized spell:

> Lance Warrick ... held the audience mesmerized. At times, Nancy felt certain he was playing and singing especially to *her*.
> From the corner of her eye, she stole a swift glace at her girl friends. Both Bess and George were staring at the rock king entranced, their eyes wide open, lips slightly parted.
> With a shock, Nancy realized that she had been doing the same thing herself! [35].

Later, at an after-concert party, Bess tells one of the band members, "You really had the audience turned on!" (42). Of course, what has stunned Nancy into silence at this moment is that, indeed, she is perhaps for the first time in her incarnation *turned on*, in the sexual parlance of the phrase, and is quickly losing control over — and the autonomy of — her feminine space. Later at the same party, Nancy thanks Lance for sending her the concert tickets, and when he tells her he did not send them, she remonstrates herself:

> Nancy felt like falling through the floor. How could she have been so vain as to think a world-famous star like Lance Warrick would go out of his way to invite her to his sell-out concert?! — as his personal guest yet!
>
> Most humiliating of all, she'd exposed her nitwit fantasies! And now he had obviously sized her up as one more groupie candidate ... [45–6].

What is most shocking to Nancy in this scene is not that Lance considers her a possible sexual conquest (the remark about the "groupies") or that Nancy herself has considered the notion (her "nitwit fantasies") but that Lance will see her as nothing *more* than a sexual conquest. Nancy Drew, Detective, Nancy Drew, virginal goddess and autonomous inhabitor of feminine space, is now worried about being considered ... a slut?

In a review of the newly sexualized Nancy Drew, Robert Basler notes that "it is the 1980s. Men can wear jewelry. Women can run for vice-president. And Nancy Drew can finally feel tingly when she gets kissed."[48] The newly sexualized Nancy does not feel tingly, however; she feels terror, not at the thought of sexuality, nor its consequences, but at not succeeding in this new venture. After fifty-five years of total and welcomed celibacy, Nancy has entered the sexual arena with no small amount of trepidation and determination. When she receives a note from Lance, Nancy's hands shake when opening it, "much to her annoyance" (94). To ensure success in this new endeavor, not only does Nancy continue to pursue Lance when she arrives in England (and vice-versa), but when she meets a local reporter, Alan Trevor, she also enjoys romantic interludes with him:

> He drew her close and kissed her. Nancy resisted at first, then found herself yielding willingly to his embrace.
>
> When they said good night moments later, she was less sure than ever which of the two she found more attractive, Lance or Alan [137].

Two men in one book! Poor Ned Nickerson is left behind in more ways than one: "Ned and I've been going together so long we found ourselves taking each other for granted. So we decided to date other people until we make up our minds" (73). Ned Nickerson has always represented a simulacrum of male passivity, in both his sexuality and his masculinity; for all his college athleticism and "fratboy" bravado, he is cut from the same cloth as Nancy is, at least as far as his rejection of sexuality is concerned. The difference is that Nancy's fashioning of her own gender and sexuality suggests empowerment; Ned's fashioning smacks of disempowerment, since he has surrendered his male social privilege to the teen sleuth who has captured his heart (but rejected his body). It is *Nancy* who has chosen his path for him, just as she chose her own way forward (sexually speaking) for herself.[49] Thus the rejection of ineffectual Ned is the first indication of Nancy's acceptance of her newly found sexuality; whereas previously only the non-threatening "masculinity" of Ned Nickerson had been allowed into Nancy's feminine space, she now eagerly seeks the intimacy of not one but two sexually active men.

In labeling Perrault's "Bluebeard" as a conflict between husband and wife, Tatar adds that the legend also reflects a conflict "between the family (mother, sister, two brothers) and a foreigner (one whose blue beard marks him as an exotic outsider)."[50] It seems no accident then that Nancy's new sexuality blooms in a foreign land with foreign beaus whose "exotic" nature marks an exotic entry of sexuality into Nancy's space. The Bluebeard room itself is also indicative of this alien space. Nancy first encounters the room during a tour of the castle with Lisa. Coming across a "stout, iron-bound oak door," Nancy asks Lisa what is inside. Lisa's response — "I don't know" — suggests the test of her own wifely fidelity, a test immediately heightened by the presence of the girl sleuth: "Aren't you curious?" (89). The incident reminds Nancy of the Bluebeard legend itself, though she says nothing to her friend. Later, though, she overhears an argument between Lisa and Hugh about the contents of the room:

> "I've told you before — what's in that room is none of your business!" Hugh was saying stormily.
> "But why not, if I'm your wife?" Lisa pleaded.
> "Because I say so, and I'm your husband! What kind of marriage do we have if you can't trust me that far?"
> "Doesn't trust work both ways? Oh, Hugh, I felt so foolish and ashamed, having to admit to Nancy that you wouldn't even tell *me* why you keep that room shut up and locked!"
> "Nancy's here as our guest, not as a detective!" Lord Penvellyn retorted. "Why I choose to keep that room closed is none of her business, either!" [96].

Nancy's reaction to overhearing the argument is atypical of the sleuth; embarrassed, she flees to her room and broods over what she has heard. One would expect intrepid, determined Nancy to more than ever seek out the mystery of the room, but instead, she does not mention it again, even in her own thoughts, until much later in the book. This reaction may seem the proper, "feminine" response to witnessing an embarrassing argument between husband and wife, but it is certainly not the response of the dogged sleuth who has seventy-six previous mysteries notched on her belt.

Unlike the wife in the "Bluebeard" story, Nancy is never given a key to the room, though the temptation to enter does prove so great that she eventually attempts—unsuccessfully—to pick the lock. Whereas Hugh's actual wife, Lisa, never decides to explore the room (she passes *her* test of temptation), Nancy with her inquisitive nature cannot resist the mystery of the room's contents. Thus, even more than Hugh's own wife, Nancy now takes on the guise of Bluebeard's wife, the female whose insatiable curiosity leads her into danger in the transformative confines of the Bluebeard room.[51] Yet what is most surprising about the scene is not that Nancy gives into her curiosity's temptation — indeed, this is a hallmark of the successful detective — but rather how long it takes her to do so. The mystery of the forbidden room should have been irresistible to a girl sleuth, but distracted by Lance and Alan — distracted by the first blushes of sexuality — Nancy falters in entering the room. Her thoughts are consumed by passion, not by mystery; her central identity, as detective, is subsumed by thoughts perhaps unbecoming for a girl sleuth.

Eventually, though, Nancy pushes thoughts of romance aside, at least temporarily, and contrives to enter the room. She believes that an outside, underwater tunnel might lead to the room, and she and Lance plan a sortie to see if she is right. The initial entry into the room is a dank underwater cave, reachable only through scuba diving. The enclosed space of the cave suggests a masculine space, and the circular iron cage hanging in the space reinforces this notion of female confinement that Bluebeard's room also reflects. Upon spying the cage, Nancy "gasped in surprise. 'What on earth is that?!'" she asks of Lance, who replies that he is as baffled as she is. Soon, however, Lance, taking the lead, "entered the cage and pulled [Nancy] up to join him." Being drawn into the cage, and being led by a man, suggests the symbolic culmination of Nancy's sexual journey; she has entered into male confinement willingly, where she "shivered with excitement" (148). Now constrained in a stronghold of the masculine, like the wives before her, Nancy has seemingly wholly adapted into the role her newfound interest in sexuality has created for her.

Or has she? Though the room in the Bluebeard legend is masculine, the water here adds both a literal and metaphorical element to the space. Water is constantly changing, and as an elemental space, cannot be easily contained. Plus, water is reflective of nature, and, as Nedra Reynolds points out, "nature, historically, has been feminized."[52] The antechamber to the Bluebeard room is a dark, wet recess, reminiscent of the home of Grendel's mother in the saga *Beowulf*. In the tale, the hero Beowulf must journey to an underwater cave to do battle with Grendel's mother, a terrible monster. The home of Grendel's mother has long been seen to symbolize the female sexual organs, especially the vagina, and, by extending the allegory, the threat of female sexuality itself since, as Michael R. Near notes, the cave is "more a psychological space than a physical location."[53] Thus the wetness and natural component (a cave as opposed to a man-made space) of the antechamber and its symbolic correlation to the womb are suggestive that the space is designed to be feminine, and not masculine, in dynamic. Nancy's entering the realm is thus not wholly the journey of Bluebeard's wives, for it is not *his* sexuality she is exploring but, rather, her own.

The first cover art for *The Bluebeard Room*, as designed by Hector Garrido, depicts the scene of Nancy and Lance discovering the antechamber cave. In the scene, Nancy is in the foreground, her hair slicked back, her lips and cheeks both red with make-up (which still adheres after being completely submerged), and her hand grasping a large, phallic flashlight. Her facial expression is identical to the one she experiences during Lance's concert; eyes wide open, lips slightly parted, she is completely entranced by the scene before her. Unfortunately, it is not the door to the room that fulfills her gaze, but rather the masculine figure and backside of Lance himself, who is boldly moving forward while the brave girl sleuth falters back. In the picture, she is allowing the male to dominate both the mystery and her traditional space, while Nancy is more concerned with holding the gaze of the viewer, her "to-be-looked-at-ness" (as Laura Mulvey astutely labels it) more important than solving the crime against her feminine sense of space.[54] The image as depicted creates a contrast with the symbolism of the room itself: masculine versus feminine, detective versus lover, Nancy is trapped between both worlds; her confinement is secure, but her reconstruction is not.[55]

The Bluebeard room itself is very different from the one in Perrault's narrative, and largely anticlimactic after the antechamber. Lance pushes through the door and is first to enter into a "beamed and vaulted stone room, richly furnished in antique style" (149). In the room the pair uncovers two icons of *feminine* authority: a golden statue of the Celtic goddess Mab, and a portrait of Lady Phoebe Penvellyn, who had been burned at the stake for witchcraft in the early eighteenth century. The domestic nature of the room likewise suggests it is a feminine space, as does the depiction of feminine figures. This space likewise reflects this dualistic and combative nature of masculine versus feminine: the space is designed to contain feminine embarrassments from the Penvellyn past, but also reflects notions of feminist authority, in both the figure of the goddess and Hugh's ancestor. Thus, while the room is confused, there really is no doubt: this room, this man-made room, has a perspective that is quite uniquely feminine.

The question, then, is why does the Nancy Drew narrative transform the Bluebeard room from a masculine to a feminine place, and what does this entail for the character of Nancy herself? In Perrault's narrative, the space was designed not only to contain but also to lure female hegemony, and thus to curtail the autonomy of the body as female space. In the Nancy Drew narrative, the space is so much more reflective of Nancy's body itself, and the dark mystery surrounding it, that she only now seems willing to explore. Nedra Reynolds writes, "Only bodies can make places meaningful, and the bodies that occupy a place give it meaning."[56] This is true whether the bodies are dead (Bluebeard's wives) or alive (Nancy Drew). Thus the true transformation in *The Bluebeard Room* only occurs when Nancy herself enters the antechamber — a transformation wrought by the very sexuality Nancy has been exploring throughout the text. It is Nancy that feminizes the room, Nancy who reclaims it from the realm of the masculine and restores to it notions of female hegemony.

Yet in order to accomplish this task, Nancy has had to sacrifice her own hegemony — or, at least, the previously constructed notion of her own feminine space. Now that Nancy is no longer virginal, no longer consumed only by thoughts of mystery, the reader is left to conclude that if Nancy's body has changed the Bluebeard room, then *The Bluebeard Room* has likewise changed Nancy's body. Her initial foray into the cave reflects her initial foray into the murky depths of her own sexuality. Her hesitancy at the door of the room — and Lance's bold thrust forward into the cave — are reflective of Nancy's loss of independence. Her autonomy and "soloness" are incongruous with the intimacy the cave and the Bluebeard room represent. In exchange for a sexual identity, Nancy has diminished her detective one.

At the end of the book, Nancy kisses both her suitors good-bye, and Lance asks her which of the two men she prefers. Nancy laughingly replies, "I guess that's one riddle I haven't solved yet!" (159). Indeed, the "riddle" of Nancy's sexuality has only begun confounding the formerly formidable girl sleuth. In her next adventure, *The Phantom of Venice*,[57] Nancy likewise faces two suitors, though one, an Italian lothario, becomes a sexual predator, alarming Nancy into retreat on several occasions. The formerly impenetrable fortress of Nancy's sexuality has now been breached, and it lies open for any male conqueror, invited or otherwise; as Massey notes, Nancy's mobility and ability as detective are now curtailed.

Two years would pass before Nancy's subsequent adventure, *The Double Horror of Fenley Place*, and in this mystery, the "classic" Nancy would return as she was before *The Bluebeard Room*. Ned re-debuted as Nancy's plain, stalwart, ineffectual boyfriend, and sexuality was again banished from the series. It is not surprising that after the foreignness of England and Italy, this adventure is a homegrown tale, set in River Heights, where Nancy can clearly reestablish her autonomy and reconstruct herself as a virgin domicile once again. Yet, despite this change, the character of Nancy Drew remains forever altered. In exchanging sexuality for her own woman space, Nancy has forever altered the design of the world she inhabits. Hélène Cixous writes, "Woman must write her body ... must make up the unimpeded tongue that bursts partitions, classes and rhetorics, orders and codes, must inundate, run through, go beyond the discourse with its last reserves."[58] By allowing her body to be re-written in *The Bluebeard Room*, and not just by herself, Nancy Drew has impeded her own ability to exist as she formerly had, an autonomous and incredibly successful solo identity in a unique and unassailable woman space. Like the wife in Charles Perrault's original version of the tale of "Bluebeard," Nancy Drew learns too late the consequences of curiosity; though both are saved in the end, they remain forever altered, their unique woman space torn down by the ravages of the Bluebeard room and the always savage design of patriarchy itself.

Notes

1. Deborah Siegel notes that the character of Nancy Drew was optimally timed, since she "arrived on the heels of an era that witnessed the rise of the revolutionary demographic and political phenomenon known as the New Woman." A response to and rejection of the Victorian fashioning of girlhood and womanhood, "with the rise of the New Woman, Victorian constructions of femininity underwent drastic reconfiguration. In 1930 and beyond, the nation was still in the process of assimilating women's new sociopolitical status, as well as re-orienting to the ever-shifting ideological construct of 'the feminine.' Images of 'womanhood'—and with it 'girlhood'—figured varyingly in the nation's popular imagination." Without these emerging configurations of girlhood and womanhood, a character like Nancy Drew may never have existed, and most likely would never have become as enduring and impactful as she did. Deborah L. Siegel, "Nancy Drew As New Girl Wonder: Solving It All for the 1930s," in Sherrie A. Inness, ed., *Nancy Drew and Company: Culture, Gender, and Girls' Series* (Bowling Green, OH: Bowling Green State University Popular Press, 1997), 160.

2. C. M. Gill, "Hardy Camraderie: Boy Sleuthing and Male Community in the Hardy Boys Mysteries," in Michael G. Cornelius, ed., *The Boy Detectives: Essays on the Hardy Boys and Others* (Jefferson, NC: McFarland, 2010), 38.

3. Carolyn Keene, *The Mystery of Lilac Inn* (New York: Grosset and Dunlap, 1961 [revised]), 180.

4. Betsy Caprio, *Girl Sleuth on the Couch: The Mystery of Nancy Drew* (Trabuco Canyon, CA: Source Books, 1992), 37.

5. *The Bluebeard Room* was written by series ghostwriter James Lawrence. Lawrence had been instructed by publisher Simon & Schuster, who had just outright purchased the Nancy Drew series and other holdings of the Stratemeyer Syndicate, to "update" Nancy (see Plunkett-Powell 106). Lawrence writes that he agreed, and then "asked the big questions: Can Nancy date other boys than Ned Nickerson? Can she kiss them?"

(Plunkett-Powell 106). Clearly, the answers to Lawrence's "big" questions were "yes." For more on Nancy Drew ghostwriters, see James D. Keeline, "Who Wrote Nancy Drew? Secret from the Syndicate Files Revealed" (16 March 2006, keeline.com/Nancy_Drew.pdf).

6. Anne McGrath, "Eye on Publishing," *Wilson Library Bulletin* (December 1984), 268.

7. Karen Plunkett-Powell, *The Nancy Drew Scrapbook* (New York: St. Martin's Press, 1993), 107.

8. Maria Tatar, *Secrets Beyond the Door: The Story of Bluebeard and His Wives* (Princeton: Princeton University Press, 2004), 20.

9. Lydia Millet, "The Wife Killer," in Kate Bernheimer, ed., *Mirror, Mirror, on the Wall: Women Writers Explore Their Favorite Fairy Tales* (New York: Doubleday, 1998), 230.

10. Charles Perrault, "Bluebeard," in Maria Tatar, *Secrets Beyond the Door: The Story of Bluebeard and His Wives*, 179.

11. *Ibid.*

12. Ruth Salvaggio, "Theory and Space, Space and Women," *Tulsa Studies in Women's Literature* 7.2, 274.

13. Theresa de Lauretis, *Technologies of Gender: Essays on Theory, Film, and Fiction* (Bloomington: University of Indiana Press, 1987), 25.

14. Jessica Benjamin, "A Desire of One's Own: Psychoanalytic Feminism and Intersubjective Space," in Teresa de Lauretis, ed., *Feminist Studies/Critical Studies* (Bloomington: University of Indiana Press, 1986), 94.

15. Salvaggio, 275.

16. de Lauretis, 25.

17. Salvaggio, 269.

18. Alice Jardine, *Gynesis: Configurations of Women and Modernity* (Ithaca: Cornell University Press, 1985), 38.

19. Daniela Hempen, "Bluebeard's Female Helper: The Ambiguous Rôle of the Strange Old Woman in the Grimms' 'Castle of Murder' and 'The Robber Bridegroom,'" *Folklore* 108 (1997), 45.

20. Caprio, 33.

21. Marion Woodman, *The Pregnant Virgin* (Toronto: Inner City, 1985), 169.

22. Caprio, 34.

23. Tatar, 17.

24. Perrault, 176.

25. *Ibid.*

26. *Ibid.*

27. Ann R. Tickamyer, "Space Matters! Spatial Inequality in Future Sociology," *Contemporary Sociology* 29.6 (Nov. 2000), 806.

28. Salvaggio, 262.

29. Doreen Massey, *Space, Place, and Gender* (Minneapolis: University of Minnesota Press, 1994), 147–48.

30. Michel Foucault, "Other Spaces: The Principles of Heterotopia," *Lotus* 48/49 (1986), 12.

31. Tickamyer, 806.

32. Caprio, 33, 37.

33. Anne Scott MacLeod, "Nancy Drew and Her Rivals: No Contest," *Horn Book* 63 (1987), 427.

34. Michael G. Cornelius, "'They blinded her with science': Science Fiction and Technology in Nancy Drew," in Michael G. Cornelius and Melanie E. Gregg, eds., *Nancy*

Drew and Her Sister Sleuths: Essays on the Fiction of Girl Detectives (Jefferson, NC: McFarland, 2008), 78.

35. Sally E. Parry, "The Secret of the Feminist Heroine: The Search for Values in Nancy Drew and Judy Bolton," in Sherrie A. Inness, ed., *Nancy Drew and Company: Culture, Gender, and Girls' Series*, 152.

36. *Ibid.*

37. Margaret Sutton, *The Vanishing Shadow* (New York: Grosset and Dunlap, 1932), 53.

38. Ilana Nash, *American Sweethearts: Teenage Girls in Twentieth-Century Popular Culture* (Bloomington: Indiana University Press, 2006), 46, 47.

39. Carolyn Keene, *The Mystery of the Tolling Bell* (New York: Grosset and Dunlap, 1973 [revised]), 181.

40. Carolyn Keene, *The Witch Tree Symbol*, (New York: Grosset and Dunlap, 1975 [revised]), 88.

41. Caprio, 33.

42. Bobbie Ann Mason, *The Girl Sleuth* (Athens: University of Georgia Press, 1975), 99.

43. Parry, 150. Other critics who have discussed Nancy Drew as a feminist besides Parry include Carolyn Heilbrun (cited below); Melanie Rehak (*Girl Sleuth: Nancy Drew and the Women Who Created Her*, [Orlando: Harcourt, 2005]; JoAnne Furtak ("Of Clues, Kisses, and Childhood Memories: Nancy Drew Revisited," *Seventeen* [May 1984], 90); Hope E. Burwell ("Nancy Drew, Girl Detective, Nascent Feminist, and Family Therapist," *The English Journal* 84.4 [April 1995], 51–53); and Carol S. Chadwick ("Nancy Drew — The Perfect Solution," in Nancy Owen Nelson, ed., *Private Voices, Public Lives: Women Speak on the Literary Life* [Denton: University of North Texas Press, 1995], to name a few. Ilana Nash suggests that while Nancy herself may be interpreted in feminist ways, the series itself is not feminist, because the other women in the texts are not afforded the same qualities and opportunities Nancy is (42).

44. Carolyn G. Heilbrun, "Nancy Drew: A Moment in Feminist History," in Carolyn Stewart Dyer and Nancy Tillman Romalov, eds., *Rediscovering Nancy Drew* (Iowa City: University of Iowa Press, 1995), 11, and Diane Reynolds, "Nancy Drew: Is She a Virgin?," *The Whispered Watchword* 99–10 (Dec./Jan. 1999–2000), 2.

45. Caprio, 37.

46. Carolyn Keene, *The Bluebeard Room* (New York: Wanderer Books, 1985), 16. Hereafter, page number citations for *The Bluebeard Room* will appear in text.

47. *Ibid.*, back piece.

48. Robert Basler, "A New Image for Nancy Drew," *Philadelphia Inquirer* (29 June 1986), C2.

49. Ned here is somewhat akin to the wives in the "Bluebeard" legend, who allow their own sexuality to be re-made and re-cast by another. Yet the result is opposite; whereas Bluebeard destroys his wives for their altered sexuality, Nancy, at least until she enters *The Bluebeard Room*, would not allow Ned into her realm if he espoused any real spark of sexuality more than she, thus preserving their relationship and his identity as her "special friend."

50. Tatar 17,

51. This creates, in actuality, two wives for Hugh — one who is faithful and subservient (Lisa) and one who is disloyal and subversive (Nancy). This is interesting because Nancy's disobedience allows Lisa to stay in the role of faithful wife while ultimately solving the mystery of *The Bluebeard Room* and fixing the unhappy marriage. Thus, in a way, both obedience and disobedience are rewarded in the end, creating perhaps the "happy" ending that Perrault's tale could never manage (because Bluebeard has only one wife at a time).

52. Nedra Reynolds, *Geographies of Writing: Inhabiting Places and Encountering Difference* (Carbondale: Southern Illinois University Press, 2004), 59.
53. Michael R. Near, "Anticipating Alienation: *Beowulf* and the Intrusion of Literacy," *PMLA* 198.2 (1993), 325.
54. Laura Mulvey, "Visual Pleasure and Narrative Cinema," *Screen* 16.3 (1975), 17.
55. Garrido's cover art is the first of three for *The Bluebeard Room*. The second cover art, crafted by Bob Berran and released in 1988, removes the masculine altogether, placing Nancy on top of Penvellyn Castle watching Lisa as she sleepwalks by. Both women are dressed in long formal gowns (an oddity since both were supposed to be asleep at the start of this scene) which somehow, coupled with the absence of any male presence, emphasizes the feminine aspect of Nancy in art. Tellingly, the third cover art, designed in 1992 by Aleta Jenks, inverts Garrido's original scene, with Nancy now leading Lance up a stair, taking more familiarly the role to which she is most comfortably assigned — detective — and asserting her more usual feminist leanings. These competing versions of Nancy all suggest the inherent difficulty in depicting the balanced nature of the character's feminine/feminist space, especially when such a nuance must be represented in two-dimensional images against a narrative as sexualized as this.
56. Reynolds, 144.
57. *The Phantom of Venice* was likewise penned by Lawrence.
58. Hélène Cixous, "Sorties," in Cixous and Catherine Clement, eds., Betty Wing, trans., *The Newly Born Woman* (Minneapolis: University of Minnesota Press, 1986), 94–95.

Works Cited

Basler, Robert. "A New Image for Nancy Drew." *Philadelphia Inquirer*. 29 June 1986: C2.
Benjamin, Jessica. "A Desire of One's Own: Psychoanalytic Feminism and Intersubjective Space." *Feminist Studies/Critical Studies*. Ed. Teresa de Lauretis. Bloomington: University of Indiana Press, 1986. 78–101.
Burwell, Hope E. "Nancy Drew, Girl Detective, Nascent Feminist, and Family Therapist." *The English Journal* 84.4 (1995): 51–53.
Caprio, Betsy. *Girl Sleuth on the Couch: The Mystery of Nancy Drew*. Trabuco Canyon, CA: Source Books, 1992.
Chadwick, Carol S. "Nancy Drew — The Perfect Solution." *Private Voices, Public Lives: Women Speak on the Literary Life*. Ed. Nancy Owen Nelson. Denton: University of North Texas Press, 1995. 41–53.
Cixous, Hélène. "Sorties." *The Newly Born Woman*. Eds. Cixous and Catherine Clement. Trans. Betty Wing. Minneapolis: University of Minnesota Press, 1986.
Cornelius, Michael G. "'They blinded her with science': Science Fiction and Technology in Nancy Drew." *Nancy Drew and Her Sister Sleuths: Essays on the Fiction of Girl Detectives*. Eds. Cornelius and Melanie E. Gregg. Jefferson, NC: McFarland, 2008. 77–95.
de Lauretis, Teresa. *Technologies of Gender: Essays on Theory, Film, and Fiction*. Bloomington: University of Indiana Press, 1987.
Foucault, Michel. "Other Spaces: The Principles of Heterotopia." *Lotus* 48/49 (1986): 10–24.
Furtak, Joanne. "Of Clues, Kisses, and Childhood Memories: Nancy Drew Revisited." *Seventeen* (May 1984): 90.
Gill, C. M. "Hardy Camaraderie: Boy Sleuthing and Male Community in the Hardy Boys Mysteries." Ed. Michael G. Cornelius. *The Boy Detectives: Essays on the Hardy Boys and Others*. Jefferson, NC: McFarland, 2010. 35–50.

Heilbrun, Carolyn G. "Nancy Drew: A Moment in Feminist History." *Rediscovering Nancy Drew*. Eds. Carolyn Stewart Dyer and Nancy Tillman Romalov. Iowa City: University of Iowa Press, 1995.
Hempen, Daniela. "Bluebeard's Female Helper: The Ambiguous Rôle of the Strange Old Woman in the Grimms' 'Castle of Murder' and 'The Robber Bridegroom.'" *Folklore* 108 (1997): 45–48.
Jardine, Alice. *Gynesis: Configurations of Women and Modernity*. Ithaca: Cornell University Press, 1985.
Keeline, James D. "Who Wrote Nancy Drew? Secrets from the Syndicate Files Revealed." 16 Mar 2006. <keeline.com/Nancy_Drew.pdf>.
Keene, Carolyn. *The Bluebeard Room*. New York: Wanderer Books, 1985.
_____. *The Double Horror of Fenley Place*. New York. Pocket Books, 1987.
_____. *The Mystery at Lilac Inn*. Rev. ed. New York: Grosset and Dunlap, 1961.
_____. *The Mystery of the Tolling Bell*. Rev. ed. New York: Grosset and Dunlap, 1973.
_____. *The Phantom of Venice*. New York: Wanderer Books, 1985.
_____. *The Witch Tree Symbol*. Rev. ed. New York: Grosset and Dunlap, 1975.
MacLeod, Anne Scott. "Nancy Drew and Her Rivals: No Contest." *Horn Book* 63 (1987): 422–450.
Massey, Doreen. *Space, Place, and Gender*. Minneapolis: University of Minnesota Press, 1994.
McGrath, Anne. "Eye on Publishing." *Wilson Library Bulletin* (December 1984): 268–269.
Millet, Lydia. "The Wife Killer." *Mirror, Mirror, on the Wall: Women Writers Explore Their Favorite Fairy Tales*. Ed. Kate Bernheimer. New York: Doubleday, 1998. 230–246.
Mulvey, Laura. "Visual Pleasure and Narrative Cinema." *Screen* 16.3 (1975): 6–18.
Nash, Ilana. *American Sweethearts: Teenage Girls in Twentieth-Century Popular Culture*. Bloomington: Indiana University Press, 2006.
Near, Michael R. "Anticipating Alienation: *Beowulf* and the Intrusion of Literacy." *PMLA* 198.2 (1993): 320–332.
Parry, Sally E. "The Secret of the Feminist Heroine: The Search for Values in Nancy Drew and Judy Bolton." *Nancy Drew and Company: Culture, Gender, and Girls' Series*. Ed. Sherrie A. Inness. Bowling Green, OH: Bowling Green State University Popular Press, 1997. 145–158.
Perrault, Charles. "Bluebeard." In Maria Tatar, *Secrets Beyond the Door: The Story of Bluebeard and His Wives*. Princeton: Princeton University Press, 2004. 176–179.
Plunkett-Powell, Karen. *The Nancy Drew Scrapbook*. New York: St. Martin's Press, 1993.
Reynolds, Diane. "Nancy Drew: Is She a Virgin?" *The Whispered Watchword* 99–10 (Dec./Jan. 1999–2000): 2–4.
Reynolds, Nedra. *Geographies of Writing: Inhabiting Places and Encountering Difference*. Carbondale: Southern Illinois University Press, 2004.
Salvaggio, Ruth. "Theory and Space, Space and Women." *Tulsa Studies in Women's Literature* (7.2): 261–282.
Siegel, Deborah L. "Nancy Drew As New Girl Wonder: Solving It All for the 1930s." *Nancy Drew and Company: Culture, Gender, and Girls' Series*. Ed. Sherrie A. Inness. Bowling Green, OH: Bowling Green State University Popular Press, 1997. 159–182.
Sutton, Margaret. *The Vanishing Shadow*. New York: Grosset and Dunlap, 1932.
Tatar, Maria. *Secrets Beyond the Door: The Story of Bluebeard and His Wives*. Princeton: Princeton University Press, 2004.
Tickamyer, Ann R. "Space Matters! Spatial Inequality in Future Sociology." *Contemporary Sociology* 29.6 (Nov. 2000): 805–813.
Woodman, Marion. *The Pregnant Virgin*. Toronto: Inner City, 1985.

2. Not-So-Nice, Indeed
Mabel Maney, Girl Detectives, and Sexual Awakenings
Jennifer Mitchell

A (Perhaps Too) Personal Foreword

I have never had a particularly vexed relationship with Nancy Drew. She simply occupied my early readerly self. Of course, it is nearly impossible for me to approach anything related to my childhood life as a reader in purely objective, critical terms. I have distinct and warming memories of hiding myself under the covers, with an awkwardly large flashlight and whatever Nancy Drew book I was into at that moment. Now, though, I understand the parallel of watching a villain get caught and being on the precarious edge of getting caught myself—staying up past bedtime, reading in the dark, "straining my eyes." An avid reader, I'd plow my way through a case in a day or two, cultivating my own ability to identify potentially telling clues and subtly suspicious characters. My engagement with Nancy and her cases became a test of intellect and of my potential authorial chops; could I beat Nancy to it? Could I, someday, write my own mysteries, craftily leading readers astray only to have the deliberately chosen pieces of evidence fall into place to surprise the characters and readers alike?

Allow Me to Introduce the Nancys

Nancy Drew is, without question, an icon; questions arise, though, about the implications of that status. Jennifer Woolston reads Nancy as "the antithesis of passivity, therein promoting the idea of outward action and effectively serving as a subversively positive role model for young female readers."[1] Yet, Woolston's declaration that Nancy's perpetually proactive stance is the "recipe for success,"[2] does not ring true for other scholars of the series. Reading Nancy as inspiringly active presents a problem for Ilana Nash, who suggests that the "biggest fallacy in calling the Nancy Drew Mysteries a feminist series" is that "Nancy is the *only* female who embodies multiple admirable traits."[3] Although Nash and Woolston agree that Nancy is the site of oft-impressive, albeit also complicated, feminist-inspired characteristics, their readings of the series are importantly oppositional. That the same sets of characteristics can incite such dramatically divergent interpretations is a testament to what Kathleen Chamberlain identifies as the "contradictions" at the "core of Nancy's appeal": "Nancy Drew is a powerful cultural icon because of, not despite, the paradoxical nature of the lessons she teaches."[4] Chamberlain locates such contradictions in the series' representations of gender, race, economics, and wholesomeness. Michael Cornelius further articulates those contradictions as having their roots in the girl sleuth's "impossibly" gendered self:

> Many of the qualities that are largely unique to the girl sleuth character — her independence, her puissance, her sense of justice, her fearlessness — are those qualities that are more often described as emanating from traditional masculine realms. More feminine characteristics — her gentility, her compassion, her dedication to appearance — are often viewed negatively, not as weaknesses, but as qualities that do not distinguish the characters beyond other examples of girl-driven literary creations of the twentieth century.[5]

Cornelius reads the gendered dichotomy of traits ascribed to the girl sleuth as indicative of a seemingly impossible self, and as particularly revealing when it comes to the angle of the critic approaching the text. Thus, it is not at all surprising that almost a hundred years after her inception, Nancy Drew continues to divide critics about issues that range from the obviously controversial — class and gender — to the seemingly trivial — wardrobe, pleasantries, food.

For the purposes of this piece, I am interested not simply in Nancy as a figure, but in Nancy as a deliberately heterosexualized girl that invites Mabel Maney's contemporary rewriting of her — and of another famed girl detective, Cherry Ames — in *The Case of the Not-So-Nice Nurse* (1993). Maney's text, a campy and hilarious look into the infrastructure of early girl detective novels, is actually a project of revision — and, more notably, a re-envisioning — of what Nancy Drew has represented to girls during the twentieth-century. Maney extrapolates elements that are quintessentially Nancy Drew, and, perhaps surprisingly to some readers, Sherrie A. Inness identifies lesbianism as one of those elements: "Lesbianism cannot easily be separated from the text, despite the book's apparent allegiance to heterosexual values."[6] Despite the text's seeming adherence to heterosexuality, there is room for interpretation and, of course, reinterpretation. Maney's texts are a testament to some of the powerful, latent or explicit, sexualized elements within the earlier series.

In order to understand the implications of the conversation that Maney sets up between her revised and revamped characters and their foundations, I analyze a variety of the most representative aspects of the Nancy Drew series — her distinct family, her diverse friends, the text's use of food, her implicit sexual self—in conjunction with Maney's reframing of those same elements. As Maney herself explains, "I don't want just to lift a character, but to talk about Nancy as an icon of proper middle-class America and to create characters that show the hidden world of women that's always been there. I wanted to create a world that was a whole lot nicer."[7] "Nicer," for Maney— a well-meaning jab at the discourse of the original series—means the incorporation, exploitation, celebration, and subversion of elements that define not only the *Nancy Drew* texts, but also the teenage detective genre as a whole. Through Nancy Clue and Cherry Aimless, the text's complicated, campy, and sexualized heroines, Maney replaces a set of implicit gender and sexual stereotypes with more explicit commentary about gender and sexuality; broader sexual identities ascribed to a variety of characters in the text are, for Maney, organic to the characters, the narrative of the text and the girl detective genre as a whole. Maney utilizes the genre to create the space for questions of sexual identity to become a part of the mysteries within the narrative; as Carolyn Keene's Nancy Drew seeks out villains and uncovers crimes, so Mabel Maney's Cherry Aimless and Nancy Clue also seek out villains and uncover crimes. But, further, Cherry Aimless and Nancy Clue are also seeking out and uncovering sexual possibilities—identities, experiences, choices, and expressions. Contemporary readings of *The Case of the Not-So-Nice Nurse* foster a reconsideration of the politics of innocence, discovery, heroics and friendship. Ultimately, Maney's text begs to be approached as more than simply a revision, but rather a re-invention of the genre and the sexual identities that have been a part of that genre for almost the last century.

Oh, Daddy's Girl

Nancy Drew presents readers with a life that, although it may feel "normal" within the confines of the text, is far from the life of a typical teenage girl. The seeming contradiction here lies in the way that Nancy's life is crafted as ordinary, even despite its extraordinariness. As Ilana Nash so rightly points out, Nancy, like other adolescent heroes and heroines, is a "semi-orphan": "teenagers, in order to effect the kind of perfect agency which Stratemeyer excelled at portraying, needed freedom of movement."[8] A useful narrative mechanism, removing a parent—or, later, multiple parents—is a strategic way of removing some of the ties that inhibit a young, developing character. Yet, as Nash also declares, the absence of Nancy's mother in the series does more than simply allow her an extended curfew: "In the case of Nancy Drew the absence of a mother also loosens gender-related constraints.... Mrs. Drew's death during her daughter's childhood frees Nancy to grow up as the lady of the house, the mother of her own identity, and the apple of her father's eye."[9] Mrs. Drew is not only physically absent, but theoretically, as well; without so much as a first name, Mrs. Drew is a character comprised entirely of vague, peripheral reference. As a result, Jennifer Woolston contends "Nancy is not oppressed by a female influence and experiences no sense of feminine rivalry. There are no older women, other than the occasionally present housekeeper, to limit her decisions or actions ... instead of being confined by the rules (or laws) or the father, Nancy is allowed to engage in adventures of her own choosing, thereby proving to be active within the adult world of decision-making."[10] Because Woolston reads the absence of a mother-figure as *the* positive foundation for an active, adult-like Nancy, she refuses to acknowledge the presence of alternative motherly possibilities.

Nancy is not entirely the lady of the house, as some version of a traditional two-parent household can be located within the series. Hannah Gruen, the Drews' loyal housekeeper does play a usefully maternal role, providing Nancy with comfort and outlets for her emotion while never fully being able to encroach on her freedom, a matter of class distinction. In the 1959 version of *The Hidden Staircase*, Hannah is introduced, in fact, as a surrogate mother: "Mrs. Gruen had lived with the Drews since Nancy was three years old. At that time Mrs. Drew had passed away and Hannah had become like a second mother to Nancy. There was a deep affection between the two, and Nancy confided all her secrets to the understanding housekeeper."[11] While Hannah is introduced as the primary female in Nancy's life and put in direct comparison to Mrs. Drew, her status as housekeeper is still a constant reminder of the constraints of her position. Furthermore, Hannah's subsequent declarations of reassurance in the face of somewhat bleak circumstances, "I'm sure everything will come out all right for everybody" (*Hidden Staircase*, 11), reassure readers of her motherly potential while simultaneously making her look hopelessly optimistic in comparison to Nancy.

Contemporary readers of the series might be perplexed by the family dynamic presented. A successful, attractive lawyer living with his housekeeper would, of course, beg a variety of questions from even the least invasive reader. Attune to contemporary concerns, Maney presents readers with a much darker possibility. Cherry Aimless, Maney's primary protagonist in *The Case of the Not-So-Nice Nurse*, reads the following headline in complete disbelief: "ATTORNEY CARSON CLUE MURDERED! *Longtime housekeeper admits the dastardly deed!*"[12] Although Cherry's shock mirrors that of *Seattle Post* readers of the headline, it also mirrors that of *Nancy Drew* readers: "Nancy Clue's father dead at the hands of kindly housekeeper Hannah Gruel! It just couldn't be!" (*Case*, 8). Maney utilizes the familiarity of the Drew family dynamic to draw readers in but immediately unsettles such familiarity by destroying the core relationships within that family. Of course, the mystery at the heart of Cherry's reaction to the news—"It just couldn't be!"—parallels the series of mysteries that surface within the novel. Preoccupied by the breakdown of Nancy Clue, a girl she "practically worshipped" (*Case*, 9), Cherry continues to ponder Hannah's descent into murder:

> Try as she might, she just couldn't stop thinking about the murder. Something just didn't seem right. "Hannah's been like a mother to me," Nancy had been quoted in the *Girls' Life* article. "How strange," Cherry mused, "that helpful Hannah, who had given a lifetime of care to Mr. Clue and his motherless daughter, should turn out to be a murderess...." Perhaps there was something she had missed, something that would explain the odd turn of events [*Case*, 10].

Again, Cherry's response to Nancy Clue's family turmoil is virtually the same as the informed reader's response to this potential representation of Nancy Drew. After the novel's primary mystery is solved—the case of the missing nuns, to which I will later return—Cherry's focus turns to the death of Carson Clue. After an overwhelming display of emotion, Nancy finally declares, "My father was not killed by Hannah Gruel! It was *I* who shot him!" (*Case*, 160). Nancy's confession shocks those around her as the destruction of the family suddenly results from a true insider, rather than Hannah's still-othered self.

Nancy's explanation reflects Nash's assertion that the death of Mrs. Drew allows Nancy to grow up as *the* woman of the house: "He became obsessed with my appearance, insisting I wear grown-up dresses and stylish hair-dos. After we'd fight he'd always buy me something big and flashy, like a new car. The neighbors thought he was the greatest" (*Case*, 161). In this small explanation, Maney addresses some of the most defining aspects of Nancy's life, and of the *Nancy Drew* narratives overall: Nancy's continuously perfect appearance and the car that "allows her mobility."[13] Of course, these are elements that further distance Nancy's reality from the reality of her readers. Maney addresses the "unreality" of these elements by complicating their existence; rather than testaments to Nancy's ideal lifestyle, they are evidence of a domineering and abusive father.[14] The insinuation of abuse here is made more explicit with Nancy's next confession: "When I was thirteen I started maturing; I was becoming a woman. It was then he ... well, he forced me to do things" (*Case*, 161). Carson Clue, in readers' minds a representation of the familial support and respect associated with Carson Drew, is suddenly depicted as a monster. As Nash reads Carson Drew "more like a peer" than a father, Maney extends those implications substantially: "It was as if I were his wife!" (*Case*, 161). Nancy is made the "woman of the house" in every capacity; not only is she the prime female figure by virtue of an absent mother, but she is made into a wife as a result of her father's sexual molestation. Importantly, the abuse begins as Nancy physically transitions from girl to woman, suggesting a peculiarity about the original series—that Carson Drew functioned without a sexual or romantic outlet. Whereas Nancy is given the occasional and fleeting date, like Dirk Jackson in *The Hidden Staircase*, or, in later stories, the consistent, though almost lifeless boyfriend, Ned Nickerson, Carson Drew is never given a replacement partner. Interestingly, as the diverse values celebrated by the variety of writers who filled Carolyn Keene's shoes present readers with various, at times conflicting representations of Nancy herself, virtually all of the authors of the series seem to agree that Carson ought to remain a bachelor.[15] Maney's assertion that Nancy could prove such a viable, though catastrophic, surrogate is a testament to the possibility that Nancy is invited to be viewed—consciously or not—as an implicit surrogate in this regard.

In her interview with Laura Harris and Liz Crocker, Maney explains her version of the father daughter relationship: "I feel that there is a very incestuous subtext in the original Nancy Drew books. Her mother is dead and Nancy is paired with her father in a curious way."[16] That curiosity allows Maney to exploit what she sees as the latent possibility of incest in the original texts. For Maney, the subtext is precisely sub-text, as Carson's peripheral presence in the text—often away on business trips thereby communicating with Nancy through abbreviated phone calls—is one protective layer against the accusations of incest. Yet, Maney's reading of the incestuous father-daughter matrix allows her to bring to the forefront what she sees as the problematic placement of single women in the original series; regardless of how subtly it is presented to reader, Nancy, the "woman" of the house *must* fill every role that such a designation entails.

Just as Maney rewrites Nancy's father as a "monster" and a "bully," she rewrites Hannah accordingly. More akin to a mother in Maney's version, Hannah is used by Carson as a way of preventing Nancy from squealing: "When he started bothering me, he told me that if I told anyone he'd harm Hannah" (*Case,* 161). Hannah's primary role in Nancy's life makes her the ideal target for Carson's threats, which encompass not only Hannah but Nancy's birth mother as well: "No one else knows it, but Mother died in an asylum and he used to say I was crazy, just like her! And he'd add, I could have you put away, just like I did her!' (*Case,* 161). All possible representations of mother and wife are targeted here; the lineage between Nancy and her biological mother—a sacred subject virtually off limits in the original series— is made potentially disastrous in Maney's version. Moreover, Maney emphasizes the problematic roots of Carson's power in this situation by his usage of gender and weakness; he defines his power in contrast to a "crazy" wife, a potentially "crazy" daughter, and the foolish praise of unknowing neighbors.

Although Maney's primary critique against the originally crafted family dynamic is presented in sexual terms, she deliberately ties that sexual argument to an economic one, emphasizing Hannah's marginalized class position. Critics of the original series have suggested that, at its core, it is "very racist and very classist and very judgmental."[17] Such scholarship presents readers with an abundance of lower-class, ethnically-othered villains, yet Maney further exploits such clearly delineated lines in her characterization of the final altercation between Hannah and Carson. When Hannah's anticipated absence finally encourages Nancy to speak up—"I just knew it would get worse with her gone. I broke down and told her, and when my father came home, she confronted him"—Carson's response is a testament to his adherence (and, according to Maney, the entire series' adherence) to catastrophic class divides: "...he just laughed. 'Who'd believe you over me?'" (*Case*, 161). Hannah's attempts to protect Nancy, Maney's reinforcement of her motherly qualities, are initially overwhelmed by Carson's presentation of himself as all-knowing and all-powerful: a wealthy, well-educated, white man. Regardless of Hannah's merits and heroics, Nancy quickly realizes that Carson is, in fact, absolutely correct in his logic; here, Maney's reading of the series' economic and cultural bias is at its most potent. Carson, with his race, class, reputation, appearance, and status will always present a more alluringly reliable witness than his housekeeper.

Thus, during the pseudo-parental confrontation between Carson and Hannah, as Nancy "thought he was going to kill her," she realized that the only way to eliminate Carson as a threat is to actually eliminate him altogether, yelling "Father," grabbing "one of his guns," and shooting him "right through the heart" (*Case*, 162). The guns, obviously phallic testaments to Carson's masculinity and power, are usurped by Nancy in this momentary reversal of power. Nancy's last word to her father, a loud denunciation of his position relative to her, is quickly trumped by Hannah's motherly interjections: "Hannah begged me to let her say she did it, and I agreed.... She told me to forget and never tell anyone what had happened" (*Case*, 162). Hannah's sacrifice is the quintessential maternal gesture, and Maney's reinforcement of Hannah's status as Nancy's *only* parent. Despite Carson's physical absence from the text, Nancy remains overburdened by the stress of his murder and Hannah's unjust incarceration. Nancy cannot simply forget, and her newfound friends chime in to reassure her that she's not alone. Herein lies Maney's violent destruction of the latent gender inequalities in the nuclear (and not quite so nuclear) family within the original books, and a revision that highlights the criminal sexualization of Nancy, the creation of "wife," and the ultimate elimination of the problem.[18] Furthermore, killing Carson is vital for Maney's creation of an all-queer space. Once Carson is removed from the body of the text, almost every character that readers are introduced to is queer — in sexual, gender, political, legal, and other regards. For Maney, Carson is the last embodiment of a wealthy, sterile, destructive, mistakenly empowered conservatism that must and will undoubtedly be replaced by a dispersed and multifaceted queerness.

Best Friends Forever (and Ever and Ever)

Critics often argue, in the words of Kathleen Chamberlain, that "what young readers see in Nancy is not themselves as they are, but as they *would* be,"[19] and use her exaggerated best friends as a way to help prove Nancy's allure. Bess Marvin and George Fayne are almost always introduced to readers as two cousins who "could hardly have been more different."[20] Bess, constantly caught in a flirting or feeding frenzy, is usually described as "plump" and full of "enthusiasm" while George is "pretty ... trim-figured," and "as active and adventurous as her boyish nickname suggested" (*Bluebeard*, 2, 3). While contemporary young adult novels might utilize the three girls to make a complete and complementary threesome, the original series uses Bess and George to help isolate and define Nancy. Ilana Nash cites Susan Brownmiller's memories of the series: "I mean her friend George dressed like a boy and Bess was fat, so you didn't want to be her. Nancy had the car, Nancy had the boyfriend."[21] Nash reads Brownmiller's look back at the cast of Nancy's life as indicative of the "failed femininities of Nancy's friends."[22] It seems important, though, that Bess and George do reflect characteristics that can be located within Nancy herself: Bess's flirtatiousness and attention to detail, George's athleticism and beauty. However, by characterizing the girls to excess—Bess's inability to function in the face of a handsome fellow or George's masculine overtones—the original series undercuts traits that are otherwise ideal in Nancy.

Maney, though, presents readers with a cast that picks up on one of the implicit characteristics that she locates in George. In an interview with Owen Keehnen, Maney explains, "Plus in Nancy Drew you had George, 'The giggly girl with the boy's name.' Come on, everybody knew George was a dyke. It was great."[23] Maney outs George as an obvious dyke while Sherrie A. Inness utilizes sexology in order to "diagnose" George: "She fits neatly into the category of the mannish lesbian, which was described by late nineteenth-century sexologists, such as Richard von Krafft-Ebing, who discussed in the 1880s what he named the 'female urning' who ignored 'girlish occupations,' neglected her toilet, and affected 'rough boyish manners'" (418).[24] Inness's contextual reading of George provides a telling explanation of what Stephanie Foote identifies as Maney's "fidelity to, not their knowing divergence from, the Nancy Drew books."[25] Foote's understanding of Maney's project prioritizes Maney's reliance upon the tropes and patterns set up in the original series; highlighting the relationship between George and Bess as latently lesbian, Foote declares that Maney had "not all that much to change":

> George and Bess, Nancy's two best friends, are a classic butch-femme couple: George is a slim, boyish young woman with short, dark hair, and Bess is a blowsy blond bombshell. They appear everywhere together, and when Nancy goes out with her boyfriend Ned ... she tends to double date with George and Bess. All Mabel Maney needs to do in the case of those characters is import.[26]

Although Foote reads George and Bess in a way that highlights the original series' reliance upon implicitly homoerotic dynamics, she refers to such dynamics as "strangeness."[27] In some ways, that ambiguity is a telling adherence to the way that sexuality is simultaneously ubiquitous and absent from the *Nancy Drew* texts. While Nancy's heterosexuality is peripherally mentioned in virtually every book in the series, it is not a particularly revealing element of her character. Instead, the brief reference to Dirk Jackson in *The Hidden Staircase* establishes Nancy as an active part of a dating, heterosexual community, yet no part of that date is of substantial importance — an element of the text that contributes to what Sherrie A. Inness astutely deems "superficially heterosexual."[28] Rather, it is simply the mention of the date itself that reminds readers that although Nancy does seem to step outside of the bounds of ladylike propriety, her heterosexuality eases concerns associated with gender deviance. That Dirk was added during the 1950s Stratemeyer Syndicate revisions is a testament to the strength and pervasiveness of those concerns; the revisions themselves, an attempt at making Nancy less overtly independent and brash, highlighted Nancy's tangential participation in heterosexual courtship rituals. Ilana Nash targets the almost irrelevant nature of that participation when she suggests that "Nancy does not suffer the same fate as typical heroines; her boyfriend Ned may drop hints about marriage, but Keene keeps him on a short tether, never allowing his fantasies of domestic bliss to stick to Nancy. Indeed, Nancy dodges all projections, domestic and otherwise. At no point is her behavior successfully constrained by others' definitions of her sex or her age."[29] Despite the encompassing nature of the revisions, Nancy's heterosexuality rarely extends beyond the surface.

Reaching underneath the hetero-road-markers in the original series, Maney is able to build up on the gap between sexuality and self that the original text cannot seem to close. Despite Maney's loyalty to early George's apparent lesbianism, the explicit homosexuality within Maney's text reinforces its implicit role within the earlier series. As Foote declares, "George and Bess's existence in the first Nancy Drew series makes Nancy's adherence to gender norms seem more parodic than natural, something Maney also exploits in her updated books."[30] Maney introduces readers to a cast of women that span the sexual spectrum — sort of. Because Cherry Aimless's mother is a staunch advocate of the "*Single* doctors" that her daughter works with, she reminds Cherry of the importance of settling down: "no man would want to marry her if she didn't begin to act more interested in dating" (*Case*, 37–8). Indeed, the Aimless parents are representations of the quintessential 1950s nuclear family — a mother who is "such a dear" and a father who is "demanding," "in one of his moods," and career-obsessed (*Case*, 37, 36, 177, 33). Yet, while Maney does not spare Mr. Aimless from a series of harsh criticisms, she does give substantially more depth to Mrs. Aimless. When Cherry declares that she intends to visit her Aunt Gertrude, estranged from Mr. Aimless, her mother smoothes her path: "I made a deal with your father. He lets you visit Gert, and I promise not to put arsenic in his coffee!" (*Case*, 40). Mrs. Aimless may play nice and domestic, over-accommodating her grumpy husband and diligently preparing cheese balls for guests, but she is certainly able to play sassy, as well.[31]

Furthermore, Maney utilizes the cast of characters within her text as a way of emphasizing the variety of roles available to women, both sexually and otherwise. Take the reader's introduction to Lauren, for example: "Cherry peeked and saw a slender lad clad in baggy overalls and a plaid shirt with a newsbag slung over his shoulder" (*Case*, 93). Continuously referred to as "he" by all of the women at Aunt Gert's, Lauren is only revealed as a girl when Cherry "gave the lad a consoling hug," discovering "the soft curves of a young girl!" (*Case*, 95). Two and a half pages after Lauren surfaces in the text, the rest of the girls find themselves in shock at the revelation of her identity as "girl." Maney seems to be playing with the masculine traits that critics often identify in Nancy Drew and her fellow girl sleuths; such masculine traits are, of course, internal characteristics and reading them as masculine means forcing personalities to be gendered. Maney uses Lauren's first appearance as a reminder to readers that Nancy Drew's "independence" is no more necessarily masculine than her "appearance" is necessarily feminine. With the introduction of Lauren, and the immediate processing of Lauren as boy, Maney suggests that a seamless reading of gender, especially on the surface level, is simply impossible. Indeed, Maney seems to be exploiting the troublesome — and ultimately false — ease with which Nancy Drew's heterosexuality is presented to readers. While no reader would mistake Nancy for a boy, Nancy's heterosexuality is far from clear-cut and legible.

While Lauren might be the most overt example of Maney's playfulness in this regard, she certainly is not on her own. When Midge decides that Cherry needs a disguise, Midge declares, "We need to make you look so different that even your own mother wouldn't recognize you" (*Case*, 78). Right after Midge and the hairstylist chop and buzz off most of Cherry's curly hair, she shrieks, "Eek!" and cries, "I look like a boy!" (*Case*, 80). The planned disguise reflects the gap between appearance and self; even though Midge reassures Cherry that "no one could ever mistake you for a boy," part of the plan for the disguise rests on the assumed misinterpretation of Cherry by those who do not know her (*Case*, 80). By changing Cherry's hair and ultimately dressing her in men's clothing, Midge introduces Cherry to the distinction "butch," a signifier that Cherry misreads entirely: "And who is this Butch person you're always talking about?" (*Case*, 83). While Cherry's question remains technically unanswered, "butch" in the text is what ultimately allows her to be simultaneously girl and boy: to appear as boy, thereby throwing off the villains after her, but to be girl, a part of her identity that she sees as irreplaceable.

When faced with the question "When you are writing, are you thinking about the butch-femme codes—that you are putting out a code that only a certain kind of subculture is going to pick up on?" Maney explains the relationship between butch and femme that she crafts within the text: "Oh, absolutely.... I have met people who say, 'Oh, Nancy [Clue] can't be a butch, because she wears a dress.' But I see her as definitely a butch. She is sort of upper-class butch; she conforms to her culture."[32] Not only does Maney utilize the potential gap between appearance and identity as a way of subverting the original series' reliance upon appearance as the prime indicator of character, but she removes "butch" from the realm of narrow lesbian identities and positions it as an open-ended category of self with a variety of individual connotations.[33] Moreover, Maney presents readers with a reality that, while subversive and new, feels familiar; she explains, "One reason for the [butch-femme universe] is that it is just a mimicry of the originals; keeping it in the fifties keeps this layer of innocence that you could never have now."[34] Cherry's shock at the range of identities she could put on (literally) does indeed capture the innocence that defined the original series. Yet, just as Maney incorporates both implicit and explicit designations of "butch" and "femme" that seem to mirror earlier designations of "masculine" and "feminine," she also presents readers with a range in between such oppositional binaries. Midge, Velma, flirty Sally, Officer Jones, Lana, and Peg allow Maney to establish a spectrum of identities that expands notions of specific types of women. Maney sets up rules that she herself even refuses to play by; contemporary audiences of Maney's text are instructed to reopen and reposition types of selves, with potentially large-scale, dramatic consequences.

Chock Full of Chocolate

Early on in *The Case of the Not-So-Nice Nurse,* Cherry has a somewhat peculiar conversation with herself about chocolate:

> Cherry took her time selecting an assortment of chocolates. "Coconut crèmes or caramels?" she wondered, furrowing her pretty brow. She laughed when she caught a glimpse of herself in the mirror behind the counter. "I look so serious," she thought. "Just a few days ago, I was making life-or-death decisions, and today I'm selecting candy with the same earnestness! Although, when a girl's ready to get her visitor, sometimes chocolate can be pretty serious," Cherry had to admit [*Case*, 44].

Prior to this stressful selection of chocolates, food has been front and center in the text. Right before Cherry's departure to visit her family en route to San Francisco, Cherry ate a "delicious breakfast of soft-boiled eggs, melba toast and fruit cup" and on the road enjoys "a nourishing lunch of an egg salad sandwich, jello and milk" (*Case*, 24, 27). Once at home with her family, Cherry prepares to enjoy one of her mother's "award-winning strawberry waffles" and a vanilla soda at Tilly's Drugstore (*Case*, 35). She goes home to a "special supper of pot roast, baked potatoes and green bean casserole," "strawberry cake [with] vanilla icing" (*Case*, 36). I could literally spend several pages just rehashing the discussions of food in Maney's text; during my first reading of it, I remember thinking that she simply got the picture — the early emphasis on all aspects of domesticity that again reinforces ideas of Nancy's wholesomeness and adherence to certain gender rules of behavior.

Elizabeth Marshall writes about Nancy's notable relationship to food: "Unlike Bess, who can wolf down five sandwiches at one time, Nancy's appetite isn't excessive.... Nancy often stops for lunch or dinner, and even indulges in dessert; however, mysterious events or clues tend to interrupt her meals."[35] Marshall critiques the series for its prioritization of Nancy's body, "taut, athletic, and slim ... usually under control."[36] Suggesting that the original texts present readers with problematic messages about appetite, with "Nancy, Bess, and George ... portrayed as being 'ashamed' of their hearty appetites," Marshall highlights Nancy's status as ideal — never overindulgent, never excessive, never boyish. Beth Younger, in her survey of contemporary Young Adult texts, echoes the importance of this "shame":

> Young Adult fiction encourages young women's self-surveillance of their bodies ... unless the weight of a character is specifically mentioned, the reader will most likely assume the character is thin. Only if the character is considered abnormal, i.e., fat or chubby, is her weight mentioned at all. Women and girls who are heavy are *always* identified as such. Even in diverse and otherwise progressive texts, the fat person is marked as Other.[37]

Although Nancy and George have rather svelt figures—despite the presentation of Nancy's in significantly more feminine terms than George's—Bess's chubbiness concerns Nancy, George, and readers alike. Bess's physical and personal excesses manifest themselves in her inability to control her body, her laughter, her fear, and her flirtations, while Nancy is presented to readers as embodying the ideal amount of self-control. Accordingly, Woolston's reading of Nancy's body "as a vehicle through which she can pursue her curiosity, where she feels physical reactions pertaining to her adventures, and where numerous (primarily male) villains seek to restrain her" relies on her respect of Nancy's "autonomous female body."[38] That autonomy, though, is compromised by the body's adherence to a set of problematic cultural associations; indeed, for Marshall, the texts' reliance upon the oft-criticized relationship between "slenderness" and "heterosexual restraint," allows for the implicit criticism of Bess as oversexualized, a characteristic emphasized by her interest in "romance." Younger, too, suggests that "heavy characters are all represented as sexually promiscuous, passive, and powerless, while thin characters appear responsible and powerful."[39] Although George is certainly not the star of the show, she helps Nancy out in significantly more productive ways than silly, girly Bess.[40]

Importantly, Nancy's eating habits are not universally agreed upon; Sherrie A. Inness approaches Nancy's eating habits from a vastly different perspective: "Even her eating patterns are not typically 'lady-like.' Between adventures, she always makes it home for a snack, lunch, or dinner produced by Hannah.... Nancy thinks nothing of consuming a meal consisting of cream of mushroom soup, tomato salad, lamb chops, French fries, peas, and chocolate pie. Chasing crooks must burn a lot of calories, because she maintains her svelt figure...."[41] The divergence of critical opinions on food suggests that the revisions that Maney makes to the eating habits of her characters are far from trivial, which they might initially appear to be. Even the review from *SF Weekly* quoted on the back cover of the book celebrates Maney's lampooning of "the torpid style of both children's books and lesbian mysteries where similarly nothing happens without at least three changes of clothing and a good, hot meal." An integral part of the genre, the focus on food that proves so unsettling for Marshall actually helps to mark Cherry's movement throughout the text. While fretting over chocolate, Cherry is ascribed a moment of bodily awareness that extends beyond her "ungainly size-nine feet" in which eating becomes associated with femininity and the female body (*Case*, 27); rather than Nancy Drew's awareness of and seeming appreciation for food, Maney allows Cherry the freedom to genuinely enjoy it. Moreover, the linkage between food and the body—however playfully that linkage is presented, considering the relationship between a menstruating woman and her chocolate supply — suggests that Cherry is able to make a connection between self and desire, something it takes her the entire rest of the text to realize and understand. Indeed, Cherry's relationship with food suggests a significantly active and positive connection, deviating not only from the original series but also from contemporary texts that still adhere to a model of self control vis-à-vis a girl's eating habits.

Uncovering a Whole Bunch of Truths

In her introduction to *The Case of the Not-So-Nice Nurse*, Mabel Maney explains her timeless interest in the Cherry Ames series: "They are a homoerotic, fetishistic cheese fest, escapism of the purest form. Who wouldn't want to live in an all-girl dorm, giggle late into the night, and wear a starched uniform and jaunty cap? Finally, a girlfriend my mother would approve of!" Maney's understanding of the Cherry Ames texts — and, of course, her girl detective counterparts like Nancy Drew — reflects her interest in the possibilities associated with an all-female space. That is, of course, what readers find themselves amidst in her rewriting. Maney takes the idea of an "all-girl dorm" and exploits it, utilizing a convent and an order of nuns as the backdrop for the prime mystery within the text. While Katharine M. Rogers, in her exploration of eighteenth-century fictional convents, dismisses the "lurid sexual fantasies ... about nuns," the relationship between sex and nunneries is a substantial one, at least in literary terms.[42] Contrary to the idea that Susan P. Casteras puts forth, "that the nun might qualify as a perfect embodiment of the Victorian idealization of womanhood, particularly with her qualities of virginity, docility, dedication, spirituality, and modesty," pornographic interest in the nunnery could be located in tendencies to mistrust the convent itself.[43] Casteras cites Mrs. Anna Jameson: "I conceive that any large number of women shut up together in the locality, with no occupation connecting them actively with the world or humanity outside, would not mend each other, and that such an atmosphere could not be perfectly healthy, spiritually, morally, or physically."[44] Mrs. Anna Jameson locates within the all-female space of the convent the potential for idleness, personal decay and, perhaps, bawdy and lewd behavior. Maney doesn't quite play by these rules, choosing instead to celebrate the convent as a harmonious and productive safe-haven — for girls who have been abused, for women needing to escape their lives, and for lesbians seeking a sanctioned outlet for their expressions of emotion.

Maney highlights the importance of this female-only space in the unfolding of the text's main mystery — the disappearing nuns. When the gang finally tracks down their whereabouts, the importance of the nunnery reveals itself.

During their time locked up, Midge tells the rest of the girls her real history including her shooting of the father who was "horrible ... beating the bejesus out" of her (*Case*, 126). On the run, Midge went to the Mother Superior who provided her with papers, identification, money—all of the tools necessary for Midge to survive on the run. Midge's story reveals the nature of the nunnery itself—"an important institution for females on the run" (*Case*, 129). The threat to the nunnery takes the form of a group of sinister and greedy priests—the most sustained representation of men in the entire text. Directly contrasted to the generosity of the women, these men will stop at nothing— including murder—to acquire the land that belongs to the nunnery. When put side by side, the priests line up quite well with the abusive fathers, husbands and boyfriends from which the nunnery protects women; moreover, the priests are presented as creating villains-in-training with their use of dangerous and threatening altar boys. Just as the convent itself creates generations of grateful women who seek to help others in return, so the evil priests attempt to create mini-evil-priests, one of Maney's major comparisons of the two genealogies.

Overall, Maney allows for a complete division of traditional genders and sexualities; while gay men in the novel, including Cherry's brother, his partner, Midge and Velma's neighbors, are presented as perpetual allies, other types of men are represented as constant sources of villainy. Again, Maney seems to be picking up on and subsequently revising a trope common to the original texts—the presentation of the male characters. Ellen Brown points out, "Men were secondary to Nancy Drew's world; boyfriends, Dad, captains of police forces—all were at Nancy's disposal to help with a case, but they remained in the background, arriving in time to clean up and arrest after Nancy had solved and caught."[45] Brown's assessment of the role of men within the original series suggests that Nancy is able to shine as the hero and star of the series because all of the men within that series are only marginally involved. Although Maney counters the earlier reliance on racial and economic "Others" as villains by constructing the villains as powerful white men, virtually all men in the novel abuse the power at their disposal.

The presentations of the convent and the villains threatening it are the most overt elements of the mystery that unfold in the text; yet, it is certainly not the only set of circumstances that warrant uncovering. Stephanie Foote explains Maney's queer rewriting in terms that highlight her motivations and her means:

> The covers lovingly borrow the lurid elements of the classic Nancy Drew book covers, the prose mimics the breathless excitability of the mysteries, and perhaps more importantly, the texts pick up on some of the strangeness of the Nancy Drew cast of characters.... Finally, there is no doubt that the

genre of the mystery, in combination with the girls' book, is the engine of queerness for Maney, for it supposes that there are secrets to read and reread in the texts addressed to "normal" girls.[46]

Although the *Nancy Drew* stories certainly had their fair share of crimes, mysteries and secrets, Maney unfolds seemingly limitless other mysteries within the confines of that same type of mystery tale. In spite of Maney's assessment of her own texts—"I think of them as romances disguised as mysteries"[47]— the mystery genre is ideal for her project; in fact, the detective fiction genre is the only medium that allows Maney to layer such local mysteries as the missing nuns, the identity of Lana, and the disappearance of Aunt Gert within such broader social "mysteries" including the development of one's sexual self, the ability to accurately read someone else's identity and desires, and the sexual codes that give way to knowledge. Maney's seeming prioritization of romance over mystery is perhaps a testament to her girlhood crush on Cherry Ames and does not necessarily undercut the way that she presents the constant unfolding of one's sexual identity as parallel to the clue-hunting, case-solving infrastructure of the detective novel.

While the missing convent itself is clearly one of the typical elements of a detective story, Cherry's progressive awareness of herself and the world around her is equally mysterious. Sherrie A. Inness points out that

> one of the reasons for the appeal of the Drew books to lesbian readers is that their formulaic plots suggest a possible path through a lesbian's life. The young lesbian who has yet to discover her sexual identification has a secret in her life (her lesbianism) that she must search to discover, although she will be hindered at every step of the way by individuals who would prefer that she did not solve this mystery.[48]

Reading Nancy Drew as potentially queer allows for an alignment of the mystery of sexual identity with the mystery within the detective novel — something that Maney clearly picks up on in Cherry's character. Notably, though, *The Case of the Not-So-Nice Nurse* is filled, not with individuals who "hinder" Cherry's discovery, but rather those who provide Cherry with ample support and opportunity to discover that aspect of herself. Early on in the text, Maney deliberately highlights Cherry's innocence, choosing to focus on her perpetually telling blush, first revealing itself when a fellow nurse asks about her "shrine" to Nancy Clue. Maney uses Cherry's blush to reinforce her development throughout the novel; its appearance signals to readers Cherry's discomfort with her disappointments and insecurities, the knowledge she slowly acquires and the spotlight she unexpectedly finds herself in. The earliest sexually-tinged usage of Cherry's revealing blush comes from nosing around Lana, the beautiful amnesia patient: "'Why, if I were a man, I'd marry her,'

Cherry thought, blushing furiously at the idea" (*Case*, 14). The blush, of course, indicates Cherry's awareness of the problematic nature of such a thought — a potentially misdirected expression of a seemingly improper desire. Although Cherry's conditional reaction proves itself ultimately useless, Cherry's interpretation of Lana's response — "She realized Lana was looking at her with a penetrating gaze that made Cherry feel all flustered. 'Why, it's as if she can read my mind,' Cherry thought, feeling a flush race up her cheeks" (*Case*, 14) — is spot on. Lana can, in fact, read Cherry's mind, in addition to her body language, her insecurities, and the self that Cherry has yet to figure out. Lana is the first character in the text to recognize a kinship in Cherry that is constantly referred to throughout the rest of the novel.

Cherry's innocence is further emphasized through the explanations of queer behavior filtered through Cherry's mind. In order to explain her father's estrangement from her Aunt Gert, Cherry rehashes the story in details that suggest an excessive naiveté:

> Gert had never married, but with her vivacious personality and striking good looks, she made friends easily. The first week in Pleasantville she became fast friends with the town librarian, Miss Hathaway ... they spent the summer days swimming, hiking, and picnicking. In the evening, they had often sat on the front porch, sewing and talking. Her father had arrived home a week early to find Gert and Miss Hathaway napping in the spare bedroom. He forbade them to set foot in his house again, and that was the last Cherry saw of Aunt Gert [*Case*, 38–9].

Clearly, Mr. Aimless did not simply find Aunt Gert and Miss Hathaway "napping," yet Cherry's explanation comes across as earnest. Readers, though, are clued in to the reality of the situation, a reality unintentionally reinforced when Mrs. Aimless declares, "You were always like two peas in a pod. The older you get, the more you become like Gert" (*Case*, 40). Despite Mrs. Aimless's advocacy of (heterosexual) dating, this comparison between the two women — one that Cherry takes as the strongest of compliments — suggests that Mrs. Aimless intuits a bit more than she lets on, though not quite enough to comprehend Cherry's twin brother: "It pleased her to know that Cherry's twin, Charley, was settled in a good job in the interior design business in New York, even if it was so far away. She did wonder, however, if he was ever going to settle down and get married, or if he was planning on living with that roommate for the rest of his life" (*Case*, 42). Readers are quick to understand that Charley's roommate is more than just a roommate, yet neither Cherry nor Mrs. Aimless seems able to pick up the intricacies of their relationship, at least not until Cherry learns about herself first. In fact, Mrs. Aimless's lack of awareness in this regard is heightened when Charley and Johnny come to visit, eagerly volunteer to share a bedroom, compliment Cherry on her new short hairstyle and take complete control over the design and display of a parade float. Yet again, Maney is not quite content with leaving Mrs. Aimless in the dark entirely as she hugs Cherry, Charley and Johnny, calling them "the best children in the whole world!" (*Case*, 176). Critics of Maney's project may think this characterization of Mrs. Aimless is simply unfair — that Maney wants her to play both sides of the equation: batty, clueless lady and subtly supportive mother; yet, this is perhaps the most subtle of Maney's revisions. Although the original Nancy Drew was seen as the girl who had it all — the independence, the financial stability, the looks, the car, the boyfriend — she lacked the space to develop as a character. Even the college Nancy Drew of the 1990s is strikingly similar in her priorities and characteristics to 1950s, a testament to the longevity and power of her one-dimensional self. The ambiguity surrounding Mrs. Aimless, however, allows Cherry the freedom to figure things out on her own. Maney utilizes Mrs. Aimless in order to solidify Cherry's position as the detective of her own self and sexuality, neither of which are presented to readers as static.

If Mrs. Aimless is *endearingly* oblivious, Cherry, for much of the novel, is *hopelessly* oblivious. Wandering into a lesbian bar in search of Nurse Marstad's friend, Cherry is completely unaware of the motivations behind the gestures of niceness from complete strangers; when one girl offers the "telephone back at my place" to Cherry, a clear come-on, Cherry thinks, "What a nice girl" (*Case*, 47). While watching the girl's friends try to stop her with reminders of her girlfriend, Cherry "wasn't sure what had just happened" (*Case*, 48). Of course, Maney has her fun with Cherry's inability to comprehend her surroundings when, upon the realization that Cherry and Velma look almost identical, Cherry declares it "the queerest thing," both a throwback to the language of the original series and a tease regarding the queerness of the parties involved (*Case*, 48). Cherry's interaction with Midge and Velma reveals the relationship between the two girls as well as Cherry's misreading of that relationship; like Charley and Johnny who volunteer to share a room, so Midge gives up her bed, claiming that she doesn't "mind sleeping with Velma. Really," to which Cherry swoons, "touched by their hospitality" (*Case*, 54). Midge, though, attempts to clarify things by claiming a kinship with Cherry based on being a "fellow Girl Scout" and explaining with a wink that "we can always spot another Scout" (*Case*, 54). Overall, this introduction to Midge and Velma establishes them as a well-meaning, compassionate and generous couple, though Cherry still seems to read them as simply generous roommates, another testament to her naiveté. Such innocence initially seems to be simple mimicry on Maney's behalf, a striking loyalty to the tone of the original series. Yet, Maney uses the seeming excess of innocence as a way of experimenting with the processes by which a sexualized self is uncovered. As Cherry gets closer and closer to the "truth" about her companions and ultimately herself, the misinterpretations ascribed to her trump the broader mystery of the nuns, again a testament to Maney's reliance upon the detective story overall.

Even in more intimate settings and despite Midge's insinuations, Cherry cannot seem to pick up on the cues. When Midge asks, "What's a nice girl like you doing all alone?" and Cherry compares Midge to her mother, Midge declares, "I bet your mother and I don't have the same thing in mind" (*Case*, 63). Cherry thinks this over, wondering what Midge meant by such a thing but only gets so far as admitting her lack of interest in the doctors at the hospital when Midge confesses being "involved with Velma" (*Case*, 64). Cherry's response highlights her shock at the revelation: "'You mean ... you and Velma...' Cherry blushed a deep crimson. 'Golly! I mean ... oh!'" (*Case*, 64). Again, Cherry's blush marks the stages in her development from innocent unsexed girl to sexually aware, sexually active woman. Although Cherry is shocked to find out that Velma and Midge are involved, she is quick to translate her ingrained awareness of heterosexual romance fantasies and apply them to Velma and Midge: "You fell madly in love with each other, and you've lived happily ever after" (*Case*, 64). Cherry's reliance upon hetero-heavy fairy tale endings immediately suggests another interpretive misstep on her behalf. However, as Midge — and readers—critique Cherry's incorporation of a seemingly inappropriate fantasy, the ease with which Cherry transitions such connotative ideas from heterosexual space to queer space imbues the fantasy with new life and possibility. Thus, what initially appears to readers as a typical Cherry goof actually foreshadows her introduction as a visible participant in an alternative sexual space.

Though Cherry has previously found herself in lesbian bars, she was completely unaware of her surroundings. As she searches for Nancy Clue, who the team perceives of as its only chance to find Aunt Gert and the missing nuns, Cherry finds herself back in those all-female spaces. Much more aware of the girls in the bar, and much more aware of her own position therein, Cherry is able to configure and present herself accordingly this time around. Her desires, instead of causing her to blush uncomfortably, as with Lana earlier in the text, are presented as exciting and full of possibility: "Cherry had never heard an accent like hers before. It sent shivers up and down her spine" (*Case*, 104). Entertained and flattered by the attention paid to her by pretty girls, Cherry has to remind herself that she is on a mission and readers are privy to the impending success of that mission far before Cherry catches on. The "titian-haired girl"— a description that appears in some form or another to describe Nancy Drew, herself— mesmerizes Cherry and makes her super attuned to her nerves and her appearance. Cherry "felt wonderful" after talking with the unnamed girl, though readers are invited to assume the girl is Nancy Clue based upon the slow revelation of details about the girl's appearance and personal history. As the mysterious girl pays Cherry a series of sexually loaded compliments—"I like looking at you" (*Case*, 109)—Cherry's insecurities about, but enjoyment in, her sexualized self are magnified: "Cherry began to wish she had worn panties" (*Case*, 109). As Cherry confesses the extent of her newfound desires to readers, the girl takes matters into her own hands, kissing Cherry "first on her neck and then full on her mouth" moving down to "caress her breasts" (*Case*, 109). Importantly, Cherry's reservations are based upon her lack of knowledge, "Why, I don't even know her name," rather than on the gender or sex of her partner (*Case*, 109). The gap between Chapter 15 ("A Special Kiss") and Chapter 16 ("An Unexpected Awakening") allow readers to assume that Cherry and the girl had sex, despite Cherry waking up with no knowledge of the girl's identity. Of course, Cherry's realization that her first sexual foray has been with none other than the girl she "worshipped"— the girl she was searching for—leads to much more than a one night stand with Nancy Clue.

The match-up enables Cherry to feel more comfortable with herself in the more intimate all-girl space that opens up at the end of the novel. When Cherry awakes from her fainting spell, concerned with her inability to "dine in this outfit," Aunt Gert's slacks tell Cherry that it's "come as you are"— the motto for the end of the text when all secrets are revealed (*Case*, 149). Cherry's previous innocence is replaced by a graceful awareness of those around her; when Midge declares that she's not going to sleep after finally recovering Velma, Cherry "saw the look that passed between the two girls ... tears of happiness welled up in her eyes" (*Case*, 150). With her complete knowledge of and appreciation for Nancy, Cherry no longer misses the cues and insinuations between the girls. The blush that surfaces in this setting is indicative of a desire that Cherry is proud of, rather than a desire she has yet to identify, is insecure about, or deems improper. Seeing Nurse Marstad paired with Jackie, Midge and Velma reunited, and Aunt Gert with Lana, Cherry fundamentally feels that she belongs.[49] The slumber party that ensues, with the revelation of each of the girls in their "cute" or "luxurious" pajamas, is yet another reminder of the original series; the wholesomeness of the girls is emphasized *in conjunction with* their desire for one another. Maney constructs a world in which same sex desire exists within a sphere of previously vanilla, heterosexed wholesomeness.

Accordingly, Cherry's partnership with Nancy yields a variety of successes; not only are the two able to find and rescue the missing nuns and catch the manipulative priests, but Cherry is empowered by her discovery of the sexual version of herself, a discovery that the original Nancy Drew is never able to make. Devoid of sexual terms, Nancy's romantic relationship with Ned Nickerson is perpetually compared to her relationship with her girlfriends, rather than her father's relationship with her mother or any other representation of heterosexual romance. Elizabeth Marshall emphasizes the peripheral role of the male figures in the *Nancy Drew* series, reading Ned as an "accessory": "Ultimately, Nancy is less thrilled by Ned's physique or his attentions than by solving mysteries with her girl chums. In this way, Ned surfaces as an accessory."[50] Maney replaces Ned's secondary status with Nancy's primary position as Cherry's sexual partner, close friend, and co-detective, further expanding the productive role of women in the novel. Although Sherrie A. Inness suggests that Nancy is "able to twist any man around her little finger,"[51] Maney presents both Nancy and Cherry as wholly separate from men; although men had peripheral roles in the original series, they're almost eliminated entirely from Maney's text. Explicit about her motivations, Maney explains her prioritizing of girls and their potential: "So there are a lot of problems with them, which I think that I address. I try to take the best of them — particularly the idea that there is this exciting world of girls who have this incredible freedom, and they're smart, and people respect them, and they give them all this power, and they get to go home and put on nice clothes!"[52]

Maney does indeed pick up on the "I can have it all mentality" that has its home in some of the most indicative aspects of the *Nancy Drew* books. Beyond the wardrobe, the freedom, the girl community, Maney also utilizes the girl detective genre's consistent incorporation of tools that make decoding people, places, and things possible. Sherrie A. Inness provides readers with insight into the importance of Nancy's methodical crime solving: "Her obsession with codes and clues shows readers that the world is an understandable, logical place, but only for those who look closer."[53] Considering the formulaic nature of the original series, the emphasis on Nancy's ability to decode mysteries, people, and secrets presents readers with the option to imagine the outside world as easily comprehensible. Maney takes the question of comprehensibility to new levels; not only are traditional mysteries solvable, but the configuration of oneself in relation to the world is equally mysterious and equally "solvable." The complicated, albeit probably liberating, process by which one becomes a fully sexualized adult is at the heart of Maney's project; thus, the confident, engaged Cherry Aimless that readers leave at the end of the novel is far from the wide-eyed, clueless (literally and figuratively!) insecure girl that readers met at its inception. Readers leave *The Case of the Not-So-Nice Nurse* simultaneously reminiscing about the original series and the feelings of potential invincibility it inspired—feelings that may have subsequently been overshadowed by relationships and careers, given the lives of its readers—and thinking about the ways in which Maney has encouraged her characters to embrace their sexuality (and the constant unfolding of the identity that corresponds with it) in a way that Nancy was never quite allowed to. Maney transforms that "I can do anything" mantra into an "I can be anyone" reality.

Notes

1. Jennifer Woolston, "Nancy Drew's Body: The Case of the Autonomous Female Sleuth," *Studies in the Novel*, 42.1/2 (2010), 173.
2. Ibid.
3. Ilana Nash, *American Sweethearts: Teenage Girls in Twentieth-Century Popular Culture* (Bloomington: Indiana University Press, 2006), 41.
4. Kathleen Chamberlain, "The Secrets of Nancy Drew: Having Their Cake and Eating It Too," *The Lion and the Unicorn*, 18.1 (1994), 2.
5. Michael G. Cornelius, "Introduction: The Mystery of the Moll Dick," *Nancy Drew and her Sister Sleuths: Essays on the Fiction of Girl Detectives*, Michael G. Cornelius and Melanie E. Gregg, eds. (Jefferson, N.C.: McFarland, 2008), 2.
6. Sherrie A. Inness, "Is Nancy Drew Queer? Popular Reading Strategies for the Lesbian Reader," *Women's Studies*, 26.3 (1997), 349.
7. Owen Keehnen, "The Case of the Oh-So-Successful Sequel: Nancy Drew and Beyond — A Talk with Mabel Maney," *GLBTQ: An Encyclopedia of Gay, Lesbian, Bisexual, Transgender, & Queer Culture*, 1995, www.glbtg.com/sfeatures/interviewmmany.html.
8. Nash, 36. While the semi-orphan, as Nash suggests, is typical of Stratemeyer and later of Walt Disney (*AS*, 36), it has much earlier roots that are quite significant. In their introduction to "Growing Up (is Hard to Do)," in *Folk and Fairy Tales*, Martin Hallet and Barbara Karasek write of "the presence and power of the mother": "the Grimms chose in later editions to turn mother into stepmother, no doubt because they did not wish to confront their child-readers with such unnatural maternal behavior" (140). Even prior to Walt Disney, the development of fairy tales suggests a growing reliance upon the trope of the orphan, or the semi-orphan, not only as it allows for a child with fewer restrictions and limitations, but also because it seems to demand the cultivation of resourcefulness and survival instincts on behalf of the child in question. See Martin Hallet and Barbara Karesek, eds. *Folk and Fairy Tales* 4th edition (Ontario, Canada: Broadview Press, 2009).
9. Ibid., 37.
10. Woolston, 175.
11. Carolyn Keene, *Nancy Drew Mystery Stories: The Hidden Staircase*, (New York: Grosset & Dunlap, 1930, 1959, 1987), 2.
12. Mabel Maney, *The Case of the Not-So-Nice Nurse* (San Francisco: Cleiss Press, 1993), 8; hereafter abbreviated as *Case*.
13. Nash, 36.
14. It seems useful here to discuss the potential relationship between Carson Clue and a representation of broader, male-dominated society.
15. For a detailed history of the series, as well as the Stratemeyer empire, see Carol Billman's *The Secret of the Stratemeyer Syndicate* (New York: Ungar, 1986).
16. Laura Harris and Liz Crocker, "Mysteries, Mothers, and Cops: An Interview with Mabel Maney," *Femme: Feminists, Lesbians, and Bad Girls* (New York: Routledge, 1997), 71; hereafter abbreviated as "Mysteries."

17. Harris and Crocker, "Mysteries," 71.
18. What is, of course, interesting in Maney's text — and among contemporary detective television shows— is the specific associations of criminality.
19. Chamberlain, 5.
20. Carolyn Keene, *Nancy Drew: The Bluebeard Room* (New York: Simon & Schuster, 1985), 3.
21. Quoted in Nash, 41.
22. *Ibid.*
23. Keehnen. Even George's serious boyfriend, Will Blackfeather, who surfaces in *Nancy Drew: The College Years*, is ultimately killed off in a motorcycle accident.
24. Inness, 362.
25. Stephanie Foote, "Bookish Women: Reading Girls' Fiction: A Response to Julia Mickenberg," *American Literary History*, 19.2 (2007), 525.
26. *Ibid.*
27. *Ibid.*
28. Inness, 360.
29. Nash, 47.
30. Foote, 525.
31. Of course, Mrs. Aimless's depth is at its most indicative when she reveals that she still keeps in touch with Aunt Gert: "What your father doesn't know ... won't hurt him!" (*Case*, 40). While Mrs. Aimless often seems like the butt of jokes— with her seeming inability to successfully read her daughter — more credit is given to her than it may have initially seemed.
32. Harris and Crocker, 69. Maney's reading of Nancy as butch is based upon her prioritization of class values as well as her sexual forwardness.
33. Elizabeth Marshall chronicles some of the ways in which the series relies upon a presumed concrete relationship between appearance and character, especially when it comes to the villains in the texts: "Unsavory characters usually exhibit a 'flashy' fashion sense and are often depicted as racial minorities or as 'lower class.' For the most part, one can predict that nasty culprits will fail to share Nancy's WASP background." Elizabeth Marshall, "Red, White, and Drew: The All-American Girl and the Case of Gendered Childhood," *Children's Literature Association Quarterly*, 27.4 (Winter 2002), 205–6; hereafter abbreviated as "Red."
34. Harris and Crocker, 70.
35. Marshall, 205.
36. *Ibid.*
37. Beth Younger, "Pleasure, Pain, and the Power of Being Thin: Female Sexuality in Young Adult Literature," *NWSA*, 15.2 (Summer 2003), 47.
38. Woolston, 178.
39. Younger, 47.
40. Although Younger focuses on texts from 1975 to 1999, the connection between appetite and desire reaches farther back, as Carina Garland writes of Lewis Carroll that "food and appetite are corrupting and extravagant forces" (28). Garland makes a distinction that is incredibly useful when considering the implications of conflicting appetites in the original series: "the male author doesn't acknowledge the heroine's hunger and has her consume without appetite, this being an attempt to maintain her purity by separating her appetite and consumption" (28). The interpretive space generated between appetite and consumption allows Nancy Drew to be viewed as necessarily fueling herself and Bess to be viewed as indulging her weaknesses. Carina Garland, "Curious Appetites: Food, Desire, Gender and Subjectivity in Lewis Carroll's Alice Texts," *The Lion and the Unicorn*, 32.1 (January 2008).

41. Inness, 356.
42. Katharine M. Rogers, "Fantasy and Reality in Fictional Convents of the Eighteenth Century," *Comparative Literature Studies*, 22.3 (Fall 1985), 299. Contrastingly, Tracy Fessenden, in her exploration of Protestant women's spaces, locates the inventory of the "nun-as-prostitute figure ... in Western cultures: in one or another incarnation she inhabits medieval hagiography; the works of Boccacio, Chaucer, Erasmus, Shakespeare, Rabelais, and Diderot; eighteenth-century No-Popery tracts; Victorian pornography; and contemporary camp." Fessendan's location of the nun-as-prostitute can simply, for our purposes, be the nun-as-sexualized female figure. See Tracy Fessenden, "The Convent, the Brothel, and the Protestant Woman's Sphere," *Signs*, 25.2 (Winter 2000), 452.
43. Susan P. Casteras, "Virgin Vows: The Early Victorian Artists' Portrayal of Nuns and Novices," *Victorian Studies*, 24.2 (Winter 1981), 157.
44. *Ibid.*, 165.
45. Ellen Brown, "In Search of Nancy Drew, the Snow Queen, and Room Nineteen: Cruising for Feminine Discourse," *Frontiers: A Journal of Women Studies*, 13.2 (1993), 7.
46. Foote, 525.
47. Harris and Crocker, 69.
48. Inness, 353.
49. Maney plays with this sense of belonging by incorporating a series of playful lesbian stereotypes: "Cherry was surprised to find the convent had a Physical Education nun, a well as a nun whose single duty it was to train the convent's collies" (*Case*, 151).
50. Marshall, 209.
51. Inness, 359.
52. Harris and Crocker, 71.
53. Inness, 357.

Works Cited

Billman, Carol. *The Secret of the Stratemeyer Syndicate*. New York: Ungar, 1986.
Brown, Ellen. "In Search of Nancy Drew, the Snow Queen, and Room Nineteen: Cruising for Feminine Discourse." *Frontiers: A Journal of Women Studies*, 13.2 (1992): 1–25.
Casteras, Susan P. "Virgin Vows: The Early Victorian Artists' Portrayal of Nuns and Novices." *Victorian Studies*, 24.2 (Winter 1981): 157–184.
Chamberlain, Kathleen. "The Secrets of Nancy Drew: Having Their Cake and Eating It Too." *The Lion and the Unicorn*, 18.1 (1994): 1–12.
Cornelius, Michael G. "The Mystery of the Moll Dick." *Nancy Drew and her Sister Sleuths: Essays on the Fiction of Girl Detectives*. Edited by Michael G. Cornelius and Melanie E. Gregg. Jefferson, NC: MacFarland, 2008. 1–12.
Fessendan, Tracy. "The Convent, the Brothel, and the Protestant Woman's Sphere." *Signs*, 25.2 (Winter 2000): 451–478.
Foote, Stephanie. "Bookish Women: Reading Girls' Fiction: A Response to Julia Mickenberg." *American Literary History*, 19.2 (2007): 521–6.
Garland, Carina. "Curious Appetites: Food, Desire, Gender and Subjectivity in Lewis Carroll's Alice Texts." *The Lion and the Unicorn*, 32.1 (January 2008): 22–39.
Hallet, Martin, and Barbara Karesek, eds. *Folk and Fairy Tales*, 4th ed. Ontario: Broadview Press, 2009.
Harris, Laura, and Liz Crocker. "Mysteries, Mothers, and Cops: An Interview with Mabel Maney." *Femme: Feminists, Lesbians, and Bad Girls*. New York: Routledge, 1997. 68–81.

Inness, Sherrie A. "Is Nancy Drew Queer? Popular Reading Strategies for the Lesbian Reader." *Women's Studies*, 26.3 (1997): 343–372.
Keehnen, Owen. "The Case of the Oh-So-Successful Sequel: Nancy Drew and Beyond — A Talk with Mabel Maney." *GLBTQ: An Encyclopedia of Gay, Lesbian, Bisexual, Transgender, & Queer Culture*, www.glbtq.com. 1995.
Keene, Carolyn. *Nancy Drew Mystery Stories: The Bluebeard Room*, New York: Simon & Schuster, 1985.
Keene, Carolyn. *Nancy Drew Mystery Stories: The Hidden Staircase*. New York: Grosset & Dunlap, 1930, 1959, 1987.
Maney, Mable. *The Case of the Not-So-Nice Nurse*. San Francisco: Cleiss Press, 1993.
Marshall, Elizabeth. "Red, White, and Drew: The All-American Girl and the Case of Gendered Childhood." *Children's Literature Association Quarterly*, 27.4 (Winter 2002): 203–211.
Nash, Ilana. *American Sweethearts: Teenage Girls in Twentieth-Century Popular Culture*. Bloomington: Indiana University Press, 2006.
Rogers, Katharine M. "Fantasy and Reality in Fictional Convents of the Eighteenth Century." *Comparative Literature Studies*, 22.3 (Fall 1985): 297–316.
Woolston, Jennifer. "Nancy Drew's Body: The Case of the Autonomous Female Sleuth." *Studies in the Novel*, 42.1/2 (2010): 173–184.
Younger, Beth. "Pleasure, Pain, and the Power of Being Thin: Female Sexuality in Young Adult Literature." *NWSA Journal*, 15.2 (Summer 2003): 45–56.

LONG AGO, IN PLACES FAR AWAY:
GENDER SUBVERSION IN DETECTIVE
FICTION PERIOD PIECES

3. Repopulating the Margins
Rhys Bowen's Treatment of Gender, History, and Power

KELLEY WEZNER

In the late 1990s, three critical examinations of the history of the mystery genre and the role of diversity in the mystery tradition provided the framework and justification for examining how factors like gender shape and are shaped by the mystery formula.[1] These texts, and subsequent scholarship, have mapped a set of challenges to the genre. Critics recognize that today's detective stories can participate within the tradition, permitting readers to rely on generic expectations, while writers exploit those very traditions and expectations. Kathleen Gregory Klein and other critics note that the mainstream detective novel can become a space for exploration of social issues and the renegotiation of gendered roles.[2] Adoption of this social or political function has not curtailed the popularity of this formulaic genre fiction though. Priscilla Walton and Manina Jones' work in *Detective Agency* demonstrates that over the last fifteen years, mysteries featuring female detectives and/or detective stories written by female authors experienced phenomenal growth.[3] Participating in that explosion, Rhys Bowen's award-winning series featuring private investigator Molly Murphy premiered in 2001 with *Murphy's Law*.[4] Bowen uses the setting of the Murphy novels (turn-of-the-century New York) and Murphy's status (a single, independent-minded, and outspoken Irish immigrant) to explore social and political reform movements, institutionalized corruption, and discrimination against women as well as ethnic and religious minorities.

However, Bowen's examination of gender identity is not limited to her female private investigator, who clashes with social injustice as much as she does with miscreants. Rather, a comparison between Molly Murphy and Bowen's male detective, Constable Evan Evans of Llanfair, Wales, provides a clearer sense of how Bowen exploits the mystery formula to address and redefine gender and power.[5] Bowen places both Evans and Murphy in struggles for autonomy and power, and she complicates this examination of gender and power with the way she locates her protagonists in relation to history. The male Evans embodies an attempt to retreat into the presumed safety of the past, while the female Murphy is literally written into historical events, including the assassination of McKinley, the birth of the Ladies Garment Workers Union, and the early suffrage movement. Murphy's agency in shaping American culture and history provides a perspective from the margins of culture and society — a female Irish immigrant in early 1900s America — whose voice had previously been silenced because her class, gender, and nationality limited her access to power. In contrast, Evans's relation to history and power occupies the ideological space usually assigned to women — influence within a more domestic, private realm. By crafting a male detective who attempts to avoid involvement with modern, changing culture and a female detective who shapes historical events, Rhys Bowen subverts conventions in her Constable Evans and Molly Murphy detective series, and this subversion prompts a reevaluation of both femininity and masculinity across the two series.

The comparison of her lone male detective with her most popular female detective illustrates Bowen's manipulation of the traditional mystery formula, which many critics have considered male-dominated.[6] In particular, the first two works in the Evan Evans series, *Evans Above* (1997) and *Evan Help Us* (1998), and the second and third books in the Molly Murphy series, *Death of Riley* (2002) and *For the Love of Mike* (2003), invite readers to evaluate and redefine gender roles. My decision to focus on these four novels is motivated by the two detectives' analogous status as liminal figures particularly in these early texts in their respective series. Patricia Linton observes that it is common for the detective to be partially marginalized, "ambiguously positioned as an insider/outsider figure."[7] Despite having lived in Llanfair, Evans' move away to urban Swansea as a child and his subsequent education and employment in Wales' second-largest city marks him as a partial outsider when he returns to his home village, located in remote Northern Wales. Moreover, his decision to drop out of detective training and take a post as rural Llanfair's local constable places him in a border position within the institution of law enforcement. He has exposure to urban crime and investigative techniques, but in his current job, he cannot carry a weapon or investigate serious crimes. Murphy also experiences marginalization: she is female, an Irish immigrant in the United States, and an untrained amateur seeking acceptance as a professional private investigator. Evans and Murphy are both outsider and insider: while aspects of their identity, experience, or worldview coincide with the societies they investigate, they are distanced from or even barred from resources and people that would help them in their investigation.

Nevertheless, their liminal standing situates them to investigate their respective mysteries. In his seminal essay "The Guilty Vicarage," W. H. Auden argues that the detective novel follows the model of Greek tragedy: a closed society, troubled by a crime, can only return to its normal state by solving the crime.[8] The detective's instrumental role in solving the crime places him or her in a liminal position, at least temporarily. As the person responsible for solving the crime, the detective restores social order and is aligned with conservatism, law and order; as the person investigating the crime, the detective associates with transgressors. This provisional standing as both insider and outsider offers two benefits. First, the detective's ability to solve the crime requires both a familiarity with culturally specific details and the disinterest needed for ratiocination. Second, as Bowen's two protagonists demonstrate, detectives serve as proxy for readers by offering access to a different world while acknowledging some distance from that world, an experience with which readers would relate. This second advantage also provides a vehicle for explorations of identity politics, particularly since they can portray diversity in an accessible medium. As John G. Cawelti posits, formula fiction affirms social norms and values while it invites readers to assimilate changes to those very norms and values.[9] Evans and Murphy offer insight into their respective social milieus while they simultaneously challenge or complicate the construction of their cultures. Evans' Llanfair and Murphy's turn-of-the-century New York are different enough from our contemporary society to safely invite critiques, yet similar enough to draw useful parallels between Bowen's settings and the audience's own cultural contexts.

Bowen uses the subversion of conventions represented by these two protagonists to address both historical and current views of femininity. She relies upon conventional conceptions of gender roles, anticipating that her audience will recognize the departure from them, and that the readers' customary identification with the detective will provide a safe mechanism for challenging those assumptions. Maureen T. Reddy argues that

> men tend to define themselves through individuation and separation, valuing autonomy over connections with others and perceiving relationships in terms of rules and procedures ... whereas women tend to define themselves in terms of relationships, valuing affiliations with others over autonomy and perceiving relationships in terms of balancing needs and negotiating responsibilities in order to maintain the relationship.[10]

The traditional male desire is to "see themselves as autonomous individuals in a world of other autonomous individuals: confrontation is the key."[11] Building on Reddy's gendered distinction between detectives, Samuel Coale concludes that "the male detective remains an essential loner at odds with his society and estranged from it."[12]

Rejecting autonomy, Evans' success within the circumscribed sphere of Llanfair requires him to acquire knowledge and skills that Reddy's distinction labels as feminine. Much of Evans' energy is spent on interceding between two feuding parties to defuse potentially volatile situations and maintain his relationships with the village residents. His efforts to mediate — between a long-feuding Evans-the-Milk and Evans-the-Meat, between the two small churches competing for members among the local population, between tourists and local residents, and between British newcomers and Welsh nationalists — are not carried out through confrontation or with appeals to social order, laws, and regulations, but through cooperation and compromise. In fact, Evans' success in solving crimes often relies on his sympathetic demeanor and his eventual privileging of cooperation over competition or even autonomy. These qualities — conventionally coded as female — allow him to build key interpersonal relationships that provide him with resources and insights necessary to solve the crimes.

Although Bowen ultimately attributes Evans' success to his rejection of competition and autonomy and his endorsement of cooperation and affiliation, she complicates his participation in these gendered behaviors with his reintegration into Llanfair, his reactions to class differences, and his membership in the North Wales police force. Tension between autonomy and affiliation surfaces in Evans' liminality: he is a native villager, but has been gone long enough that his reintegration into the village is cautiously undertaken and incomplete. The series begins with Evans in his position for only a year, although he remembers fondly "his early childhood spent among these mountains" and knows "these mountains like the back of his hand."[13] Bowen establishes Evans' stance of belonging to and separate from Llanfair with his introduction, which locates him in church, where the "words of that favorite old Welsh hymn, *Cwm Rhonda*, resounded around Chapel Bethel as only Welsh voices can sing it.... Only one person was not joining in lustily"; Constable Evans was "only mouthing the words" (*Above*, 7). While it is soon explained that the particular hymn unfortunately reminds Evans of childhood taunting, it is nevertheless notable that the novel — indeed the series — starts with Evans *not* fully joining in the activity of a larger community. Bowen's initial image of Evans performing as culture and situation dictate yet maintaining an individual ethos separate from that public role foreshadows his negotiations between affiliation and autonomy that characterize the series.

These feelings of alienation from society also appear in Evans' marked lack of respect for the wealthy and powerful. Evans' conflict with British upper class superiority not only fuels his decisions between competition and cooperation, but also the audience's reassessment of Evans' values when Bowen reveals some of his assumptions to be unfounded. Evans must deal with a range of unpleasant characters; however, his strongest negative reactions—ones that also interfere with his investigation—are reserved for those who speak with posh British accents and are dismissive of Welsh culture. The resulting conflict between class-based distrust and necessary cooperation colors Evans' relationship with Major Anderson, a British business owner who relocated to Llanfair around the same time that Evans did. Despite the major's money, status, and connections, Evans refuses to comply with a request the major makes because of his previous imperiousness (10). Evans' subsequent explanation locates his dislike in class differences: "He reminds me of my old headmaster at school—he had the same accent and he was always looking down at me because I was only a scholarship boy" (22). Evans' dislike deepens into suspicion when inquiries reveal that the Army has no record of a "Major Anderson." While this information should, logically, remove the major from the list of potential suspects with military connections to the victims, Evans maintains his suspicion:

> "But that shoots down my little theory about his being mixed up in Danny Bartholomew's death because he was the officer in charge. All the same," he went on, "it might be worth checking up on him, don't you think, sarge? A man who goes around calling himself something he's not might just be doing it for a reason" [122].

His antipathy toward Major Anderson, reflecting his attitude toward the oppressive English upper class, is challenged in the novel's climax. Anderson, whom Evans suspects may be another killer, actually helps Evans restrain the real one. In the middle of the mist upon Crib Goch, Evans catches a glimpse of Anderson, and sees him as "his mirror image" (206), a doubling the major himself identifies when he praises Evans for his bravery, saying he's a "man after my own heart" (209). The ensuing conversation reveals that as an officer in the Marines, Anderson does, in fact, deserve the military title he uses, and his courageous attempt on Crib Goch demonstrates his willingness to help the locals (210). The parallel between Evans and Anderson, initially established by their mutual performances—Evans as a fully integrated local and Anderson as a "major"—transmutes into another parallel that gestures toward Evans' potential affiliation with ostensibly differing groups in the performance of his duties. Just as the upper class, British Major Anderson can work cooperatively for the good of Llanfair, so can Evans develop cooperative and effective relationships with groups he resents being judged by or excluded from.

As a policeman, Evans is a member of a male-dominated community that regulates itself through hierarchy, rules, and regulations and fosters competition for prestige and resources, yet requires—even mandates—some amount of cooperation. Significantly, Bowen peoples the North Wales police force, and two similar institutions, Scotland Yard and the military, with only male characters, associating masculinity with these organizations. Moreover, the majority of police and military personnel seem preoccupied with hierarchy and rules, evincing an acute awareness of potential responses from superiors and concerns about control and power. Bowen situates Evans' struggles reconciling his marginalized occupational role as a mere village constable with his innate instincts for investigation against this backdrop of tensions between masculine competition and necessary cooperation.

A key part of that struggle lies in Evans' relationship with Detective Sergeant Watkins, an investigator for the region of North Wales in which Llanfair is located. Detective Sergeant Watkins would traditionally be competitive with Evans: he is Evans' superior officer; he is responsible for a large city rather than a small village; and he is commissioned to investigate more important crimes, which gives him access to restricted resources and the law enforcement hierarchy. Their initial relationship displays the hallmarks of competition, with Watkins wondering why Evans had bothered to call them in for a straightforward climbing accident, given that they're "busy down at headquarters ... and don't have time to check out climbing accidents" (*Above*, 25). He assumes that Evans has exploited the accident as a way to get noticed: "Look, I can understand. It must be boring stuck out in a little village with only old ladies and their missing pussycats to keep you occupied. A nice juicy murder would spice things up, wouldn't it?" (27). Watkins contrasts his view of Evans' marginal, limited responsibilities with his current case, an unsolved child rape and murder, "a real murder," according to Watkins (26). Despite this rocky start, the two work well together, with Watkins supporting Evans' hypotheses even at the risk of his own reputation. What could have been competition becomes a successful cooperative relationship, based on negotiating responsibilities and mutual respect.

Their collaboration ensues primarily from Evans' suppression of competitive responses in favor of empathy. Evans only competes with Watkins once, early in their interaction, when they both make claims for authority through displays of resources. Watkins announces his superior connections with a reminder that he has access to a helicopter; Evans responds by promoting his local connections. Regarding the possibly perilous removal of a corpse from a mountain, Evans volunteers:

> "My lads can probably do it.... We have a local mountain rescue squad in our village. All the men there grew up when the slate quarries were still working. They're used to walking up and down cliffs. Born to it, they are around here. They walk up and down these mountains like they're crossing an open field — and in their best Sunday polished shoes if there's a real necessity for it" [27].

Evans' use of "my lads" emphasizes his possession while it suggests his command over and familiarity with men equipped with specialized, dangerous skills. Moreover, Evans' challenge that local, working-class men can outperform a state-of-the-art helicopter, suggests that he views their conflict at least partly in terms of class differences.

However, Evans' subsequent responses to Watkins' reminders of his authority bypass competition and, instead, are empathetic. Evans' genuine recognition of Watkins' situation or experience results in Watkins' increasing willingness to include Evans in the investigation: at first, Watkins tacitly agrees that Evans can investigate unofficially, then he invites Evans to participate in interviews, and eventually recognizes him as a colleague. When another murder is discovered while the chief suspect is in custody, Watkins realizes that they have not yet caught the real killer and that his immediate superior, Inspector Hughes, will "definitely want to take over this case himself, as soon as he gets back," but until he returns from Scotland Yard, "it's up to us at the moment" (109). This new camaraderie is noted both by Evans—who "noticed he had said 'us,'" and who remarks silently that it was gratifying that "he was no longer thought of as the stupid village bobby" (109)—and by Hughes, who is less gratified when he later notices Watkins' inclusive "we":

> "We?" D.I. Hughes asked. "Have you been assigned to this department, Evans?"
> "No, sir. I just wanted to help out," Evans said.
> "I'm sure we're very grateful for all your help," D.I. Hughes said. "But I suggest you get back to your assigned duties and leave the criminal investigation to those trained to do it. And that's an order" [186].

Hughes is described as a stickler for procedure, and his dismissal of Evans and his contributions follows his passion for structure; Hughes' assessment of Evans as an "untrained amateur" only capable of "bumbling interrogations" (187) illustrates his correlation between worth and rank, endorsing the value of hierarchical order. Hughes' demand that Watkins "follow his lead" (187) reflects one method by which institutions like the police privilege cooperation over autonomy: cooperation mediated by hierarchical relationships. Watkins and Evans' working relationship, however, provides another model — one that counters Coale's definition of the confrontation at the heart of traditional male's view of "themselves as autonomous individuals in a world of other autonomous individuals."[14]

Bowen redefines masculinity to include civility and sympathy, in part by equating civility with success within masculine enclaves, seen in the interaction between her protagonist Evans and the most prestigious investigative officer to appear in the series, D.C. I. Harmon from Scotland Yard. Evans anticipates that Harmon will be too busy or officious to provide useful aid, yet Harmon answers his own phone, offers information immediately and willingly, stating, "We coppers have to help each other, don't we?" (*Above*, 191). Evans attributes Harmon's civility to his success, reflecting that Harmon is a "nice chap. No wonder he'd gone to the top. He was the sort that his men would willingly put in overtime for. Not like that cold fish Hughes" (191).

Bowen's revised model of masculinity also incorporates emotional sympathy reminiscent of mid–eighteenth-century sensibility, which includes "a readiness to be touched (particularly by others' distress), to display tender feelings, to be susceptive to sympathy."[15] Both Evans and Watkins betray strong emotional reactions to the tragedy to which their jobs expose them, including other people's suffering. Finding an eleven-year old girl who had been sexually assaulted, strangled, and dumped in a ditch haunts Watkins:

> "I don't think I'll ever forget how she looked when we found her in that ditch. I'll never be able to get that little face out of my mind as long as I live. Looked as if she was asleep at first — just like our little Tiffany when I check on her."
> His voice cracked and he put his hand to his mouth and coughed as if embarrassed about showing such emotion [*Above*, 30].

Watkins admits that if a woman became hysterical, and he "has her and her little kids crying all over [him], it gets [him] started too" (38), which leads him to question whether he is in the right line of work. In both *Evans Above* and *Evan Help Us*, Constable Evans demonstrates his sensitivity in handling other people, whether village girls, grieving mothers, or his police superiors. One of the things he enjoys most about his job was the connection with the place and its inhabitants:

> Checking out the neighborhood on foot was one of the things he liked about being a village policeman. You just didn't get that same feel of a place from the interior of a police car. And now it had been proved — there was less crime when areas were patrolled on foot and policemen built up a rapport with the locals. Evan could have told them that when they experimented with centralization a few years ago and closed down all the local stations in favor of cruising police cars. He was glad they'd gone back to village bobbies again [*Above*, 104–05].

Evans reiterates this awareness in *Evan Help Us*, noting that his position, though low in rank and marginal in position, "was the best kind of policeman to be."[16] The job requirements fit "what he liked doing most, walking around and talking to people" (8). Bowen notes, in both books, that Great Britain had experimented with a "national movement to modernize and streamline the police force," using car patrols from centralized headquarters instead of a community police presence (8). They found, however, that this more isolated approach to crime prevention and surveillance was less effective than building stronger relationships with communities. Bowen's attribution of success to this older and traditional model, which promotes civility and sensitivity through the village bobby's "rapport with the locals," illustrates that experience of strong or tender emotions in response to others' suffering does not necessarily emasculate or weaken. Civility and sensitivity encourage the cooperation and affiliation aligned with success in the Evans series.

Ultimately, Evans' successful apprehension of the killer in *Evans Above* rests on his rejection of competition and embrace of cooperation or, as Reddy posits, "valuing affiliations with others over autonomy."[17] Evans is fleeing from the killer, who is armed with a gun, along mist-covered Crib Gogh, a "knife-edged crest" right below the summit of Mount Snowdon, with a sheer, thousand-foot drop on either side (203). When the killer loses his nerve and surrenders in exchange for help down Crib Gogh, Evans must decide whether to attempt to bring him in alone or go for help:

> Evan stood like a statue, unable to make up his mind between prudence and valour. He could imagine Inspector Hughes' face if he brought in the murderer, single-handed. Then he found himself thinking of his father. Had his father dreamed of being a hero too when he went alone to intercept that drug shipment in the Swansea docks? Better to play it safe, Evan decided [205].

Bowen attributes Evans' immobilization to a forced decision between autonomy, with a concomitant possibility of individual glory, and cooperation, with a tacit admission of needing help. Evans' impotence in the face of this decision triggers a recollection of his father's death, which occurred while Evans was in investigative training and he and his father were both police officers assigned to a patrol that included the rough docks of Swansea. His father tried to intercept a drug shipment alone and was shot and killed. Evans' initial identification with his father, visible in his adoption of the same occupation, is rejected when he is unsuccessful in his attempts to deal with his father's murder. As a result, Evans retreats to Llanfair, denying his place in the traditional male succession and abandoning his training in investigation, which would have ensured his access to higher rank and greater investigative resources and enabled his participation in the regional criminal investigation unit. In Evans' evaluation on Crib Gogh, his father, representing a definition of masculinity couched in individuation and separation, lost his life because of his quest for autonomy. Evans rejects identification with his father a second time, reaffirming his alignment with the more feminine model of affiliation and confirming his abrogation of his access to power and success.

Evans nearly gives into a choice fueled by competition, as he would dearly love to best Inspector Hughes, who has diminished and marginalized him. His choice to be prudent is immediately challenged with the appearance of another rival, Major Anderson, the British hotel owner who also appeared contemptuous and dismissive of Evans and his position. Taking charge of the situation, Anderson immediately moves to apprehend the killer; Evans worries, however, that Anderson may be on the spot because he is connected to the murderer or that Anderson will be walking into a trap — that the killer is not unarmed as he has promised:

> Major Anderson had already begun to walk out onto the knife edge. Evan realized he might be walking into a trap and yet he couldn't just stand there and watch the major trying to rescue Doug alone either. It had become a matter of honor. Maybe his father had felt the same way when he recognized the drug dealers and knew he had to go on anyway...
> He took a deep breath and walked out onto Crib Goch [206].

The intervention of a competitor and reappearance of multiple decisions reanimate Evans' feelings of impotence and confusion, which, again, paralyzes him as he "just stand[s] there," unable to decide. And again, these feelings recall his father; however, in this reenactment, Evans reevaluates his father by projecting his mixed feelings of fear and weakness onto his father. His reevaluation prompts his identification with him, as Evans posits whether "his father had felt the same way"; this identification galvanizes him into action. Evans chooses the needs of the situation over individual honor and, in doing so, combines the apprehension of the criminal with the conventionally feminine privileging of cooperation over competition. Perhaps ironically and perhaps fittingly, both the identification with the father-figure and the "matter of honor" ultimately become part of the feminized self-definition which recovers access to power and success.

In *Evan Help Us*, Evans acts alone when he identifies the killer, a decision he recognizes nearly immediately as an error, when he "realized now that he had acted impulsively, rushing out alone into the dark" (195). Despite his adrenaline-fueled act of autonomy, Evans relies on more feminine characteristics when his life is threatened at the climax. Dawson, a much smaller man, uses a revolver to force Evans over a ledge for an "unfortunate fall" (199). Rejecting physical avenues to escape or overpower Dawson, Evans appeals to Dawson's paternal feelings, reminding him of important relationships in his late daughter's life and of another parent-child relationship that will be destroyed by murder. Evans' empathetic assessment of Dawson is successful; Dawson's guilt about his role in his daughter's death prevents him from killing Evans and from allowing his daughter's friend — a parent herself — to take the blame for his crime. Instead, Dawson flees, sending his car over the cliff in the very fall he planned for Evans (201). Evans' accurate judgment of Dawson's strong paternal affection demonstrates two ways in which Bowen endorses femininity: Evans' use of empathy rather than physical confrontation expands the attributes associated with success; additionally, both men value affiliations with others over autonomy. Despite the appeal to Dawson's *fatherly* feelings, the emphasis on emotional attachments and on privileging relationships over individual desires code these behaviors as feminine. In both Constable Evans novels, Evans' reliance on behaviors characteristic of feminine gender roles rewards him, preserving his life and resolving the crime. Moreover, these confrontations, in which Evans must choose between gendered options, tacitly stigmatize masculine norms when they are rejected. Accordingly, Bowen redefines and heightens the value of femininity by linking the acquisition of power and success to traditionally feminine norms.

Bowen's more explicit elevation of femininity in the Molly Murphy series stems, in part, from a focus on female agency. Rather than the limited omniscient third-person narrator employed in the Constable Evans series, Molly Murphy narrates her own story, creating a vicarious personal perspective for readers. Murphy, a spirited, outspoken, well-educated young woman, bridles at attempts to constrain her. She stands up to foremen, and gets fired. She refuses to participate in some contemporary feminine behavior, such as wearing corsets and fainting, a habit that she says is for ninnies.[18] She is aware of contemporary demands for propriety and gentility yet is selective about when to adhere to them.

Unemployed at the beginning of *Death of Riley*—partly because of the limited job opportunities for Irish immigrants, partly because of her personality, and partly because she is unwilling to stoop to jobs she feels are beneath her—she desires to become a private investigator (7). Two characters representing the societies that she would like to become part of—law enforcement and New York City gentry—pass judgment on her career aspirations. Her sometime beau, New York City Police Captain Daniel Sullivan, informs her, repeatedly, that "women do not become investigators" (7). When she reminds him that her preference would be to help reunite families who have become separated because of immigration, not criminal cases, Sullivan lists the real limitations for women even in non-criminal investigations: relatives may not wish to be found; she would need to be able to rent and advertise; she might need to travel; and she will need capital (7). Sullivan observes that she only needs "a pleasant, dignified job that pays the rent, for the time being," a temporary position until she can take up her more permanent and suitable career as wife and mother, since she is not "a man [who] needs to be thinking of a future career" (8). Miss Van Woekem, another eventual supporter, employs Murphy temporarily as a companion, and admires her spirit and tenacity. Even though she enjoys the control over her own life and family that her wealth and status provide and thus might sympathize with Murphy's independence, Van Woekem also tells Murphy that a private investigator is "not a suitable job for a woman" (33).

Murphy rails against the institutions that repress and oppress her and other women yet clings tenaciously to the desire to be a member of one. Accordingly, she talks her way into being taken on as an apprentice to Paddy Riley, a talented private detective and known misogynist. After his death, she retains his name on the business, adding "and associate" to the agency's name, and promoting herself to junior associate, complete with business cards that announce her status. Aware of the realities of 1901 New York City, Murphy thus acquires the mantle of respectability that his name provides, as well as his reputation for competence that garners clients. She adopts male dress as a disguise, and attempts to use the same network that the male private investigators use. This protective coloration has limited efficacy: Murphy's male disguise is penetrated by other investigators; despite the male figurehead, clients still express distrust in relying on a female operative; and, with one exception, the network of police, informants, and criminals that Riley used is shown to be closed, even hostile, to Murphy. Sullivan is the only police officer who provides even limited intelligence, and his assistance comes at too high a price for Murphy's integrity and pride as his offers of help are often accompanied by commands, warnings, lectures, or requests that she reconsider his offer to wait until he can break off his engagement.

Characters who are less supportive than Sullivan and Van Woekem criticize and even challenge Murphy for deviating from contemporary gender expectations. Her critics are primarily male authority figures, such as police officers, judges, and wealthy businessmen, but women who consider themselves in competition with Murphy also expose her transgressions. Her detractors act as blocking devices, thwarting her ability to investigate as they frustrate her personally, and forcing her to find alternative solutions. When Murphy's investigator mentor, Paddy Riley, is murdered, Lieutenant Wolski, the investigating officer immediately locks horns with Murphy. When she asserts herself, Wolski pushes back: "I'm the law around here.... You shut up until you're asked a question" (*Riley*, 70). When Murphy asks one too many questions about the investigation, Wolski immediately — and correctly — assumes that she's trying to tell him how to do his job, and Murphy is forced to return "to [her] humble female mode" (73). When she finds the key to Riley's locked client files, which Wolski is searching for, she remains "humble" and quiet, secreting the key for her own future use. Murphy's feigned resignation outwardly complies with the constraints that Wolski imposes on her; however, Murphy's manipulation of that appearance of compliance for her own ends undermines those controls. Wolski's relief that he has successfully contained the subversive "creature of a lower order" (73) is, in fact, subverted by Murphy's reappropriation of hegemonic controls.

Murphy is not always successful in subverting hegemonic controls, and Bowen uses Murphy's failures not to demonstrate Murphy's weaknesses, but to illustrate the socially-imposed limitations for women and the potential costs of crossing those boundaries. By doubling key events from *Death of Riley* and *For the Love of Mike*, Bowen encourages a comparison between Riley and Murphy engaging in similar surveillance. When Murphy first meets her mentor, Paddy Riley is staking out a client's wife (*Riley*, 17). His remarkable ability to conduct surveillance, particularly his patience and seeming invisibility, speaks to his expertise. The subsequent book, *For the Love of Mike*, opens with Murphy attempting to replicate her mentor's fortitude and skill, as she is staking out her client's spouse. However, Murphy's gender complicates her ability to engage in surveillance, a common and necessary skill for private investigators. She is in a "highly respectable neighborhood, only one block from the patricians of Fifth Avenue," when she is arrested for being a suspicious person, either a prostitute and/or a moll for the Hudson Dusters, a local criminal gang.[19] Murphy, infuriated by the unfairness of the situation and at the limitations to which her gender subjects her, thinks,

> This would have never happened if I'd been a man. Men were free to walk when and where they chose in this city. But a lone female, out unchaperoned at night, was immediately suspected of being up to no good. I had already realized that there were many things that Paddy Riley had been able to do that were just not open to me. He had contacts with gangs, and with the police. He frequented various taverns. He could move freely and unobtrusively through the worst areas, and could change his appearance easily by means of a beard or a moustache [14].

Murphy's reaction focuses on her sense of vulnerability in the face of society's immediate reading of her as "up to no good" if unsupervised — not the potential dangers of being alone at night, interacting with gangs and police (both corrupt), and frequenting taverns and "the worst areas." Murphy's assumption that "this would have never happened if I'd been a man" elides other logical explanations also prompted by the comparison Bowen creates: she has no training in surveillance and she has little experience. Bowen fails to acknowledge, or has Murphy fail to acknowledge, these other alternatives, narrowing the cause for Murphy's failure to gender alone.

Bowen's focus on the injustice ensuing from restrictions placed on women also results in her avoidance of subjecting Murphy to disciplinary correction for female gender transgressions. In fact, the books reward her by tying those deviations to her successful handling of dangerous situations or the solving of the crime. Murphy's willingness to take risks and to violate feminine decorum saves herself and her fellow workers from the fire in Mostel's garment factory (*Mike*, 261–63). The women manage to break windows in their attic workroom and crawl out onto the rooftop, but find no way down. She removes her boots, outer clothing, and petticoat, remaining clad in only her drawers and stocking, an act that "produced a gasp of horror almost as great as the original flames had done" (263). Freed from the restricting clothing, Murphy is able to jump to a neighboring rooftop and construct a temporary bridge for the others to crawl to safety (264). Bowen's depiction of the onlookers' near inability to distinguish between actual danger (death by immolation) and socially-constructed danger (a necessary breach of propriety) invites readers to mock such confining views of female behavior. The congratulations, tears of relief, and hugs for the escaped factory workers, including Murphy, provide a corrective view of what is truly valuable.

At times, Bowen's exploration of gender as a social construction lends itself to Murphy's *agon* of whether appropriating the male role model for autonomy and achievement requires relinquishing femininity. In *For the Love of Mike*, Murphy is asked to investigate the thefts of clothing designs and goes undercover at two sweatshops, both run by immigrants who exploit other immigrants. She does identify the guilty party — and in true classic mystery style, it is the most unlikely party. However, the novel identifies the real crime as poverty and limited options for immigrants that provide the thieves few real alternatives. The two sisters, Russian immigrants who copied Mostel's designs and sold them to his chief competitor, Lowenstein, were not allowed to work for the same company (288). Their mother's serious illness increases their need for money, as the doctor demands payment immediately and they are docked money for arriving to work late. Justifying their behavior as a response to their employers' tactics of docking their pay for minor or imaginary infractions, Sarah and Fanny resort to industrial espionage:

> "Ten cents for sneezing. Ten cents for going to the washroom, for coming back one minute late from lunch. And don't think we don't know about turning back the clock hands to get extra minutes out of us. We were cheated every single day, so don't preach to me about cheating" [288].

Sarah complains bitterly about Murphy's decision to tell her employer her discovery, wondering, "Then what? We get arrested and go to jail and our mother will die. That's good American justice" (288). Murphy reports "feeling like a heel" and "really sick" about following through on her commission, and wonders whether she could, in fact, not turn them in (289). However, she concludes that

> if I made personal judgments about each case that I undertook, I wouldn't be making much money in my chosen profession. I had to learn to keep myself remote. I had been hired to do a job. I had done that job and now my duty was to report my findings to my employer [289].

Murphy's reflection that to be successful she must "learn to keep [herself] remote" suggests that she equates success in her "chosen profession" with the masculine model that Reddy outlines, yet her very questioning of her own use or potential misuse of power gestures toward a reworking of that formula. She recognizes that her job and new knowledge would necessitate an aggressive act against women who had already been victimized. She directly addresses and questions her own participation in systems that perpetuate inequality; she interrogates her agency and, in doing so, redefines the parameters of success. Her solution is not to name the thieves, but to assure the client that it will not happen again (293). Murphy tries to fix the real source of the crime, suggesting that Mostel "make the conditions bearable" for his employees and "relax the rule about not hiring members of the same family," which might eliminate the likelihood that they would be tempted to betray him (294). She negotiates between her duty to her client and professional code, her solidarity with other oppressed women, and her integrity, and finds a solution that completes the assignment, earns her reward, retains her agency, and limits the further victimization of the two immigrant seamstresses.

Bowen historicizes Murphy's independence and agency, encouraging readers to contrast turn-of-the-century and present-day views of women. Murphy's story is joined to the McKinley assassination, the unionizing of the garment workers, and early suffrage efforts, articulating the manner in which the personal, the public, and the political are linked. Accordingly, readers understand changes and — more notably — absence of changes in terms of the social and political developments integral to the series' setting. Readers are encouraged to judge characters, ideas, and movements that repress or oppress women as flawed, deficient, or hostile. Bowen imbues characters evincing negative views toward women with traditionally masculine qualities or labels and, accordingly, prompts the protagonist and readers to critique masculinity.

However, Bowen's tendency to simply reverse the binary by aligning masculinity with injustice and oppression becomes reductive. Murphy's most hostile encounters are uniformly with oppressive males, such as her identification as a criminal by the government and police. After trying unsuccessfully to warn police and the security detail that an anarchist will attempt to shoot the president, once the president is shot, Murphy and her friend Ryan O'Hare are arrested as co-conspirators (*Riley*, 272–73). They are alternately ignored, harassed, and manhandled by the police. The next morning, the Buffalo Chief of Police interviews Murphy in front of a crowd of fellow officers:

> "Ah yes, Miss Murphy. The one who uncovered the plot single-handed." The man at the desk had several chins and was leering at me. "I understand you are one of our more promising detectives, Miss Murphy. I should keep you on here, to give my boys some lessons." Chuckles from those standing around him [280].

The police chief's performance for a like-minded audience emphasizes the unfairness and pervasiveness of the attitudes responsible for Murphy's mistreatment. Bowen repeats this technique in *For the Love of Mike*, when hired enforcers, corrupt police officers, and a bribed judge collude to break the picket line that Murphy has helped to organize. The involvement and complicity of these flawed and male-dominated groups represent the prevalence and the danger of their ideas and instructs the readers to associate masculinity with oppression and injustice.

The hostility of the male-dominated world reaches its peak when Murphy is attacked near the climax in both mysteries. Her vulnerability stems from both her autonomous actions as an investigator and her aspirations to participate in the institutions responsible for her victimization. As Sandra Tomc outlines, some mysteries engage in feminist critique by collapsing the victim and detective through their shared identity as a subordinated object, manifested literally when the detective becomes the killer's next target.[20] Like other feminist mysteries, Murphy's search for the criminal reveals "a network of problematic social and institutional mechanisms of which the crime itself is only one manifestation."[21] While Bowen often identifies social institutions as ultimately responsible for the crimes they foster, she still relies upon a simplistic equation of masculinity with oppressive social and institutional mechanisms.

The killer in *Death of Riley* is an anarchist, inspired by Emma Goldman's mission to call attention to social issues that require change. The anarchist attacks Murphy when he believes that she will interrupt his plan to "do something spectacular at the exposition" (258), and endangers her again after he successfully shoots President McKinley, when her efforts to expose and disrupt his plan make her appear to be an accomplice. Spectators and police threaten her safety, and she is nearly a scapegoat. Ostensibly wishing to draw public attention to the government's oppression of the poor and marginalized, the anarchist's goals are extremes of Murphy's; the resulting comparison makes Murphy's desires seem reasonable. The crowd's inability to distinguish between Murphy (an outspoken, crusading female), her friend Ryan O'Hare (a flamboyant homosexual playwright), and Leon Czolgosz (a foreign anarchist and assassin) demonstrates how transgressive Murphy's behavior appears to her contemporary society. Notably, Bowen only identifies males as belonging to the groups who misjudge and threaten Murphy, including the many policemen who manhandle, threaten, imprison, and interrogate her, and the mob, gendered in the shouts to recapture her: "Over here, boys. Here's one of 'em trying to slip away" (282).

Similarly, Bowen's pattern of females victimized by male oppression appears in Murphy's efforts to locate the killer in *For the Love of Mike*, which ultimately place herself, her surrogate child, Bridie, and another young woman — all three female Irish immigrants — in mortal peril, as they are hoisted on the half-built tower for the East Street Bridge (302–08). Bowen acknowledges the social contributions to crime with the setting, which represents the progress associated with increasing industrialization of New York City through the exploitation of the vulnerable immigrant population, as well as in the power exercised by the male killer, who is member of one of the local gangs, also an exploiter of immigrants. While Murphy identifies the killer and all three females exhibit bravery in the face of danger, they escape death only by the intervention of the police, who use a sharpshooter to kill the murderer (308). This rescue, as well as police captain Sullivan's similar last-minute intervention in *Death of Riley*, could reflect a desire for verisimilitude, but regardless of intent, Bowen's conformity to a traditional formula of female dependency on male intervention undercuts Murphy's agency.

Ultimately, Bowen's novels betray an oversimplification of the intersections between gender and other identity factors, despite her willingness to embrace complexity — seen in her redefinition of masculinity and femininity in the Evans series — and her recognition of the underlying and remaining social disorder that fosters the crime — apparent in her avoidance of a tidy resolution in the Molly Murphy mysteries. Indeed, Bowen's mysteries present an uneven consideration of gender definitions. At first glance, Bowen's Molly Murphy series would appear to offer more latitude for challenges to or revision of conventional views of femininity and masculinity. Murphy's idealism and agency are hallmarks of the series; reviews and blurbs emphasize her advocacy for women's rights and her feisty temperament. Murphy's limited options as an immigrant female private investigator in turn-of-the-century New York City paradoxically highlight her agency. Without consistent access to police procedures or contemporary technology, Murphy has to solve mysteries with her logic, native observational skills, persistence, and ingenuity. Bowen's setting provides the opportunity to discuss or engage social issues and complicated relationships among power, race, religion, gender, and sexuality; the Murphy books do provide a more overtly feminist protagonist and include a wider range of characters representing marginalized communities than the Evans series. Murphy struggles with identity formation; she takes on various roles — companion, seamstress, detective, radical, bohemian, surrogate mother and wife, business owner, romantic partner, and suspect or person of interest — throughout the series. She cannot work in her own name, which indelibly identifies her as an immigrant. Murphy's first person account provides a gendered voice with complex reactions, and thus a counterpoint to the historical narrative with which readers might be more familiar.

Murphy's idealism is attractive, as is her energy or desire for change; however, juxtaposing how both detectives reconsider gender demonstrates that the feminist message in the Murphy series, while attractive, in the end, is slightly reductive, especially when compared to the more subtle but farther-reaching social reevaluations in the Evans series. Bowen elevates femininity in both series: Evans' success is predicated on the adoption of skills and attributes conventionally coded as feminine; similarly, Murphy is rewarded for female agency and judicious transgressions of female behavior. Bowen's treatment of femininity in the Evans series is complicated by intersections with class and nationalistic loyalty, which betray biases in the protagonist. While Bowen has the opportunity to examine class, nationality, and other factors of identity affecting gender definitions in the Murphy series, she overlooks these opportunities in her focus on the social injustices that oppress and repress women. As a result, rather than a nuanced, complicated consideration of femininity and masculinity, Murphy's world casts oppressive social forces and institutions as masculine, simply inverting the traditional binary and homogenizing masculinity. In contrast, Bowen expands the model for success as a detective in the Evans series to include feminine qualities, such as cooperation and affiliation, and redefines masculinity to incorporate civility and sensitivity. In this way, the Evans series moves closer toward the possibility of an androgynous detective in which sharply drawn distinctions between genders are blurred or even erased.

Notes

1. Kathleen Gregory Klein, ed., *Diversity and Detective Fiction* (Bowling Green: Bowling Green State University. Popular Press, 1999); Catherine Ross Nickerson, *The Web of Iniquity: Early Detective Fiction by American Women* (Durham: Duke University Press, 1998); Priscilla L. Walton and Manina Jones, *Detective Agency: Women Rewriting the Hard-Boiled Tradition* (Berkeley: University of California Press, 1999).

2. See, for instance, Klein, *Diversity and Detective Fiction*; Nickerson, *The Web of Iniquity*; Walton and Jones, *Detective Agency*; Sally R. Munt, *Murder by the Book? Feminism and the Crime Novel* (London: Routledge), 1994; Adrienne Johnson Gosselin, ed., *Multicultural Detective Fiction: Murder from the "Other" Side* (New York: Garland, 1999); and Samuel Coale, *The Mystery of Mysteries: Cultural Differences and Designs* (Bowling Green: Bowling Green State University Popular Press, 2000).

3. Walton and Jones, *Detective Agency*, 24–33.

4. Rhys Bowen's Evans and Murphy mystery novels have received the following awards and nominations: *Evan Help Us* (1999), Barry Award nomination; *Murphy's Law* (2002), Agatha Award winner, Reviewer's Choice Award winner, Herodotus Award winner, Mary Higgins Clark award finalist; *Death of Riley* (2003), Agatha Award nominee, Reviewer's Choice Award nominee; *For the Love of Mike* (2004), Anthony Award winner, Bruce Alexander Memorial Award winner, Freddy winner, Macavity Award nominee; *Evan's Gate* (2005), Edgar Award nominee; *In Like Flynn* (2006), Macavity Award nominee; *Oh Danny Boy* (2007), Macavity Award winner, Barry Award nominee; *Tell Me Pretty Maiden* (2009), Bruce Alexander Memorial Historical Mystery nominee.

5. Under her pen name, Rhys Bowen, Janet Quin-Harkin writes three mystery series: the two examined in this essay, as well as the "Her Royal Spyness" series, which follows the penniless Lady Georgie, the cousin of King George V, in 1932 London.

6. See, for instance, Klein, *Diversity and Detective Fiction*; Nickerson, *The Web of Iniquity*; Walton and Jones, *Detective Agency*; Johanna M. Smith, "Hard-Boiled Detective Fiction: Gendering the Canon," *Pacific Coast Philology* 26, n0.1/2 (199): 78–84; Munt, *Murder by the Book?*; Phyllis M. Betz, "Playing the Boys' Game," in *Multicultural Detective Fiction: Murder from the "Other" Side*, ed. Adrienne Johnson Gosselin (New York: Garland, 1999), 85–103; Glenwood Irons, ed., *Feminism in Women's Detective Fiction* (Toronto: University of Toronto Press, 1995); and Kimberly J. Dilley, *Busybodies, Meddlers, and Snoops: The Female Hero in Contemporary Women's Mysteries* (Westport, CT: Greenwood Press, 1998), among others.

7. Patricia Linton, "The Detective Novel as a Resistant Text: Alter-Ideology in Linda Hogan's *Mean Spirit*," in *Multicultural Detective Fiction: Murder from the "Other" Side*, ed. Adrienne Johnson Gosselin (New York: Garland, 1999), 18.

8. W. H. Auden, "The Guilty Vicarage," in *Detective Fiction*, ed. Robin Winks (Englewood Cliffs: Prentice-Hall, 1980),16.

9. John G. Cawelti, *Adventure, Mystery and Romance: Formula Stories as Art and Popular Culture* (Chicago: University of Chicago Press, 1976), 34–36.

10. Maureen T. Reddy, *Sisters in Crime: Feminism and the Crime Novel* (New York: Continuum, 1988), 9–10.

11. Coale, *The Mystery of Mysteries*, 84.

12. Ibid.

13. Rhys Bowen, *Evans Above* (New York: Berkeley Prime Crime, 1997), 12. Hereafter, references to this work will be provided in text.

14. Coale, 84.

15. John Mullan, "Sentimental Novels," in *The Cambridge Companion to the Eighteenth Century Novel*, ed. John Richetti (Cambridge: Cambridge University Press, 1996), 238.

16. Rhys Bowen, *Evan Help Us* (New York: Berkeley Prime Crime, 1998), 8. Hereafter, references to this work will be provided in text.

17. Reddy, *Sisters in Crime*, 10.

18. Rhys Bowen, *Death of Riley* (New York: St. Martin's/Minotaur, 2002), 4. Hereafter, references to this work will be provided in text.

19. Rhys Bowen, *For the Love of Mike* (New York: St. Martin's/Minotaur, 2003), 5–8. Hereafter, references to this work will be provided in text.

20. Sandra Tomc, "Questing Women: The Feminist Mystery After Feminism," in *Feminism in Women's Detective Fiction*, ed. Glenwood Irons (Toronto: University of Toronto Press, 1995), 47.

21. Ibid., 46–47.

Works Cited

Auden, W. H. "The Guilty Vicarage." In *Detective Fiction*, edited by Robin Winks, 15–24. Englewood Cliffs: Prentice-Hall, 1980.
Bowen, Rhys. *Death of Riley*. New York: St. Martin's/Minotaur, 2002.
_____. *Evan Help Us*. New York: Berkeley Prime Crime, 1998.
_____. *Evans Above*. New York: Berkeley Prime Crime, 1997.
_____. *For the Love of Mike*. New York: St. Martin's/Minotaur, 2003.

Cawelti, John G. *Adventure, Mystery and Romance: Formula Stories as Art and Popular Culture*. Chicago: University of Chicago Press, 1976.
Coale, Samuel. *The Mystery of Mysteries: Cultural Differences and Designs*. Bowling Green: Bowling Green State University Popular Press, 2000.
Gosselin, Adrienne Johnson, ed. *Multicultural Detective Fiction: Murder from the "Other" Side*. New York: Garland, 1999.
Klein, Kathleen Gregory, ed. *Diversity and Detective Fiction*. Bowling Green: Bowling Green State University Popular Press, 1999.
Linton, Patricia. "The Detective Novel as a Resistant Text: Alter-Ideology in Linda Hogan's *Mean Spirit*." In *Multicultural Detective Fiction: Murder from the "Other" Side*, edited by Adrienne Johnson Gosselin, 17-36. New York: Garland, 1999.
Mullan, John. "Sentimental Novels." In *The Cambridge Companion to the Eighteenth Century Novel*, edited by John Richetti, 236-54. Cambridge: Cambridge University Press, 1996.
Munt, Sally R. *Murder by the Book? Feminism and the Crime Novel*. London: Routledge, 1994.
Nickerson, Catherine Ross. *The Web of Iniquity: Early Detective Fiction by American Women*. Durham: Duke University Press, 1998.
Reddy, Maureen T. *Sisters in Crime: Feminism and the Crime Novel*. New York: Continuum, 1988.
Tomc, Sandra. "Questing Women: The Feminist Mystery After Feminism." In *Feminism in Women's Detective Fiction*, edited by Glenwood Irons, 46-63. Toronto: University of Toronto Press, 1995.
Walton, Priscilla L., and Manina Jones. *Detective Agency: Women Rewriting the Hard-Boiled Tradition*. Berkeley: University of California Press, 1999.

4. Assuming Identities
Strategies of Drag in Laurie R. King's Mary Russell Series

MEGAN HOFFMAN

Genre fiction is a potentially powerful tool for placing women characters in positions of agency and exposing the ways in which women have been overlooked or represented one-dimensionally by traditional narratives. Detective fiction is a genre which offers particular promise for feminist reimagining since the gender anxiety found in the genre, in spite of its apparent glorification of masculinity, makes it a prime site for examination of the potential flexibility of gender roles. Sir Arthur Conan Doyle's Sherlock Holmes stories provide one example of "classic" detective fiction that has been appropriated by women writers seeking to create new narrative paradigms by reinterpreting conventional plots. The Holmes of Conan Doyle's stories is a paragon of masculinized rationality, a seemingly all-knowing father figure who polices gender roles and social order. This chapter will explore the implications of the use of the Holmes character and "canon" in Laurie R. King's contemporary Mary Russell series. The Mary Russell novels use strategies of drag in order both to question genre stereotypes by undermining the assumptions that typically accompany the masculine detective figure and to expose the potential for gender ambivalence already present in the Holmes stories.

King's series undermines the Holmesian myth of masculine rationality by using devices such as disguise, particularly cross-dressed disguise, to show the fluidity of gender boundaries and how, in transgressing them, the position of agency represented by the detective can be re-imagined in ways that include feminine perspectives. In *Gender Trouble*, Judith Butler writes: "*In imitating gender, drag implicitly reveals the imitative structure of gender itself— as well as its contingency.*"[1] Feminist detective novels that use strategies of drag rewrite traditional detective narratives by exposing gender as a performance. The nature of gender as a compulsory performance enables the subversive potential of drag. Butler argues:

> Gender parody reveals that the original identity after which gender fashions itself is an imitation without an origin ... it is a production which, in effect — that is, in its effect — postures as an imitation. This perpetual displacement constitutes a fluidity of identities that suggests an openness to resignification and recontextualization; parodic proliferation deprives hegemonic culture and its critics of the claim to naturalized or essentialist gender identities. Although the gender meanings taken up in these parodic styles are clearly part of hegemonic, misogynist culture, they are nevertheless denaturalized and mobilized through their parodic recontextualization. As imitations which effectively displace the meaning of the original, they imitate the myth of originality itself.[2]

As a form of gender parody, drag exposes the artificiality of understood gender categories through its displaced repetition of those categories. This framework can also be used to recognise the effect of feminist reinterpretations of traditional forms. Detective fiction is an ideal site for such revisions because of its repetitive formula: its derivative nature allows for constant re-workings, thereby revealing the inherent instability in the very idea of a fixed formula. In novels such as those in the Mary Russell series, the cross-dressed female character is subverting *genre* conventions that can be compared to *gender* conventions. By becoming a transgressive reversal of the masculine detective figure, a character like Mary Russell can expose the artificiality of masculine characteristics traditionally associated with that character through her physical and metaphorical cross-dressing.

King's series of detective novels featuring Sherlock Holmes and his "partner" Mary Russell — which chronicles Russell's teenage apprenticeship to Holmes and their subsequent partnership and marriage — attempts to give the traditional Sherlock Holmes a feminine (and feminist) counterpart in the character Mary Russell. This character is in many ways as exaggerated as Holmes in her intelligence and talents: an Oxford graduate and skilled knife-thrower, Russell is as capable as Holmes in observing and drawing conclusions from seemingly insignificant details. Instead of simply embodying a feminine version of Holmes who has absorbed his traditionally masculine and English modes of knowledge, Mary Russell in fact has many characteristics that make her more subversive than appearances might suggest: first, even as Holmes's female counterpart, she is a young woman with sexual potential and so is at once the dangerous "other" of the original Conan Doyle stories. She is also, in spite of her Oxbridge accent, marginalized in that she is not associated with the traditional England represented by Holmes — she is the product of a Jewish mother from England and an American father. This makes Russell inherently dangerous because she represents not only women but foreign women — the most sexually menacing kind, according to Holmes stories such as "The Noble Bachelor," in which Conan Doyle mentions the phenomenon of American women marrying into the British aristocracy: "One by one the management of the noble houses of Great Britain is passing into the hands of our fair cousins from across the Atlantic."[3] The sexuality of American women threatens to infiltrate the English sense of identity Holmes symbolises and upholds. Like Irene Adler, another American woman who appears in the Conan Doyle story "A Scandal in Bohemia," Russell often navigates gender boundaries through cross-dressing; in fact, when she first meets Holmes he thinks she is a boy because she is dressed in her dead father's clothing. Not only does Russell physically cross-dress, she also does so in a narrative sense: whereas in most of the Conan Doyle stories Dr. Watson is the first-person narrator, in King's series Russell takes Watson's place as relater of events. However, Russell differs from Watson in that she has agency as a detective herself. Russell is constantly part of the action, makes accurate deductions of her own, and is usually privy to Holmes's motivations; she does not simply and admiringly describe Holmes's exploits and wait for him to reveal the solution. In addition, in their depiction of Holmes, King's novels use a well-known characteristic of Doyle's original Holmes—an aptitude for disguise—to exploit the potential instability of the conventions surrounding the archetypal male detective figure.

The Woman in Drag: Irene Adler's Influence

Any novel that offers a female detective counterpart to Sherlock Holmes must surely owe a debt to one of the best-known of the original Holmes stories, "A Scandal in Bohemia." This story is provocative because of its depiction of Holmes matching wits with a worthy female antagonist and failing due to his underestimation of her abilities. Significantly, "A Scandal in Bohemia" was the first Holmes short story published, appearing in *The Strand* in 1891.[4] None of the stories or novels to follow would depict a woman character as capable as Irene Adler of crossing social and gender boundaries. Perhaps the fact that this story appeared so early in the Holmes canon would account for the willingness to transgress such boundaries and the depiction of Holmes's patriarchal authority as fallible. In any case, "A Scandal in Bohemia" provides a template for future revisions of the Holmes stories by feminist writers and a strategy—cross-dressing—for how a feminist counterpart to Holmes might be constructed.

Many critics concur that Irene Adler's presence is subversive and that "A Scandal in Bohemia" can be read as questioning masculine authority and the power of the male gaze. Rosemary Jann writes that "[Irene Adler] seriously threatens male authority"[5]; Joseph Kestner asserts that "Adler ... threatens the patriarchal order in the tale"[6]; and Andrew Smith concludes that "ultimately the tale suggests that Adler is a deeply disturbing presence for Holmes because she confounds his preconception that women are not able to think rationally and so challenges his own claims for the dominance of a superior, masculine, rational gaze."[7] On the other hand, some argue that Adler's transgression of gender norms and possibilities as a feminist figure ultimately fails. Rosemary Jann, after acknowledging Adler's threatening implications, goes on to write: "The potential subversiveness of her powers is blunted ... by her willingness to hold her hand and rise above petty revenge. Domesticated love, woman's true vocation, leads her to submit in the end to voluntary exile as a devoted wife."[8] Significantly, Irene Adler's most subversive act in the story, her cross-dressed foray into the streets of London following Sherlock Holmes back to Baker Street, occurs *after* she is married. She also eludes capture by patriarchal authority figures Holmes and the King of Bohemia and keeps the incriminating photograph as insurance against further attempts to contain her, none of which are entirely consistent with the actions of a properly "domesticated" Victorian wife. Adler's subversive potential stems from the fact that she is a cross-dressed figure. Her possible duality becomes apparent very early in the story, as the King of Bohemia describes her to Holmes: "She has the face of the most beautiful of women, and the mind of the most resolute of men."[9] Irene Adler is an ideal character to illustrate the performative nature of gender: not only is she identified as having a body and mind of different genders, she is an actress by profession and so is used to performance. She herself states in her letter to Holmes: "Male costume is nothing new to me. I often take advantage of the freedom which it gives" (28). Her statement is empowering: she "takes advantage" of the "freedom" of male dress, easily sliding between gender identities by choice. Marjorie Garber argues that "cross-dressing is a classic strategy of disappearance in detective fiction. The lady vanishes by turning into a man — or the man by turning into a woman."[10] Adler's escape from London is due to the failure of the detective's gaze when it came to her gender, both when she is dressed as a man and when she is dressed as a woman. In underestimating her intelligence and making assumptions about the limited capabilities of women, Holmes's powers of observation fail when it comes to meeting Irene Adler on his own masculine ground when she is cross-dressed.

The two photographs of Adler in the story, the "scandalous" one which incriminates the king and the photograph of herself that she leaves behind, are further symbolic of her duality. Though she does not take revenge with the photograph, a move Jann criticizes as "blunting her subversiveness," Adler's restraint must be examined through her own explanation of her actions in her letter to Holmes: "I keep it only to safeguard myself, and to preserve a weapon which will always secure me from any steps [the king] might take in the future" (28). The language Adler uses is not that of feminized passivity; she keeps the letter as a "weapon" to use in her own defense. Her language and her actions demonstrate that she has the power to control the situation. The photograph that Irene Adler leaves behind depicts her alone, in evening dress—the most feminine of female costume; it is the tame alternative that she presents as her "public face." The "scandalous" photograph that she keeps as a weapon with which to defend herself represents the other, transgressive side that she can bring out to use when she needs to, much like her flair for male disguise that fools Holmes.

Irene Adler can also be read as a double for Sherlock Holmes. Her skill in disguise and acting are comparable to Holmes's; in the story, Watson remarks upon seeing Holmes's clergyman disguise that "the stage lost a fine actor ... when he became a specialist in crime" (21). Adler usurps Holmes's privileged position as detective—it is she, not Holmes, who explains her methodology in "solving the case" to her astonished audience of the King of Bohemia, Watson, and Holmes in the letter she leaves behind. Her explanation of how she deduces who Holmes is and the meaning of his actions and motives echoes Holmes's display of his own deductive abilities to Watson at the beginning of the story. Adler appropriates the detective's all-seeing masculine gaze, as well; when she walks down Baker Street in male costume, bidding him goodnight, Holmes is bemused: "'I've heard that voice before,' said Holmes, staring down the dimly lit street. 'Now, I wonder who the deuce that could have been'" (26). Though Holmes is aware that there is something he should be observing, he is too much "in the dark" to detect Adler's duplicity. "Who the deuce" is in fact Irene Adler, the cross-dressed figure who sees clearly through Holmes's disguise as another masculine authority figure and addresses him by name.

Some critics have pointed to the fact that Irene Adler is American as one aspect of her threatening potential. Joseph A. Kestner writes:

> The querying of female nature and its encroachments along male borders is especially reflected in Doyle's conjunctions of two elements which contribute to the late nineteenth-century crisis of masculinity—women and America—reflected in his particular stress ... on the subversive and transgressive nature of American women.[11]

Certainly a woman character, already representative of a dangerous and irrational "other," can be shown to be even more transgressive by making her American as well. Marjorie Garber writes that in detective fiction, "'American' ... marks an ambivalent and liminal place as regards not only courtship customs but also dress and social behavior—much as it did with Conan Doyle's Irene Adler."[12] Adler's liminality, already demonstrated by the ease with which she can slip back and forth across gender boundaries through cross-dressing, is compounded by the fact that she is American: she speaks English, she "lives quietly," and "she is the daintiest thing under a bonnet on this planet," yet her position in English society is uneasy and undefined (17). Is she a "woman ... of dubious and questionable memory," as Watson labels her, or is she, as Holmes comes to respectfully call her, a "lady ... on a very different level" than the King of Bohemia (5, 28)? Holmes implies that even though Irene Adler has transgressed sexual mores and gender codes, she has proven herself, in his opinion, to be morally and intellectually a cut above the King of Bohemia. This obviously upsets accepted social categories: how can an actress with a dubious sexual history be the superior of a king? Adler's status as an American makes her social position ambiguous and so, as with her cross-dressing, her liminal status has made it possible for her to exist both outside and inside accepted definitions of a "lady."

Laurie R. King's Mary Russell novels take advantage of the strategy utilized in "A Scandal in Bohemia" of American woman as transgressive outsider to present Russell as a liminal figure. Though Russell seems on the surface to be perfectly English, she has in fact spent many of her formative childhood and adolescent years in America, and she proves herself able to comfortably embody both typically American and English characteristics, making it easy for her to belong to both categories. This position proves to aid her in her crime-fighting activities, as well: at the climax of the first case she solves without Holmes, she stops a running thief by knocking his leg out from under him with a well-thrown rock. When Holmes asks her where she learned to throw so accurately, Russell responds, "My father thought all young ladies should be able to throw and to run. He was not amused by cultivated awkwardness. He was a great lover of sports, and was trying to introduce cricket into San Francisco."[13] The active skills her American father teaches her help Russell to cross gender boundaries of presumed limitations on women's capacity for physical activity. Russell's father's introduction of cricket, a British game, into San Francisco also hints at his daughter's future capacity to draw on aspects of both national identities. Russell can also employ her learned "Englishness" to aid her when she needs to; she frequently uses the English accent she has acquired from her mother in order to make herself heard in certain situations. When Russell and Holmes are called upon to aid in a kidnapping investigation and are detained at a police station while dressed as gypsies, she uses her voice to get a policeman to *see* her: "For the first time he actually looked at me, drawn up short by the thick Oxford drawl emerging from the gipsy girl, and I reflected upon the extraordinary effect gained by speech that is incongruous with one's appearance" (99). Russell's assumed upper-class Englishness gives her authority when she is in official settings like the police station or academia in which she needs to be properly English to be understood. She uses her speech as another form of drag, illustrating the gap existing between who a person is assumed to be and who she is.

The skills that Russell learns from both her parents, her American father Charles and her English mother Judith, plant the seeds of her future duality. The education of Russell's body has been Charles's domain: he teaches her to throw accurately, certainly a talent that proves useful in her later detective days when she frequently brings down criminals with knives and convenient stones. The correspondence of Russell's body to her father is further underscored by the fact that she often wears his old clothing after he is dead, not her mother's. When she grows older and becomes comfortable with her sexual capacity as a woman, Russell is already adept at disguising herself as a man, giving her a useful advantage as a woman in the position of detective. Her mother, Judith, begins Russell's academic education, and in doing so shapes her daughter's mind in ways that will make her significantly different from Holmes. Judith is Jewish and begins teaching her daughter theology from an early age, and this interest will have as considerable an impact on Russell as Holmes's deductive methods. When Russell goes to Oxford, she chooses to focus on "chemistry and theology, the workings of the physical universe and the deepest stuff of the human mind" (40). The chemistry is due to Holmes's influence, the theology her mother's. Here, the physical, rational, and concrete is gendered masculine while the intellectual, psychological, and spiritual is gendered feminine, but these areas of study are shown to be not entirely incompatible.

In *The Beekeeper's Apprentice* (1994), Russell and Holmes retreat to Palestine on an undercover mission for the British government to escape from mysterious attempts on their lives in London. Russell is the one who chooses the assignment, and she finds unexpected "comfort, shelter and counsel" in her visit "to the birthplace of [her] people" (243). In Palestine, Russell's personal and spiritual growth draws her closer to gaining equality in her partnership with Holmes. Russell's increasing confidence in her abilities is reflected in her relating of the apocryphal story of Judith and Holofernes to Holmes as a hint that she has matured enough to allow her to take on greater challenges as a detective.[14] The story, the first Russell studied with her mother when learning Hebrew as a child, tells of Judith, a beautiful widow who determines to end a war by dressing in attractive clothing and using her appearance to gain access to the enemy camp to kill the general, Holofernes. Judith's manipulation of her sexualized appearance to enable her to carry out her violent intentions is suggestive of Russell's own transgressive employment of gender performance. Russell uses the language of theology learned from her mother, whose name was also Judith, to signal her willingness and desire to play an active role in the subsequent entrapment of the would-be assassin stalking her and Holmes by drawing a parallel between herself and another Jewish woman whose agency stems from subverting gender norms.

In a later instance, Russell again uses a theological means of describing her experiences and separating herself from the masculinised language of detection by working out the identity of the criminal through a suggestive dream stemming from a mental state in which she describes hearing "the *bat qol*, the daughter of the voice of God, she who speaks in whispers and half-seen images" (292). This state, she explains, is when the mind

> continue[s] worrying away at a problem all on its own, so that when the "Eureka!" comes it is as mysterious as if it were God speaking.... When active, strained vision only obscures and frustrates, looking away often permits the eye to see and interpret the shape of what it sees. Thus does inattention allow the mind to register the still, small whisper of the daughter of the voice [292].

Russell also mentions that Holmes experiences a similar state when he is playing the violin or smoking his pipe; but while they have the same understanding, they use different ways of describing it. Holmes "compare[s] this mental state with the sort of passive seeing that enables the eye ... to grasp details with greater clarity by focusing slightly to one side" (292). The process that Holmes and Russell are describing seems to jar with the masculinised, rational deductive methods Holmes is known for, but it is shown to be just as effective. While Holmes calls this intuitive condition "passive seeing," Russell describes it using feminized theological language. To her, it is more active listening than passively receiving insight, as the mind "worr[ies] away at a problem all on its own." Their ways of reaching this state of mind also differ; Holmes uses masculinized means, such as smoking his (phallic) pipe, and he does so alone. Russell seeks out a female friend for dinner and a concert, after which she retires to bed early and experiences a dream that brings her "the daughter of the voice"— the key to the villain's identity.

The dream that comes to Russell after she decides to stop thinking about the problem directly and listen for the "daughter of the voice" is suggestive of the gender flexibility explored in *The Beekeeper's Apprentice*:

> A shadowy face had leered at me from the bookshelf in the corner, half-hidden by blonde hair, and held out a clay pipe in a twisted hand. "You know nothing!" the figure cackled in a voice both male and female, and laughed horribly. His/her gnarled fist tightened over the pipe, which I knew to be Holmes', and then opened [294].

The figure of uncertain gender in Russell's dream smashes Holmes's pipe, phallic symbol and aid to his ratiocination, suggesting that Holmes's masculinized deductive methods, represented by his pipe, will not lead to the solution in this case. Maggie Humm writes that in feminist detective fiction,

> one major example of the representation of Otherness—the investigation of those parts of meaning that are customarily repressed—occurs most often in dreams. Dreams are a common way of introducing a character's irrational or unconscious feelings into a realistic narrative.... In detective fiction by feminist women the contradictions in dreams spill over with gusto into the daily world.[15]

This analysis is apt when applied to Russell's dream. Certainly, the knowledge that comes to her from "the daughter of the voice" is "Other" when compared to the concrete, measurable data that comes from the strategies of deductive analysis she has learned from Holmes.[16] The "contradictions" in Russell's dream do indeed "spill ... into the daily world" when she discovers that though the villain is female, she is a complex, doubled character who occupies an ambiguously gendered position. Russell takes her dream seriously and does not dismiss it as nonsensical and irrelevant, and the dream-hints ultimately lead her to work out the mathematical code that reveals the name of the criminal: Moriarty.

The Moriarty of *The Beekeeper's Apprentice* is not Holmes's nemesis Professor Moriarty of the original Holmes stories, but his daughter Patricia Donleavy. The strategy of using Moriarty's daughter as super villain in opposition to Holmes's female protégée echoes the mirroring of Holmes and Professor Moriarty, and Moriarty's daughter also functions as a double to Holmes and to her father, extending the play with gender categories that has gone on throughout the novel. Holmes reacts with frustration at the cunning of his adversary when he recognizes that she is a woman—but one whose identity he does not yet know:

> "How does one defend against a mirror-image?... A woman! She has turned my own words against me, caused me considerable mental and physical distress, kept me off my balance.... [This] person has even penetrated into one of my bolt-holes!... I still cannot believe that a woman can have done this, deducing my deductions, plotting my moves for me, and all the time giving the impression that to her it is a ... game. Even Moriarty did not go so far, and he was a master without parallel. The mind, capable of such *coups de maître. Maîtresse.*" He stopped, and straightened his shoulders with a jerk as if to settle his clothing back into place [230].

Holmes is disconcerted not just because his adversary seems to think exactly the way he does and anticipate his thoughts, but that she is a *woman* who does so. He has thus far mostly ignored Russell's femininity, but when confronted with another person who thinks in the same way and happens to be a woman, he can no longer presume that a mind like his is exclusively linked to gender. When he "straighten[s] his shoulders with a jerk as if to settle his clothing back into place," Holmes is putting the mantle of masculinity back on after his identity is threatened by a woman. Donleavy has even "penetrated" into one of the bolt-holes around London where Holmes keeps his disguises; the phallic language Holmes uses to describe the break-in suggests that Donleavy has appropriated his assumed masculinity and exposed it as a disguise in itself. Indeed, "even Moriarty did not go so far."

Like her father, Patricia Donleavy is a mathematics professor; she is, in fact, Russell's mathematics professor. As an authority figure whom Russell respects and wants to please, Professor Donleavy is again a double for Holmes; finding out that she is the villain gives Russell feelings of betrayal and sadness. She is, of course, also Russell's double; Donleavy is the student of a master in his field (crime, in this case) and, in addition, she is a woman who functions easily in spheres usually presumed to be dominated by men (again, crime and mathematics). Rosemary Erickson Johnsen argues that

> King very cleverly plays on assumptions ... that an Oxford maths tutor would be male to surprise readers with the revelation of Moriarty's daughter as the criminal. Any satisfaction in this demonstration of gender assumptions in action, however, is dampened by the vision of a thwarted woman tormenting her father's nemesis, using one of her own (female) students to do so.[17]

Certainly Patricia Donleavy is used to playing with gender assumptions, but Johnsen's reading of the character is somewhat simplistic. Donleavy functions as double for both Holmes and Russell, and, in defeating her, Russell achieves full agency as detective. Donleavy is a formidable adversary, made more so by her seemingly endless duality. At the moment when she corners Holmes and Russell in Holmes's cottage and they realize they have been outmanoeuvred, Donleavy greets them with "Good morning, Mr. Holmes ... Miss Russell" (311). This is a pointed reference to Irene Adler's triumphant "Good evening, Mr. Sherlock Holmes" in "A Scandal in Bohemia." Here, Donleavy is shown to be Adler's double as well as Holmes's and Russell's, not only because she is a woman who has outwitted them but also because she is, like Adler, adept at transgressing gender boundaries. When Donleavy is holding Holmes and Russell at gunpoint at the climax of the novel, Russell thinks: "The woman was more dangerous than her gun, as volatile as petrol fumes and malignant as a poisonous spider ... I could only sit, still and unimportant, to one side, and leave the field to Holmes's vast experience" (321). Russell recognises that the really perilous aspect of the situation is the woman, not the phallic weapon with which the woman is holding them captive, but at this point she still views her own agency as an inferior copy of Holmes's and does not take action. However, at the scene's climax, Russell is the one who wrestles the gun away from the other woman and survives the shot that goes through her shoulder and into Donleavy's heart. The novel concludes with Holmes asking Russell to play chess with him and offering to spot her a piece, but Russell refuses:

> "We'll start equal, then."
> "I shall beat you if we do."
> "I don't think so, Holmes. I really don't think you will" [341].

Russell now has the confidence to see herself as Holmes's match in intelligence and skill. In her struggle with her own Moriarty, Russell has gained agency as a detective. She has also indirectly confronted Holmes by killing his female double and replacing her, and in doing so establishing herself in the Irene Adler role assumed by Donleavy. By overcoming Donleavy, Russell now recognizes herself not only as Holmes's equal but as a *woman* who is Holmes's equal.

The Case of the Cross-Dressed Detective

The Mary Russell novels also take cues from "A Scandal in Bohemia" in their frequent use of cross-dressing as an empowering strategy. In fact, the first meeting between Holmes and Russell seems to make playful allusion to Holmes's difficulty in recognizing a woman dressed as a man: when Russell stumbles over Holmes on a hill watching bees, she is dressed in an old suit that belonged to her dead father, her long hair tucked under a hat, and Holmes, despite his legendary capacity for observation, fails to perceive that she is female:

> "Young man, I—"
> "'*Young man*'!" That did it. Rage swept into my veins, filling me with power. Granted I was far from voluptuous, granted I was dressed in practical, that is, male, clothing—this was not to be borne...With a surge of glee I seized the weapon he had placed in my hands and drew back for the coup de grâce...With that I reached for the brim of my oversized cap and my long blonde plaits slithered down over my shoulders [9].

Russell's cross-dressing gives her power over Holmes; she knows who he is at this point but he does not know her, and she becomes aware of the "weapon" she has when she realizes that the "great detective" has not discerned her sex. Even though Russell acknowledges that male clothing is more "practical" and that her adolescent body has a boyish shape, the fact that it is still a *female* body enables the gender fluidity that gives her the power of disguise, unintended in this particular case but successfully deployed in later instances.

Russell's flair for cross-dressing develops throughout the novels, and each episode increases her sense of her own agency. The first time that she deliberately cross-dresses is literally for the sake of performance; she plays Petruchio in an amateur, all-female production of *The Taming of the Shrew* at Oxford, a humorous reversal of Renaissance drama's traditionally all-male casts. In another episode at Oxford, Russell involves herself in a complicated prank in which she disguises herself as a male, Indian student called Ratnakar Sanji who appears at parties and pubs with other male undergraduates. Such activities would have been heavily restricted for female students at Oxford at the time, but Russell comments, "Many girls found these rules infuriating; I found them less so, but perhaps that was only because I was more agile at climbing the walls or scrambling between hansom roof and upper window in the wee hours" (42). Russell is already a liminal figure adept at moving between states; her skill in transgressing gender roles is by now apparent. When the Oxford authorities eventually get wind of the fact that Ratnakar Sanji is a woman, Russell escapes reprimand: "Miss Mary Russell walked demurely away from the pub's back entrance, leaving Ratnakar Sanji in the dustbin behind the door ... scandal was averted, largely because no one ever found the woman who rumour said was involved" (44). Such episodes support Marjorie Garber's perspective, quoted earlier, that "cross-dressing is a classic strategy of disappearance in detective fiction." Russell is able to "disappear" when she realizes the potential for freedom that comes with the transgression of gender boundaries. In this situation, though not yet a detective, Russell uses cross-dressing to navigate rules that discriminate between acceptable social activities for men and women and to humorously subvert authority. Russell concludes of the prank: "The conspiracy left me with two legacies, neither of which had been in my original expectations of University life: a coterie of lasting friends ... and a distinct taste for the freedom that comes with assuming another's identity" (45). The resulting changes in Russell's life after the hoax are significant; her violation of authority has not only given her a liking for "the freedom" of cross-dressing (a phrase that echoes Irene Adler's words to Holmes, "I often take advantage of the freedom which [male costume] gives"), it has also brought Russell "lasting friends," an advantage she had not anticipated which separates her from the "lone detective" figure of Holmes, who uses disguise to confuse and show off to Watson, clients, and police, but not to build a shared sense of the exhilaration of transgression, as Russell's disguise has done.[18]

These beginning forays into cross-dressing, humorous though they are, reveal Russell's future potential for agency as a female detective. Sally R. Munt writes:

Parody has played an important part in destabilizing dominant myths of gender and sexuality in feminist culture, and we also find that it is integral to the crime form itself. The cross-dressed feminist heroine lays bare the artifice of gender via an investigation into patriarchal effects.[19]

Russell's Ratnakar Sanji disguise allows her to take part in university activities that are barred to her as a woman, and her transgression of authority uncovers feminist possibilities for her future: as a detective, particularly as a counterpart to Holmes, Russell would presumably assume the detective's patriarchal authority. However, Russell's ability to dress as a man when she chooses — instead of making her complicit in upholding the patriarchal status quo — enables her to subvert those rules and to expose, through the humorous aspects of her disguise, the artificiality of traditional gender roles and the conventions that accompany them. Butler argues that "part of the pleasure, the giddiness of the performance is in the recognition of a radical contingency in the relation between sex and gender in the face of cultural configurations of causal unities that are regularly assumed to be natural and necessary."[20] Russell's cross-dressing is an instance of the "pleasure" Butler refers to; the "freedom" of cross-dressing is enjoyable to Russell and, as in the case of the Ratnakar Sanji prank, it reveals the construction of societal restrictions on gendered activities.

Another significant example of cross-dressing occurs in *A Monstrous Regiment of Women* (1995), just after Holmes has mocked the idea of marriage (and, implicitly, an equal partnership) between him and Russell. Russell, once again dressed as a man for the sake of comfort, is not amused at his mockery and eludes him, slipping away into the streets of London:

> I stood motionless in a doorway while a patrolling constable shot his light's beam down the alley ... and the incongruity of my furtive behaviour struck me: Here went Mary Russell, who six months previously had qualified for her degrees ... from the most prestigious university in the world, who should in seven — six — days attain her majority and inherit ... a fortune, who was the closest confidante and sometime partner of the almost-legendary figure of Sherlock Holmes (whom, moreover, she had just soundly outwitted) and who walked through London's filthy pavements and alleys a young man, unrecognised, unknown, untraceable.... In an extremity of exhilaration, intoxicated by freedom and caught up by the power in my limbs, I bared my teeth and laughed silently into the darkness.[21]

The cross-dressed Russell avoids the patriarchal authority represented by the policeman by standing in a doorway, a liminal moment in which she recognizes the "incongruity" of her actions. Like Irene Adler, Russell is empowered by her ability to walk the streets of London as a man. As a woman, Russell is academically accomplished and financially privileged, but her "exhilaration" comes from disappearing into her cross-dressed identity, where she can subvert the authority represented by Holmes, academia, and the responsibilities that accompany the coming of age and inheriting her father's fortune.

Physically cross-dressing as a man is not the only strategy of drag used in the series to expose and destabilize conventions of gender roles and detective fiction. As previously mentioned, Russell uses her voice as another form of disguise to cross boundaries of class, to *disappear* and *reappear* at will depending on which accent she is using and to instill trust in her authority when she puts on her "Oxford drawl." Another strategy of drag used in the series is the placement of Russell as first-person narrator, the position that belongs to Watson in the original Sherlock Holmes stories. Rosemary Jann writes of Watson:

> Doyle planned Watson as "commonplace" foil and comrade to Holmes, someone who could give a first-hand description of the adventures he had participated in but who was sufficiently excluded from Holmes's thoughts to maintain the suspense.... No matter how many times he is witness to Holmes's reasoning abilities, he never quite learns how to duplicate them.[22]

Watson is a passive figure; he observes the action but does not understand its implications until Holmes reveals the meaning. Though Watson often assists Holmes on cases, he does not have the agency of a detective figure and is always deprived of the knowledge that would allow him the ability to work out solutions. As Jann argues, "Watson may tell the story ... but Doyle allows Holmes to control the knowledge that is power in the world of detection."[23] Watson's admiring, subordinate position to Holmes also, as Joseph Kestner suggests, functions to affirm the dominance of Holmes's patriarchal authority: "Hero-worship becomes in the Holmes tales the very manifestation of the detective as masculine paradigm."[24] As a strategy of drag, Russell's occupation of Watson's position as narrator challenges these conventions; the role of storyteller in King's novels is used not to create distance but to break down the barrier between narrator, detective figure, and reader through shared knowledge, thereby subverting the detective's conventional role as authority figure.

Like Watson, Russell observes and describes Holmes's actions from her own point of view and works side-by-side with him. Unlike Watson, Russell is not awed by Holmes's methods and conclusions or locked into the position of inferior assistant; she has agency as a detective herself. In her first major case with Holmes, an investigation into the kidnapping of a child, Russell finds herself in the passive role of observer but does not stay there for long:

> What if I did not wait for Holmes to effect the rescue tomorrow? Madness. To take a child's life into my own absurdly inexperienced hands— I shook my head as if to discourage an irritating fly and settled myself more firmly into my post of observer. My assigned post. My vital and agreed-to post.... In a moment the niggling thought had returned, stronger, surer ...

how could Holmes hope to reach her but across these narrow branches? Holmes, approaching sixty and becoming just the least bit hesitant about risking his bones, would have to balance his greater weight and height on the same branch.... My mind veered wildly between obedient caution and reckless insanity, between a sensible preparation for future action and the hard knowledge that we might never have the chance to use it, between carrying out Holmes' direct orders and seizing what even common sense told me might be the only chance offered us [*Beekeeper's Apprentice*, 127].

In this scene, Russell is performing Watson's usual function as general lookout and assistant, waiting for Holmes to burst in and act as the heroic detective, but instead of staying in her "post of observer," she considers Holmes's potential weaknesses and rationalizes that she is in a better position to take action than he is. While Watson would not have disobeyed "direct orders," Russell does so and successfully carries out the rescue, placing herself firmly into the position of agency occupied by the detective figure. Holmes's reaction to Russell's exploit is telling; when she asks him if he regrets letting her join him on the case, he informs her:

I work alone. I always have. Even when Watson was with me, he functioned purely as another pair of hands, not in anything resembling true partnership. You, however ... are not the type to be content to follow directions ... It was something Watson could never have done, even discounting his bad leg ... It was, in fact, precisely what I myself might have done, given the circumstances [142–43].

Russell, unlike Watson, is a fellow detective figure and a true partner; she has performed the function of detective "precisely as [Holmes] might have done." Significantly, during his entire response to Russell's question Holmes is struggling to light his pipe, "which seem[s] to be giving him considerable difficulty" (143). Holmes's discomfort with being supplanted as the lone detective is apparent as he grapples with his iconic pipe, a widely-recognised sign of his identity. The unlit pipe also functions again as a phallic symbol; instead of affirming Holmes's masculinity as Kestner argues Watson does with his admiration, Russell has not only appropriated Holmes's place as sole agent but has also cast doubt on his masculine and investigative authority when she decides that his age and size make him the inferior choice for carrying out the rescue of the kidnapped child. Russell's occupation of Watson's position, both as first-person narrator and as Holmes's "assistant," is a strategy of drag that is not a simple role reversal but a means of obtaining power. In reinterpreting Watson's traditional role in the narrative, the Russell character is used to exploit the instabilities of the Holmes stories' formulaic conventions, thereby creating space for a woman detective's potential agency.

The use of cross-dressing throughout the Russell series is continued in the depiction of Holmes. Though Holmes dons many disguises throughout the canonical Conan Doyle stories, the only occasion when he actually dresses as a woman is in "The Adventure of the Mazarin Stone" (1921). He is not actually shown in this disguise during the course of the narrative's action, but the costume is described to Watson by Holmes's young assistant, Billy: "To-day he was an old woman. Fairly took me in, he did, and I ought to know his ways by now."[25] Holmes later boasts to Watson, "I was never more convincing. [The suspect] actually picked up my parasol for me once" (8). Holmes's surprisingly believable turn as an old woman in this Conan Doyle story provides a site of gender ambivalence that is exploited in King's novels when he is depicted several times cross-dressing as a woman, providing an intriguing counterpart to Russell's male cross-dressing. Significantly, in these situations after relating to each other as women, Holmes and Russell share a sexually charged moment, but only when Holmes has divested himself of his disguise. At one point in *The Beekeeper's Apprentice*, Holmes breaks into Russell's rooms at Oxford disguised as a spectacularly unattractive elderly woman (155–56). Holmes assumes a motherly role towards the rain-soaked Russell, fetching her some brandy and handing her food from a picnic basket. After Russell demands that he change out of his disguise and he "s[its] down again as Sherlock Holmes, more or less," Holmes refers to himself as "a cold-blooded thinking machine," echoing Dr. Watson's famous description of him from "A Scandal in Bohemia" (*Apprentice*, 158). Russell almost flirtatiously responds, "*I* [author's emphasis] have never called you cold-blooded" (158). Another instance of Holmes in drag occurs in *A Monstrous Regiment of Women*, when Holmes dons the costume of "a massive woman whose full bust strained the bright yellow satin of her dress above the tray she bore, a selection of glittering geegaws" (286). Russell, who is herself disguised as a young prostitute and about to embark upon a risky and stressful investigation, is reassured by Holmes's presence and by the friendly banter they engage in. After Russell has gathered her information and escaped, she finds Holmes, who has changed into "the costume of an indeterminate labourer," and "seiz[es] his hand, which surprised [her] as much as it did him" (304). In both instances, the tentative sexual overture is not made until Holmes is "more or less" in his masculine guise again and Russell is dressed in a way that explicitly suggests femininity, in her bathrobe in the first case and in her prostitute disguise in the second. These occasions both reinforce and complicate the seemingly rather conventional marriage plot between the two. Holmes's masculinity is not compromised by engaging in romantic behavior while he is in drag, but that these episodes occur directly after he sheds his female disguises indicates a degree of gender ambivalence that underlies the more traditional masculine and feminine roles that Holmes and Russell assume for their first forays into what will eventually become a romantic relationship. Just as Russell's male cross-dressing complicates her gender identity and enhances her reshaping of the detective role, Holmes's female cross-dressing uses the strategy offered in "The Adventure of the Mazarin Stone" to suggest the possibility of gender ambiguity in his character, destabilizing the paradigm of the masculine detective figure.

The Holmes of the Russell novels is also reinterpreted as being more accepting of conventionally feminine attributes like open displays of emotion than the character in the Doyle stories — or at least more capable of possessing them. For example, in one instance when Holmes is attacked he assumes that Russell is also in danger so he rushes to make sure she is uninjured even when there is no indication that she might have been a target. Russell is puzzled by Holmes's actions and asks him if he has any reason to believe that she might have been harmed. Holmes responds, "to tell you the truth, I found it impossible to retain a logical train of thought" (*Apprentice*, 188). This Holmes, unlike the man depicted by Watson, is capable of acting from an emotional motive even when there is no compelling reason to do so — a somewhat different man than the "reasoning and observing machine" described in the Doyle stories. Russell, in another twist on her occupation of Watson's narrative position, describes Holmes's capacity for emotion in a revision of Watson's famous portrayal of Holmes as a "machine":

> I had known Holmes for a third of my life and had long since accustomed myself to the almost instantaneous workings of his mental processes, but even after two years of the intimacy of marriage, I was able to feel surprise at the unerring accuracy of his emotional judgement. Holmes the cold, the reasoner, Holmes the perfect thinking machine was, in fact, as burningly passionate as any religious fanatic. He had never been a man to accept the right action for the wrong reason.[26]

According to Russell, Holmes has always been capable not only of understanding emotion but also of feeling it. Perhaps, then, the Holmes of the Russell series is more a rereading of the original character as a multidimensional being than an entirely new Holmes who is suddenly able to experience emotion as well as reason. Lee Horsley argues of the Doyle stories:

> In the case of Holmes, conflicting tendencies are apparent, for example, in the way his methods of detection combine the artistic and the scientific, the intuitive and the rational. He is a melancholy, drug-taking bohemian aesthete but also an energetic exemplar of intellectual power and rational penetration.[27]

The potential for duality in Holmes's character is present in the Conan Doyle stories as well as in the King novels. The strategy of Russell as narrator allows for development of Holmes's character in King's series, revealing potential for the questioning of conventionally accepted readings of his motivations. At the beginning of *The Beekeeper's Apprentice* is a prologue in the form of a letter from Russell to the reader in which Russell states, "Watson's stories, those feeble evocations of the compelling personality we both knew, have taken on a life of their own, and the living creature of Sherlock Holmes has become ethereal, dreamy. Fictional" (xix). Russell's letter to the reader rejects the notion of Conan Doyle's Holmes stories as the authentic representation of the character. This presentation of Holmes complicates the concept of an "original" character, suggesting an identity for Holmes that includes the possibility for multiple interpretations.

Conclusion

> "Holmes," I asked ... do you find that there are aspects of yourself with which you feel most comfortable?..."
> "'Who am I?' you mean." He smiled at the question and gave what was at first glance a most oblique answer. "Do you know what a fugue is?"... I thought in silence for some distance before his answer arranged itself sensibly in my mind. "I see. Two discrete sections of a fugue may not appear related, unless the listener has received the entire work, at which time the music's internal logic makes clear the relationship" [*Beekeeper's Apprentice*, 205].

Laurie R. King's Mary Russell novels explore through various strategies of drag the ways in which an identity can be constructed for a woman detective that reinterprets conventions of traditional detective narratives yet still allows her agency in the genre's terms. As the quote above suggests, an identity can consist of many different facets yet still be cohesive; the Mary Russell novels use drag to investigate how masculine and feminine aspects can be integrated to create a new image of the detective figure. In order for the woman detective's identity to be effective she must be able to be read within the formula that renders detective fiction recognisable as a genre. At the same time, with approaches such as placing Russell in the first-person narrator position previously occupied by Watson, the practices of traditional narratives can be subverted and rewritten to promote a feminist agenda. Drag is also employed in King's novels in order to question the original depiction of Holmes as masculine authority figure, revealing possibilities for multiplicity in his character that go beyond long-established interpretations. The drag strategies used in King's novels expose the performative nature of both gender and genre categories, using an understanding of both to subversively repeat, reinterpret, and transgress them. Marjorie Garber writes: "Transvestism is a space of possibility structuring and confounding culture: the disruptive element that intervenes, not just a category crisis of male and female, but the crisis of category itself."[28] Drag in the Mary Russell novels reveals the "crisis of category" in rules of both gender and genre, dramatising the fluid nature of gender identity and the promise of agency to be found in variations on the detective fiction formula.

Notes

1. Judith Butler, *Gender Trouble: Feminism and the Subversion of Identity* (New York: Routledge, 1999), 175. Italics in original.
2. *Ibid.*, 175–76.
3. Sir Arthur Conan Doyle, "The Noble Bachelor," in *The Adventures of Sherlock Holmes*, ed. Richard Lancelyn Green (Oxford: Oxford University Press, 1993), 224.
4. Rosemary Jann, *The Adventures of Sherlock Holmes: Detecting Social Order* (New York: Twayne, 1995), xvi.
5. *Ibid.*, 113.
6. Joseph A. Kestner, *Sherlock's Men: Masculinity, Conan Doyle, and Cultural History* (Aldershot, and Brookfield, VT: Ashgate, 1997), 77.
7. Andrew Smith, *Victorian Demons: Medicine, Masculinity, and the Gothic at the Fin-de-Siècle* (Manchester: Manchester University Press, 2004), 135.
8. Jann, *The Adventures of Sherlock Holmes*, 113.
9. Sir Arthur Conan Doyle, "A Scandal in Bohemia," in *The Adventures of Sherlock Holmes*, ed. Richard Lancelyn Green (Oxford: Oxford University Press, 1993), 14. Hereafter, citations from this work will be provided in text.
10. Marjorie Garber, *Vested Interests: Cross-Dressing and Cultural Anxiety* (Harmondsworth: Penguin, 1993), 186.
11. Kestner, *Sherlock's Men*, 36.
12. Garber, *Vested Interests*, 199.
13. Laurie R. King, *The Beekeeper's Apprentice* (1994; New York: Bantam, 2002), 83. Hereafter, citations from this work will be provided in text.
14. Russell's use of an apocryphal story, a scriptural text that is excluded from the Hebrew canon, is suggestive; the King novels are set up as relating events that occur after or outside of the original Holmes stories, which are often referred to by readers and critics as the "canon."
15. Maggie Humm, *Border Traffic: Strategies of Contemporary Women Writers* (Manchester: Manchester University Press, 1991), 209.
16. Like Russell's understanding and application of the Jewish concept of the *bat qol* to the conclusions she reaches through her dream, non-rational and often culturally specific means of processing information, including dreams, telepathy and clairvoyance, occur as a strategy in other novels by American women detective writers including Barbara Neely, Lucha Corpi and Sujata Massey. The protagonists in these series provide an alternative to the traditional, masculine Euro-American detective figure.
17. Rosemary Erickson Johnsen, *Contemporary Feminist Historical Crime Fiction* (Basingstoke: Palgrave Macmillan, 2006), 103.
18. For example, in "The Adventure of the Dying Detective" (1913), when Holmes alters his appearance to make it look as though he is suffering from a highly contagious,

inevitably fatal tropical disease, he insults and alienates Watson rather than tell him that he is actually pretending to be ill in order to flush out a criminal.
    19. Sally R. Munt, *Murder by the Book? Feminism and the Crime Novel* (London: Routledge, 1994), 206–7.
    20. Butler, *Gender Trouble*, 175.
    21. Laurie R. King, *A Monstrous Regiment of Women* (London: HarperCollins, 2000), 18.
    22. Jann, *The Adventures of Sherlock Holmes*, 24.
    23. *Ibid.*, 25.
    24. Kestner, *Sherlock's Men*, 16.
    25. Sir Arthur Conan Doyle, "The Adventure of the Mazarin Stone," in *The Case-Book of Sherlock Holmes*, ed. W.W. Robson (Oxford: Oxford University Press, 2009), 5. Hereafter, citations from this work will be provided in text.
    26. Laurie R. King, *A Letter of Mary* (New York: Bantam, 1998), 296.
    27. Lee Horsley, *Twentieth-Century Crime Fiction* (Oxford; Oxford University Press, 2005), 31.
    28. Garber, *Vested Interests*, 17.

Works Cited

Butler, Judith. *Gender Trouble: Feminism and the Subversion of Identity*. New York: Routledge, 1999.
Conan Doyle, Arthur. "The Adventure of the Mazarin Stone." In *The Case-Book of Sherlock Holmes*, 5–22. Edited by W.W. Robson. Oxford: Oxford University Press, 2009.
_____. "The Adventure of the Noble Bachelor." In *The Adventures of Sherlock Holmes*, 223–248. Edited by Richard Lancelyn Green. Oxford: Oxford University Press, 1993.
_____. "A Scandal in Bohemia." In *The Adventures of Sherlock Holmes*, 3–28. Edited by Richard Lancelyn Green. Oxford: Oxford University Press, 1993.
Garber, Marjorie. *Vested Interests: Cross-Dressing and Cultural Anxiety*. Harmondsworth: Penguin Books, 1993.
Horsley, Lee. *Twentieth-Century Crime Fiction*. Oxford: Oxford University Press, 2005.
Humm, Maggie. *Border Traffic: Strategies of Contemporary Women Writers*. Manchester: Manchester University Press, 1991.
Jann, Rosemary. *The Adventures of Sherlock Holmes: Detecting Social Order*. New York: Twayne, 1995.
Johnsen, Rosemary Erickson. *Contemporary Feminist Historical Crime Fiction*. Basingstoke: Palgrave Macmillan, 2006.
Kestner, Joseph A. *Sherlock's Men: Masculinity, Conan Doyle, and Cultural History*. Aldershot, and Brookfield, VT: Ashgate, 1997.
King, Laurie R. *The Beekeeper's Apprentice*. New York: Bantam, 2002.
_____. *A Letter of Mary*. New York: Bantam, 1998.
_____. *A Monstrous Regiment of Women*. London: HarperCollins, 2000.
Munt, Sally R. *Murder by the Book? Feminism and the Crime Novel*. London: Routledge, 1994.
Smith, Andrew. *Victorian Demons: Medicine, Masculinity, and the Gothic at the Fin-de-Siècle*. Manchester: Manchester University Press, 2004.

5. Genre–Bending in Neely's Blanche White Series
Testing the Limits of Crime Fiction

BETSY YOUNG

A central question in detective fiction criticism over the past few decades has been whether or not the genre is conducive to, and appropriate for, furthering any real social or political agenda. Is it best left to reinforcing the current cultural climate, as classic crime fiction — especially the hardboiled — has always done?

While detective fiction had played out on a conservative landscape ever since Holmes met Watson, that landscape has been redrawn by the pens of a large and diverse set of authors during the last 30 years. And many of these authors are working to shift the paradigm. In her Blanche White series written and set in the 1990s, black feminist Barbara Neely purposely sets forth on this mission, remarking on her debut, *Blanche on the Lam*, "The mystery genre seemed like a very good place to talk about serious issues.... One of my major goals with this book was really to talk about the relationship between domestic workers and their employers in a way that gets at race and class,"[1] and, of course, gender. Neely pays a great deal of attention in each novel to revealing Blanche's own self-identity, her unique take on what it means to be a female, working-class African American, so that Blanche can be the instrument that Neely needs to put forth this discourse. But critics like Andrew Pepper propose that the dialogue doesn't work, and that Neely is too constrained by the genre to advance her agenda successfully. Pepper postulates, "One could argue that her subversive political agenda is undermined by formal conventionality."[2] I contend that the opposite is true: it is precisely by putting her protagonist and her stories into a genre that's conservative in both ideology and form that Neely is able to showcase, by contrast, a black feminist voice and viewpoint. Neely imbues this voice with power and exigency by giving her protagonist a strong female individuality shaped by personal and ancestral relationships, influenced by historical awareness, and empowered by the mantle of double-consciousness.

Paradoxically, although the genre itself does not undercut the persuasiveness of that voice, Neely's own urgency eventually does. The series appears to have concluded prematurely after only four novels, the last published in 2000. Fans and scholars have wondered why, and even Neely herself has said that she had more Blanche stories to write. Here I argue that Neely's ability to succeed in the genre was ultimately undermined by her social agenda. By the fourth and final book, Neely's passion for black feminist principles impels her to push the boundaries of the detective fiction form so far that they snap, depositing her character outside the genre.

The debate on the viability of detective fiction as a suitable vehicle for anything but reaffirming the status quo has been waged since female writers entered the hardboiled landscape in droves in the 1980s, laying claim to it as a valid setting for a spectrum of feminist positions. Authors like Sue Grafton and Sara Paretsky introduced series in which their female private detectives challenged many of the assumptions on which the hardboiled tradition had rested. Though fans embraced the burgeoning subgenre — making these and similar series into long-running bestsellers— scholars were at first more skeptical. In an early study of the subject, Kathleen Gregory Klein famously named the seeming paradox in play: "Either feminism or the formula is at risk."[3] She further indicted these authors for "allow[ing] the genre to triumph over feminism."[4] The discussion expanded during the 1990s to include emerging series that, grouped as a whole, can be classified as "multicultural detective fiction." Adrienne Johnson Gosselin, editor of *Multicultural Detective Fiction: Murder from the "Other" Side*, describes the category simply but significantly as "the detective story in the hands of authors whose cultural communities are not those of the traditional Euro-American male hero ... and whose cultural aesthetic alters the formula itself."[5] She further defines multiculturalism in terms of cultural communities and their relation to (i.e., lack of traditional) social power, so that the subcultures include those based on race and ethnicity, gender, sexuality, and socioeconomic status.[6] Ultimately, time and cultural temperament have shifted enough to create a space for agency within these works, a view presaged by Maureen Reddy back in 1988 when she explored this topic in *Sisters in Crime*, suggesting that "feminist crime novels ... participate in the larger feminist project of redefining and redistributing power."[7] While I am not conflating all feminisms nor all minority perspectives, it is reasonable to extrapolate that if there is agency for one previously-marginalized voice in detective fiction, there is room for others, an idea that the ongoing expansion of the genre supports.

There is even a strong argument that positioning ethnicity at the center of a crime narrative provides a natural opportunity for examination, and, by extension, for instruction. Dorothea Fischer-Hornung and Monika Mueller call the pairing of ethnicity and crime fiction symbiotic, explaining that both share the exploration of "the self and other, the borderlands of minority and majority relations, dominance and alterity, as well as marginality and centrality."[8] In other words, since both ethnic study and the detective genre each have the compelling need to question these binaries, they can join together in an effort to expose or even shift them — at least, in the literary landscape — as well. Reddy exposes one of the principal ways that black detective fiction writers begin to achieve this, by "treating racism as a fundamental fact of life and as an absolutely central component of the dominant ideology."[9] Because traditional detective fiction has reaffirmed that ideology, confronting racism head-on in this landscape is a blatantly subversive move — a move that Neely makes at every turn. Even among her sisters in authorhood, Neely's work stands out for its explicit undertaking: "On the whole, Neely's series is far more overtly political than any of the other series by black women, with Blanche deeply committed to the emancipatory project of black women's liberation from racism, sexism, heterosexism, and classism."[10] In terms of the literary field, Neely's novels straddle the feminist and African American subgenres without fitting neatly into either. I think she is in a very workable space; she has identified a natural intersection of multicultural issues. Ironically, it is the boundaries of the umbrella genre of detective fiction that she ultimately finds too constraining.

Blanche on the Lam, and thus the series, opens with an everyday courtroom scene where Blanche, a domestic day worker with multiple clients, is appearing before a judge on charges of bouncing checks. It's a situation caused by her (white) employers' negligence, not her own, and yet she, of course, is the one who suffers. What should be routine becomes serious when the judge decides to set an example with Blanche and sentences her to jail time. The judge offers her the chance to speak and then immediately cuts her off, rendering her voiceless and therefore powerless. Being disempowered in the face of the law is something most people can identify with, but it clearly runs deeper for this black southern woman. Lack of trust in the legal system is a recurring theme in detective fiction, but it is often magnified when the protagonist is female and/or a minority, because "law" and "justice" are simply not equated in their world.[11] Blanche's instance of mistreatment here is a perfect example of why that is; it's a victimization of race and class by "the system," by the dominant ideology. When Blanche goes "on the lam" and ends up as the maid and cook in a country house where murder and other crimes take place, she quickly assumes the role of amateur detective out of very personal motives. Unlike her professional counterparts in the hardboiled novels or the amateur detectives of cozy mysteries, Blanche is not coming from a place of detachment, autonomy, or power; instead, she is forced into the role in order to survive.

This survival theme is central to a black feminist worldview, often identified as "a legacy of struggle." Katie Cannon explains, "Throughout the history of the United States, the interrelationship of white supremacy and male superiority has characterized the Black woman's reality as a situation of struggle — a struggle to survive in two contradictory worlds simultaneously, one white, privileged, and oppressive, the other black, exploited, and oppressed."[12] The setting of *Lam* primarily in this southern country house is a perfect microcosm of the contradictory worlds that Cannon identifies. This fact mitigates Pepper's assertion that the country house venue "acts as kind of a screen, distancing the narrative, detective, and reader from such problems [as the brutal suppression of the black population]."[13] Instead, the pristine setting provides a stark background from which the issues of racism, the legacy of slavery, and the crimes of murder and fraud stand out in pointed contrast.

Pepper's argument that the medium undermines the message is echoed by reviewer Kathy Phillips, who claims that by the fourth and final story, *Blanche Passes Go*, the forum of the detective novel is no longer appropriate for Neely's increasingly strident tone.[14] This opinion may stem in part from Phillips's erroneous characterization of the entire Blanche series as part of the cozy subgenre, from which readers are likely to be expecting light, escapist fare. The cozy, one of the earlier forms of detective fiction popularized by Agatha Christie, is distinguished by its removed, rural setting, and a murder that takes place "off-stage," often prior to the opening of the story itself. These characteristics are in sharp contrast to the hardboiled novels, in which the detective braves the "mean streets" of the city to solve what's often been a brutal and cold-blooded murder. *Blanche Among the Talented Tenth* in particular does fit the cozy mold in a few ways: it takes place in the remote, protected vacation setting of Amber Cove, an exclusive resort for wealthy — and conspicuously, all light-skinned — African Americans. No one is ever in any real physical danger, and the "crime," which isn't even identified until half way through the book, turns out to be an accidental death. Other pivotal deaths in *Talented Tenth* are a suicide and a natural demise. This removed, privileged setting gives Neely ample opportunity to explore the themes she really wants to: colorism, classism, the complex relationships that black women have with each other and with black men.

But the rest of the series is decidedly not cozy material. Even though *Lam* primarily takes place in a remote country house, criminal activity including murder repeatedly violates any illusion of a safe, protected setting. In fact, the penultimate scene of the book has Blanche literally running for her life across the manicured property. Blanche is often in physical jeopardy throughout the series, which is another point of difference from the cozy tradition where the amateur detective herself is usually removed and protected from violence, just as the setting appears to be. The third novel, *Blanche Cleans Up*, takes place in Boston — much of it on the gritty streets of Roxbury — and in *Blanche Passes Go*, though the story is set in Farleigh, North Carolina, violence is literally brought to Blanche's front door in the form of physical attacks on herself and the physical abuse of a neighboring woman. As each of the novels progresses, it is not just violence that is exposed, but the more socially embedded crimes of fraud and corruption. It is these offenses — hallmarks of the hardboiled tradition — that provide Neely more ammunition for the political statements she wants to make. Neely's works, in terms of setting, tone, and feel, fall somewhere between the cozies and the hardboileds. Adding in the multicultural angle — the African-American, feminist viewpoint — it's clear that Neely has found a unique place in the canon of detective fiction.

Neely has freely admitted that the mystery itself is the least interesting part of the story for her,[15] so it is not surprising that she gives it nominal regard in the plot of *Talented Tenth*. This subjugation of sleuthing is a distinction of black crime fiction, where "blues detectives are interested in the social and political atmosphere, often to the exclusion of detection."[16] Neely has also confessed that she wasn't planning to follow up *Lam* with another Blanche story, and that her initial impetus to do so was largely financial.[17] In retrospect for the reader, this makes sense for two reasons: *Lam* is not written as a set-up for a series, in that the landscape of Blanche's life, including the important secondary characters who help paint her identity and community, is not well-established. Indeed, the fact that each novel in the series has a completely different locale is atypical of a detective series and suggests that Neely was fighting the conventions in perhaps even unrecognized ways. Second, as *Talented Tenth* is a crime fiction novel in only the most cursory manner — and without the frame of the other Blanche titles around it, it might not even be identified as such — it also has the feel of a stand-alone novel. This observation might help to identify one of the reasons the series was ultimately short-lived; if Neely herself was not committed to the idea of a series, she might not have been paying enough attention to the needs her audience had vis-à-vis "their" detective and the critical mystery-solving facet of the stories. As other authors and critics have identified, a series character allows for greater agency in putting forth a social or political agenda or any issue that might dilute the whodunit investigation that initially attracts the genre reader.[18] The audience develops a very real though parasocial relationship with the protagonist and is willing to invest in her causes, at least for the duration of the narrative. But the conventions of the genre must be attended to sufficiently as well.

Because Blanche is the vessel for Neely's feminist agenda, the character is drawn with depth and nuance. Blanche herself is no subtle woman, which is symbolized by the ironic double-punch of her name — Blanche White — all the more contradictory because Blanche is very dark-skinned. This deliberate naming of her protagonist provides Neely with a continual opportunity for edification, as not only does Blanche reflect on the blunt irony of her name, often in the context of colorism, but she also uses it as a barometer of potential prejudice by gauging other characters' reactions to it. This is most evident in *Blanche on the Lam*, when her affluent white male employer, who is subsequently revealed to be a completely unscrupulous and unsympathetic character, openly teases her by drawing her full name out tauntingly in conversation.[19] In the second novel, *Blanche Among the Talented Tenth*, the contradiction of Blanche's name is raised so that Neely can call out not only ignorance ("Giggles, shocked silences, stupid and disdainful looks, she was accustomed to all of that"[20]), but also, more pointedly, the inevitable mistreatment that comes with her color and gender. Blanche opines, "Some people just ain't smart enough to figure out how to hurt me with it. The rest get at least as good as they give" (27). Note that in this small snippet of dialogue, Neely establishes Blanche's awareness of her own intelligence and perceptiveness, along with her penchant for fighting back. Blanche is also suggesting here that virtually no one simply accepts the incongruity of her name, or shows any grace towards her in this regard. This narrative begins to reveal a pattern of isolation for the character, as though on some level, everyone is the enemy. It foregrounds Blanche's fundamental dissociation with anyone she perceives as "other."

The reader learns a lot more about Blanche's life and especially about her viewpoints on myriad personal and social issues than most genre authors would take the time to reveal. Possibly the most intriguing aspect is Blanche's choice of career. Why would a proud, independent, sufficiently educated black woman choose to be a domestic servant over a more "professional" career? Especially when the job of servant is fraught with a history of mistreatment, subjugation, and even abuse? Blanche ruminates on this choice in each of the novels; it is a necessary point of illumination for explication since it is, at first blush, a surprising decision. In *Lam*, Blanche reflects on the difference between this and other job opportunities like clerical work or nursing, offering the following rationale: "She was really her own boss, and her clients knew it. She was the expert. She ordered her employers' lives, not the other way around" (86). Blanche further drives home the distinction of being a day worker, not a live-in, thus asserting even more autonomy and independence from each of her employers. By casting Blanche's choice of career in this light, Neely reinscribes the role of domestic servant by removing the exploitation and subordination traditionally associated with it.

But there is greater significance to Blanche's profession; I suspect Neely herself chose it with great care, and not solely for the opportunities it would provide for operation from that position as an amateur detective, though this, too, warrants further examination. By virtue of African American history in this country, the role of the black female domestic servant is paradigmatic. As Trudier Harris explains, "Domestic work has been the job most consistently available to black women in this country"[21]; and further, the image of the black domestic is "one with which the majority of black women can identify and empathize,"[22] either from their own experience or from generations before. This role cements Blanche's representation of a black "everywoman" and plants her firmly in the working class. Embedded in this identity of the black domestic is what Patricia Hill Collins calls an "outsider-within stance, a peculiar marginality."[23] Thus Blanche is solidly cast in the "other" position with regard to gender, race, and social strata — the perfect position from which to scrutinize ... sermonize ... subvert.

Black domestics were traditionally called on to be — demeaningly, absurdly — *invisible* by their employers. It's no wonder Neely would want to countermand this presumed edict by making her heroine outspoken and unwilling to yield much deference to her clients; Blanche symbolically provides a strong and empowering voice for her silenced forebears. When an employer in *Blanche Cleans Up* fails to greet her but instead begins barking out orders, Blanche responds in a tone we can only assume has just the allowable measure of sarcasm, "'And a good morning to you, too, ma'am,'"[24] which immediately elicits the contrite apology she expects. Neely exploits the invisibility theme even further to subvert the employer/employee power structure, since it is the very lack of attention that her clients pay her that allows Blanche to play out the role of amateur detective right in their own homes. But Reddy reminds us to recognize the root of this "ability"; she notes that *Lam* "depicts Blanche as hiding in plain sight, a possibility created by racism."[25]

This concept of invisibility ties in directly with one of the key tropes of African American detective fiction identified by Stephen Soitos: double-consciousness, often symbolized by the figurative imagery of "the mask" or "the veil." Though W.E.B. Du Bois initially conceived of the term to represent the conflict of unifying an identity that is both Black and American, Soitos reinterprets the phrase with positive connotations as it applies to the detective persona, suggesting that double-consciousness provides the African American detective with unique insight, even "a spiritual gift" of "extraordinary powers."[26] Soitos further explains, "Double-consciousness becomes a tool of detection, allowing characters to assume identities and masks in the trickster tradition, hide their detective personas behind their blackness, and use hoo-doo powers in their detective work."[27] Reddy further articulates how this dynamic functions by elucidating Du Bois's veil metaphor: "Blacks — who wear the veil as well as live behind it — can see through the veil easily, viewing the white territory and its inhabitants clearly, while whites cannot penetrate the veil to see the truths of black life."[28] Once again, then, there is the opportunity to harness something powerful and effective from a legacy of oppression.

In her role as domestic servant, Blanche is perfectly situated to wield this power. The veil that Blanche wears is made all the more opaque to the white world by her gender, even more so by her station. She is aware of both its burden and its benefit, resisting the former and embracing the latter at any opportunity. Though Blanche is not a trickster through and through — she's too faithful to her own self-identity to put on any act for too long — she is absolutely willing to perform the stereotype of the doting, deferential servant when the need arises. Consider the scene in *Lam* when Blanche is trying to elicit a (fake) bond with her employer, Grace, in order to extract some information from her:

> She was tempted to launch into a full-fledged, lay-it-on-my-bosom number, complete with wet eyes and hand-patting.... Instead Blanche let her arms fall to her sides and was attentively silent. Her head slightly bowed, she waited for her employer to bestow the privilege of confidence.
> "Are you married, Blanche?"
> Blanche raised her head. "Yes, ma'am," she lied.
> "Any children?"
> "No, ma'am.... That man is more than enough child for me." She gave Grace a version of that pained, puzzled and indignant look which is part of all women's male vocabulary [143].

For Blanche, this is an exaggerated act since, as she tells us repeatedly in the series, she does not suffer from "Darkies Disease"— that is, essentially, mistaking the professional relationship between black servant and white employer as a personal, even familial, loving one (*Lam*, 48). But since she understands how she is perceived by her employers, she can "don the mask" and perform an expected role, and she knows they will not be able to detect her deception. Blanche uses the act in a different way in *Cleans Up*, when she's trying to keep her employer Allister Brindle from uncovering another bit of her trickery. Clearly, she's in complete control of the exchange: "She looked him hard in the eye and held him for a few moments before he remembered he was supposed to be in charge" (74). After the thrust-and-parry conversation that ensues, in which Blanche maintains her innocence through sheer effrontery, she formulates her last deflection while thinking, "She'd never seen anyone's eyes get bloodshot while she watched. Could she make him froth at the mouth next?" (74). In both cases, she can assume control because she has a more clear-eyed view of the dynamics in play. Thus Blanche's lens of double-consciousness is magnified by her role as a servant, supplying her with even more facility to act as an amateur detective. With this, Neely further reinforces her ongoing subversion of the traditional hierarchy.

All of this empowerment, however, would fall flat if it were not for the inherent strength in Blanche that compels her to harness this power for the causes she deems important. Neely gives us ample opportunity to examine this source of strength, as the very fact of it — the very *possibility* of it, that a single, black working woman can be independent, successful, and self-defined — is a crucial part of her message. In some ways, Blanche's positive self-valuations are not unique to her: she's proud of her ability to support herself, to do her work well, to raise her children[29] "right." Blanche is also defined by her community, which is not a literal, physical one so much as an emotional, spiritual one that she defines and maintains for herself. With the exception of the young son she is raising, Blanche's is a community of *women*. It is a small circle, too; the only women we hear from in every book are Blanche's mother and her best friend, Ardell, and, except in *Passes Go*, these relationships are maintained solely through phone calls. Still, it's clear that Blanche considers these women her touchstones and their conversation, her lifelines. With Ardell in particular, Blanche looks for and receives validation of her own worldviews. Beyond these two women, Blanche has an authentic connection to two other women who influence her life: Miz Minnie, the matriarch of Blanche's community in Farleigh, and Madame Rosa, a spiritual guide she met in New York. Both of these women possess otherworldly gifts of insight and understanding, and they take turns providing pivotal guidance to Blanche throughout the four novels. It is noteworthy that Blanche, street-savvy and skeptical by nature, never questions the wisdom or authority of these two women.

In fact, these are the only two people whose almost-mystical directives Blanche follows without question. This illuminates another significant aspect of her character, and it ties into another of the tropes that, according to Soitos, characterizes African American detective fiction: the use of hoodoo. Carmen Flys-Junquera defines hoodoo generally as a wide-ranging African American folklore that incorporates elements of ritualism, ancestralism, clairvoyance, dream visions, and animism, and in the context of black crime fiction, as the practice of these elements by the protagonists in the course of their detection.[30] Neely introduces us to this concept slowly; in *Lam*, we learn of Blanche's belief in animism upon her arrival at the country estate: "The house was anxious, as though something of which it did not approve had taken place on its premises, or was about to" (35). Similarly, Neely presents Blanche's sixth sense as an inalienable talent, as the character reflects on her newfound and disquieting connection to Mumsfield: "She always knew when her mother was around, or Ardell, or which one of the children was about to fling open the door and bound through the house. This ability to sense Mumsfield's approach was of the same nature but different" (45).

As the series progresses Neely reveals more of her character's faith in hoodoo, from her dreams to her altars and ancestral prayers. Where she strays from the genre is that these elements of hoodoo are not simply devices for detection. Hoodoo is a central part of Blanche's life, and Blanche's brand of hoodoo is distinctly feminine in all aspects. In *Talented Tenth*, we learn that Blanche was sent to Amber Cove with a mission from Madame Rosa to commune with "Mother Water" (both a symbol of the unconscious and a celebrated African spiritual figure), so that she can help Blanche interpret a disturbing recurrent dream and restore her sense of equanimity. Neely also discloses more about Blanche's arrival at her unique belief system, having rejected Christianity as belonging to her ancestors' enslavers and other organized religions for their male-centric systems (60). True to her own spirit, Blanche self-determines a spiritualism that works for her: "She already knew who and what to worship.... She turned her tendency to talk to her dead grandmothers into ancestor worship.... [and] She routinely called on all the forces in the universe for power" (61). Or, as she explains her practice more bluntly to a would-be suitor, "It's taken me a long time to figure out what I needed. I should have figured it would be old and African" (137). We see these beliefs evidenced by the ancestral altar she constructs in her various homes and in the frequent appeals in her daily vernacular ("Ancestors bless me!" "Ancestors save us!"). These invocations provide Blanche, and therefore Neely, with a natural platform to expound on the struggles faced by both her ancestors and herself, thus connecting her personal story to the historical, which allows for greater social examination. As she's setting up her new altar in *Passes Go*, Blanche stops to ruminate, and what follows is a thought-provoking if perhaps discordant passage. Reflecting on her ancestors, she thinks,

> They knew about rape, they knew about fear, and they hadn't been stopped by either. They'd found ways to fight back—from running away to killing as many slave owners as they could, from aborting the slaver's issue to hexing his penis so he'd never want to touch that particular woman again, to putting pepper in the slop pot and spit in the soup. They had not run from their enemies, except to rest up and find another way to fight.[31]

This is powerful text; it connects Blanche's experiences directly to those of the domestics and slaves that came before her. And this linkage is based not on the victimization itself, but on the rebellion these women show in the face of it. This passage and others like it are what make Neely's social agenda so conspicuous in her writing.

Flys-Junquera asserts that by participating in the hoodoo traditions, the black detective is exhibiting a high degree of ethnic awareness and pride.[32] In Blanche, this equates to personal dignity; as she considers her self-created spiritualism, she reflects, "She was her own priest and goddess" (*Passes Go*, 12). Soitos characterizes this pride "in her background and her black skin" as what provides Blanche with "the anchor for her personality as well as the fulcrum for her investigative behavior,"[33] thus reaffirming the significance of hoodoo in these books. Soitos takes the theme further, explaining that the roots of hoodoo lie in slavery, specifically in the slave owners' attempts to suppress their slaves' freedom of religion.[34] Thus hoodoo is a very deliberate statement of freedom for those, like Blanche, who embrace it so fully and openly.

As the above excerpt also highlights, Blanche appears to acknowledge a connection with female ancestors only. If Blanche's personal and spiritual connections are only with women, then what is conspicuously absent in her life is a strong and sympathetic — adult, black — male. Nicole Décuré claims that in the series men are "nonexistent, marginalized.... Blanche wants a man, but there are none good enough."[35] Why is this? I'm not sure Neely ever provides a completely satisfactory answer. Blanche is clearly desirable and desired; throughout the series, she holds onto the affections of Leo, her longtime love whose marriage proposals she repeatedly turned down. Even after he marries someone else, Leo expresses his continuing preference for Blanche. (One might wonder why, when she seemingly never gives him so much as the time of day.) Blanche plainly sees marriage as an institution that subjugates women. In *Talented Tenth* she opines, "All the married women she knew worked hard in somebody else's house, field or plant and came home to take care of a full-grown man and a houseful of kids who seemed to think her labor was their due" (11). She views marriage through a harsh, hyper-feminist lens, as though all it has to offer is another role of servitude. She refers to being married as "hogtied" (11) and maintains, "She simply could not marry" (12). Blanche later stalls a budding relationship with the attractive and attentive Thelvin in *Passes Go* because of one minor show of jealousy and his expressed desire to protect her. As Blanche reflects to Ardell, "You ever notice how close being protected and taken care of are to being held prisoner?" (49).

Reddy offers a compelling reason for this seemingly militant stance, explaining that "historically women have been defined by their relationships with men and have been refused the right to self-definition,"[36] with the result that — in terms of these heroines—"Relationships with men are always possible threats to their hard-won autonomy and independence."[37] In her book about contemporary black women's literature, *Saints, Sinners, Saviors: Strong Black Women in African American Literature*, Harris laments that what's missing from this body of work are black female protagonists who are "self-sufficient without diminishing anyone else, who are secure in their own identities, who are sexual and spiritual beings,"[38] although she acknowledges that these characters are a little more prevalent in popular fiction. Neely has firmly established Blanche's secure identity, her sexuality and her spirituality; what's missing from Harris's prescription is the self-sufficiency *without* diminishment of others. In the opening to her book, Harris illuminates one reason for the perpetual limitation, that "the landscape of African American literature is peopled with black female characters who are almost too strong for their own good," such that this strength "overshadow[s] the complexity of their femininity and humanity."[39] In other words, if the otherwise positive attribution of strength is overplayed, it becomes a liability in terms of characterization. When that happens, as in the case with Blanche, it may begin to strain the readers' affection for her.

It's not just romantic men that are missing from Blanche's milieu. She has no male friends or adult male family members; her life is virtually devoid of positive male figures. Mention of Blanche's father is notably absent throughout most of the series, until a pivotal, dramatic scene late in the fourth novel, *Passes Go*. As Blanche is railing about what she perceives as the weakness of an abused woman who won't leave her husband, her mother calls her up short, revealing for the first time that Blanche's father had abused her both verbally and physically, often while drunk. Blanche's response is palpable: "Pain pricked [her] entire body, as though all of her circulation had been cut off. Her mother's words ricocheted around her brain, bouncing off Blanche's attempts to make them mean something other than what her mother was saying. Her mother. Her father" (216). It's a watershed moment of understanding for Blanche, who had always perceived her mother as being too strong and too independent — an ironic accusation, since Blanche doesn't recognize the limitations of those qualities magnified in herself. This scene exposes Blanche's own mother as a victim, and at the hands of a black man, no less. It sheds further light on the character's deep-seated mistrust of men. Perhaps, then, Blanche's convictions on remaining single are justified as a symbolic rebellion against this continued victimization.

The subplot of abuse underscores a central matter in *Blanche Passes Go*: Blanche's attempt to bring down the white man who raped her years before so she can finally come to terms with that event. Blanche repeatedly reflects on this theme, at one point identifying a "circle of bruised women" and wondering "if there were women in the world who hadn't been slapped, or probed, or punched, or shouted out or down..." (218). These issues of abuse frame the main crime of the novel—the murder of a poor young woman whom we ultimately learn was killed in a jealous rage by her boyfriend, in reaction to the affair she was having with a wealthy, privileged male who was simply using her. In a more typical detective novel, the context of investigating this murder might allow for a little reflection on the use and abuse of women, but here Neely spotlights the issue so that it far overshadows the mystery angle.

With the exception of *Lam*, each novel features social themes and subplots which all but bury the actual crime and detection thereof, and each of these gives Blanche/Neely the opportunity to lecture. *Talented Tenth* brings the issues of colorism, classism and feminism to the forefront of the narrative, and Blanche doesn't miss the chance to pontificate on any of them; she has sharply defined views on just how the world should be. *Cleans Up* presents the same situation, with the issues in play being environmentalism, heterosexism, abuse of political power and civic corruption. All of these, of course—along with the issues of racism, oppression, abuse, and tyranny that the other novels include—are critical matters that deserve the raised awareness that Neely is trying to give them. But at some point, they simply overwhelm the genre. Mueller astutely recognizes this problem as a "cumbersome didacticism."[40]

Phillips makes the related claim that, as the series develops, Blanche's point of view—and thus the tone of each book—becomes angrier and more polemical.[41] Neely has subsumed plot for character to such a degree that she's boxed in her protagonist, thereby rendering her less effective as a voice of agency. Phillips describes the Blanche of *Passes Go* like this: "Nothing satisfies this woman, nothing encourages her, no one reaches her, everything angers her. In the midst of battles—gender wars, race wars, class wars—Blanche finds nowhere that she can simply *be*."[42] Harris has suggested this inability to "just be" is common in black women featured in late 20th-century literature written by black females, offering that this agitation may be the result of great energy spent in an effort "to hold on to an essence of self against forces that would stereotype them, force them to conform, or dehumanize them."[43]

This unresolved and unyielding resentment is demonstrated in part through Blanche's relationships, specifically her inability to forge authentic new connections. In both the first and last novels of the series, Blanche rejects a true friendship with the sweet, sympathetic Mumsfield, first because he is nominally part of the white aristocracy, and later because of his wife's prejudices. Blanche is judging him not on who he is but rather on who and what he represents. The few connections she does make are always with other marginalized characters (the aging black gardener in *Lam*, the lesbian masseuse in *Cleans Up*, the poor country girl in *Passes Go*). While true to Blanche's character to champion these disempowered voices, it is telling that even these relationships are always defunct by the end of each story. Effectively, Blanche's overriding need to assert her independence thwarts her ability to develop solid new relationships, even with those to whom she initially connects. And while she will feel an affinity with their "otherness," it is not enough to compensate for the otherness she feels *towards* them. A thoughtful and very sympathetic reader might take the time to understand how she got to this point, but a casual reader is likely to dismiss Blanche's posturing as overzealousness, therefore limiting what he or she may relate to or draw from the character. Neely might be missing two opportunities here: first, the chance to showcase how authentic, individual relationships can transcend socially prescribed boundaries; second, to consider the empowering possibilities that might come from marshalling the marginalized voices together.

Perhaps Neely has, consciously or not, gone so far as to paint Blanche as a separatist, a feminist position defined as one "where Black women withdraw from other groups and engage in exclusionary politics."[44] Barbara Smith explains why this stance runs counter to a productive, progressive feminism: "Whereas autonomy comes from a position of strength, separatism comes from a position of fear. When we're truly autonomous, we can deal with other kinds of people, a multiplicity of issues, and with difference, because we have formed a solid base of strength."[45] While it is clear that Blanche has done much to avow her autonomy — her choice of career right down to the detail of being a day worker, her rejection of marriage and partnership, her self-created brand of spiritualism — the motivation of fear rings true. This is a woman whose life has been scarred by rape and marred repeatedly by poverty, abuse, death, prejudice (even from other blacks), and discrimination. But while the fear is understandable, it keeps Blanche at arms' length not only from other characters, but also from the reader.

Neely's stridency is revealed through the panoply of other characters as well. Blanche's small circle — her family, her best friend, and a few well-chosen community matriarchs— are presented as positive, multi-dimensional people. Virtually everyone else who is cast in a positive light represents some kind of marginalized minority, be it other working-class blacks, homosexuals, or as with Mumsfield, the disabled. As for the rich, upper-class characters who appear in each title? White or black, they are always drawn as villains ... bigoted, shallow, greedy, insensitive, and ruthless. And the more "other" they are from Blanche, the more one-dimensionally villainous they are likely to be.

Nowhere is this more evident than in *Blanche Cleans Up,* in which Allister Brindle, the rich white male employer and gubernatorial candidate, is immediately sized up by Blanche as arrogant and aggressive. He's also a known philanderer, and soon Blanche suspects him of being a coldblooded murderer.

Though Blanche eventually realizes his (relative) innocence, Neely doesn't give this character any kind of pass. To serve the story it would be enough for Brindle to be having some kind of scandalous sex outside of his marriage, thus allowing for the important plot element of an incriminating videotape. Instead, Neely takes this so much further; Brindle is not merely having unconventional sex, he's having sex with dogs and with extremely young children. In itself this is distasteful enough as to seem extreme. But from a realism standpoint, it's hard to imagine that, even in the pre-web and wireless days of the 1990s, a candidate for governor would think that he could hide such monstrous proclivities. By pushing the behaviors of such characters beyond the boundaries of believability, Neely may again be compelling her readers to disconnect. This is an especially valid consideration for the genre of detective fiction, in which verisimilitude is a necessary component for maintaining audience engagement.

"A literature ... can be stifled or contained in many ways. It can labor under the burden of advocacy.... Black female characters are so dominant in many of the works in which they appear, so morally and physically strong, so otherworldly at times, that [they] raise questions about the direction in which the literacy is going, the authors' conscious or inadvertent complicity in that single-mindedness...."[46] So concludes Harris in *Saints, Sinners, Saviors.* While she's again speaking to the broader body of African American works and does not reference Neely directly, the Blanche series perfectly exemplifies her point. Neely's passion for her agenda seems to have, by the fourth novel, outstripped her ability to succeed in the form.

Feminism and "the formula" *can* work together, but only if the needs of each are acknowledged and attended to. The genre *is* pliant enough to absorb alternative viewpoints and ideological shifts, as the success of myriad contemporary series has shown. The audience is willing to go along for the ride with a protagonist they like ... to a point. But a balance must be struck between passion and prescription. Blanche's craving for self-determination leads her to a separatist position from which she has nowhere to go as a compelling protagonist of detective fiction. Thus what had once provided the power and urgency for Neely's feminist voice ultimately, ironically, and with the demise of the series, renders it mute.

If Neely's message was in the end weakened by her zeal, we should not let that detract from what she has accomplished along the way. Nor should it suggest that the forum she chose was not appropriate and effective, or that her audience was not open to her agenda. As Reddy states, "Rethinking assumptions is an activity favored by both crime fiction readers and feminists,"[47] so that to engage fully in the reading experience of either genre, one's mind must be open to new ideas and possibility. Complementing that is another dynamic in play, as described by Flys-Junquera, that "ethnic detective fiction ... forces the mainstream popular audience of the detective novel into an outsider perspective."[48] Throughout the Blanche series, through the eyes and voice of Blanche, Neely gives her audience — crime fiction devotees or otherwise — many meaningful ideas and issues to consider. She gives us "outsiders" a worldview that we might not be exposed to had it not been presented in the guise of a very popular genre. And she may have had an even more profound effect on the genre as a whole, one that would, in turn, influence millions more readers than just her own. Reddy asserts that the collective impact of writers like Neely is that they have encouraged many of the pioneering white feminist crime fiction writers to explore a broader set of societal conditions that incorporate race and class issues. Similarly, these writers have opened up the genre to even more possibility — to new voices and alternative perspectives.[49]

Neely has in fact helped to identify just where the boundaries of detective fiction lie even as she tried to push them farther, a lesson from which other authors-on-a-mission might benefit. So while Neely's series may have been short-lived, her legacy endures. I think Blanche would be proud.

Notes

1. Rosemary Herbert, "An Interview with Barbara Neely," *Harvard Review* no. 5 (Fall 1993): 112, http://www.jstor.org.helin.uri.edu/stable/27559921.
2. Andrew Pepper, "Black Crime Fiction," in *The Cambridge Companion to Crime Fiction*, ed. Martin Priestman (Cambridge: Cambridge University Press, 2003), 222.
3. Kathleen Gregory Klein, *The Woman Detective: Gender and Genre* (Urbana: University of Illinois Press, 1988), 202.
4. *Ibid.*, 226.
5. Adrienne Johnson Gosselin, ed., *Multicultural Detective Fiction: Murder from the "Other" Side* (New York: Garland, 1999), xi-xii.
6. *Ibid.*, 12.
7. Maureen T. Reddy, *Sisters in Crime: Feminism and the Crime Novel* (New York: Continuum, 1988), 149.
8. Dorothea Fischer-Hornung and Monika Mueller, eds. *Sleuthing Ethnicity: The Detective in Multiethnic Crime Fiction* (Madison: Fairleigh Dickinson University Press, 2003), 320.
9. Maureen T. Reddy, "Women Detectives" in Priestman, *Cambridge Companion*, 202.
10. *Ibid.*, 203–4.
11. Maureen T. Reddy, *Traces, Codes, and Clues: Reading Race in Crime Fiction* (New Brunswick: Rutgers University Press, 2003), 57–62. Reddy offers several examples of contemporary black female detective series in which the protagonists have uneasy relationships with law enforcement, and she explores some of the social issues surrounding this common theme.

12. Katie G. Cannon, "The Emergence of a Black Feminist Consciousness," in *Feminist Interpretations of the Bible*, ed. Letty M. Russell (Philadelphia: Westminster Press), 30, quoted in Patricia Hill Collins, *Black Feminist Thought: Knowledge, Consciousness, and the Politics of Empowerment* (New York: Routledge, 1991), 22.
13. Pepper, "Black Crime Fiction," 222–3.
14. Kathy Phillips review of *Blanche Passes Go*, by Barbara Neely, *The Women's Review of Books* 17, no. 10/11 (July 2000): 43, http://www.jstor.org/stable/4023497.
15. Alison D. Goeller, "An Interview with Barbara Neely," in Fischer-Hornung/Mueller, *Sleuthing Ethnicity*, 303.
16. Stephen F. Soitos, *The Blues Detective: A Study of African American Detective Fiction* (Amherst: University of Massachusetts, 1996), 31.
17. Goeller, "An Interview with Barbara Neely," 303.
18. Priscilla L. Walton and Manina Jones, *Detective Agency: Women Rewriting the Hard-boiled Tradition* (Berkeley: University of California Press, 1999), 44–85. Walton and Jones provide an explication of the relationship of character, author, and reader in detective series and all that this relationship allows for in terms of feminist agency and other socio-political agendas—including anecdotal testimonials from series readers themselves—in the chapter "Gumshoe Metaphysics."
19. Barbara Neely, *Blanche on the Lam* (New York: Penguin Books, 1993), 67. Hereafter, citations from this work will be provided in text.
20. Barbara Neely, *Blanche Among the Talented Tenth* (New York: Penguin Books, 1995), 27. Hereafter, citations from this work will be provided in text.
21. Trudier Harris, *From Mammies to Militants: Domestics in Black American Literature* (Philadelphia: Temple University Press, 1982), 8.
22. *Ibid.*, 22.
23. Collins, *Black Feminist Thought*, 11.
24. Barbara Neely, *Blanche Cleans Up* (New York: Viking, 1998), 87. Hereafter, citations from this work will be provided in text.
25. Reddy, "Women Detectives," 204.
26. Soitos, *Blues Detective*, 34.
27. *Ibid.*, 69.
28. Reddy, *Traces*, 82.
29. The children Blanche is raising throughout the series are the son and daughter of her deceased sister. The fact that they are not her biological children gives Blanche the license to articulate at various points in the series her discomfort in the position of "mother," and the fact that she would not have chosen to be a mother were it not for the extraordinary circumstances of her sister's death. This is another way in which Blanche rejects a traditional black female role, that of caregiver. It is notable that the children are not present throughout much of the series, underscoring Blanche's mental distance from the role. In spite of all this, Blanche is painted as a loving and nurturing mother, and the act of raising children provides the character with another platform for edification: Neely uses conversations and minor subplots involving the children as yet more opportunities for Blanche to put forth her worldview.
30. Carmen Flys-Junquera, "Detectives, Hoodoo, and Brujeria," in Fischer-Hornung/Mueller, *Sleuthing Ethnicity*, 99, 102.
31. Barbara Neely, *Blanche Passes Go* (New York: Viking, 2000), 29. Hereafter, citations from this work will be provided in text.
32. Flys-Junquera, "Detectives, Hoodoo, and Brujeria," 102.
33. Soitos, *Blues Detective*, 47.
34. *Ibid.*, 47.
35. Nicole Décuré, "In Search of our Sisters' Mean Streets: The Politics of Sex, Race,

and Class in Black Women's Crime Fiction," in *Diversity and Detective Fiction*, ed. Kathleen Gregory Klein (Bowling Green: Bowling Green State University Press), 166.
  36. Reddy, "Women Detectives," 197.
  37. *Ibid.*, 198.
  38. Trudier Harris, *Saints, Sinners, Saviors: Strong Black Women in African American Literature* (New York: Palgrave MacMillan, 2001), 177.
  39. *Ibid.*, 11.
  40. Monika Mueller, "A Cuban American 'Lady Dick' and an African American Miss Marple? The Female Detective in the Novels of Carolina Garcia-Aguilera and Barbara Neely," in Fischer-Hornung/Mueller, *Sleuthing Ethnicity*, 126.
  41. Phillips review, 43.
  42. *Ibid.*, 43.
  43. Harris, *Mammies*, xiii.
  44. Collins, *Black Feminist Thought*, 35.
  45. Barbara Smith, *Home Girls: A Black Feminist Anthology* (New York: Kitchen Table Press, 1983), xl, quoted in Collins, *Black Feminist Thought*, 35.
  46. Harris, *Saints, Sinners, Saviors*, 174.
  47. Reddy, *Sisters in Crime*, 2.
  48. Flys-Junquera, "Detectives, Hoo-doo, and Brujeria," 111.
  49. Reddy, "Women Detectives," 63.

Works Cited

Collins, Patricia Hill. *Black Feminist Thought: Knowledge, Consciousness, and the Politics of Empowerment*. New York: Routledge, 2000.

Décuré, Nicole. "In Search of our Sisters' Mean Streets: The Politics of Sex, Race, and Class in Black Women's Crime Fiction." In Klein, *Diversity and Detective Fiction*, 158–185.

Fischer-Hornung, Dorothea, and Monika Mueller, ed. *Sleuthing Ethnicity: The Detective in Multiethnic Crime Fiction*. Madison: Fairleigh Dickinson University Press, 2003.

Flys-Junquera, Carmen. "Detectives, Hoodoo, and Brujeria." In Fischer-Hornung and Mueller, *Sleuthing Ethnicity*, 97–113.

Goeller, Alison D. "An Interview with Barbara Neely." In Fischer-Hornung and Mueller, *Sleuthing Ethnicity*, 299–307.

Gosselin, Adrienne Johnson, ed. *Multicultural Detective Fiction: Murder from the "Other" Side*. New York: Garland, 1999.

Harris, Trudier. *From Mammies to Militants: Domestics in Black American Literature*. Philadelphia: Temple University Press, 1982.

_____. *Saints, Sinners, Saviors: Strong Black Women in African American Literature*. New York: Palgrave MacMillan, 2001.

Herbert, Rosemary. "An Interview with Barbara Neely." *Harvard Review*, no. 5 (Fall 1993): 107–116, http://0-www.jstor.org.helin.uri.edu/stable/27559921.

Klein, Kathleen Gregory. *The Woman Detective: Gender and Genre*. Urbana: University of Illinois Press, 1988.

_____. ed. *Diversity and Detective Fiction*. Bowling Green: Bowling Green State University Press, 1999.

Mueller, Monika. "A Cuban American 'Lady Dick' and an African American Miss Marple?: The Female Detective in the Novels of Carolina Garcia-Aguilera and Barbara Neely." In Fischer-Hornung and Mueller, *Sleuthing Ethnicity*, 114–132 .

Neely, Barbara. *Blanche Among the Talented Tenth*. New York: Penguin, 1995.
_____. *Blanche Cleans up*. New York: Viking, 1998.
_____. *Blanche on the Lam*. New York: Penguin, 1993.
_____. *Blanche Passes Go*. New York: Viking, 2000.
Pepper, Andrew. "Black Crime Fiction." In Priestman, *Cambridge Companion*, 209–26.
Phillips, Kathy. Review of *Blanche Passes Go*, by Barbara Neely. *The Women's Review of Books* 17. no. 10/11 (July 2000): 42–43, http://www.jstor.org/stable/4023497.
Priestman, Martin, ed. *The Cambridge Companion to Crime Fiction*. Cambridge: Cambridge University Press, 2003.
Reddy, Maureen T. *Sisters in Crime: Feminism and the Crime Novel*. New York: Continuum, 1988.
_____. *Traces, Codes, and Clues: Reading Race in Crime Fiction*. New Brunswick: Rutgers University Press, 2003.
_____. "Women Detectives." In Priestman, *Cambridge Companion*, 191–207.
Soitos, Stephen F. *The Blues Detective: a Study of African American Detective Fiction*. Amherst: University of Massachusetts, 1996.
Walton, Priscilla L., and Manina Jones. *Detective Agency: Women Rewriting the Hardboiled Tradition*. Berkeley: University of California Press, 1999.

6. "W" Is for Woman
Deconstructing the Private Dick in Sue Grafton's Alphabet Series

HEATH A. DIEHL

> "I don't even remember now how I pictured the job before I took it on. I must have had vague, idealistic notions of law and order, the good guys versus the bad, with occasional court appearances in which I'd be asked to testify as to which was which. In my view, the bad guys would all go to jail, thus making it safe for the rest of us to carry on. After a while, I realized how naïve I was .... I'm wiser now than I used to be and I'm more experienced, but the fact remains that when a client sits down in the chair across the desk from me, I never know what's going to happen next."
> — Sue Grafton, *"B" Is for Burglar*[1]

Begun in 1982 with the publication of *"A" Is for Alibi*,[2] Sue Grafton's alphabet series is a long-standing staple of women's hardboiled detective fiction, and its author along with her contemporaries Marcia Muller and Sara Paretsky are widely regarded as "mothers" of the genre. Over the nearly three decades of its existence, this series has generated a modest but compelling body of criticism, one very prominent strain of which focuses on the "feminist" politics of the series and its author. Such self-described "feminist" critics generally are torn between two competing (and, given their either-or nature, equally problematic) interpretations. On one hand are critics who view the protagonist of the series, Kinsey Millhone, as a gender traitor — a female P. I. who (figuratively) masquerades as a male in order to "survive" within the (historically patriarchal) world of the hardboiled private dick. More common are critics who view the series as a "radical" feminist intervention into a conventional, and oftentimes conventionally patriarchal, genre.

This essay locates itself at the interstices of these two competing perspectives, arguing that Grafton's alphabet series centers not on the "feminist/not-feminist" dynamic that has preoccupied critics for nearly thirty years, but rather on an ambiguity regarding women's roles within the traditionally male-dominated professions of law enforcement and within the traditionally patriarchal genre of the hardboiled detective novel. I will focus specifically on Grafton's *"K" Is for Killer*[3] (1994, hereafter *"K"*)—to date one of only three novels[4] in Grafton's now twenty-one-book series that foregrounds this ambiguity. What is fascinating to me about these three novels (and *"K"* in particular) is the absence—some might even say resistance to—narrative (and ideological) closure. Traditional hardboiled detective fiction, according to Maureen T. Reddy,[5] presents readers with "an authoritative central figure [i.e., a male private investigator] who separates the false from the true clues and satisfactorily solves the problem,"[6] ultimately allowing for the "bad guys" to be punished according to the law. In these three novels, however, what I find most interesting is "the contrast between what is expected [i.e., narrative closure] and what actually occurs in the story [i.e., ambiguity, open-endedness]."[7] Focusing specifically on Grafton's *"K,"* I contend that Kinsey occupies a conflicted position in relation to institutions of jurisprudence—both outsider and insider—and that this conflicted position is engendered by her unwillingness and/or inability to conform to traditional expectations for appropriate (female) gendered behavior within hardboiled P. I. fiction. In the tension between "vague, idealistic notions of law and order" and the certainty of "never know[ing] what's going to happen next," Grafton offers readers a thought-provoking investigation into the institutionalization of liberal feminist rhetoric, the potential use-value of a radical feminist standpoint, and the cultural and historical legacies of American second wave feminisms between 1960 and 1990.[8]

As I note above, one strand of feminist criticism regarding Grafton's series casts its protagonist as a gender traitor. In *The Woman Detective: Gender and Genre*,[9] Kathleen Gregory Klein expresses a common assumption undergirding this view—namely, that "adopting the [hardboiled] formula traps ... [female] authors."[10] Two critics who share this view are Jean Swanson and Dean James. In *By a Woman's Hand: A Guide to Mystery Fiction by Women*, Swanson and James neatly sidestep the important issue of Kinsey's gender difference, seeing her instead as "definitely a descendent of the wise-cracking, hard-boiled male private eye who has been a staple of American detective fiction for 70 years." And while Swanson and James go on to note that Kinsey, despite being part of this well-established tradition, "remains an individual,"[11] they attribute this "individuality" to "an author well in command of her voice"[12] without considering the provocative ways in which gender and genre clash in Grafton's fiction.

In *Murder by the Book? Feminism and the Crime Novel*, Sally R. Munt initiates a cursory investigation into the clash between gender and genre in women's hardboiled detective fiction. Reading Grafton's fiction through a liberal feminist lens, Munt suggests that Kinsey occupies an unstable subject position "between dominant and subordinate cultural locations."[13] This unstable subject position — one simultaneously inside and outside of dominant forms, such as the hardboiled detective novel, and one that both conforms to and deviates from traditional expectations for appropriate gendered behavior — prohibits Kinsey (at least initially) from "fit[ting] seamlessly into the male model."[14] Nonetheless, in the tradition of such critics as Catherine Belsey and Jill Dolan,[15] Munt ultimately concedes that the conservative ideological pull of the hardboiled form disallows the emergence of a sustainable feminist polemic. As Munt explains, "The threat [of the unstable liberal feminist subject] is defused by ... the predetermination of the genre."[16] In other words, the form of the hardboiled detective novel allows for the presence of a female-gendered private investigator precisely because the ideological underpinnings of that genre predetermine the containment and concomitant erasure of gender difference. Woman becomes man through the (re-)inscription of the private dick.

A more common reading of the series casts Kinsey and/or her creator as feminist revolutionaries working against the ideological pull of a patriarchal genre. Patricia E. Johnson begins her analysis of "Sex and Betrayal in the Detective Fiction of Sue Grafton and Sara Paretsky"[17] by identifying as her central focus two novels—Grafton's *"A" Is for Alibi* (1982) and Paretsky's *Bitter Medicine* (1987)—in which "the professional detective ... becomes sexually involved with a suspect who then turns out to be implicated in the crime."[18] Of these novels, Johnson asks, "Are [they] simply a misguided attempt to appropriate a form inherently sexist? Or can there emerge a different relation both to the form and the issues of violence, crime, and power?"[19] And while some critics—like Swanson, James, and Munt above— would be quick to reply to this last question in the negative, Johnson holds out much more hope that the form of the hardboiled detective novel not only can be appropriated (by female authors), but also can be inhabited (by female private eyes) without either having to sacrifice her gender difference. As she writes, "Detectives Kinsey Millhone and V. I. Warshawski have deliberately defined themselves against most cultural norms of the feminine, yet, at the same time, their authors want us to know that both are feminine and not only feminine but (hetero)sexually desirable and active."[20]

Critic Scott Christianson would agree with Johnson that the form of the hardboiled detective novel is recuperable for a feminist author and/or from a feminist subject position. In "Talkin' Trash and Kickin' Butt: Sue Grafton's Hard-boiled Feminism,"[21] Christianson contends that "Grafton's series of hardboiled mystery novels ... challenges patriarchy and asserts feminine autonomy."[22] Of particular interest to Christianson is Kinsey's tough talk —

"her appropriation of [the] language" that typifies the writings of Raymond Chandler and Dashiell Hammett. For Christianson, this appropriation of the masculine and patriarchal discourse of the traditional hardboiled detective novel "transforms the classic private eye genre into a place from which a woman can exercise language as power."[23] Like many cultural critics in a postmodern moment, Christianson views language not merely as a communication tool but also as a social and cultural institution that determines and that is determined by our individual and collective identities. In this respect, language represents a means to and a vehicle for the exercise of power in the Foucauldian sense, thereby allowing female characters a location from which they can assert their gendered identities in a traditionally patriarchal genre.[24]

Like Christianson, Reddy begins with the assumption that "women creators of professional private detectives also have to deal in some way with the aggressively masculine, patriarchal tradition of the hard-boiled detective that posits woman as dangerous, destructive, 'other.'"[25] But whereas Christianson views the appropriation of the "tough talk" typical of Philip Marlowe and Sam Spade as an exercise of feminist "power" (read autonomy) within the hardboiled genre, Reddy views "the tough talk from the detective" as a mere "superficial" commonality between male- and female-authored hardboiled detective novels. In a much more radical move, Reddy suggests that "[e]very feature of male hard-boiled detective novels [aside from a few such superficial commonalities] is transformed in women's novels, with the detective's isolation or connectedness, attitude toward violence, sense of justice, and sense of self essentially different."[26]

In this essay, I, like Reddy, am chiefly concerned with the "feminist possibilities" of "*K*"—with the ways in which the novel both fits within the series, and the genre, of which it is part, and resists the ideological prescriptions of both. Of the plot of "*K*," an author for SueGrafton.com summarizes:

> Lorna Kepler was beautiful and willful, a loner who couldn't resist flirting with danger. Maybe that's what killed her. Her death had raised a host of tough questions. The cops suspected homicide, but they could find neither motive nor suspect. Even the means were mysterious: Lorna's body was so badly decomposed when it was discovered that they couldn't be certain she hadn't died of natural causes. In the way of overworked cops everywhere, the case was gradually shifted to the back burner and became another unsolved file. Only Lorna's mother kept it alive, consumed by the certainty that somebody out there had gotten away with murder. In the ten months since her daughter's death, Janice Kepler had joined a support group, trying to come to terms with her loss and her anger. It wasn't helping. And so, leaving a session one evening and noticing a light on in the offices of Millhone Investigations, she knocked on the door. In answering that knock, Kinsey Millhone is pulled into the netherworld of unavenged murder, where

only a pact with the devil will satisfy the restless ghosts of the victims and give release to the living they have left behind.[27]

Like this author, I would contend that "*K*" marks "a darkside turn, pitching [readers] into a shadow land of pain and grief where killers still walk free, unaccused, unpunished, unrepentant."[28] Indeed, "*K*" arguably stands as Grafton's darkest novel to date — not necessarily for its subject matter (which is certainly rivaled if not surpassed in gritty realism by "*T*" *Is for Trespass*[29]), but for its bleak view of human nature and its indictment of the social institutions that are designed to curb human nature's most base and violent urges.

From the beginning of the novel, Lorna Kepler is painted as a "risk-taker"— a would-be pornography starlet turned prostitute who, in some characters' view, courted danger with her every move. Despite the common perception of Lorna as a self-destructive outsider, her mother, Janice, pleads with Kinsey in their initial meeting to "remember [that] Lorna really wasn't like what you see" (18). And, as Kinsey digs deeper into Lorna's past, she realizes not only that there is much more to Lorna than initially meets the eye, but also that she and Lorna share some striking similarities. Two passages taken from the initial chapters of the novel clearly point up the parallels in demeanor that readers are encouraged to draw between Lorna and Kinsey. In the first, Lorna is described by her mother as

> antisocial: bullheaded and uncooperative. She had a streak of defiance, I think because she was used to being by herself, doing what *she* wanted. And I might have spoiled her some. Children sense when they have the power to cause you distress. Makes them tyrants to some extent. Lorna didn't understand about pleasing other people, ordinary give-and-take. She was a nice person and she could be generous if she wanted, but she wasn't what you'd call loving or nurturing [9].

In the second, Kinsey describes herself as a "misanthrope," going on to explain, "Since my principal means of employment involved exposure to the underside of human nature, I tended ... to keep other people at a distance. I have since learned to be polite. I can even appear friendly when it suits my purposes, but I'm not really known for my cute girlish ways" (21). As "a person who hates or distrusts humankind,"[30] a "misanthrope" can fairly accurately be characterized as "antisocial," as someone who "keep[s] other people at a distance." Both Lorna and Kinsey have learned to "appear friendly" or "be generous" "when it suits [their] purposes," but neither is especially sociable. Furthermore, both women were raised in environments that fostered the "lone wolf" mentality, environments that encouraged them to do only "what [they] wanted." Janice Kepler admits to indulging Lorna and worries that as a child Lorna's overindulgence might have empowered her to the point of tyranny over adult authority figures. As for Kinsey, she was reared by her "spinster" Aunt Virginia (Gin, for short) after her parents were killed in an automobile accident when Kinsey was just five years old. Unaccustomed to interacting with children, Aunt Gin treated Kinsey more as a peer than as a charge, instilling in Kinsey a precociousness that later translates to a willfulness (minus the "tyranny") akin to Lorna's.

As the story unfolds, readers quickly begin to realize that the parallels between Kinsey and Lorna run deeper than their shared antipathy toward and distrust of other human beings. Specifically, both women are painted as outsiders. In Lorna's case, she is described as a woman decidedly on the margins of "normality." From Janice, Kinsey learns that Lorna lived in a small cabin at the back of a rural property owned by J. D. and Leda Burke. As Janice explains, "She didn't want to live around other people. She liked the feel of being in the woods. The property wasn't all that big.... I guess it gave her the sense of isolation and quiet" (10). Lorna's desire for isolation and "privacy" is echoed in a flashback of Kinsey's a few pages later as Kinsey recalls "retreating into the solace of [the] compact space" of her mobile home after her Aunt Gin's death many years earlier (19). This self-isolation and the strong independent streak (Janice describes Lorna as "an independent little cuss," 8) for Lorna extends as far back as her childhood — a product of genetic circumstance as much as of environment or of some misanthropic predisposition. As Janice explains, "Poor thing was allergic to just about everything. She didn't have many friends. She couldn't spend the night at anybody else's house because other little girls always seemed to live with pets or house dust, mold, or whatnot" (8–9). These early experiences of segregation from her peer group contributed, according to Janice's theory, to a young woman who "did everything her way. She didn't care what other people thought, and she didn't feel what she did was anybody else's business" (8). Lorna's lack of concern for other people's approval becomes increasingly apparent as Kinsey sinks deeper into the underbelly of Santa Teresa nightlife and learns about Lorna's short-lived venture into the pornographic film industry (14–15), her engagement to a mafia bigwig from Los Angeles (178–80), and her employment as a high-end escort/call girl. The secrecy combined with the self-isolation leads to a general perception of Lorna as someone who, in the words of Lorna's sister Trinny, "wasn't close to anyone. She lived in her world and we lived in ours" (150).

In Kinsey's case, she at times operates at the margins of institutionalized law enforcement. During her initial interview with Roger Bonney, Lorna's boss at a local water treatment plant where she works part-time, Kinsey is asked, "You're not with the police department?" to which Kinsey responds, "I was, once upon a time. Temperamentally, I'm better suited to the private sector" (115). The distinction that Kinsey draws here between the public (i.e., police department) and private (i.e., private investigation) sectors points up the parallel distinctions between institutionalized and rogue law enforcement and is illustrated in the contrasts between Santa Teresa Police Department (hereafter STPD) Detective Cheney Phillips and Private Investigator Kinsey. Though Kinsey and Cheney hardly represent absolute antithesis of each other, I would like to highlight contrasts between private investigation and conventional law enforcement — between Kinsey and Cheney — to underline a larger thematic that I think Grafton is developing regarding institutional oppression of unconventional gendered identities. In this novel, Cheney often is set up as strict, unbending — a stickler for statutory law and civil order — and Kinsey, by contrast, is often set up as his foil, especially in this novel where Kinsey is time and again linked to the night (symbolic of chaos, disorder). Throughout the novel, Kinsey continually presses the ever-rational, law-abiding Cheney to guess at and to theorize about the circumstances surrounding Lorna's death — whether she was murdered, how she died, who might have been responsible — and, toward the end of the novel, Cheney finally tires of Kinsey's prodding, saying simply, "I think it's dumb to guess." Kinsey's response to Cheney is telling: "Quit being such a stickler and play the game" (274). That Kinsey refers to her investigation into Lorna's death as a "game" does not belie the seriousness with which Kinsey approaches her work; rather, the term "game" merely suggests a more intuitive approach to crime solving than typically is permissible within the bounds of institutionalized law enforcement and it points up, again, the sharp contrasts being drawn in "*K*" between the public and the private sectors of law enforcement. From the beginning, Cheney is very aware of these contrasts, even perhaps anticipating the climactic action that Kinsey takes in this novel, when he warns, "Just make sure that you keep us informed. And play it straight. If you come up with something, we don't want it thrown out of court because you've tainted the evidence" (32). In these passages, Kinsey is cast in the classic tradition of the (male) hardboiled P. I. — as the solitary figure who "works alone and drinks alone, operating outside established social codes." According to Kimberly J. Dilley in her book *Busybodies, Meddlers, and Snoops: The Female Hero in Contemporary Women's Mysteries,* this hero-figure is someone who "isolates himself[/herself] from normal human relationships," someone "doomed to solitude" precisely because "[h]is[/her] toughness and moral convictions conflict with the values of civilization."[31]

While Grafton makes clear that, in Lorna Kepler's case, traditional law enforcement and private investigation are at odds (with the latter linked closely to outsiderhood, marginality), she also underscores the point that even within the field of private investigation, Kinsey is something of an anomaly in 1985 (the year during which this novel is set). The following passage depicts the first moments of the initial encounter between Kinsey and Janice 127Kepler:

> "Sorry to bother you, but the directory downstairs says there's a private investigator up here in this suite. Is he in by any chance?"
> "Ah. Well, more or less," I said, "but these aren't actual office hours. Is there any way you can come back tomorrow? I'll be happy to set up an appointment for you once I check my book."
> "Are you his secretary?" Her tanned face was an irregular oval, lines cutting down along each side of her nose, four lines between her eyes where the brows were plucked to nothing and reframed in black....
> I tried not to sound irritated since the mistake is not uncommon. "I'm him," I said. "Millhone Investigations. The first name is Kinsey" [3].

Janice Kepler's assumptions that the private investigator whose name appears on the board downstairs must be male, and that Kinsey (a female) must be the P.I.'s secretary, underlines then-prevailing notions of what constitutes "proper" work for men and women.[32] Even in 1985 — the period during which, in the United States, the conservative ideological backdrop of Reaganism allowed the sex and culture wars to blossom and second wave feminism to reach its political stride — traditional expectations regarding appropriate gendered behavior held firm in the personal and professional lives of many everyday Americans. Specifically within the professional arena, women often still were confined to very traditional occupations and those who challenged the ideological prescriptions that confined them to these occupations were marked as "abnormal." That Janice Kepler initially "misidentifies" Kinsey as a secretary to a male P. I. highlights the anomalous position that Kinsey occupies within the American workforce and within the field of private investigation.

Over the course of the novel this parallel outsiderhood that Kinsey and Lorna share begins to consume and transform Kinsey, disrupting her natural circadian rhythms and enfolding her into the nocturnal and dangerous underbelly of the Santa Teresa landscape. Early in the novel, as Kinsey ventures out into the darkness of night to meet up with Cheney at the Caliente Cafe, Kinsey off-handedly remarks, "I'm not often out at such an hour" (26). Throughout much of the alphabet series, Kinsey proves herself to be a dedicated creature of "early-to-bed-early-to-rise" habit; indeed, despite her unconventional profession, Kinsey typically is, like clockwork, awake in the early morning hours for a three-mile jog around Santa Teresa before she showers and heads to the office for a pretty conventional nine-to-five-ish workday. In "*K*," however, Kinsey quickly begins to notice the "inverted pattern [her] life [has] taken" (146), describing this transformation as follows: "By some curious metamorphosis,

I was being drawn into the shadowy after-hours world Lorna Kepler had inhabited. Night turf, the darkness, seemed both exotic and familiar" (188). As a female private investigator, Kinsey already to some degree operates on the margins of conventionality (both ideologically and professionally) and therefore she experiences this world-turned-upside-down as not wholly unfamiliar. At the same time, this "inverted pattern" that her life takes on feels "exotic," pointing up not only the ways in which outsider Kinsey sometimes attempts to conform but also the conflicted subject position she occupies as a result. As Kinsey "begin[s] to feel at home in the late night world" (104), she experiences her "usual sense of [self] breaking down" (146) and worries that she is "turning into a vampire or a werewolf, repelled by the sunlight, seduced by the moon" (159). And toward the end of the novel, Kinsey reveals that "having completed my transmigration into the nocturnal realms, I found the notion of getting up any time before two repugnant" (265).

This night into which Kinsey transmigrates has long been associated with the seedier elements of society (e.g., violent crime, human degradation, sexual taboo), and in this novel, Grafton consistently links Kinsey to night and to darkness as a means of foreshadowing the climax of the novel and the concomitant shift in Kinsey's character. In the *Dictionary of Symbolism*, the authors note that "[n]ight is typically associated with the obscurity and mystery of darkness ... [i]t is the symbol of ignorance ... and is represented by the goddess Nyx, who is the mother of sleep, dreams, sexual pleasure, and death."[33] Interestingly, it is under the cover of night (symbolic of ignorance, obscurity) that Kinsey conducts the bulk of her inquiries into the murder of Lorna Kepler—an investigation for which, as Kinsey admits, she has "no direction and no hard line to take." Kinsey goes on to note of the investigation, "I didn't even have a theory about why she had died. I felt as though I were fishing, fly casting in the hopes that I'd somehow snag myself a killer" (143). With her "internal clock ... no longer synchronized with the rest of the world's" (146) and faced with a crime marked by "the absence of concrete evidence" (24), Kinsey travels into the world of obscurity—a night whose darkness mirrors the "bad fortune" and the "primitive chaos"[34] of the Kepler investigation—in the hopes of finding a killer.

Although Kinsey is painted as an outsider perpetually linked to the dark, the mysterious, the unknown, she also (and simultaneously) is depicted as an upstanding, law-abiding member of the Santa Teresa (law enforcement) community. It is, I think, no coincidence that the novel begins as follows:

> The statutory definition of homicide is the "unlawful killing of one human being by another." Sometimes the phrase "with malice" is employed, the concept serving to distinguish murder from the numerous other occasions in which people deprive each other of life—wars and executions coming

foremost to mind. "Malice" in the law doesn't necessarily convey hatred or even ill will but refers instead to a conscious desire to inflict serious injury or cause death. In the main, criminal homicide is an intimate, personal affair insofar as most homicide victims are killed by close relatives, friends, or acquaintances [1]

Under statutory law, definitions of specific actions (like "homicide") do not merely delimit and clarify the meanings of terms—as is the case for standard, dictionary-type definitions—but rather they simultaneously establish codes of conduct for appropriate (read lawful) behavior, and they demarcate what constitutes criminal behavior punishable under the law. This statutory definition of "homicide" frames the action of "*K*," providing a backdrop for the narrative that develops around Kinsey's investigation into Lorna's murder and intimating that Kinsey is the type of private investigator who abides by and operates within the strict letter of the law.

Not only does the existing legal system frame the action of the novel, but also throughout much of the narrative, Kinsey voices an unwavering faith in the ability of the law to enforce justice. Janice Kepler is especially suspicious of the STPD, offering Kinsey many "conspiracy theories" from incompetence of the officers to a botched undercover sting with Lorna as bait (13, 15) for why they have failed to solve her daughter's murder. Time and again Kinsey responds to these conspiracy theories with pleas for Janice to exercise reason, to trust Kinsey's assessment of members of the STPD as "serious professionals" (15). That Kinsey works closely with Cheney throughout this novel and consults other members of the STPD for their theories about the death of Lorna—most notably Lieutenant Con Dolan—clearly indicates the respect that Kinsey holds for law enforcement. Moreover, even in the absence of "proof" that Roger Bonney murdered Lorna, that Kinsey presents the information to Cheney before she goes rogue (a point addressed more fully below) underscores the faith that she places in the institution of the law to enforce justice.

Despite the faith that Kinsey invests in the law, the investigation into Lorna's murder paints a narrative principally about the failure of the existing justice system, a realization that Kinsey makes early in the novel and that is reinforced over and again throughout her investigation. On one hand, a resolution to Lorna's case is forestalled by a lack of evidence. Early in the novel during the initial consultation with Janice, Kinsey laments the "absence of concrete evidence" in Lorna's case (24). Given the lapse of time between when Lorna was murdered and when her body was "discovered" by Serena Bonney, "[d]ecomposition ha[d] erased most of the definition from Lorna Kepler's face" (77), though toxicology and bone marrow tests confirmed with absolute certainty the identity of the victim (76). Given the virtual absence of physical and trace evidence due to advanced decomposition of the body,[35] the coroner could not determine the cause of Lorna's death, though, as Kinsey discovers, "the police had proceeded on the assumption that she'd been struck down by a person or persons unknown" (24). But even this official "fact" of the case is marked by uncertainty — it is, after all, framed as merely an assumption and the assumption itself fails to identify the means by which Lorna was killed (i.e., struck down by what? And how many assailants?) as well as any possible motive that the person or persons unknown might have had for committing the crime.

The failure of the justice system is compounded by the fact that a number of the characters — including significantly some members of the STPD — exhibit a prejudice against Lorna, almost going so far as to suggest that Lorna courted her own murder by leading a "deviant" lifestyle. When Kinsey asks him if he has a theory about Lorna's death, Cheney remarks, "I think somebody killed her, if that's what you're after. Rough trade, jealous boyfriend. Maybe some other hooker thought Lorna was treading on her turf. Lorna loved risk. She's the kind who liked to teeter right out on the edge" (32).[36] Cheney's remarks about Lorna's lifestyle are echoed later in the novel by Con Dolan: "The life [prostitutes] live is so damn dangerous. Night after night, connecting up with strangers. Get in a car and you have to be aware it might be the last ride you ever take" (75). Even among Lorna's "friends" her lifestyle is painted as "dangerous," self-destructive, deviant. When interviewed by Kinsey, Hector Moreno, a local radio DJ, admits, "Lorna flirted with disaster every day of her life. If you want my theory, fear was the only real sensation she felt. Danger was like a drug" (42). Similarly, fellow prostitute Danielle Rivers reveals, "Lorna was a wild one, and she didn't like to be controlled" (91). Cheney Phillips, Con Dolan, Hector Moreno, and Danielle Rivers all operate under very stereotypical assumptions about Lorna based on a few of the lifestyle choices that she made. And, like Lorna's sister Trinny, many who knew her (with perhaps the exceptions of Hector Moreno and Danielle Rivers) seem to come to the conclusion that Lorna "wasn't pure. She wasn't even *good*" (154). Under statutory law, the morality (or lack thereof) of Lorna's lifestyle choices does not preclude the fact that she was murdered, and certainly it does not excuse the guilty party from due punishment under the law. But within the world of the novel, Grafton suggests that assumptions about a victim's morality, especially if that victim was a woman, can (and in Lorna's case do) forestall the execution of justice by shifting the focus of blame to the victim, thereby derailing, possibly indefinitely, the search for Lorna's killer.[37]

In large part, it is precisely these prejudices that many of the characters exhibit toward Lorna's "deviant" behavior that motivate Janice to seek help from outside of the justice system. During their initial meeting, Janice laments to Kinsey that nearly a year after Lorna's body was discovered, she feels "like nobody cares. [Lorna's death is] not even something people talk about anymore" (7). Janice suggests that the police have "dropped" the case, explaining, "You know how they do those things. Something else comes along, and they concentrate on that" (13). Even worse, Janice claims that she "can't get anyone to listen." She admits that she "do[esn't] trust the police" and even goes so far as to suggest that she has not turned over the copy of Lorna's unreleased pornographic film to the police because "I've heard of cases like this. Evidence they don't like disappears into thin air. Get to court and it's mysteriously vanished" (16). While Janice does not outright accuse the STPD of misconduct, she does strongly imply that the inability of the police with regard to resolving Lorna's case is caused by more than simply a lack of evidence. And given Cheney Phillips' and Con Dolan's comments to Kinsey about Lorna's "dangerous" lifestyle, it is certainly not illogical to assume that prejudices regarding appropriate gendered behaviors contribute to (if not determine) the STPD's failure to resolve Lorna's murder investigation. In other words, Lorna's "wanton" sexuality and the concomitant radical sense of autonomy that it engenders, coupled with her lack of "purity"—both bodily and morally—perhaps precipitate (in a case of "she was asking for it") the institutional neglect that her case receives.

Kinsey, too, eventually is motivated to take the Kepler case because she feels as if the justice system has failed Lorna. From the initial meeting between Kinsey and Janice, Grafton underscores important values that the two women share with regard to their beliefs about "justice."[38] When Janice talks about what drove her to seek Kinsey's help, she explains, "Whoever did this, I want him *punished*. I want this laid to rest. I want to know why he did it. I want to tell him face-to-face exactly what he did to my life the day he took hers" (8). Janice's heart-felt pleas in this passage are laced with a desire to know what happened to her daughter, to understand why Lorna was killed. This desire to know, to understand, consumes Janice; she admits, "I think about Lorna's killer way more than I should," and later, Janice's husband Mace confirms that Janice simply cannot let the matter rest (51–53). In part what drives Janice is the pursuit of justice, a need to see Lorna's killer "punished." But "punishment" in Janice's view does not merely involve jury trials and prison sentences; rather, the "punishment" that she envisions for Lorna's killer includes a "face-to-face" confrontation during which she intends to tell him "exactly what he did to [her] life the day he took [Lorna's]." In this respect, knowledge is regarded as both blessing and curse. For Janice, knowledge is the means by which she moves past ignorance regarding her daughter's final moments but it also is, once known, the graphic and awful burden that she must carry for the rest of her life. For the murderer, Janice imagines—or, at least, hopes — that knowledge of how his actions have impacted Lorna's family and friends will weigh heavily on him and his conscience, a kind of psychological torture that he must endure every day.

Like Janice, Kinsey is driven by a desire to know and to understand what happened to Lorna and others like her. From the beginning of the novel, Kinsey explains to the reader that she is haunted by "the unruly dead," her name for victims of unsolved homicide, whom she describes as

> persons who reside in a limbo of their own, some state between life and death, restless, dissatisfied, longing for release.... I've talked to homicide investigators who've been caught up in similar reveries, haunted by certain victims who seem to linger among us, persistent in their desire for vindication. In the hazy zone where wakefulness fades into sleep, in that leaden moment just before the mind sinks below consciousness, I can sometimes hear them murmuring. They mourn themselves. They sing a lullaby of the murdered. They whisper the names of their attackers, those men and women who still walk the earth, unidentified, unaccused, unpunished, unrepentant. On such nights, I do not sleep well. I lie awake listening, hoping to catch a syllable, a phrase, straining to discern in that roll call of conspirators the name of one killer. Lorna Kepler's murder ended up affecting me that way [1-2].

For someone (like Kinsey) who admittedly does not "like loose ends" (188), cold cases like Lorna's are troubling. On one hand, these cases devalue human life, leaving only the dead to mourn themselves. But they also are troubling because they suggest that the justice system has somehow failed — that despite the best efforts of law enforcement officers, some crimes go unsolved, some criminals go unpunished. That the name of the murderer remains just out of ear-shot when "the unruly dead" sing their "lullaby" intimates the sense of impotence that Kinsey and her fellow law enforcement officers feel when faced with cold cases for which very little hard evidence exists. Kinsey expresses this feeling of impotence near the end of the novel once she has identified Lorna's killer. Although Kinsey does not possess sufficient evidence for him to be tried and convicted in a court of law, she is certain that Roger Bonney is Lorna's killer. In the absence of substantive proof of Roger Bonney's guilt, Cheney, ever a man of the law, tells Kinsey to "Face it. There's nothing you can do," to which she responds, "Cheney, I'm tired of the bad guys winning. I'm sick of watching people get away with murder. How come the law protects them and not us?" (282)[39]

At work in this scene (and, indeed, throughout the novel) are two competing conceptions of "justice": one prescribed by the law that Kinsey, as a P.I. licensed by the state of California, is sworn to uphold and the other derived from a shared feminist polemic — a collective identity of "sister outsiders," that Kinsey shares with both Lorna Kepler and Danielle Rivers (who late in the novel also is murdered by Roger Bonney).[40] The first definition, that regarding the law, which opens the novel and frames its action, is discussed above. The second conception of "justice" centers on what might be termed a "shared sisterhood":

> I laid out the canceled checks like a hand of solitaire. At the bottom, under "Memo," she'd dutifully written in the purpose of the payment: groceries, manicure, haircut, linens, sundries. There was something touching about the care she'd taken. She hadn't known she'd be dead by the time these checks came back. She hadn't known her last meal would be her last, that every action she'd taken and each endeavor she'd engaged in were part of some finite number that would soon run out. Sometimes the hardest part of my job is the incessant reminder of the fact that we're all trying so assiduously to ignore: we are here temporarily ... life is only ours on loan [158].

The value of human life derives in large part precisely from its finite nature; life is, as Kinsey notes, "only ours on loan." To cheat another human being of his/her already finite amount of time, to call in the "loan" before it is due, devalues human life and the sense of personhood associated with the victim. Moreover, in her line of work, Kinsey regularly witnesses the brutal and destructive ways in which patriarchy physically manifests itself on the bodies of real women in cases of rape, domestic violence, and murder. In her search for Lorna's killer, then, Kinsey not only seeks legal "vindication" for a violation of the law, but also seeks to affirm the value of Lorna's life, to restore (to some degree) the dignity of a human life cut short by violence and greed. In her actions, too, Kinsey gives "voice" to feelings of solidarity that she shares with other, especially female, outsiders.

Ultimately the conflict between these two notions of "justice"—as well as Kinsey's mounting feelings of impotence—precipitates an unexpected climax to the novel. About three-quarters of the way into the narrative, Kinsey is grabbed by two men outside of the Caliente Cafe and escorted to a limousine. Inside, Kinsey meets a "Los Angeles attorney" (179) who represents the man to whom Lorna was engaged; he explains to Kinsey that his boss would "appreciate it if [Kinsey would] apprise [him] of the information [she has] acquired" (180). During the exchange, Kinsey assesses the situation as follows: "The word M-A-F-I-A formed at the back of my mind.... These guys were professionals. They killed for business, not pleasure" (179). Initially Kinsey refuses to abet these "hired guns" in their search for rogue justice, but when told by Cheney later that "there were no options open to [her]," Kinsey's long-held allegiance to the law is tested:

> What was this? What was happening? How could ... Roger [be] beyond reach? At first, I felt nothing. My initial response was a curious blank, no sensation at all attached. I took in the truth content of what Cheney had

told me, but there was no corresponding emotional reaction.... I remained motionless for perhaps a minute, and when feelings finally crept back, what I experienced wasn't grief, but a mounting fury. Like some ancient creature hurtling up from the deep, my rage broke the surface and I struck [283].

In rage, in desperation, and in utter helplessness, Kinsey locates the business card given to her by the Los Angeles attorney, dials the number, "a combination of digits that spelled death" (283–284), and —"giving absolutely no thought to what [she] was doing" but only "propelled by the hot urge to act"— Kinsey tells the person who answers on the other end, "Roger Bonney killed Lorna Kepler" (284).

While Kinsey's climactic act of desperation and rage certainly is out of character, the actions that follow in some respects bring her back into the fold of conventional jurisprudence. Almost instantly Kinsey regrets the impulsive action —"Oh, Jesus. What had I done? I picked up the phone and dialed the number again. Endless rings. No answer" (284). When retracting her accusation over the telephone proves impossible, Kinsey grabs her gun and heads out for the water treatment plant to warn Roger Bonney. But Roger Bonney is expecting Kinsey, and before she can give voice to her warning, he tasers Kinsey, rendering her momentarily paralyzed and mute — perhaps a metaphor for Kinsey's role in the justice system being represented within the novel (288). Roger Bonney's intention is to kill Kinsey in much the same way that he killed Lorna, but before he can do more than taser her, he is called away by an employee to deal with a "[g]uy up here to see you" (289). At this point, dramatic irony weighs heavily on readers and the paralyzed Kinsey, both of whom know that the "guy" Roger Bonney is called away to deal with is the very threat about whom Kinsey came to the plant to warn Roger.

"*K,*" then, ends in moral ambiguity — at the interstices of the two competing notions of "justice" where human dignity has been restored but seemingly at the price of conventional statutory law. Roger Bonney has been "punished" for the murder of Lorna Kepler, but the "punishment" (itself an act of murder to which Kinsey is an abettor) violates the very law that Kinsey spends the majority of the novel trying to uphold. In the Epilogue to the novel, Kinsey reflects on the complicated emotions that she has regarding the resolution of her investigation into Lorna's murder:

> I spent a long time in conversation with Lieutenant Dolan and Cheney Phillips and, for once, I told the truth. Given the enormity of what I'd done, I felt I had to accept the responsibility.... Now, in the dead of night, I ponder the part I played in Lorna Kepler's story, in the laying to rest of those ghosts. Homicide calls up in us the primitive desire to strike a like blow, an impulse to inflict a pain commensurate with the pain we've been dealt. For the most part, we depend upon the judicial processes to settle our grievances.

Perhaps we've even created the clumsy strictures of the courts to keep our savageries in check. The problem is that so often the law seems pale in its remedies, leaving us restless and unfulfilled in our craving for satisfaction. And then what? As for me, the question I'm left with is simple and haunting: Having strayed into the shadows, can I find my way back? [291–92].

Interestingly, "K" begins and ends with two related, but different types of hauntings. At the opening of the novel, Kinsey is haunted by what she calls "the unruly dead"—those victims of murder whose cases have run cold. At the conclusion of the novel, and as a result of "closing" one of those cold cases and laying to rest its "unruly dead," Kinsey is haunted by "the enormity" of the consequences of her impulsive action. Clearly, Kinsey does not fear punishment by the law for "the part [she] played in Lorna Kepler's story"; otherwise, she would not have "accept[ed] the responsibility" for her actions and "told the truth" to Con Dolan and Cheney. Rather, Kinsey worries over the dramatic shift that she has witnessed in herself—an uneasy and complicated journey into the "shadows" of criminality, a walk on the other side of the law that leaves Kinsey "restless" and unsettled by the realization that sometimes "the law seems pale in its remedies." The question with which Kinsey ends the Epilogue of this novel—that is, "Having strayed into the shadows, can I find my way back?"—captures so clearly the sense of moral and legal ambiguity that circumscribes (nay, haunts) the narrative of "K" and the figure of Kinsey Millhone.

The shadows into which Kinsey strays, the ambiguity that haunts the close of the novel, must be read within and against the politics and the history that defined the 1980s—the decade during which Grafton's series debuted and "K" specifically is set. As Dilley notes, series fiction "provides the scholar with the unique opportunity to examine ... a community and its codes over time."[41] Bethe Schoenfeld, too, argues that women writers of serial mysteries "[use] their fiction to explore the ideas, values, and feelings through which they experience their world at this particular time in history."[42] For Sue Grafton, a self-proclaimed "feminist from way back,"[43] the most influential "ideas" that shaped her lived experience while writing "K" concerned the place of women "in a society where gender prescribes behavior, expectations, and limitations."[44] Like Priscilla L. Walton and Manina Jones,[45] I would contend that Grafton in her fiction draws on "an established popular formula ... to investigate not just a particular crime but the more general offenses in which the patriarchal power structures of contemporary society itself is potentially incriminated."[46] And Kinsey's investigation into the impact of patriarchal social structures on women is most clearly witnessed in the ambiguous ending of the novel.

This ambiguity not only calls into question the efficacy of the institutions of law and order that circumscribe human civilization, but also points to tensions within late-stage second wave feminism, most pointedly between liberal and radical feminisms. On one hand, Kinsey (as a female P. I. working within a profession dominated by males) and Grafton (as a female author writing within a tradition of hardboiled detective fiction dominated by male authors) must to some degree align themselves with the very traditions that historically have contributed to their silence and marginality, actions that ultimately reflect a liberal feminist polemic. In *The Feminist Spectator as Critic*,[47] Jill Dolan explains that "[r]ather than proposing radical structural change, [liberal feminism] suggests that working within existing social and political organizations will eventually secure women social, political, and economic parity with men."[48] Dolan goes on to note that liberal feminism "relies on values claimed to be universally human"[49] and, as such, "would subsume the female gender into the (male) generic, or universal, category."[50]

That Kinsey for much of the novel places her trust in Cheney and the STPD reflects her desire to collaborate with (male) law enforcement officers, to work within "existing social ... organizations." Her goal in doing so is to ensure that Lorna's murderer is punished and Lorna herself can finally rest in peace; in the end, though, Kinsey's faith in Cheney and the institution of the law proves misplaced as the "social organization" of the law fails to provide closure to the case with the execution of swift and certain justice. The failure of the STPD in some sense reflects the ways in which working within existing social structures can threaten to institutionalize the "rogue" outsider, rendering her impotent in her pursuit of justice. The narrative of "*K*," then, traces Kinsey's coming to terms with the realization that any social institution that "relies on values claimed to be universally human" (e.g., "justice is blind") will never give women like Lorna Kepler the closure that they need. For Kinsey, a liberal feminist approach to this case proves ineffectual precisely because that polemic is always and only implicated in the self-same institutionalized forces of patriarchy that it seeks to oppose.

This realization leads Kinsey to explore a more "radical," or cultural, feminist polemic, most particularly in her final, climactic (albeit temporary) rebuke of the institution of law. Radical, or cultural, feminism, as Jill Dolan argues, "bases its analysis in a reification of sexual difference based on absolute gender categories."[51] This "reification of sexual difference" translates to "a fundamental change in the nature of universality by suggesting that female gender values take the place of the generic male." As Dolan argues, cultural feminism "seeks to reverse the gender hierarchy by theorizing female values as superior to male values."[52] When the law proves unable to dole out justice, Kinsey takes matters into her own hands, essentially overthrowing the existing power structure operative within the novel (a power structure to which she has devoted the majority of her adult life, both as a police officer and as a private investigator). In doing so, Kinsey upholds the values of equity, justice, and above all altruism, but she does so from within a feminist standpoint. This standpoint asserts itself as in opposition to institutions (like the STPD) that would permit petty moral judgments against unconventional gendered behavior to forestall the execution of justice. And while Kinsey ultimately is unsettled by the moral and legal implications of her own decision, she does not doubt that it was the "right" choice.

Readers, too, are torn between what is moral — based on preconceived expectations for mystery fiction — and what is "right," or just. In *Private Dicks and Feisty Chicks: An Interrogation of Crime Fiction*,[53] Cathy Cole notes that "[c]rime fiction is ... a genre that deals heavily in expectations."[54] For Cole, some such expectations include the female reader's ability to "identify with the female investigator's strength, take comfort in the story's highly moral tone and the restoration of social order, and revel in the scientific neatness of its problem-solving."[55] Certainly the conclusion of "*K*" fulfills two of the aforementioned expectations, allowing readers to identify with Kinsey's strength of character and to revel in the "neatness of ... problem-solving." But despite the sense of closure that Roger Bonney's death provides the narrative, the tone in the novel's Epilogue is anything but "highly moral" and the social order (both within and outside the diegesis) is rendered even more confusing. For me, as a reader, it is precisely the thwarting of convention, the disrupting of expectations that I find so compelling in this novel. At that moment when Kinsey dials the "digits that spelled death" (284), readers are reminded of the "vague, idealistic notions of law and order, the good guys versus the bad" ("*B*" 1) with which they began reading the novel. But readers also are made aware of the naïveté of such expectations. By the final page of the novel, readers are wiser, more experienced, and if there is one thing of which we are certain it is that we "never know what's going to happen next" ("*B*" 2). It is this certainty of uncertainty that I think is one of the most important legacies of second wave feminisms. That movement — if it can even be referred to by such an all-encompassing term — not only called into question the overarching framework of patriarchy that historically defined social institutions, kinship relationships, and individual/collective identities, but also introduced us to the concept of differences within the cohort till then known simply as "women." Second wave feminisms took us on a journey into the shadows and the recesses of American culture both past and present, and that movement identified all who fight against institutionalized forms of oppression as part of the "unruly dead" who struggle to have our voices heard. Perhaps, then, Kinsey misspeaks a bit in the final line of the Epilogue; instead of asking, "Having strayed into the shadows, can I find my way back?"—a question that privileges Light, Truth, Justice, Law/Order — I think she might more aptly have asked, "Having strayed into the shadows, why would I want to find my way back?"

Notes

1. Sue Grafton, *"B" Is for Burglar* (New York: Bantam, 1985), 1, 2.
2. Sue Grafton, *"A" Is for Alibi* (New York: Bantam, 1982).
3. Sue Grafton, *"K" Is for Killer* (New York: Fawcett Crest, 1994). Citations for this work will appear in text.
4. The other two novels to which I allude here are: Sue Grafton, *"D" Is for Deadbeat* (New York: Bantam, 1987); and Sue Grafton, *"J" Is for Judgment* (New York: Fawcett Crest, 1993).
5. Maureen T. Reddy, *Sisters in Crime: Feminism and the Crime Novel*, (New York: Continuum, 1988).
6. *Ibid.*, 13.
7. Bethe Schoenfeld, "Women Writers Writing about Women Detectives in Twenty-First Century America," *The Journal of Popular Culture* 41.5(2008): 836–853, 842.
8. To be sure, I acknowledge that within feminist circles there is some confusion and/or disagreement regarding the dating of the various "waves" of feminist histories. Katie King offers, for example, an interesting exploration of this idea in her book *Theory in Its Feminist Travels: Conversations in U. S. Women's Movements* (Bloomington: Indiana University Press, 1995). Some feminist critics locate second wave feminism in the 1960s and 1970s, and identify the 1980s (the focus of the current essay) as part of the "third wave" of feminism (which many see as continuing into the present moment). Like any historical movement, though, feminism is difficult (if not impossible) to date precisely and our attempts to do so are as much the product of our own histories and our own institutional positionalities as they are inherent within the movements themselves. Like a number of prominent feminist critics, I see the 1980s as a continuation of the second wave of feminism because feminist groups during that decade were continuing to discuss, examine, and combat a constellation of issues— most particularly in relation to inequalities within the workforce, the law, the family, and the media — similar to those issues that earlier second wavers were discussing, examining, and combating. To not include under the umbrella of "second wave feminism" the decade during which the Sex and Culture Wars rocked the American political and social landscape ignores the important relationship between the Sex and Culture Wars and earlier struggles that second wavers had long been addressing. Thus, for the purposes of this essay, "second wave feminism" will refer loosely to an American political movement that took place over the three decades that spanned between 1960 and 1990.
9. Kathleen Gregory Klein, *The Woman Detective: Gender and Genre* (Urbana: Illinois, University Press, 1988).
10. *Ibid.*, 201.
11. Jean Swanson and Dean James, *By a Woman's Hand: A Guide to Mystery Fiction by Women* (New York: Berkeley Books, 1994), 85.
12. *Ibid.*
13. Sally R. Munt, *Murder by the Book? Feminism and the Crime Novel* (New York: Routledge, 1994), 31.
14. *Ibid.*, 48.
15. See Catherine Belsey, *Critical Practice* (New York: Routledge, 1991), and Jill Dolan,

Presence and Desire: Essays on Gender, Sexuality, Performance (Ann Arbor: University of Michigan Press, 1994), especially Dolan's chapter on lesbian subjectivity in realism.
 16. Munt, 58.
 17. Patricia E. Johnson, "Sex and Betrayal in the Detective Fiction of Sue Grafton and Sara Paretsky," *The Journal of Popular Culture* 27.4 (1994): 97–106.
 18. *Ibid.*, 97.
 19. *Ibid.*
 20. *Ibid.*, 99.
 21. Scott Christianson, "Talkin' Trash and Kickin' Butt: Sue Grafton's Hard-boiled Feminism," in *Feminism in Women's Detective Fiction*, ed. Glenwood Irons (Toronto: University of Toronto Press, 1995), 127–147.
 22. *Ibid.*, 127.
 23. *Ibid.*, 128.
 24. For more on this point, see Michel Foucault, *Power/Knowledge: Selected Interviews and Other Writings, 1972–1977*, ed. by Colin Gordon (New York: Vintage, 1980).
 25. Reddy, 99.
 26. *Ibid.*, 120.
 27. "'K' Is for Killer," *Alphabet Series*, Sue Grafton, accessed December 26, 2010, http://www.suegrafton.com/titlepage.asp?ISBN=0805019367.
 28. *Ibid.*
 29. Sue Grafton. *"T" Is for Trespass* (New York: Putnam, 2007).
 30. "Misanthrope," *Merriam-Webster Dictionary*, Merriam-Webster, Incorporated, accessed December 26, 2010, http://mw1.merriam-webster.com/dictionary/misanthrope?show=0&t=1293370373.
 31. Kimberly J. Dilley, *Busybodies, Meddlers, and Snoops: The Female Hero in Contemporary Women's Mysteries* (Westport, CT: Greenwood Press, 1998), 21. While Dilley does acknowledge some commonalities between the female hero in contemporary women's mysteries and the classic hardboiled male hero (à la Sam Spade and Phillip Marlowe), she goes on to argue that "[t]he 'lone wolf' is part of the pack in the mysteries of women" (31). Dilley explains that the woman PI "implicates the men who came before her ... not simply a substitute ... [but] a critique of the ... solitary male figure" (33).
 32. Dilley makes a similar observation about women's mystery fiction, noting: "Assumptions regarding 'proper' work for women can still be found in women's mysteries. The PI, herself, is sometimes surprised that a woman is at her door, ready to work. She may refer to a person as 'he,' only to be reminded that women are often doctors, plumbers, glaziers, and so on. The PI, too, is a victim of such misunderstandings" (40).
 33. "Night," *Dictionary of Symbolism*, University of Michigan, accessed December 23, 2010, http://www.umich.edu/~umfandsf/symbolismproject/symbolism.html/N/night.html.
 34. "Darkness," *Dictionary of Symbolism*, University of Michigan, accessed December 23, 2010, http://www.umich.edu/~umfandsf/symbolismproject/symbolism.html/D/darkness.html.
 35. This is one of the most graphic novels of Grafton's career — with explicit allusions to the state of Lorna Kepler's body upon discovery repeated over the course of the novel. Neither gratuitous sensationalism nor mere homage to the hardboiled genre, such allusions rather point up one of the central themes of the novel: "In some ways, it's hard to know which is more sordid, the pornography of sex or the pornography of homicide. Both speak of violence, the broken and debased, the humiliations to which we subject one another in the heat of passion. Some forms of sex are as cold-blooded as murder, some kinds of murder as titillating to the perpetrator as a sexual encounter" (77).
 36. And, of course, the irony here is that none of these assumptions about the

dangerous consequences of Lorna's lifestyle proves true when the identity of Lorna's murderer (and his motive: personal greed) is revealed.

37. Dilley, too, argues that one of the functions (whether implicit or explicit) of many women's mystery novels is to critique existing social structures and their material impacts on real women. As Dilley explains, "[Women authors] bring attention to the constraints and sometimes damaging consequences of stereotypes on the women, as well as society as a whole" (22).

38. By highlighting parallels between (here) Janice Kepler and Kinsey Millhone and (above) Kinsey Millhone and Lorna Kepler, I assume, as does Dilley, that one of the significant ways in which women writers modify the traditional hardboiled detective novel is by eschewing the "lone wolf" figure (at least to some degree) and by highlighting the affinities between and among individuals that allow for the formation of substantive human relationships. As Dilley writes, "The woman PI highlights the human drive for connection, the potential flexibility of social roles, and the primacy of commitment" (34).

39. Interestingly, early in the novel during her initial consultation with Kinsey, Janice Kepler makes a similar observation about the justice system; she notes, "System's set up to keep [murderers] all alive while our kids are dead for the rest of the time" (7).

40. Some readers of "K" might argue that Kinsey's relationship with Danielle Rivers seems conspicuous by its absence in this essay, even going so far as to suggest that Danielle's death, and not Lorna's, is what ultimately prompts Kinsey's climactic call to the mafia. Certainly I agree that the relationship between Kinsey and Danielle Rivers is ripe for analysis. However, I also think that reading Danielle's murder as the catalyst that prompts Kinsey's telephone call is to mis-read the novel and to ignore the initial three-quarters of the novel when the specter of Lorna figures so prominently in Kinsey's investigation and in her own evolving sense of identity. In my reading of the novel, Danielle always and only serves as a mere touchstone connecting Kinsey to Lorna (whom Kinsey has never and will never personally meet). The centrality of Lorna (and not Danielle) to Kinsey's investigation and pursuit of "justice" can be seen, for example, during the scenes when Kinsey imagines herself *as Lorna* when she and Danielle "hang out." So, for me, Danielle's absence in this essay is reflective of her (at first metaphorical and later physical) absence in Grafton's novel; that is, Danielle is never meaningful in her own right, but merely serves to connect Kinsey more intimately to Lorna (on both a plot and a character level). Therefore, one avenue for further analysis is to explore the feminist "implications" of the relationship between Danielle and Kinsey. Such analysis simply falls outside of the scope of the current essay.

41. Dilley, xii.
42. Schoenfeld, 839.
43. Sue Grafton, interview by Bruce Taylor, *Armchair Detective* 22, no. 1 (Winter 1989), 4–13.
44. Dilley, xix.
45. Priscilla L. Walton and Manina Jones, *Detective Agency: Women Rewriting the Hard-Boiled Tradition* (Berkeley: University of California Press, 1999).
46. *Ibid.*, 4.
47. Jill Dolan, *The Feminist Spectator as Critic* (Ann Arbor: University of Michigan Press, 1991).
48. *Ibid.*
49. *Ibid.*, 3.
50. *Ibid.*, 6.
51. *Ibid.*, 5.
52. *Ibid.*, 6.

53. Cathy Cole, *Private Dicks and Feisty Chicks: An Interrogation of Crime Fiction*, (North Fremantle, Australia: Curtin University Books, 2004).
54. *Ibid.*, 141.
55. *Ibid.*

Works Cited

Belsey, Catherine. *Critical Practice.* New York: Routledge, 1991.
Christianson, Scott. "Talkin' Trash and Kickin' Butt: Sue Grafton's Hard-boiled Feminism." *Feminism in Women's Detective Fiction.* Ed. Glenwood Irons. Toronto: U of Toronto, 1995. 127–147.
Cole, Cathy. *Private Dicks and Feisty Chicks: An Interrogation of Crime Fiction.* North Fremantle, Australia: Curtin University Books, 2004.
"Darkness." *Dictionary of Symbolism.* University of Michigan. n.d. Web. 23 Dec. 2010.
Dilley, Kimberly J. *Busybodies, Meddlers, and Snoops: The Female Hero in Contemporary Women's Mysteries.* Westport, CT: Greenwood Press, 1998.
Dolan, Jill. *The Feminist Spectator as Critic.* Ann Arbor: University of Michigan Press, 1991.
_____. *Presence and Desire: Essays on Gender, Sexuality, Performance.* Ann Arbor: University of Michigan Press, 1994.
Foucault, Michel. *Power/Knowledge: Selected Interviews and Other Writings, 1972–1977.* Ed. Colin Gordon. New York: Vintage, 1980.
Grafton, Sue. *"A" Is for Alibi.* New York: Bantam, 1982.
_____. *"B" Is for Burglar.* New York: Bantam, 1985.
_____. *"D" Is for Deadbeat.* New York: Bantam, 1987.
_____. *"J" Is for Judgment.* New York: Fawcett Crest, 1993.
_____. *"K" Is for Killer.* New York: Fawcett Crest, 1994.
_____. *"T" Is for Trespass.* New York: Putnam, 2007.
_____. Interview with Bruce Taylor. *Armchair Detective* 22.1 (Winter 1989): 4–13.
Johnson, Patricia E. "Sex and Betrayal in the Detective Fiction of Sue Grafton and Sara Paretsky." *The Journal of Popular Culture* 27.4 (1994): 97–106.
"K" Is for Killer. Sue Grafton.com. n.d. Web. 26 Dec. 2010.
King, Katie. *Theory in Its Feminist Travels: Conversations in U.S. Women's Movements.* Bloomington: Indiana University Press, 1995.
Klein, Kathleen Gregory. *The Woman Detective: Gender and Genre.* Urbana: Illinois University Press, 1988.
"Misanthrope." *Merriam-Webster Dictionary.* n.d. Web. 26 Dec. 2010.
Munt, Sally R. *Murder by the Book? Feminism and the Crime Novel.* New York: Routledge, 1994.
"Night." *Dictionary of Symbolism.* University of Michigan. n.d. Web. 23 Dec. 2010.
Reddy, Maureen T. *Sisters in Crime: Feminism and the Crime Novel.* New York: Continuum, 1988.
Schoenfeld, Bethe. "Women Writers Writing about Women Detectives in Twenty-First Century America." *The Journal of Popular Culture* 41.5 (2008): 836–853.
Swanson, Jean, and Dean James. *By a Woman's Hand: A Guide to Mystery Fiction by Women.* New York: Berkeley Books, 1994.
Walton, Priscilla L., and Manina Jones. *Detective Agency: Women Rewriting the Hard-Boiled Tradition.* Berkeley: University of California Press, 1999.

LANGUAGE AND GENDER, NARRATIVE AND
SEXUALITY: RHETORICS OF IDENTITY AND DESIRE

7. Melancholia, Narrative Objectivity and the Eyewitness
The Role of the Narrator in Barbara Vine's A Dark-Adapted Eye *and* The Minotaur

ANDREW HOCK SOON NG

The reliability of first person narratives has become suspect in much contemporary literature (beginning in late twentieth century) partly because of postmodernism's deconstruction of the stable, uncomplicated subject, and partly because of psychoanalysis's revelation that within each self resides an unconscious that symptomatically manifests—such as in writing—to subvert allegedly conscious acts. Admittedly, the unreliable narrator is not a device specific to twentieth-century literature, but the prominence of realist writing (which emphasizes rational, truthful and unprejudiced representations) throughout the eighteenth and nineteenth centuries, with its tacit claim to accurately and truthfully represent veracity, had more or less left the honesty of first person narratives unchecked and taken for granted.[1] Narratives that otherwise depended on unreliability to create an atmosphere of uncertainty, like the ghost story, inadvertently end up reinforcing realist fiction's prominence by employing the trope of the hysterical woman as narrator, which also reiterated these centuries' sexist ideology. Nineteenth century *fin-de-siècle* Gothic works, for example, were rife with such a representation, either locating incongruence in the woman herself (Henry James's *The Turn of the Screw*, 1898), in men whose moral reprehensibility or weakness renders them feminized (Stevenson's *The Strange Case of Dr. Jekyll and Mr. Hyde*, 1886) or in monsters who transgress gender boundaries (Stoker's *Dracula*, 1897). Moreover, such narratives, often because of their fantastic premise, did not pose a significant challenge to the dominant literary mode. However, in the decades following the 1960s, critical theories inflected by poststructuralist and psychoanalysis have derailed such unproblematic claims of realism. Not only are realist classical works written in the first person being reread for the potential unreliability of their telling, but contemporary narratives have also increasingly turned to this device to reflect the fractured subject as the result of erratic memories, contradictory histories and/or the dangerous, if unconscious, propensity for self-deception.

Despite crime fiction's affinity with the Gothic (it is, after all, Edgar Allan Poe who single-handedly created the genre), it is noteworthy that scholarship is drawn more to its realist dimension instead, often focusing on socio-ideological issues such as race, gender, and sexuality. This may partly be due to the fact that the genre, for most of its history, is inextricably tied to the no-nonsense, rational male *par excellence*—the detective. From C. Auguste Dupin, Sherlock Holmes, and Hercule Poirot, to the hard-boiled American detective stories, these men are *grounded* in reality, and use deductive reasoning (and even violence) to divest crime of its ambiguity and mystery. Even during the Golden Age of crime narratives (1920s–1930s), when writers such as Agatha Christie, Dorothy Sayers, Josephine Tey and Ngaio Marsh dominated the genre, the male detective's prominence remained uncompromised. Clearly, even women writers colluded in reinforcing such a sexist dimension that was more or less correlative to the genre. Crime fiction, especially the type that features "gentlemen" detectives (whom Gill Plain terms "professors of logic"[2]), also usually eschews the first person detective's viewpoint to solidify the distinction between reader and character. Such a strategy will hold the latter in thrall of the former's elevated cleverness (and therefore, the superior masculine mind) in bringing the narrative, predictably, to "closure and explicability."[3]

But the traditional detective fiction has seen a gradual decline in recent years. Technological superiority (DNA, advancements in criminal detection) and feminist criticism have rendered the Descartian male detective anachronistic, while the surge in female detectives (or women who become involved in, and endeavor to, solve a crime) in the genre in the last thirty years has also redefined its emphasis from *who* the killer is to *why* a crime has been perpetrated. That much contemporary crime fiction eschews closure is a consequence of such a shift. Instead of an alpha rational male, the resignified crime fiction, as Gill Plain sees it, frequently features perplexed and helpless female "detectives" in their "struggles to 'make sense' of an increasingly alien world." Such a strategy has the value of bridging the gap between reader and detective because the detective is now "a figure who reassures not through authority, but through his or her proximity to the reader's own disenfranchisement."[4]

Because the "new" detective struggles with confusion, the premise of the narrative becomes dangerously unstable. She is unable to piece together clues accurately, and faces variegated obstructions which hamper her work, one of which is the unreliability of her witnesses. When the detective is also the narrator tasked to re-evaluate a crime — especially one in which she was somehow involved, and that had happened many years back[5] — the obvious gaps in her memory inadvertently render her account questionable as well. A narrative tension enters the story as the earnestness to accurately recall is frustrated by retranscriptions (or reinterpretations) of memories and, more importantly, the influence of unconscious desires. The novels of Barbara Vine (the *nom de plume* of Ruth Rendell) often depict such a circumstance. Her first person narrator is almost always the text's detective reviewing a past crime in which she is implicated, either directly or otherwise.[6] In *A Dark-Adapted Eye* (1986), Faith revisits the murder of her Aunt Eden by the latter's sister, Vera, after she is approached for assistance by a writer, Daniel Stewart, who specializes in reappraising past murder cases "by looking at them afresh and from the viewpoint of [...] the perpetrator."[7] While seemingly reliable in her account of an event which occurred more than thirty years ago (239), it is my contention that there is also an unconscious dynamic which censors or modifies her story in order to *protect* an unacknowledgeable, homoerotic-inflected dimension within herself. As such, rather than the unified subject of the traditional detective, Faith conforms to contemporary crime fiction's representation of the detective as, in Sally Munt's observation, a fractured self struggling against "frustrated pleasures" that "conspire to usurp complacent representations of an uncomplicated individual self."[8]

Munt encourages a psychoanalytical approach to interpreting contemporary crime fiction,[9] and this essay, to a significant degree, responds to her suggestion. By deploying Melanie Klein's revision of the Freudian melancholia, I argue that the reliability of the narrator in *Eye* is called into question precisely because she cannot objectively evaluate the scenario. This is due to a homoerotic desire for her aunts which she cannot acknowledge, and thus, has unconsciously "ingested" them as objects of scrutiny, and which now structure her ego. To re-evaluate the crime would force her to acknowledge desires that must remain unspoken and admit that she may not be the innocent observer that she believes of herself. That Faith manifests melancholia is not so much due to her familial association with the two women but a desire to preserve them as signifiers of her homoerotic desire. In *The Minotaur* (2005), the narrator Kerstin reminisces about the time she lived with the Cosways, for whom she worked as a caretaker to John, an autistic and only male member of the family. Ridden with antagonism and dangerous secrets, the family will eventually dissolve in tragedy when one of the sisters is murdered on the eve of her wedding. Unlike Faith's account, which is ridden with a tone of insistence that belies an aggression against contradictions, but whose reliance on coincidence undermines her story nevertheless, Kerstin's narrative seems assured and almost effortless. This could be attributed to the fact that she does not merely rely on her memory, but on a diary she kept while in the family's service, which helps to substantiate what she recalls. Also, as an outsider and observer, Kerstin has no unconscious agenda that could potentially prejudice her viewpoint. Finally, it is also noteworthy that Kerstin does not merely rely on words to record her memory, but drawings as well, especially cartoons. Her recognition of language's doubtful ability to signify, which encourages her also to use art as reflection of experiences, will later prove invaluable for objective and unbiased recollection. To an extent then, Kerstin arguably exemplifies what Jessica Benjamin would call an intersubjective self. Her capacity to accommodate divergent views—even those whom she opposes—without attempting to reduce them to categories that reinforce her "omnipotence" is what, according to one reading, provides the certainty of objectivity and trustworthiness in her narrative. This is also the reason why, in my view, *Minotaur* is less complex a novel than *Eye,* because the former seems to replicate a familiar structure of crime fiction that deploy a detective from the "tradition of unified heroine[s] in feminist fiction."[10]

But it is precisely this storytelling strategy in *Minotaur* that also renders its credibility suspect. In *Eye,* the careful reader can intimate Faith's psychic split that leads to narrative gaps because she allows other voices to enter her story in order to complement her perspective and perhaps, to reclaim her aunts from oblivion. Correspondences from her aunts are faithfully reproduced, and conversations with individuals (at least those still alive) implicated in the tragedy are reported, resulting in a narrative that is polyvocal. All this, however, introduces an opposite effect to Faith's story; as it progresses, she finds it increasingly difficult to negotiate between voices. If her story gradually becomes more emphatic-sounding in its apparent correctness, it is a sign of desperation to prevent the exposure of her desire by these other "lives" that she has unwittingly resurrected. *Minotaur,* on the other hand, remains unwaveringly monological throughout. The assurance in Kerstin's account is premised on the denial of other voices, which she carefully filters and then assimilates into the structure of her tale. While this does not imply dishonesty or inaccuracy—the story's lack of closure evinces her attempt to be unprejudiced in her memory—it does beg the question if what she records is, indeed, objective. After all, her sympathy with John and the desire to protect him may have colored her judgment of his family. Julia, the Cosway matriarch, is consistently represented in unfavorable terms, and his sisters are all exposed for their shortcomings. Undeniable as this may be, at least in Kerstin's point of view, that their value as individuals is always circumscribed by the narrator's judgment potentially undermines Kerstin's claim to reliability.

This essay concludes with a brief consideration of the relationship between language and memory. Lacan has demonstrated the parallel structures between language and the unconscious, which directly suggests that when the former is used to articulate memory, what has been repressed or denied can possibly resurface, thereby compromising the teller's position. Faith's narrative exemplifies precisely such a dilemma. In generously attempting to recover voices silenced by time, she unwittingly exposes a carefully hidden aspect of her psyche. Her account reveals as much as it hides, and this results in a testimony that reflects the view of what Derrida would term a "blind witness"— one who (at the risk of simplifying Derrida) chooses to believe her own perspective of what had occurred, rather what *actually* did occur.[11] Unconscious proclivities are altogether inadmissible in *Minotaur* because the narrator has diligently refused other voices from complicating her tale. In doing so, Kerstin's claim to be objective is upheld. But as scholars of detective fiction have consistently argued, it is the dominance of such a narrative strategy in the genre that has rendered the entire enterprise problematic. *Minotaur*'s narrator may be, in this sense, more reliable, but the novel is, in my opinion, also less compelling than *Eye*.

Memory and Melancholia in A Dark-Adapted Eye

A Dark-Adapted Eye revolves around Vera and Eden Hillyard, two sisters whose initial devotion to each other descends into intense animosity and tragedy over the custody of Jamie, the child whom each woman claims as her own, but which the narrative never ascertains.[12] Despite Faith's resolve to unravel "the doubt at the heart of things" (291), by the end of the narrative, she not only fails but effectively derails Stewart's project in refusing to defer ambiguities in her account. It is significant that Faith's story begins with Vera's death because, as the next section of this essay will show, the latter's demise is also the consolidation of Faith's ego formation. In Vera's death, Faith's ego finally achieves the security to preserve desire in a transfixed, unchallengeable object within her psyche. This also reveals a melancholic mechanism at work, but as with most melancholiacs, Faith derives curious comfort from being able to keep her loved object pristine and unchanging for always. Faith recalls how her father, who had always held his sisters in high esteem, had refused on that fateful day to read about the execution in the papers. Turning his attention to some world news instead (he has the habit of reading aloud), he becomes somehow stuck at a particular phrase, "in the far" (10), which he is unable to complete by appending the final word, "East." In the following days, his systematic erasure of his siblings' every trace reaches a culminating point when he boxes up all material reminders of them to be shelved away.

After this, Vera and Eden are never spoken of again, consigned to a second death even as their brother reinvents himself as an only child in the family. All this will have a curious effect on Faith, although she is unaware, because the denial of mourning will consolidate the resignification of her aunts into specific images that serve to bolster her ego, one that harbors an inadmissible homoerotic desire.

Faith will subsequently retrieve the boxes her father stored away in order to recover her aunts' letters so that she can piece her story together. She will also speak to various individuals, notably Jamie and her aunt Helen, to help her fill the gaps in her memory. The letters and these conversations are faithfully reproduced alongside her perspective to give her story greater veracity, but such an enterprise will have an adverse effect on her tale. By allowing a diversity of voices to infiltrate her account, she will increasingly find it difficult to contain them within the frame of her narrative. Throughout the novel, Faith often reminds the reader that "this is Vera's story, not mine" (242, also 62); but what becomes gradually evident is the fact that Vera's story *is* inseparable from hers, and that to narrate the former is to expose herself to an encounter with an unconscious that must remain unacknowledgeable, and always be located "in the far." Lee Horsley, in her study of twentieth-century crime fiction, suggests that "if the plot moves towards an unsettling revelation of the detective's own hidden guilt, this is more likely to involve issues of sexual identity."[13] In *Eye*, although guilt associated with sexual identity is never admitted (because it is unconscious), it is nevertheless integral to Faith's narrative's ambiguity. "[R]ooted in [a] time" (25) when homoerotic desires are not only prohibited but unthinkable, it is unsurprising that Faith cannot know the existence of such a dimension in herself, although it will manifest symptomatically, as I will demonstrate, throughout her life.

The first novel written using the pseudonym of Barbara Vine, *Eye* will subsequently inform the trajectory of all her future work, which Nicola King designates as "popular versions of the need to know our origins, the temptation to create myths around them, and the fascination involved in the works of detection to discover them."[14] In *Eye*, the predisposition toward myth-making may reveal the work of an ego resignifying certain external objects, and then internalizing them to consolidate its formation. But "the temptation to create myths" and "fascination involved in works of detection" are invariably opposed because detecting is meant to dispel myth in order to establish truth. In *Eye*, Faith sets out to do the work of detection but her fidelity to the myths of her own design proves too strong, resulting in narrative ambiguity and inconsistency. She frequently expresses misgivings about her memory's reliability, and even registers surprise when she recalls fragments of her aunt's dialogues, but remains persuaded that despite possible inaccuracies, her memory is more or less correct for they capture "the gist, the essential inner sense of those remarks [that she has] often thought of [...] since" (193–94). But I find this unconvincing and begging too many questions: what does she mean by "an essential inner sense"? At what point did her "thought" first start?—was it after meeting Stewart, or since the original point of encounter? And certainly, a thirty-five year gap is too large to leave memories intact and uncolored by subsequent experiences. Conveniently as well, whenever she needs corroboration to fill the "gaps in her knowledge,"[15] she would turn to her aunt Helen, Vera and Eden's older half-sister (now in her nineties) who, in Faith's regard, has superior memory.

Under scrutiny, Faith's self-deprecation about her ability to remember, her admission that she sometimes resorts to "creating mysteries" (153) as considered reasons behind why certain events occurred, and her deference to Helen for more accurate knowledge, may belie the fundamental but inadmissible point that despite her wish to exorcise the ghost of the past, her melancholia blocks this endeavor, which she excuses as incompetence. This is most evidently suggested by the fact that, for all her misgivings, she can be surprisingly stubborn at defending the accuracy of some of her recollections which either could not possibly have happened, or is premised on an incredible, as if staged, coincidence. Two of her allegedly assured memories, both related, particularly stand out to mitigate her narrative reliability. The first is the certainty that Vera breastfed Jamie, even though Vera's maternal claim is highly suspect (she was apparently pregnant with Jamie for over ten months),[16] and despite common knowledge that Vera's moral conservatism, evidenced in her refusal to breastfeed her first son, Francis, would preclude such a possibility. Moreover, Francis and especially Eden, who are more intimately related to, and in constant contact with Vera, have never witnessed Vera breastfeeding Jamie. In fact, Vera's kitchen further confirms this, filled as it is with implements for feeding babies. Of course, one may argue that both Eden and Francis have hidden agendas to deliberately refute Vera's maternal qualities,[17] but at the point of the novel when Faith claims she has witnessed it, circumstances have not yet developed to warrant their denial. Yet, Faith remains true to her claim, and the image of Vera breastfeeding will henceforth be inscribed as concrete and unchanging in her memory for the rest of her life, often appearing in dreams that correspondingly also plot her as a child again (15).

Faith's assuredness despite evidences that suggest otherwise is a caveat that a psychoanalytically-informed reading can explicate; but to do this, we must first consider another episode which Faith unwaveringly defends as authentic, and which she will subsequently also shape into an image-memory whose significance complements by, paradoxically, opposing the other one.

The reader is informed that later in the same day that Faith witnessed Vera breastfeeding, she came across Eden with a "doctor friend" (151) and apparent courter at a London theatre, when Eden was supposed to be in Scotland as a WRNS servicewoman.[18] Faith is positive that her aunt had also noticed her: "There was no doubt that [Eden] had seen me. I knew she had seen and recognized me" (152). But when Eden, in Faith's belief, pretends otherwise, it initiates in Faith the shift from affection and esteem to utter disgust for her aunt. The detail with which she remembers the scene merits quoting at length because it reveals the possibility that her recollection is also a deeply and unconsciously compromised one:

> Eden and her man crossed the road and lost themselves in the crowd but when I closed my eyes, there she was, I could still see her, on the black retina, her beautifully made, fine-boned face like Francis's, the lipstick red as a clown's, pillar-box paint against that white skin, the eyes as blue as marbles and the hair as gilded as a cherub's on a ceiling. Her dress had been white, cross-over and draped, her legs bare and her feet in white Betty Grable shoes with heels made for a high stepping trot like a horse's [152].

In inscribing a precise image of Eden onto her "black retina," Faith unwittingly reveals the unconscious plotting of her aunt in her psyche as a libidinal object imbued with specific qualities—a motivation not dissimilar to the one that underpins her image of Vera. While Eden, on whom Faith once had a "crush" (68), is now transformed into an object of contempt and mockery (she is a lascivious clown who trots like a horse), Vera has become transfigured into Woman *par excellence*, exuding "raw earthiness" (Vera as Mother Nature), and yet "so young, so tender, so infinitely sweet and adoring" (148, Vera as Venus), and ultimately pure (Vera as the Madonna, an association Faith actually makes at one point in the novel [15]).[19] Indeed, if Vera's reputation was temporarily bruised due to the mysterious circumstances surrounding Jamie's birth, Faith's image would beatify her all over again. It is of course possible that Faith did encounter both these episodes in a single day, but in view of the way Faith has retranscripted them into specific, personal images, the coincidence seems almost affected. That both episodes occurred on the same day becomes, as such, a euphemism that belies the equal significance and power both images have for Faith in motivating subjective development. She is unshakable in her surety that Vera did breastfeed Jamie and that a libertine Eden did deliberately disregard her because she needs such images to establish an ego that will also safeguard, by hiding (even from herself), her homoerotic desire.

Psychoanalytically speaking, it is telling that Faith corresponds her eternal image of Vera to the act of breastfeeding.[20] Thus, in order to probe its significance, I turn to Melanie Klein's object-relations theory which, when applied to my reading of *Eye,* can reveal crucial insights into the dynamics of a melancholic homoeroticism that structure Faith's ego.[21] Melancholia in Freud's formulation is the condition of perpetual mourning because the patient is unable to relinquish the loved-object which has passed on; to deny the fact of loss, the patient unconsciously "ingests" the object into himself so that it now becomes part of him and can therefore never be lost. But because this ingestion directly disturbs the self's ego formation, the ego will inadvertently also end up hating the object, resulting in anxiety and guilt.[22] Freud's theory concerns subjects who have experienced the loss of a loved one, but Klein argues that long before this ever happens, melancholia is already constitutive of all subjectivities because it is an inevitable consequence of the oedipal process. In either disavowing the maternal (for the male child) or identifying with her "lack" (the female), loss already prefigures, but is never total, at the oedipal moment. Through the ingestion of mother's milk *via* breastfeeding, what is lost becomes partially restored again, but the removal of the breast reinstates the loss. It is in this sense that the breast signifies enigmatically, or ambiguously, for child because it is both a good and a bad object; as Klein puts it, the breast is the prototype for "good objects when the child obtains it and for bad when it fails him,"[23] a signifier of the tension between love, hate and guilt that will direct all the ego's subsequent object-relations for the rest of the subject's life.

As the ego develops, so would the tension increase. The ego will continually learn to identify with, and internalize, what it sees as good objects (people, things, animals, etc.), but this is always complicated by an acute awareness of "its own incapacity to protect and preserve them against the internalized, persecuting objects," which would thus reenact "the loss of the loved object" all over again.[24] And because the prototype of all good and bad objects is a single signifier (the breast), distinguishing between them can be a harrowing experience. As the need to differentiate becomes more critical, the ego resorts to

> a conception of extremely bad and extremely perfect objects, that is to say, its [the subject's] loved objects are in many ways intensely moral and exacting. At the same time, since the ego cannot really keep its good and bad objects apart in its mind, some of the cruelty of the bad objects and of the id becomes related to the good objects and this then again increases the severity of their demands. These strict demands serve the purpose of supporting the ego in its fight against its uncontrollable hatred and its bad attacking objects, with whom the ego is partly identified.[25]

Klein, if I read her correctly, is insinuating that the ego imposes upon objects, both real and imaginary, extreme qualities to clearly distinguish the good from the bad. As a consequence, a good object is also excessively moral, for this helps the ego to shore up defense against a bad object. Even so, this is never a fool-proof solution, because the ego, in its attachment to the prototype, will always be unwittingly aligned with the bad object as well. As a result, a sadistic streak becomes inherent in the ego, whose endeavor to protect the good object is always already compromised by a desire to destroy it. This leads to guilt and, for Klein, serves as the foundation of conscience (and the motivation behind its continuous development), and ego's melancholic origins. Judith Butler summarizes Klein's view of melancholia in this way: Melancholia may be understood as the very process whereby the mind becomes figured as an internal landscape, instituting the distinction between internal and external 'worlds.'"[26] We can infer from this that all our subsequent relations to objects—and the way we designate them (good, bad)—lead back to our encounter with the prototypical object. We love certain objects because they help strengthen the ego's resolve to protect the prototype, and hate others for instigating the ego with a desire to destroy it. Yet, that the ego can be thus provoked already suggests a degree of odium against the loved-object—a situation that unmistakably points to melancholia. Guilt ensures that the ego will always privilege the good, and conscience guides the ego in its internalization of the "external world" as either good or bad objects; yet, both mechanisms are enterprises whose achievements remain, at best, ambiguous.

Bringing these insights to bear on my analysis of *Eye*, it is possible to see that Faith's refashioning of her aunts into the images of the Madonna and the Whore respectively may be motivated by a melancholic foundation that is further complicated by homoeroticism. Moreover, it confirms Horsley's view, which I quoted earlier, that a female detective's hidden guilt is always linked to a sexual identity crisis. Whether or not Faith did witness it, that the image of Vera breastfeeding will come to dominate her memory, and subject all other memories to it, startlingly reveals the psychic dynamics that underpins Faith's relationship with *both* her aunts—as the contrastive image of Eden, for Faith, cannot be understood separately from this first image. It is also telling that Faith was eleven years old when she first came to stay with (to escape the bombings in London), and would become deeply enamored of, the sisters, for it suggests the point of sexual awakening (remember Faith's crush on Eden) that can subsequently find no outlet except through melancholia. In her desire for acceptance by women she esteems, it is not implausible that there is a homoerotic dimension to this dynamic. And if love/good invariably requires hate/bad, how much more profound such a conundrum would be when it is inflected with a desire that is forbidden, and thus cannot be anything *but* "bad."

The strategy with which Faith manages a love (good object) that is also forbidden (bad object) is nothing less than a feat of creative self-deception:

she transforms both aunts into images (or, she internalizes two external objects in specific ways within her unconscious) that *would simultaneously ennoble and degrade her ego.* Vera, who epitomizes Victorian severity in terms of morality and correct behavior (Faith is frequently a target for her exacting ways [46, 50]),[27] is the obvious choice (following Klein) for the good object, while Eden, already infamous for her beauty and indifference to how others perceive her, would serve well as the opposite image. In this way, Faith can persist in her secret desire for both women while at the same time repudiate it — which at once recalls the child's enigmatic relationship with the breast, and establishes the importance of Faith's image for Vera (which informs the image of Eden as well). When approached by Stewart years later, Faith, who is of course unconscious of the homoerotic melancholia that structures her desire and memory, initially believes she can finally "look things straight in the face," and dismiss Vera's importance as she "was only your aunt, it touches you at a remove, you can think of it without real pain" (14); in the end however, her recollection brings her to the edge of an unacknowledgeable self-revelation. When she tells Francis that "by the time I've finished assisting [Stewart], [...] he won't want to [continue with the project]" (266), it is the closest the narrative would come to suggesting that Faith may, after all, have an inkling of her unstated desire which, if she were to help Stewart write Vera's biography, will also expose it.

Whether or not Faith is aware (and I am inclined to believe she is not), her melancholic-homoerotic attachment to her aunts nevertheless manifest symptomatically in the way she relates to them, and in much of her future life choices and decisions. I will discuss three of them. First, Faith takes particular interest in the sisters' mutual devotion, sensitizing herself to the shifts and nuances of their affection. Initially, Faith feels closer to Eden: their nearness in age (54) and Vera's motherly treatment of Eden (39) makes Eden a potential ally, even sibling, and if Faith is able to identify with this aunt (hence her "crush"), she would perhaps also secure Vera's affection. But when Eden resorts to calling Vera "darling" (72) with alarming (at least for Faith) frequency, she suddenly becomes Faith's competition in a scenario that replicates the oedipal moment. For Juliet Mitchell, rivalry between siblings is always reminiscent of the oedipal struggle because it is ultimately a battle for supremacy over the affection of the desired parent. According to her, "once wanting becomes sexualized, it is prohibited. If the child cannot give up the desperate wanting at this point, then the retreat to being at one with the mother becomes more urgent — the child wants to be her, giving birth as she does (but without the father), as well as being her baby."[28] When a subject sees his possible displacement from his mother's love by a sibling, the need to be one with the mother — to cling even closer to the mother — becomes crucial. Faith's incorporation of Eden as bad object reflects such a scenario, but framed alongside Klein's view, the rivalry is also an ironic, and symptomatic, signifier of her homoerotic desire.

One individual who will become a significant other for Faith is Chad, Francis's homosexual lover whom everyone (including Faith, until she accidentally witnessed Chad and Francis's lovemaking one night) believed was actually Vera's secret lover and Jamie's illegitimate father. In fact, after becoming divested of her crush on Eden, it is to Chad that Faith turns her — never declared — affection. I see this as merely another symptomatic manifestation of her homoeroticism. Chad mirrors much of her own desires (secret, homoerotic, forbidden), and thereby functions as a logical extension to her unconscious ego. Through Chad, Faith can recuperate the loved-object that was lost through sibling rivalry; like Chad, Faith is also a presumed secret lover of Vera; and if united with Chad (Faith admits that she had once hoped to be his wife [167]), she can also achieve unity with Vera, if only vicariously. Finally, that Faith's homoerotic-melancholic desire for Vera continues to structure her ego is symptomatically expressed in her decision to marry Louis Cambus (after divorcing her first husband, Andrew, who is also her cousin), the lawyer son of Josie Cambus, who was Vera's only friend during her days of desperate struggle with Eden over Jamie and who would stay by and defend Vera to the end when everyone else has abandoned her. Marrying Louis allows Vera to be united with Josie, and therefore, with Vera again. This is not to say that Faith does not genuinely love her husband; but it does beg the question whether this love is not merely another symptomatic expression of a deeper, more profound desire that has become sublimated as marital bliss.

Sometime during her consideration of Stewart's proposal, Faith admits that despite the passing years and concerted efforts to forget, Vera has remained "with me, in my house like the sort of ghost that is visible to only one person, the one with the interest [...]" (25). This is true, but only partially, because Vera is not only *with* her, she (along with Eden) is effectively lodged *within* Faith as a homoerotic-melancholic object of desire. It is the unconscious refusal to relinquish this object that finally decides the fate of Stewart's project. Nicola King, despite her reservations about memory as a reliable recorder of the past, nevertheless exhorts the reader to trust Faith as a "reliable, detached and more-or-less objective" narrator, and draws attention to the significance of Faith's name to support her view, even if the name ironically also points to the narrator's "own (possibly misplaced) 'faith' in what she remembers and what she is told."[29] But in light of my argument, it would seem that King's exhortation is equally misplaced. If there is anything "faithful" about Faith, it is the unyielding, ambivalent, love for her aunts who, as images, simultaneously preserve and condemn her unspoken desire.

The Minotaur *and the Complications of Narrative Objectivity*

There are several similarities between *The Minotaur* and *A Dark-Adapted Eye*: in both, the narrator is relating an incident that occurred decades ago. Like Faith, Kerstin (pronounced Shashtin) Kvist becomes an unwitting witness to a family drama that will descend into tragedy. But not only are the Cosways dysfunctional, there is also extreme enmity between family members due to layers of secrets, the most profound of which is the fact that "there is madness in the family."[30] Kerstin is employed as caretaker to John, a mathematical genius who suffers from a then (in the 1950s) unknown mental illness, but is known today as autism, and in John's case, of the Asperger's type. His mother, Julia, is especially insistent on keeping him drugged with Lagartil at all times in order to keep him non-violent and submissive. Like Vera, Julia is acerbic, and clings stalwartly to Victorian mores. She is also suspicious of foreigners, and attempts to make (the Swedish) Kerstin's stay as uncomfortable as possible. But since it is John himself who wants a caretaker, and Kerstin's salary will come from a trust left to him by his father, Julia is helpless to prevent her son's wishes.

Like *Eye*, *Minotaur* also revolves around sibling rivalry that leads to murder. Two of John's sisters, Winifred and Ella, are locked in a battle for the affection of a visiting artist, the self-proclaimed Bohemian by the name of Felix Dunsworth. Winifred, who is soon to marry the local rector, Eric, becomes enamored of Felix, and when she "steals" him from Ella, a dangerous animosity in an already defective family is triggered. The youngest Cosway member is Zorah, the illegitimate daughter of Julia and her lover and doctor, Lombard. It is the discovery of Julia's adultery that has led to her disinheritance by her husband, whose sexist ideology also disqualifies his daughters from any inheritance as well. The novel intimates that Zorah's childhood was a miserable and ostracized one, perhaps due to her doubtful lineage. But her intelligence and successful marriage to a wealthy individual helped her escape the family, which she would later "punish" by giving — or withholding from — each member alcohol and other presents precisely to reinforce the fact of their poverty and dependence on her. John, however, she genuinely loves, perhaps because she sees in him a kindred spirit. When Winifred is murdered toward the end of the story, it is not Ella, but Ida, the oldest sibling, and Julia who become suspects, but it remains unclear to the end who is the real killer, or even what the motivation could have been.[31] This lack of closure is another similarity shared between both novels.

One significant way *Minotaur* diverges from *Eye*, however, is the manner in which the narrator is implicated in the story. Unlike Faith, Kerstin is an observer seemingly without any personal agenda apart from protecting John—whom she comes to respect and care for deeply (405)—from his mother and Dr. Lombard, the latter of whom has the claim to authority in keeping John in an induced state so that they can eventually institutionalize him and rob him of his inheritance. As a result of her outsider status, Kerstin's "study of character" (76) reads more reliably. If Faith's narrative is unreliable, it is because her story reveals an omnipotent ego that has incorporated her aunts as objects with strictly transfixed significations. Her account reflects a "self [who] recognizes the possible threat that the other poses" (such as Stewart's project), and as such, becomes suspicious in its assertion of truthfulness even as she blames poor memory to justify her inconsistency.[32] Kerstin's story, on the other hand, reflects the narrator's intersubjective position, which Jessica Benjamin describes as being inclusive "of split off feelings or blocked aspirations [that are] motivated not by a compulsion to restore unity but out of the wish to be less resentful and afraid of projected anger, less terrified of loss, less punitive toward what one desires."[33] Benjamin further asserts that "omnipotence cannot be broken up without a process of 'destruction,' which may, if survived, lead to a recognition of the other as external."[34] If Kerstin's story seems more confident in tone and assured, without sounding insistent, in its accuracy, it is because the narrator's intersubjective ego enables her to negotiate between diverse objects in a manner that modifies and enhances, rather than overwhelms and depletes, her. As such, she can tolerate Julia's "projected anger" (although this does not mean she is not exhausted or frightened or hurt by, it [212, and 401–2]), and later, endure a breakup with her boyfriend due partly to her intense involvement with the Cosways, while learning to confront her own demons at the same time.

However, to say that Kerstin is innocent of the subsequent tragedy would be untenable, although it is arguable that she, like Faith, is unaware of the part she played—apart from directly interfering with John's medication—and the effect it will have. It is interesting to note that Kerstin often wonders if Felix's presence had not inevitably set the Cosways on a path to dissolution (75) but is blind to the possibility that it may be her arrival that has initiated this—in the same way Faith remembers her father's propulsion toward repression, but is unable to recognize her own. On the one hand, Ella and Winifred's rivalry may be unconsciously *triggered by her presence*, not Felix's, as a kind of a competition with her rather than between themselves, because Kerstin's youth and beauty evoke a sense of loss in them, which they attempt to retrieve by giving into their passion. Arguably, both women are not in love with Felix (although Ella believes she is), but are exploiting him as merely a means to (symbolically) recapture their wasted youth and for Winifred, to explore her hitherto pent-up sexuality. That Kerstin also feels Winifred's "charge of sexual energy" exhibited by "a powerful sexiness in the way she breathed and the gaze of her eye and the parting of her painted lips" (342) as her relationship with Felix develops could suggest that these vibes are possibly meant also for, or at least inspired in part by, Kerstin. On the other hand, as John gradually warms to Kerstin to the point of proposing marriage in his clumsy, abrupt way (324), Kerstin would certainly appear as the *real* threat to the family, and especially to Julia. If Kerstin agrees (and she does consider it seriously, albeit briefly [341]), Julia's plan would be altogether undone.[35] Finally, there is also Kerstin's incrimination due to her non-reaction against the sisters' confessions of illicit activities, whose silence is then construed as "complicity." Of course, the narrative makes it clear that there is nothing Kerstin can actually do to avert the impending tragedy because the Cosway women are generally dismissive of her (even though, as in Ella's case, they may solicit her friendship for selfish reasons), and due to her aversion to minding other people's business. But in refusing to warn Ella or expose Winifred she indirectly deepens the familial discord and potentially endangers the life of the very person she desires to shield.

One way of understanding Kerstin's apparent objectivity is to view her as an encompassing individual, whose "acceptance of otherness" disqualifies any desire to dominate (that is, to be omnipotent over) other persons.[36] In a sense, Kerstin's strength and weakness stem from a similar source: her ability to assume an intersubjective position which, according to Jessica Benjamin, "does not constitute a transcendence (*Aufhebung*) of the intrapsychic, but rather a modification and addition to it."[37] In other words, Kerstin is able to accommodate various perspectives, even those radically at odds with hers, without attempting to overcome or transcend them, but are instead added to her own to affect or modify the repertoire of her own ego. In keeping silent, she ironically becomes the Cosways' shared but unspoken "idiom" (to borrow a term by Christopher Bollas) in order to release the family's bitterness "into being."[38] Through her, the sisters are able to finally articulate, both in word and deed, aspects of themselves which would otherwise have no outlet. As an idiom, Kerstin encourages them to leave their trace on her, even as she assumes, in their stead, the guise of what Bollas calls a "spirit."[39] This "spirit" is unlike the ghost that haunts Faith, but an ego that is capable of incorporating unqualified otherness to the point that it functions as a mirror reflecting the other's desire. This is what Bollas means when he argues that an idiom transformed into a spirit is able "to create personal effects" on those it affects *via* the gift of a trace.[40] As a trace, she poses the reflection of the self which the sisters harbor but have, hitherto, no way of acknowledging. This is why Julia is exceptionally cruel to her, while the sisters, even the usually reticent Ida, openly confide in her: as their idiom, she brings out in them facets of their identities that have been denied or repressed; as a mirror, she is able to reflect their desires (Julia's extreme hatred for John, Ella's need for acceptance, Winifred's promiscuous nature, Ida's wish for escape) to the extent that these desires, at last, find outlets.

The confidence expressed in Kerstin's narrative is also attributed to the fact that she has a diary to help her. Unlike Faith, who struggles to piece together her aunts' story by relying on letters, intermittent conversations and above all, her memory, Kerstin can fill any gaps in recollection quite easily by referring to this register that she kept during her service to the Cosways. Apart from words, Kerstin also fills her diary with drawings. And while drawings, like language, can also convey nuances and ambiguities, the kind to which Kerstin inclines, and of which she will subsequently make a successful career, are cartoons drawn with simple lines. Her specialties are caricatures, which she once used to "describe" several members of the Cosway household. This type of artwork minimizes misunderstanding: for it to be effective, it must convey exactly what the artist intends—whether a satire, a criticism, or a social concern — or it (and its creator) is deemed to have failed. In this sense, cartoons leave little room for alternative, and possibly unconscious, meanings. This does not, however, mean that the art of cartoon has no psychoanalytical significance. In fact, because cartoons are usually associated with humor, it can potentially encourage "liberating and exalting the ego."[41] Theorist Sarah Kofman suggests that humorists (of which the cartoonist is a type) are not enslaved to their ego but "overcome" and even "scorn" it instead to "hold off at a distance anything which might discredit [them], such as fear or fright."[42] Although Kerstin only began drawing during her term with the Cosways (40), the humorist is obviously already latent in her, to finally emerge at the time when she will need some self-assurance to juggle between protecting John, enduring Julia's relentless reprimands and biting criticisms, tolerating the sisters, and making conscious plans for the future. But art, whether humorous or not, is already invaluable from a psychoanalytical angle. According to the psychoanalyst Sandor Ferenczi, the "pleasure in gazing at objects" is what compels a person to become an artist because this activity compensates "for objects that as a child he had been forbidden to look at."[43] An otherwise tenuous proposition, it is nevertheless interesting, at least in theory, in implying that art can effectuate the return of the repressed and transform what is otherwise obscene into something admissible and pleasurable. Ferenczi's observation draws a clear distinction between language, which structures the unconscious even as it disguises it, and art, whose realization not only abjures the unconscious but exposes and domesticates it. In this way do the cartoons that populate Kerstin's diary serve, decades later, not merely as catalyst to her memory, but as compensation for the anxiety and unsettling feelings that would otherwise accompany, and possibly compromise, her revisiting of the past.

Yet, as mentioned earlier, although serving as another's idiom may render the "spirit" objective, this does not mean that she is uncompromised. In assuming the role of a mirror on which the Cosways' desires can find a reflection, Kerstin may have actually, if unknowingly, encouraged their release of destructive energies that will culminate in violence and death. In fact, the most insidious feature of *Minotaur* is linked precisely to the fact that Kerstin remains the family's idiom decades after the incident. A chance meeting with Ella triggers her memory, which results in the narrative — one that is also dominated by Kerstin's singular point of view. If she could be said to eschew omnipotence during her time with the family, her present narrative certainly subverts this. Moreover, although her diary enables a systematic recollection of events that led up to the tragedy, it is nevertheless shaped fundamentally by Kerstin's perspectives and opinions, which later inform the way she understands these events and the people who were implicated in them. As such, where Kerstin's narrative plot linkages are concerned:

> Characters have become objects, fixed elements in the author's design; such links bind and combine finalized images of people in the unity of a monologically perceived and understood world; there is no presumption of a plurality of equally-valid consciousnesses, each with its own world.[44]

The one-dimensionality that characterizes all the members of the Cosway family exemplifies the single-voiced imperative that underlies Kerstin's story. Each is painted in monotones, and whatever identities they bear reflect "consciousnesses" prescribed by a narrator. Throughout the novel, no individual, once his or her "element" is "fixed," ever detracts from Kerstin's "world." Ella, for example, whom Kerstin describes as someone who has "a greater capacity for getting the wrong end of the stick than anyone I have ever known" (183), never wavers from such a representation. Kerstin persistently informs the reader of the many instances when Ella evinces such a personality deficiency. This is, in my view, ironic because Kerstin, to a point, *is like Ella* in their shared propensity for dressing up "objects" to fit neatly into their design. While Ella effects this through her hobby of creating beautiful outfits for her dolls (177, 293), Kerstin does this by adorning the Cosways with preset characteristics so that they inhabit the world of her creation in precisely the manner in which she desires. It is unsurprising that Kerstin is both sympathetic toward, and most contemptuous of, Ella, who is also the focus of her first caricature. In turning Ella into a cartoon, Kerstin not only further reduces her "equally-valid" consciousness into mere object but also trivializes her so as to refute any similarity between them.

As such, Kerstin's art both reinforces and problematizes Ferenczi's postulation: although her caricatures grant her the "pleasure in gazing at objects," it is a pleasure derived not from exposing the unconscious, but from reinforcing it. By making a travesty of Ella in cartoon form, Kerstin is triggering what is possibly an unconscious defense mechanism in order to dis-identify with her. This mechanism becomes even more pronounced when read in light of my earlier discussion of the possible homoerotic tension between the sisters and Kerstin. Through art, Kerstin enacts a "degradation of others as a means of maintaining [her] own services,"[45] which, in her case, is both the maintenance of her alleged objectivity and her narrative design. Her talent is what Klaus Theweleit, with some modification to what he argues in his study of homosexuality, would call a "maintenance mechanism" whose function is to "[restore] the acting subject to 'totality'" by displaying "a distinct tendency to devivify [her] object."[46] Thus, Kerstin's drawing not only objectifies Ella, but it also blatantly renounces the latter's homoerotic vibes. Distinct from Faith, whose incorporation of her aunts as images reinforces her homoerotic desires, Kerstin reduces the sisters to cartoon images in order to preserve her ego's "totality." Tellingly, the only character who defies such a transfixing is the murdered victim. It is as if, in rejecting the omnipotent narrator's design, Winifred is therefore singled out for punishment. That the narrative does not identify Winifred's killer is also noteworthy because it suggests both Ida and her mother's exoneration of the crime. In leaving the former's fate ambiguous and allowing the latter to die in an accidental fire, the narrative is arguably "rewarding" them for conforming exactly to the narrator's plan.

Conclusion

Students of Lacanian psychoanalysis will be familiar with the theorist's assertion that the unconscious is structured like and by language.[47] Lacan also notes, in a discussion about love, that

> the subject [in love] is nothing other than what slides in a chain of signifiers, whether he knows which signifier he is the effect of or not. That effect — the subject — is the intermediary effect between what characterizes a signifier and another signifier, namely, the fact that each of them, each of them is in element. We know of no other basis by which the One may have been introduced to the world if not by the signifier as such, that is, the signifier insofar as we learn to separate it from its meaning effects. In love what is aimed at is the subject, the subject as such, insofar as is presumed in an articulated sentence, in something that is organized or can be organized on the basis of a whole life.[48]

Faith, in my view, reflects the underside of Lacan's observation; the melancholic preservation of her aunts may be impelled by (homoerotic) love, but that this preservation is also consolidated by associating specific images to them suggests an unconscious refusal to see them as anything other than what she wants. If the two women have "meaning effects" that do not correspond with the signifiers Faith imposes, the reader will never know, because Faith is obviously unable to separate them from her restricted images. And imposition is precisely what Faith must earnestly maintain as the heteroglossic nature of her narrative increasingly threatens to reveal her unconscious desires to herself. Ironically, however, such an enterprise also invariably transforms the subject into *a signifier* as well. In her unconscious preservation of images with distinct significance, Faith becomes a kind of signifier *par excellence* who holds together ("the intermediary effect") the rest, and designates their proper place (ensuring that they are "in element") in the chain of her own effecting, whose organization has now become, more or less, "the basis of [her] whole life." Faith's unreliable narrative is, in the end, reflective of the melancholia that structures it. She may lament that her memory cannot possibly fill all the "great gaps and "spaces of the past" (*Eye*, 15), but who can say that she is also not secretly comforted by this lack? After all, no one can contradict her memory now (all the other surviving members of the family have since systematically disassociated themselves from Vera, and is therefore adverse to Stewart's project), and even if someone does, it will merely be a case of whose memory is greater in accuracy.

From one perspective, Kerstin does not suffer Faith's complication because she is an outsider who remains askance from the "terrible pressures of love" (*Eye*, 24) experienced in the family. But if Faith becomes an unwitting signifier in order to sustain her homoerotic ego, Kerstin assumes the position of an idiom, perhaps in order to entice the Cosway women into expressing their repressed desires. This may not be her intention during her service to the family, but decades later, when setting the family's saga down as narrative, that she was able to function as such a signifier becomes evidently useful. Moreover, if her retrospective account relies on her diary entries, this also begs the question if she has possibly resorted to retrieving only records that serve her design. Yet, as Bakhtin has noted, "However monological the utterance may be [...], however much it may concentrate on its own object, it cannot but be, in some measure, a response to what has already been said about the given topic, on the given issue, even though this responsiveness may not have assumed a clear-cut external expression."[49] To what then could Kerstin's single-voiced narrative be responding? To answer this question requires a return to the concept of omnipotence, which I evoked earlier in my reading of *Minotaur*. If it was a younger, and somewhat guileless and helpless woman who, in enduring the Cosway women, resulted in her becoming plotted as their idiom, as a matured individual and a renowned cartoonist *now*, Kerstin can respond to their insensitivity and/or cruelty by plotting them as transfixed, disagreeable stereotypes in her narrative. In this sense, it is arguable that her story is, to an extent, enacted in order to, on the one hand, punish those who have harmed her and John, and on the other, ennoble those (such as Zorah and Eric) who have shown her ward and herself regard and kindness. Ella, while drawn with some measure of graciousness, remains emphatic in her childishness and gullibility throughout the narrative. Even when Kerstin meets her by accident decades later, thus triggering the narrative, Ella remains, in the narrator's account, unchanged in her nature.

Ultimately, when the two narratives are compared again in view of the argument that has informed their interpretation, it becomes evident that neither novel is, really, dependable in its account. In fact, Faith's narrative, despite its unreliability, seems at least more "truthful" than Kerstin's. Faith's story becomes suspect insofar that she inadvertently allows other voices to interpenetrate hers, resulting in revelations which she does not intend. In an attempt to contain those voices within the frame of her tale, she then resorts to far-fetched coincidences and insistence on correctness, all of which weakens the force of her narrative's conviction. Kerstin's story, on the other hand, is seemingly assured and confident, but this is merely because her narrative has effectively silenced all other competing "consciousness" that may imperil the certainty of her telling. If her story reads more consistently, it is because she has ensured that her plot linkages and character definitions are properly set against the frame of her design. There is no room for ambiguity in her story. But as such, if *Minotaur* is a more reliable story, it is also a less truthful one than *Eye*.

Notes

1. An excellent critique of realist writing is Lillian Furst's *All Is True* (Durham: Duke University Press, 2005).
2. Gill Plain, *Twentieth-Century Crime Fiction* (Edinburgh: Edinburgh University Press, 2001), 3.
3. *Ibid.*
4. *Ibid.*, 7.
5. In *Crime Fiction* (2005), John Scaggs argues that the historical crime fiction is further sub-divided into two: "crime fiction that is set entirely in some particular historical period, but which was not written during that period" (i.e. works written by a contemporary writer about a crime in the past solved by people contemporaneous to it); and that which "has a contemporary detective investigating an incident in the more or less remote, rather than very recent, past" (125). The limitation in Scagg's theory becomes evident when considering Vine's narratives.
6. I use the term "detective" broadly to mean the protagonist who is performing the task of detection, i.e. reassessing evidences, drawing new conclusions, and so forth. Professional detectives do not feature in Vine's oeuvre.

7. Barbara Vine, *A Dark-Adapted Eye* (London: Penguin, 1986), 23. All subsequent references to the novel are from this edition.
8. Sally R. Munt, *Murder by the Book?* (London: Routledge. 1994), 199.
9. Ibid.
10. Ibid.
11. Jacques Derrida, *Memoirs of the Blind* (Chicago: University of Chicago Press, 1988), 104.
12. Unlike in nineteenth century (and before), female criminals in the twentieth century generally received greater leniency in sentencing due to legal biases that favored them; Vera may have invited the capital punishment because she has committed what would be termed a "manly crime," thus disqualifying her of any gender-based consideration. For useful discussion, see Meda Chesney-Lind, "Women and Crime," *Signs* 12.1 (1996). For discussion on the female criminal and the legal system in the nineteenth century, see Peter J. Hutchings *The Criminal Spectre in Law, Literature and Aesthetics* (London: Routledge, 2001), esp. Chapter 4.
13. Lee Horsley, *Twentieth-Century Crime Fiction* (Oxford University Press, 2005), 251.
14. Nicola King, *Memory, Narrative, Identity* (Edinburgh: Edinburgh University Press, 2000), 94.
15. *Ibid.*, 108.
16. Later, when Eden's claim that she is Jamie's child becomes more plausible than Vera's, Faith will express her loyalty to the image of Vera breastfeeding, using "induced lactation" (296) as an argument to support her certainty.
17. Francis has never forgiven his mother for abandoning him in India with his father while she returns to England to be with Eden. For the rest of his life, he will persistently punish Vera with cruel, extreme jokes designed to vex, humiliate, or discomfort her.
18. This event occurred during the period of the second World War. Faith's conviction that the man is a doctor is based on nothing more than a particular gesture he made, which Faith would normally associate with doctors. Such is the tenuous nature of her certainty.
19. The theme of motherhood in *Eye* is briefly explored in Katherine and Lee Horsley's essay "*Mères Fatales*" *Modern Fiction Studies*, 45.2 (1999).
20. Nicola King acknowledges the significance of this image, but provides no further insights apart from directing the reader to Jean Laplanche's observation that the breast is "an 'enigmatic signifier' to the infant" (110).
21. Space disallows me from outlining what object-relations in psychoanalysis is, but here is a quote from Melanie Klein that may prove useful. Unlike Freud, who sees the ego as basically autonomous and self-defining (although this occurs through various stages), Klein states that "the phenomenon which was recognized by Freud [...] as the voices and the influence of the actual parents established in the ego is, according to my findings, a complex object-world, which is felt by the individual, in deep layers of the unconscious, to be concretely inside himself [...] an internal (inner) world. This inner world consists of innumerable objects taken into the ego, corresponding partly to the multitude of varying aspects, good and bad, in which the parents (and other people) appeared to the child's unconscious mind through various stages of his development" ("Mourning and Manic-Depressive States," in *The Selected Melanie Klein*, ed. Juliet Mitchell [New York: The Free Press, 1986], p. 166).
22. See Freud, "Mourning and Melancholia," in *Collected Papers*, ed James Strachey, trans. under the supervision of Joan Riviere (London: Hogarth Press, 1957).
23. Melanie Klein, "A Contribution to the Psychogenesis of Manic-Depressive States," 116.

24. *Ibid.*, 119.

25. *Ibid.*, 123.

26. Judith Butler, "Moral Sadism and Doubting One's Own Love," *Reading Melanie Klien*, eds. John Phillips and Lyndsey Stonebridge (London: Routledge, 1998), 184.

27. Space does not allow me to discuss a fundamental feature of both novels: a socio-ideological system heavily informed by Victorian mores (class, gender, sexuality), which governs many of Vine's characters (King treats the issue of class briefly in her essay). However, it will be erroneous to say that Vine summarily plots her female characters (often protagonists) as *always* victims (Julia Cosway clearly exemplifies such an error). As Mary S. Hartman's cautions in her study of nineteenth century middle-class female criminality in London and France: "It is tempting to view many female criminals [...] simply as victims of a rigid social code who had little chance to solve their dilemmas save through crime. It is also tempting to view at least some of these women [...] as proto-feminists, self-consciously combating constrictive social institutions and regulations. But such conclusions should be treated with caution. To be sure, in the first part of the century women do appear to have committed crimes largely to escape particular desperate situations for which they had not themselves been responsible; while at the end of the century [and, I would add, into the twentieth], more women appear to have committed crime for 'positive' reasons, that is, not merely to rid themselves of miserable circumstances but to achieve some imagined happier state [...]. It is clear that by the end of the century many women were unwilling to accept the same sort of legal and social inferiority as they had earlier, but the criminal activity of some of them was hardly a self-conscious expression of this feeling" ("Crime and the Respectable Woman," *Feminist Studies*, 2.1 (1974): pp. 53–54).

28. Juliet Mitchell, *Mad Men and Medusas* (London: Penguin, 2000), 319.

29. King, *Memory Narrative, Identity*, 95.

30. Barbara Vine, *The Minotaur* (London: Penguin, 2005), 18. All subsequent references to the novel are from this edition.

31. Ida once told Kerstin that she would do "anything for a change" (282) in her unchanging routine of slaving away for her family, which, coupled with her contempt for Winifred's adultery, could serve as a possible reason for murdering her sister. Julia, after the crime, attempts to pin the blame on John, similar to the episode in which she fell down the stairs (217). But this contradicts a fundamental characteristic of John's autism: his aversion to touch. It is this characteristic, together with Kerstin's diary, that later acquit him.

32. *Ibid.*, 94.

33. Jessica Benjamin, "Recognition and Destruction." *Like Subjects, Love Objects* (New Haven: Yale University Press, 1995), 105.

34. *Ibid.*, 90.

35. Kerstin did not manipulate John in any way, despite Julia's accusation (325), to elicit such a proposal. That John proposes may be the result of the current discourse circulating the Cosway home revolving around Winifred and Eric's upcoming marriage, which John merely mimics, or his way of signaling to her his acceptance and his nascent desire to want her by his side as friend and protector (326).

36. Benjamin, "Recognition and Destruction," 84.

37. *Ibid.*, 93. See also Jessica Benjamin, "Recognition and Destruction: An Outline of Intersubjectivity" (1995).

38. Christopher Bollas, *Being a Character* (New York: Hill and Wang, 1982), 54.

39. *Ibid.*, 63.

40. *Ibid,* When Ella and Kerstin meets by accident decades later, their mutual affection is genuine despite the strained circumstances that ended their initial friendship. Both

women bear each other no grudges, simply because Kerstin has always shown generosity and kindness to Ella (who married Eric) even though she was frequently irritated by, and sometimes even felt disgusted with, the latter for her selfishness and excessive narcissistic streak.

41. Sarah Kofman, "The Narcissistic Women," *Diacritics*, 10.3 (1980) 39.
42. *Ibid.*
43. Sandor Farenczi, "On Introjection and Transference," in *Selected Writings*, trans (primary) Jane Isabel Suttie, ed. Julia Borossa (London: Penguin, 1999) 41.
44. Mikhail Bakhtin, *The Bakhtin Reader*, trans. various, ed. Pam Morris (London: Arnold, 1994) 89.
45. Klaus Theweleit, *Male Fantasies, Male Bodies*, vol. 2, trans. Chris Turner and Eric Carter (Cambridge: Polity Press, 1989), 318.
46. *Ibid.*, 318. My argument actually reads *against* Theweleit, who views the homosexual act as devouring the other. For Theleweit, the homosexual is primarily narcissistic, and his desire for other is fundamentally self-desire. As such, the sexual act is enacted in order for him to incorporate the other into himself in order to bolster his own ego. Such a premise is, in my view, highly problematic not only because it pathologizes homosexuals, but designates them as anomalous and even criminal as well.
47. See, for example, Jacques Lacan, *On Feminine Sexuality* (New York: Norton, 1998), 48.
48. *Ibid.*, 50.
49. Bakhtin, 86.

Works Cited

Bakhtin, Mikhail. *The Bakhtin Reader*. Trans. various Ed. Pam Morris. London: Arnold, 1994.
Benjamin, Jessica. "Recognition and Destruction: An Outline of Intersubjectivity," In *Like Subjects, Love Objects*. New Haven: Yale University Press, 1995. 27–48.
_____. *Shadow of the Other: Intersubjectivity and Gender in Psychoanalysis*. London: Routledge, 1998.
Bollas, Christopher. *Being a Character: Psychoanalysis and Self Experience*. New York: Hill and Wang, 1992.
Butler, Judith. "Moral Sadism and Doubting One's own Love," In *Reading Melanie Klein*, eds. John Phillips and Lyndsey Stonebridge. London: Routledge, 1998. 179–89.
Chesney-Lind, Meda. "'Women and Crime': The Female Offender." *Signs*, 12.1 (1996): 78–96.
Derrida, Jacques. *Memoirs of the Blind: The Self-Portrait and Other Ruins*. Trans. Pascale-Anne Brault and Michael Naas. Chicago: The University of Chicago Press, 1998.
Ferenczi, Sándor. "On Introjection and Transference" (1909). In *Selected Writings*, trans. (primary) Jane Isabel Suttie, ed. Julia Borossa. London: Penguin, 1999. 31–66.
Freud, Sigmund. "Mourning and Melancholia" (1917). In *Collected Papers*, vol. IV, ed. James Strachey, trans. under the supervision of Joan Riviere. London: Hogarth Press, 1957. 152–70.
Furst, Lilian R. *All Is True: The Claims and Strategies of Realist Fiction*. Durham: Duke University Press, 1995.
Hartman, Mary S. "Crime and the Respectable Woman: Toward a Pattern of Middle-Class Female Criminality in Nineteenth-Century France and England," *Feminist Studies*, 2. 1 (1974): 38–56.

Horsley, Katherine, and Lee Horsley. "*Mères Fatales*: Maternal Guilt in the Noir Crime Novel," *Modern Fiction Studies*, 45. 2 (1999): 369–402.
Horsley, Lee. *Twentieth-Century Crime Fiction*. Oxford: Oxford University Press, 2005.
Hutchings, Peter J. *The Criminal Spectre in Law, Literature and Aesthetics: Incriminating Subjects*. London: Routledge, 2001.
King, Nicola. *Memory, Narrative, Identity: Remembering the Self*. Edinburgh: Edinburgh University Press, 2000.
Klein, Melanie. "A Contribution to the Psychogenesis of Manic-Depressive States," In *The Selected Melanie Klein*, ed. Juliet Mitchell. New York: The Free Press, 1986. 115–45.
_____. "Mourning and Manic-Depressive States," in *The Selected Melanie Klein*, ed. Juliet Mitchell. New York: The Free Press, 1986. 146–74.
Kofman, Sarah. "The Narcissistic Women: Freud and Girard," *Diacritics*, 10. 3 (1980): 36–45.
Lacan, Jacques. *On Feminine Sexuality, the Limits of Love and Knowledge, 1972–1973*. New York: Norton, 1998.
Mitchell, Juliet. *Mad Men and Medusas: Reclaiming Hysteria and the Effects of Sibling Relations on the Human Condition*. London: Penguin, 2000.
Munt, Sally R. *Murder by the Book? Feminism and the Crime Novel*. London: Routledge, 1994.
Plain, Gill. *Twentieth-Century Crime Fiction: Gender, Sexuality, and the Body*. Edinburgh: Edinburgh University Press, 2001.
Scaggs, John. *Crime Fiction*. London: Routledge, 2005.
Theweleit, Klaus. *Male Fantasies, Male Bodies: Psychoanalyzing the White Terror*, vol. 2. Trans. Chris Turner and Eric Carter. Cambridge: Polity Press, 1989.
Vine, Barbara. *A Dark-Adapted Eye*. London: Penguin, 1986.
_____. *The Minotaur*. London: Penguin, 2005.

8. Postfeminism(s) and Authority in Contemporary Glasgow Police Procedurals

PETER CLANDFIELD

In the Postscript to her 2001 book *Twentieth-Century Crime Fiction: Gender, Sexuality and the Body*, Gill Plain suggests that crime fiction "has become a literature of self-assertion, endlessly pressuring its boundaries to satisfy audience demand, and to prove its own strength."[1] This observation points to the contemporary prominence, and possible commodification, of female crime fiction protagonists defined by self-assertiveness in several intersecting spheres: professional, sexual, rhetorical. This essay focuses on two Scottish writers whose female investigators attain and maintain authority through such assertiveness yet remain notably complex figures. I will start with the recent work of Denise Mina, particularly *Still Midnight* (2009), the initial book in a series which for the first time makes one of her characteristically complex protagonists a police officer. I will go on to the three novels published thus far by Karen Campbell — *The Twilight Time* (2008), *After the Fire* (2009), and *Shadowplay* (2010) — in an ongoing series which shares both Mina's Glasgow milieu and her abrasive-yet-nuanced prose style. Mina's and Campbell's protagonists, seen critically by other characters and by themselves, are positioned within layered narratives which deal not only with particular crimes, but also with the evolving condition of Glasgow as a postindustrial city partially renewed by economic and cultural diversification, yet still subject to residual injustices and inequalities affecting gender roles and relations.

In a 2007 essay, Plain observes that until recently, Scottish crime fiction has been marked by a "literary-political coalition between the tough-guy detective and the Scottish hard man" which has been "limiting and destructive" in its foregrounding of violent and toxic masculinity.[2] Plain goes on, however, to chart the evolution of Ian Rankin's Inspector Rebus series, whose later volumes have the protagonist subduing self-destructiveness and mentoring a young female detective, Siobhan Clarke. Plain sees Clarke as "carrying the legacy of Rebus's hard-boiled integrity into a 'new' world which she can, and does, read effectively," but she argues that Clarke continues to face "the persistent handicap of gender, which remorselessly renders her 'other' within the obstinately patriarchal structure of the police force."[3] Like Rankin's, Mina's and Campbell's work locates crime in the context of persistent social and political inequities affecting urban Scotland. Yet, Mina and Campbell also treat the patriarchal structures of police and other institutions as having come to accommodate a degree of feminist influence, and they use multiple plotlines and multiple points-of-view to dramatize both potential benefits and pitfalls of authority vested in women. Crime fiction has often pitted rebelliously hard-boiled detective protagonists not only against criminals but also against office-bound superiors, and Mina and Campbell point to the dangers of merely replacing the "hard man" with the "hard woman" or of making over an old-boys' club into a gender-neutral network of careerists still obstructive of genuine justice.

Crime and detective novels construct authority not only through convincingly worked-out plots and plausibly-detailed settings, but also through calculated breaches of cultural decorum: they use startling or abrasive tricks of language and style fittingly to evoke worlds marked by devious agendas and harsh motives. In their current series, Mina and Campbell present female investigators who take on the customary maverick status—the anti-authoritarian authority—of the fictional detective partly by challenging (what are presented as) tenets and orthodoxies of contemporary feminism. Thus, their works bear on the concept or phenomenon of postfeminism. There is a basic ambiguity to the *post*-prefix: does it denote the lasting influence of the practice or condition to which it attaches, or does it assert the supersession of this practice or condition? Recent feminist writers argue convincingly that the term has increasingly been appropriated in popular media to express what Yvonne Tasker and Diane Negra, in the Introduction to their 2007 collection *Interrogating Postfeminism*, characterize as the now-widespread assumption "that it is the very success of feminism that produces its irrelevance for contemporary culture."[4] However, Tasker and Negra also note that "the posting of feminism means that feminism itself remains in the frame,"[5] while Misha Kavka, in a 2002 essay investigating "the 'Post' in Postfeminism," points out that "[w]hile the term has seemed on the one hand to announce the end of feminism, on the other hand its definition, appropriation, or rejection has itself become a site of feminist politics."[6]

I will argue that Mina's and Campbell's novels propagate a postfeminism that effectively uses critique of feminist assertion and feminist authority not in order to repudiate feminist activity or relegate it to history, but to indicate the extent to which feminist-influenced principles of justice are enduringly influential and valuable exactly because they remain subject to debate and negotiation. I will emphasize ways in which these novels, despite their generic associations with linear investigation and the trope of "interrogation," use layered plots and nuanced characterizations to treat feminism and postfeminism as much more than cases to be solved. At the same time as they challenge glibly linear constructions of Glasgow as a reinvented city where old inequities — of class or ethnicity as well as of gender — have been overcome, Mina and Campbell dramatize the live-ness, the ongoing quality, of questions of gender politics and roles, contesting over-neat and reductive bids to "post" feminism.

Mina

For several years, Denise Mina's website has offered the following statement on the origins of her career:

> At twenty-one she passed exams, got into study Law at Glasgow University and went on to research a PhD thesis at Strathclyde University on the ascription of mental illness to female offenders, teaching criminology and criminal law in the mean time. Misusing her grant she stayed at home and wrote a novel, *Garnethill*, when she was supposed to be studying instead.[7]

Together, these sentences fuse two seemingly-incompatible kinds of self-assertion. The first declares Mina's authority to write about someone like *Garnethill*'s protagonist, Maureen O'Donnell, who has been left vulnerable and volatile by the long-term effects of childhood sexual abuse from her father and by deficient psychiatric care. Yet, the second sentence enacts, in her offhand admission to "[m]isusing her grant," Mina's readiness to transgress dry academic protocols in favor of the fast-talking, wisecracking discourse of crime fiction. The statement illustrates the mixing of authoritative detail with unpredictable attitude that is characteristic of Mina's style. While one — favorable — reviewer of *Still Midnight* characterizes Mina as patrolling the "mean streets of crime fiction [...] with a full ammunition belt of radical feminist theory,"[8] Mina's work notably refuses to treat feminism as an all-purpose weapon or as a sovereign ethical force that need not attend to nuances of individual circumstances. Paradoxically, the strength of Mina's feminism is evident in the way her novels treat gender equality as a project in progress, to be investigated and re-investigated from multiple perspectives, as I will now outline before turning to a detailed reading of *Still Midnight*.

Garnethill (1998) certainly depicts a form of direct feminist justice. Central character Maureen copes with her own past; with the murder of her married psychiatrist boyfriend, Douglas Brady; with police who suspect her of the crime; and eventually with the real killer, Angus Farrell, another psychiatrist, who has sadistically abused female patients and has murdered a suspicious Douglas. Maureen and her best friend, Leslie — who runs an underfunded shelter for women — protect one of the surviving victims, Siobhain McCloud, both from insensitive police questioning and from Farrell's attempts to silence her. With Leslie's encouragement, Maureen lures Farrell to a remote island, doses him with LSD, and leaves him handcuffed to a bed for the police. As Robert P. Winston suggests, this punishment can be seen as partly analogous to what Farrell has inflicted on his female victims.[9] Winston argues that Maureen's success in subduing Farrell indicates "that it is possible for women to act on behalf of themselves and others, but the sorts of actions available to them are influenced by the socialization of a fundamentally patriarchal Glaswegian society."[10] Accordingly, Winston reads *Garnethill* and its two sequels, *Exile* (2000) and *Resolution* (2001), as concerned with "an interrogation of [...] social structures,"[11] especially legal systems, that fail to allow for the complexities of cases such as Maureen's. Winston argues persuasively that "the trilogy encourages a shift from an ethic of rights and individualism to an ethic of responsibility and collectivity" but that it eschews any "utopian fantasy" of individual actions like Maureen's leading directly to large-scale social change.[12] Yet, the trilogy also endorses individual questioning of heavy-handed institutional authority: in this respect, and in light of Mina's most recent books, its key scene may be an early one in which Maureen, under interrogation by vain and arrogant Detective Chief Inspector Joe McEwan about her visits to psychiatric clinics, reverses their roles:

"How did you find out about the Rainbow [clinic]?"
"You were seen, in the paper."
"How could they see me in the paper?"
McEwan's face flushed very red very suddenly. He bent forward, his voice was staggeringly loud. "STOP ASKING ME QUESTIONS."[13]

Inaugurating Maureen's own investigation, this exchange illustrates a rhetorical judo that counters the force of an over-assertive male, and exemplifies Mina's close observation of her feminist protagonists' negotiation of Glasgow's power structures.

However, in the novel she published immediately following the *Garnethill* trilogy, Mina complicates the feminist authority with which her work, as both academic researcher and crime novelist, has endowed her. As Plain summarizes, *Sanctum* (2002; published in the U.S. as *Deception*) "displaces the political for an examination of middle-class masculinity,"[14] as its focal character, Lachlan Harriot, a failed physician, aspiring writer, and house-husband, describes his efforts to exonerate his wife Susie, a forensic psychiatrist convicted of murdering a serial killer she has been assessing. However, Lachlan's text is framed by a Prologue and Epilogue both signed "Denise Mina, Glasgow, 2002," which open the possibility that his reported investigation has been a fabrication. The ambiguities built into *Sanctum* allow Mina to register that women too can be violent psychopaths or abusers of institutional power, while simultaneously suggesting how such possibilities may be used to demonize assertive women. To be sure, the frame narrative itself calls for sceptical reading, since in making a version of herself into a character, Mina implies the possible unreliability of her own writing, and she also skirmishes with self-subversion by centering the story on a suspect female authority figure not unlike herself in academic background. Paradoxically, though, such self-reflexive touches help in the long run to identify Mina as a feminist writer notable both for assertiveness and for readiness to invite scrutiny of her own assumptions.

Mina's long view of feminism is particularly evident in the series she began following *Sanctum*, which follows the progress of Glasgow journalist Patricia (Paddy) Meehan in the male-dominated culture of the 1980s. The retrospective focus implies that the recent past of feminism is continuous with the present; like the *Garnethill* trilogy, these books cast a critical eye on institutions that enable men to abuse power, while they also convey a sense of individuals, both male and female, as works in progress. In the second of the three volumes published thus far, *The Dead Hour* (2006), set in 1984, Paddy investigates the fate of Vhari Burnett, a respected prosecutor murdered after refusing help from police and from Paddy herself. The story puts Paddy at odds with the Thatcherite editor of her paper, who embodies crass tabloid misogyny:

"Good. Good story, it's got legs. Burnett was a good-looking bird, it'll keep going."
She couldn't disguise her lip curl and he saw it.
"Meehan, don't give me any women's lib *shit*." Ramage hissed the word. "I haven't got time for that crap."
"No, Boss." She spoke so flatly, eyes half-closed, that they both heard her telling him that she hated him.[15]

Despite his treatment of women as commodities, however, Ramage recognizes what is at stake when Paddy's investigation implicates senior policemen and endangers her (280–281). Since Mina's series gets its own "legs" by dramatizing the adventures of an attractive woman, Paddy herself, Ramage's partial redemption seems fitting, and it moderates Mina's critique of patriarchal authority by implicitly acknowledging a difference between the journalist's reflexive misogynistic rhetoric and the physical violence inflicted by the men Paddy is pursuing. Paddy goes on to accomplish what Vhari Burnett died in attempting, by saving Vhari's sister, Kate, a cocaine addict who has stolen a large quantity of the drug from her well-connected but brutal boyfriend. As the thug sent by the drug kingpin prepares to kill Kate, Paddy hits him fatally over the head with a heavy cooking pot (314). This intervention echoes climactic events in the *Garnethill* trilogy—not only from the first volume but especially from the third, *Resolution*, where, after Farrell evades legal punishment for his crimes, he again attempts to silence his former victim, Siobhain, and in self-defense she smashes his skull with "a cast-iron frying-pan."[16] In both cases the improvised weapon's domestic associations evoke the conventionally feminine and also the everyday, suggesting that self-assertion for women can be as much a response to unpredictable circumstance as an overarching programme.

However, the concluding chapters of *The Dead Hour* turn notably away from neat closure or simplistic celebration of empowered women over brutish men. Paddy meets, for the first time, her namesake, Patrick Meehan, a figure who has been a kind of double to her: "He had been found guilty of a high-profile murder when Paddy was just a child and the accident of their names meant that she followed the story all through her childhood, hearing before most people in the city that he was innocent [...]" (15). Her career has been inspired partly by the bond she feels with Patrick Meehan across boundaries of age and gender, and when they are introduced, she begins negotiations with the wary man for a project to counter the "trashy book[s]" that have sensationalized his story. Her sense, and Mina's, of what constitutes "a good book" (334) about crime and its investigation is inclusive, and the refusal to binarize gender is concisely evoked in the third book in the series, *The Last Breath* (2007), set in 1990, which has Paddy balancing single motherhood with a progressing but precarious career. Observing her newspaper colleagues at a funeral, she contemplates "a hundred and fifty men, some arseholes, some good souls, most both depending on the occasion."[17] The audacious rhyme "arseholes"/"good souls" reinforces the both/and logic: not an inane relativism but a view of gender relations as situationally specific and shaped by ongoing negotiation.

The Paddy Meehan series still appears open for volumes set in the 1990s, often identified as a key decade for "postfeminism." However, Mina's *Still Midnight* (2009) begins another series, set in the present and, as noted earlier, featuring for the first time a female protagonist who is a police officer. Despite her institutional status, Strathclyde Detective Sergeant Alex Morrow shares traits with Maureen and Paddy: her social background makes her an outsider to institutions such as the police, and her pugnacity sets her at odds with authority even while it helps her persevere. She also shares with Paddy characteristics that operate against essentialization of her femininity. Like Paddy, she uses a gender-neutral diminutive as her first name—and the narrative voice identifies her variably by first name and by surname, allowing for her gender to recede from view at times, though it is also foregrounded on occasion. Further, like Paddy, Alex has a male double: her half-brother, Danny McGrath, is a gangster, and the two of them, children of different mothers but the same father, also a criminal, are alike in age and in looks, and seemingly have a mutual regard despite their divergent career paths. Needing to keep her background obscure, since, as she reflects, "[p]olice liked the absolute value of 'them and us,'"[18] Alex is resentfully conscious of being seen as a dark horse within the police force. Thus, it is not simply her gender that makes her an outsider, and the complexity of her personal story helps generate suspense.

Still Midnight's main crime plot begins when the ordinary Glasgow home of the Anwar family is invaded by two armed, masked men who demand someone called "Bob." The thugs, Eddy and Pat, panic when they cannot identify such a person, and Pat accidentally shoots the family's 16-year-old daughter Aleesha in the hand when she impulsively attempts to unmask him. The pair then abduct the father, Aamir, a mild-mannered shopkeeper. The narrative shifts freely among the viewpoints of characters, but alternates spatially between the thugs on the run with their disoriented victim, and the police investigation centered on the Anwar household. Morrow arrives on the scene biting her own finger in suppressed resentment provoked by her colleague and rival, DS Grant Bannerman, whom she sees as the unworthy beneficiary of patriarchal cronyism: "She thought he aspired to look like a surfer but he looked like a careerist to her, a boy whose dad was in the force and introduced him to senior officers" (25). This judgement is qualified as Morrow reflects on her own personality: "If Morrow worked with herself she'd try and sit a few desks away" (26). However, having observed Bannerman's flawed management of the crime scene, she cannot keep from challenging their superior, DCI MacKechnie, over his evasively-explained decision to put Bannerman in charge:

> "Personal factors make us suitable for some cases," he said, "and not for others. You'll get the next one."
> Typical MacKechnie. Never said anything outright. Delicate situation, he wanted to say, all Asians hate women and anyway, you're a nut case [30].

The exchange is delicately nuanced in its presentation of Morrow's perception of MacKechnie's assumptions about "Asian," or Muslim, attitudes toward women. Apparently, the DCI is glibly invoking a received form of liberal feminism, insinuating that Glaswegian Muslims are out of step with enlightened attitudes that have become, supposedly, the norm in the city's institutions; at the same time, he is slighting one of his own capable female detectives— though the exchange also leaves open the possibility that she is sensing deviousness in what her superior intends as tact.

Close examination of the scene continues, with Morrow contemplating the younger son of the Anwar family, Omar, and his friend Mo, a witness to the events at the house: "Those guys didn't care if she was female or male. She was ten years older than them, she might as well have been a man and she knew the South Side. If anyone's personal factors made them suitable it was her" (31). Impelled by these thoughts, Morrow persists in her assertiveness with MacKechnie: "'Sir, that's ...' she was regretting it before the word even tumbled past her lips, 'racist'" (31). The senior policeman's understated response sustains ambiguity about his real attitudes: "MacKechnie didn't turn to speak and his voice was less than a murmur. 'Never speak to me like that again'" (31). While Paddy, in the 1980s, deals with male superiors who are overtly misogynistic, and while Maureen, in the 1990s, encounters male police detectives who are openly paternalistic, Morrow operates in an institutional culture where gender equality is, in theory, established, yet where men still wield most of the power, and where figures like MacKechnie are difficult to deal with precisely because they are fluent in a language of egalitarianism: "MacKechnie was not comfortable being in charge, she felt, and apologized for his status by pretending to listen. He had a leadership style that would be described with a lot of bullshit buzzwords: inclusive, facilitative, enabling" (77). The presence of these "bullshit buzzwords" registers a degree of feminist influence upon the traditionally masculinist environment of policing in Glasgow, even as it also suggests that gender equality may be — or appear to a woman such as Alex — an exercise in discursive performance as much as an established fact.

As the investigation proceeds under the vague direction of what Morrow labels MacKechnie's "vegetarian management style" (133), Morrow's professional capability is less at issue than her ability to restrain the urge to undermine Bannerman. When the kidnappers' van is found in a field, she and Bannerman interview the landowner and a local policeman, who ponderously reports finding nothing significant, enabling Morrow to administer an implicit insult to her rival:

> Bannerman snorted, looking to Morrow to laugh along with him: a bonding moment between colleagues.
> "Have you actually done a search?" she pointed towards the van.
> "Not yet, ma'am, no."
> "How do you know then? Get that man out beyond the tape." She walked off into the field, leaving Bannerman to stand with the two men he had been ridiculing a moment ago.
> Even she was starting to wonder if she was an arsehole [98–99].

This chapter-ending passage illustrates the text simultaneously evoking more than one postfeminist condition. Even as Morrow's self-interrogatory afterthought suggests that she is unsure her putting of the men in their place is warranted, her use of the gender-neutral "arsehole"—rather than an epithet such as "bitch"—implies that she takes a degree of gender equality for granted.

Swearing is important to the ways in which Mina's novels—and Campbell's—connect issues of gender to questions of authority. In a 2001 article, Kate E. Brown and Howard I. Kushner point to the complexities of swearing as a means of self-assertion: "Cursing always reflects the success of cultural discipline, but it does so only in the breach; cursing is at once conventional and an eruption of and within convention [....] Thus, the scandal of cursing stems perhaps less from its obscenity than from the way that the obscene refutes notions of linguistic and bodily self-possession that law itself requires."[19] This discussion suggests why cursing is often prominent in crime fiction, as an expression of eruptive forces that challenge laws and their enforcers; it also indicates why curse-words are often double-edged weapons. Brown and Kushner observe further that "the maledictory force of words like *cunt* or *fuck* is a cultural endowment over time; they are words that have absorbed the history of their past speakings. As such, their force exceeds their immediate context: curse words verge toward autonomy, congealing in themselves a quasi-magical and singular capacity to offend. [They ...] are not owned but are only voiced by the speaker."[20] Yet, given this extra-human force curse-words possess, the capacity temporarily to control them by using them in inventive and timely ways can be all the more significant. Brown and Kushner's analysis suggests why the ability to wield profanity as a rhetorical weapon can mark authority in crime fiction both for characters and for authors constructing them, and also for women in an until-recently-male-dominated world.

Swearing, then, can be identified as a tactic of feminist self-assertion in repudiation of expectations that women maintain decorum, but it may also be regarded as linguistic compensation for lack of real power.[21] Mina's characterization of Morrow evokes an ongoing oscillation between these possibilities. An exchange marking an upturn in their working relationship has Morrow and Bannerman uneasily addressing nuances of one of the most potent and significantly gendered swear-words:

> Sensing that they were getting on, Bannerman bit his lip. "You all right with me?"
>
> Morrow cleared her throat and shrugged. "Sorry I called you a cunt. I's tired..."
>
> He flinched at that. "You *didn't*. What you said was that we wouldn't get on if I was *going* to be a cunt about it, but you didn't *call* me a cunt."
>
> This semantic difference seemed to matter to him. "Yeah," she said. "No, that's right" [172–173].

While Morrow drops the subject, the text suggests that semantics do matter. Applied by one man to another, *cunt* carries definite connotations of misogyny; here, though, the word is applied under erasure to a man by a woman, and it is the man who flinches. The exchange suggests the power of the word as appropriated, or reappropriated, by a woman not just to convey contempt, but also to manipulate the history of men's abusive usage of it.[22]

Tensions between Morrow and Bannerman soon return: proceeding to see Aleesha in hospital, they pass "the Battlefield Rest, a restaurant in a converted Edwardian tram depot," and Bannerman proves oblivious to the location's significance as the site where, as Morrow tries to explain, "Mary Queen of Scots fought her last battle" in 1568 (174–175). While Bannerman's evident ignorance of this feminine dimension of Scotland's history adds implicitly to his characterization as a product of patriarchal obtuseness, it is, ironically, a form of self-feminization on his part that proves decisive in his and Morrow's rivalry: as the Anwar investigation stalls, he takes compassionate leave to attend to his hospitalized mother. Morrow is provoked into finally using "the dirtiest word she knew," albeit privately: "The cunt was ducking the cunting fucking case because he was a cunt and he was using his stinking fucking mother's pneumonia to do it" (289). Despite the apparent impotence of Morrow's profane rage, its eruption marks the point where the investigation becomes hers to conclude. Her outburst also connects to what the narrative has gradually revealed to be compelling personal reasons for her to behave like an "arsehole": she and her husband have barely spoken since the death of their young son from meningitis some months previously, a trauma that has only just been revealed (282–285). As MacKechnie hands over the case to her, she senses his veiled contempt for her background and his awareness that the "dark belligerent void" left by her personal loss makes her formidable, and she responds with a decisive moment of self-assertion:

> "This case is a great opportunity for you —"
> "This case is big fat bollocks and you know it. The family are lying out of their arses. Thirty-six hours since he was taken and every minute that passes makes it less likely that we'll find the man alive —"
> MacKechnie couldn't take it any more. He stood up and hissed at her, "Do your job. Get out" [290].

This cathartic confrontation is the turning-point of the book, setting up what will prove, somewhat unexpectedly, the most unambiguously upbeat resolution in a Mina novel to date.

Morrow's investigations reveal the home invaders' target as the Anwar family's eldest son, Billal, a seemingly solid citizen who has been operating a lucrative tax fraud on imported vehicles. (Billal's anglicized street name is Bill, which Eddy, receiving telephone instructions from a mysterious

Ulsterman behind the raid, has confused with Bob.) In a cunning twist on the text's earlier critical treatment of stereotypical European notions of Muslim family life, Billal is the most conservative of the Anwars in his religious and social views, and the profits from his racket turn up hidden in the bedroom he shares with his wife Meeshra, who has joined the household in an arranged marriage and claims to be confined to bed for postpartum medical reasons. Mina thus casts a suspicious eye on any view of women's place as domestic, even while she uses the Anwar family as a whole to indicate that Muslim families can accommodate progressive attitudes to gender roles. In the final chapters, further twists hinge on the self-assertion of Aleesha. Her independence, introduced in her attempt to unmask Pat, has been confirmed through other family members' perspectives. As her father endures his ordeal, he reflects on her: "a bad daughter: rotten, opinionated, disobedient. He adored her, she got all that from Sadiqa, all of that anger and energy was why he had fallen in love with her mother" (121). Sadiqa herself tells Morrow that "[s]tubborn girls" are a "[f]amily trait" (183). Perhaps most memorably, Omar admiringly describes Aleesha to Morrow: "'Mental. Scared of none of them. Told Meeshra to fuck off and shut up when she was in labour'" (254). However, the extent of Aleesha's independence will still prove startling.

The kidnapping of Aamir, like the rest of the book, plays out unexpectedly. The home invaders, Eddy and Pat, appear alike as low-grade "hard men," but their differences emerge as their plans go awry. Deftly, Mina registers that "hard men" are no more uniform in their identities than are (say) women or Muslims. Pat, despite having shot Aleesha, is much less brutish and more self-aware than Eddy, whom he mistrusts as having "nothing left to be but hard" (52) and whom he fears will simply murder Aamir. Pat's distance from Eddy widens with his recurring thoughts of the Anwar family's pleasant home, and of Aleesha, who has responded with favorable signals to his "frank admiration" (9) before the accidental shooting. Hidden in an abandoned warehouse, Aamir escapes to safety — in the process accidentally killing his guard, Pat's heroin-addict cousin Malki, in the book's only homicide. Abandoned by Pat, Eddy is arrested in an attempt to claim a ransom for Aamir, while the mysterious ex-terrorist Ulsterman behind the raid dies of heart failure. In a still more farfetched development, Pat, renaming himself Roy, goes to Aleesha's hospital ward, where their mutual attraction rekindles, and the two of them go off together — even though Aleesha, as she makes clear on the final page, recognizes him as the man who shot her. The book's closing lines project the couple into their future: "Despite the odds Roy and Aleesha clung tight to each other for a long, long time, until her legs were stiff and he felt very, very old" (356).

In *Still Midnight*, "despite the odds," Mina seems to embrace the utopianism she eschews in the *Garnethill* trilogy. Avoidance of over-neat closure has helped distinguish her work, but here, she deploys a romantic resolution so improbable that, in the context of her career, it both paradoxically supplies a surprise ending and invites reading as a deliberate statement. The happy ending extends to Morrow, who repudiates her gangster brother connected to Billal's fraud scheme (337), revives her bond with her husband (341–342), and gains due credit for her investigation (344). Arguably, the book amounts to another self-reflexive experiment in Mina's work: an overtly and polemically fictional vision of a world where violent conflict need not have permanently disastrous effects and old divisions of gender, race, or class, can be overcome, driven away, or driven away from. With reportedly the highest murder rate in Western Europe[23] in spite of the renewal of recent years, Glasgow may still seem a natural setting for particularly violent crime fiction, so by playing with readerly expectations and by displacing violence into verbal conflict, *Still Midnight* challenges labelling of Glasgow as an essentially "hard" city even while it contests simplistic postindustrial rebranding.[24]

Campbell

Karen Campbell's *The Twilight Time* (2008), *After the Fire* (2009), and *Shadowplay* (2010) are comparable to Mina's work in their attention to their Glasgow settings and especially in their mixture of authoritative detail — drawing on Campbell's experience as a Strathclyde police officer — with frequent twists of dialogue and characterization. Like Mina's books, Campbell's generate suspense and social resonance not only through compelling crime plots but also through close attention to procedure on a micro level. Campbell's central character, Detective Sergeant Anna Cameron, differs notably from Mina's Alex Morrow in background: where Alex's father was a gangster, Anna's was a policeman, killed in the line of duty when Anna was a child, and in circumstances that the series so far leaves open for further exposition. While Anna is less an outsider than Alex as regards social status, they share an assertiveness that empowers them yet borders on dangerous volatility.

Campbell's books also share with Mina's a directness of tone that verges on abrasiveness, thus imparting the kind of anti-authoritarian textual authority mentioned above. *The Twilight Time* begins with Anna's arrival at a new job with a "'Flexible Policing Unit'" designed to combat street crime in Glasgow's city center. Entering the unit's station, she encounters a passively hostile desk sergeant, who gives directions grudgingly, then — apparently — mutters a crude anatomical insult:

"What was that?" asked Anna.

The man kept his head down, white flakes dropping as his stubby hand stroked the grey.

"You say something?" she asked.

"Naw."

"Could have sworn I heard you say 'split-arse'?"

Viscous eyes looked up at her, a slight flush on the hollows below.

"What's that supposed tae mean?"

"You tell me."

"Naw, your hearing must be away tae buggery, hen."

"Just like your good looks, you mean?"

"First floor, like I said. Then turn left." His eyes slumped back to his paperwork.[25]

This exchange introduces the potential for small-scale conflict that Anna, as a successful female officer, meets daily. It also registers the cultural influence of feminism, through the evident fact that abusive gendered terms like "split-arse" are relegated to the uncertain borders of discourse in the once male-dominated space of a police station. Yet, as in *Still Midnight*, the now-furtive status of misogyny raises new questions. There is ambiguity about the verbal conflict — did the old sergeant utter the insulting epithet for sure? — which introduces uncertainty about the validity of Anna's assertiveness. Is she responding legitimately to a definite insult, or perhaps imagining a more virulent kind of hostility than is actually present, and thus letting the history of misogynistic abuse taint the present? While the encounter with the decrepit sergeant ends inconclusively, it signals how assertiveness will be both a vital resource for Anna and yet at times a trigger for trouble. As in *Still Midnight*, the ambiguities of such assertiveness help sustain a combined exploration and questioning of contemporary forms of postfeminism.

The opening chapter continues to invite alert reading as it characterizes Anna's new colleagues — or her perceptions of them. This is her impression of a subordinate, Derek Waugh: "ruddy, pock-marked cheeks, brown wiry hair, brown moustache, brown jacket stretched around his stocky frame — and everything with a sweaty, slightly slimy sheen. Like a wee turd on legs. Anna liked him straight off" (5–6). As often in Mina's writing, there is a sentence-level enactment of surprise; there is also a subversion of gendered expectations, here involving the assumption that a turd-like man will represent what is toxic or wasteful in masculinity. Anna goes on to meet her new boss, a Superintendent who does seem to evince, in abundance, stereotypical sexism: "'Anna, isn't it? I'm Mr Rankin. I'll be brief, dear. As you know, you weren't the first choice for the job. Granted, we need some females to deal with the hoors, but [....] I'm concerned about your background. You've not got much operational experience, have you?'"(6–7). Receiving Rankin's condescending instructions, Anna — much like Paddy Meehan with her editor in *The Dead Hour* — is silenced in anger: "She kept her face blank. *Blink twice for 'Fuck off and die'*" (8).

Campbell's inclusion of an aging and unsympathetic namesake of Ian Rankin in the first chapter of her first novel appears to be an extremely assertive proclamation of a changing of the guard in Scottish crime fiction. However, Campbell's characterization of Superintendent Rankin can also be read as an unorthodox tribute to Ian Rankin as an influential practitioner of the state-of-society novel disguised as crime fiction. Given the iconoclasm of his books, an overtly reverential allusion to Rankin would be less apt than this seemingly-antagonistic one. Moreover, Campbell's Rankin character eventually proves — in a way typical of the book's complexities — more flexible and self-aware than he seems. Well into the narrative, he rebukes Anna over what he sees as her mishandling of her authority. However, after she defends her work, he praises her for not "pull[ing] the female card," tells her that he is "a nasty bastard" because of chronic arthritis from an on-the-job kneecapping, and then alludes startlingly to an undercover operation she is undertaking among the sex workers of the area: "'I'm sure you'll look better in stockings than I do, Sergeant'" (270). While this remark might be just a friendlier version of "we need some females to deal with the hoors," it also alludes to the idea that gendered roles — like professional roles — may be performances rather than expressions of essential identity, something also suggested by the fact that the area patrolled by Anna's unit, like the book's opening chapter, is called the "Drag."

Both Anna's assertiveness and her ambivalence in this environment are highlighted as the opening chapter progresses. Exploring the "Drag," she looks askance at Derek's pragmatic familiarity with the area's prostitutes. When one of the women remarks on Anna's evident distaste — "'She aye [always] look like she's stood in shit, Mr. Waugh?'" — he jocularly replies that Anna is a "'pure ball-breaker'" (16). Detailing Anna's uncertainty over whether to treat the remark as insubordination, the narrative again indicates that her self-assertion goes hand-in-hand with self-interrogation: "A good cop learned the balance of charm and harm; always weighing up the options at her disposal. Anna, then, was not a good cop. Lash out first, before the bastards got you — that's what she always did." Reasoning, though, that "if she lost Derek, she lost them all," Anna grudgingly accepts her subordinate's assurances that his measures are effective: "'Fine.' The tiny word was painful. 'I'll take your word for it. But, Derek, don't *ever* call me a ball-breaker again'" (17). Soon after, however, Anna is accosted by a small-time would-be hard man and with some difficulty subdues him — whereupon, as the chapter ends, Derek reprises his earlier description:

"I'm sorry, Anna," said Derek, "but I have to say it. Lenny, my man, congratulations. You've just met our new ball-breaker."
   Anna smiled as enigmatically as she could, what with the blood trickling out her nose [20].

This opening to the book, and the series, positions Anna as a postfeminist figure capable of projecting power and authority under stress, but her ambivalence about the tag of "ball-breaker" also indicates her unease in the role even as she exploits the tactical value of being enigmatic.

Anna's relations with other women are at least as enigmatic as those with men. The Flexi unit includes a female officer, Jenny Heath, who is initially an antagonistic double for Anna herself. Anna's first impression of Jenny is that she is "[m]ade up with a trowel" (5), and that she and the women of the "Drag" "[p]robably swap make-up tips" (18). As the text shows through flexible deployment of multiple points-of view, Jenny's perception of Anna is equally harsh and stereotypical: "Sergeant Anna obviously had problems with women in the job [....] See the way she looked down that witch's nose, like an old film star— Bette Davis or Greta Garbo— one of those haughty cold bitches" (56). Tension between Anna and Jenny ramifies along with the book's main plotlines, which concern the unit's investigations of two seemingly distinct patterns of crime: a series of vicious knife attacks on prostitutes, and the ongoing racial harassment of local citizens. On a night patrol, Jenny resentfully confronts her fears of failing to prevent another attack and of being targeted herself: "That witch Cameron knew. That's why she chose Jenny for night shift" (62–63). Jenny goes on to discover the body of Ezra Wajerski, a gentlemanly Second World War veteran previously targeted by anti-semitic graffiti. Later, after Jenny has vented her fear and resentment by drunkenly mocking Anna (76–77), Anna herself is injured in pursuit of the slasher (122–123). Eventually, however, the "drag" operation mentioned above, where Anna and Jenny impersonate prostitutes, brings results. The description of their costumes reiterates the ambiguities of postfeminism: "Pneumatic breasts and long black legs were perverse and liberating all at once, and they both walked up and down the corridors and offices more times than they needed, feigning impatience at the catcalls and whistles" (272). Yet, perversity comes to the fore, even as the operation succeeds. While Anna is hassled by a group of young men, the slasher strikes again and is arrested; proceeding on foot to the scene, and ignoring further, drive-by, abuse, she wryly parallels her assumed role with her regular one: "It was universal then, that feeling; when what you wore overtly invited contempt. Women in uniform, pretending they didn't care" (281).

Reflections like these reiterate hints that identities, professional or personal, are performances of provisional guises more than expressions of essential being. The references to "drag" evoke Judith Butler's influential ideas. In *Gender Trouble* (1990), Butler argues that "*in imitating gender, drag implicitly reveals the imitative structure of gender itself— as well as its contingency.*"[26] Cross-dressing, in this view, does not simply parody conventional, normative conduct, but points to gendered identities as ideological constructs reinforced by ritualized repetition. A claim that Campbell's books themselves—or Mina's—treat gender or sexuality as *nothing but* performance would seem to be unwarranted. Indeed, so could a claim that gendered sexuality is all ideology and no biology: Butler's account of heterosexuality, in particular, has been challenged by critics such as Jonathan Dollimore, who argues in *Sex, Literature and Censorship* (2001) that Butler neglects "the diversity of what most straight people are, and what they might do."[27] Campbell's deployment of Anna, nevertheless, suggests how Butler's work, and the debates it has generated, has fostered mainstream awareness that gender and sexuality are not simply expressions of biological destiny, and that even heterosexual identity needs to be understood as something perilously negotiated rather than straightforwardly expressed.

Plot resolution in *The Twilight Time* extends Campbell's attention to the uncertainties of an environment no longer necessarily dominated by prescriptive gender roles. Following the arrest of the slasher, Anna confronts him in his cell, goads him into provoking her verbally, and beats him savagely in payback for her earlier injuries; only Jenny's uneasy collusion averts disciplinary disaster (284–285). As in Mina's work, summary justice meted out by assertive women to abusive men is examined as "perverse and liberating all at once"—and not as definitively representable by one case. Near the end of the book, after the slasher has been identified as a Protestant extremist and gangster, and also as (it seems) Wajerski's killer, Anna and Jenny do attain a moment of gendered bonding as Anna asks about an unusual absence of male officers from their squad room:

> "Where's the guys?'
> "Watching some vital Scotland match in the southern hemisphere. Well, in the refreshment room, but, you know what I mean." Jenny lit up a fag.
> "So, what's the drill for tonight? I brought my sussies" [334]

The book concludes, however, not by poising Anna and Jenny as a team of postfeminist action heroes complete with costumes, but with further emphasis on the open-endedness of their work. Following up Wajerski's case, Anna realizes he has actually been killed by a prostitute, Francine, when his unusually aggressive behavior during one of their regular meetings triggered her traumatic memory of an abusive grandfather (338). In the book's final paragraphs, Anna, much as Alex does in *Still Midnight* with Mary, Queen of Scots, meditates on Glasgow's neglected feminine history: "Anna kept walking down to St Enoch Square, named for St Thenew, mother of Glasgow's patron saint. Her boy, St Mungo, was everywhere — in crests, museums, schools [....] No one remembered Thenew; raped as a child, thrown from a cliff in her father's shame and left to drift to Culross in a coracle. But it was from her that Mungo had sprung" (338).[28] While she has found Wajerski charming, Anna's final action in the book reflects her sense of the war hero's less chivalrous side: she drops into the river Clyde a medal he has given her (339). Combining a plot-twist with implicit revision of earlier passages where Anna is impatient with what she sees as feminist dogma,[29] this conclusion represents a kind of stealth feminism that will recur in Campbell's series.

The series generates further plot impetus from the complexities of Anna's personal life, whose ongoing uncertainties suggest the contingency of postfeminist heterosexuality. In *The Twilight Time* Anna re-encounters Jamie Worth, an old boyfriend from police training college, who eventually left her for another young officer, Cath, but for whom she still has feelings. These feelings eventually lead her, whilst recuperating from her fall, to make advances which he only just succeeds in resisting (193) and which threaten his marriage as Cath senses his temptation. Thus superficially summarized, the Anna-Jamie-Cath triangle evokes the formulaic varieties of postfeminist fiction that Tasker and Negra's volume critiques, but here too Campbell sets up appearances to be challenged. Cath has given up her own police career to be a full-time parent, but becomes involved in the investigation of the murder of Wajerski, whom she has known, and she co-operates with Anna, albeit uneasily. Like Jenny's perceptions of Anna, Cath's serve to develop her characterization as an ambiguous figure: Cath sees her at times as a threat, yet also as a potential friend. Alongside Anna's uneasy relations with Jenny, her dealings with Cath convey that there is no one programmatically correct postfeminist career path. Further, attention to Cath's perspective links *The Twilight Time* to the second book of the series, *After the Fire*, in whose first half Cath becomes the focal character as Jamie is wrongly jailed after the shooting of an unarmed girl in a botched police operation. Cath feels dumbed-down by the demands of child-care on her own: "Food goes in your mouth, poo comes out your bum. Anything else was a bonus; or a mystery to be interrogated."[30] Yet, the ironic allusion to interrogation parallels the rigors of parenting with those of policing, and reiterates that Cath is as complex a figure as Anna.

Anna herself, meanwhile, promoted to Inspector, is in New York on secondment with a United Nations Task Force concerned with global human rights protection. Her interest in the position stems from her career ambitions, but also from her time in "the Drag" and experiences such as an encounter with young women trafficked to Glasgow from Eastern Europe (103). Hoping for a long-term UN post, Anna blows her chances under interview with the "instant and instinctive" declaration that she would "'[a]bsolutely not'" wear a veil if serving in a Muslim country (220). In the ensuing argument, Anna elaborates vehemently: "'I don't define myself by my gender. It's my uniform, and how I conduct myself, that earns respect. And it's the office my uniform stands for, which I would be representing in any country I served in. *That's* what articulates who I am, not the fact that I have breasts.'" Yet "shortly after," she rebukes herself for "blasting out loose opinions that only turned to firm conviction in the very process of uttering them" (221). Anna's undoing may be attributed to ongoing tension between egalitarian/liberal varieties of feminism and postfeminist sensitivity to cultural difference,[31] but it can also be read on a more individual level. Like Alex Morrow, she is unwilling or unable to subordinate her views to political expediencies; moreover, with Anna, as with Alex, identity is indeed shaped in its articulation or performance, rather than implemented from fixed concepts, and feminism is a lived reality rather than an inflexible programme.

Both Campbell's Anna and Mina's Alex are constructed as trustworthy partly because they repeatedly question themselves—but also because their partly-improvised methods are, partly, successful. Following Anna's return to Glasgow, she uses her UN connections to intervene clandestinely in Jamie's case, and the decisive scene in *After the Fire* is her unpremeditated showdown with the female superior officer, DCI Nikki Armstrong, who has orchestrated Jamie's scapegoating in order to protect another male officer with whom she is involved. Spotting Armstrong surrounded by sycophantic subordinates in a bar, Anna looks scornfully at the senior officer's demeanors as a "professional woman in her mid-forties, thinking it was okay to don a tight (bursting out of its half-done buttons, in fact) satin blouse and white skinny jeans for a work night out" (418). Anna's perception of Armstrong links the senior officer's corruption to what Ariel Levy critiques, in her 2005 book *Female Chauvinist Pigs*, as "raunch culture," under which sexual posturing has come misleadingly to signify real empowerment for women.[32] Following Armstrong into the women's washroom to confront her, Anna experiences a characteristic moment of ambivalence about her own clothing, assuring herself that her jeans are "[n]ot tight, just fitted" (419). Still unsure of herself, Anna confronts Armstrong with an appeal to justice, which the woman dismisses contemptuously: "'Fuck *justice*. It's survival of the fittest'" (421). Anna responds by asking, "'So you speak in stereotypes as well as act like one?'" (422). Interesting here is that Anna herself is characterized partly in terms of stereotypes, yet always in shifting and uncertain relation to them. Campbell's books, even more strongly than Mina's, indicate that there may be no escape from such role-playing, only degrees of self-awareness within it. Yet as the exchange suggests, Campbell, like Mina, treats commitment to the pursuit of justice as something that is, however complicated, perhaps the closest thing to an essential feminist trait.[33] Anna outwits Armstrong with a specific piece of role-playing: she improvises a pretence of wearing a wire and succeeds in bluffing Armstrong into panicking and eventually admitting the truth of Jamie's case. As the book ends with Jamie and Cath reunited, however, Anna's own personal uncertainty persists.

Campbell's third book, *Shadowplay*, extends her examination of complications and ironies of women's accession to authority, continuing to position Anna as both ambitious high-performer and impulsive maverick. Having earned promotion to Chief Inspector, she encounters another problematic female superior, Chief Superintendent Marion Hamilton — manipulative, arbitrary, and driven by a pre-emptive aggression that Anna diagnoses as "Margaret Thatcher syndrome," then renames as "Mrs Hamilton Syndrome."[34] The book's main plotlines, the gang murder of a young South Asian man and the disappearance of a woman from a seniors' home, converge in a crucial scene, which also exemplifies both Campbell's nuanced handling of Anna's volatility and her detailed attention to Glasgow as a site of postfeminist as well as postindustrial culture. Anna's investigations — which she, characteristically, pursues in spite of Hamilton's attempts to sideline her — take her to a lap-dancing club in the district of Govan, once a hub of the shipbuilding industry and now being gradually gentrified and redeveloped:

> It was "a hauf and a hauf" place right enough. So why not young girls in patent boots and sad, eager breasts, employed to dance in a dingy, thin townhouse that looked on to Elder Park? In their fag breaks, the girls could gaze over to the statue of Isabella Elder, a woman way ahead of her time, who dedicated her life and fortune to promoting the advancement and education of Glasgow's females, freeing her sisters to be doctors and teachers and hot-to-trot babes [369].

As Anna enters the club, the text revisits the idea of gender identity as partly a function of costume and performance. Admitted to the building by a young woman wearing a "pelmet pretending to be a skirt," Anna becomes acutely conscious of her own costume: "She too was in full uniform: black trousers, black T-shirt, black stab-proof vest. Natty bowler hat [....] Not the stern, handsome, gloss-peaked cap the male cops wore. Were women's heads a different density, a different shape? Her hat itched like buggery, an unyielding rim which was migraine-tight" (370). Anna's view of a stripper onstage extends the comparison of gendered uniforms: "Posing hands on hips, she fluttered eyes painted blue, gold and green — but the most shocking color was her pink hairless groin" (372). The idea of total nudity as anything but natural is reiterated when Anna confronts the woman, who identifies herself as the club's boss, wears "her body like a favourite outfit," and asserts that there is "'nothing freer than dancing bollock-naked with a crowd of tossers bursting their flies for you'" (374).[35] Yet, Anna's unease with her own uniform puts her on a continuum with the women she is assessing, rather than in a position of detached superiority, and the implied indictment of "raunch culture" is all the more effective for Anna's impatience with dogmatic brands of feminism and for her own demonstrated capacity to curse. Rather than a relatively predictable — if very possibly warranted — feminist censure of the exploitative practices of lap-dancing clubs, there is a forensic satirization of their crass and bizarre rituals.

The depiction of nudity as a type of costume or uniform also helps characterize stripping as the industrialized performance of a gendered and commodified identity. The characterization of the club as exploitative is reinforced with the (narratively convenient) arrival of its real owner, Jazz Chaddha, the slick gangster who — as Anna realizes during her incursion (376) — is at the center of the crimes she is investigating. In another spur-of-the-moment act of self-assertion, Anna takes over the club and arrests Chaddha. Her actions prove retroactively justified as evidence mounts of the gangster's range of crimes, including the violent exploitation of South Asian immigrants, which implies a parallel between migratory workers and the exploited women of the lap-dancing club, further linking postfeminism and postindustrial urban development.[36] Despite the positive resolution of the book, which also includes her first sustainable-looking sexual relationship, Anna's self-perceptions remain open to question: the series dramatizes postfeminism for her as an ongoing, uncertain condition. As in Mina's work, narrative open-endedness helps convey the sense that the feminist project too is an ongoing one.

Conclusion

Mina's and Campbell's novels gain strength as detective fictions by challenging and guarding against simplistic assumptions that power for women is always and only a sovereign good. In so doing, they offer evidence that gender equality has become a foundation for further investigations, rather than a subject of debate in itself. Also of interest is the way these books invite questioning of "interrogation," not just as practiced by police, but also as figured in, for example, academic book titles like *Interrogating Postfeminism*, which illustrate the way academic writing too has become a discourse of self-assertion. "Interrogating" a text implies subjecting it to a relentless critique that will force it to confess its secrets and contradictions, but the trope's frequent usage by humanities scholars might itself be interpreted as a confession of anxiety about the efficacy of academic work, or even as evidence of authoritarian tendencies. Hélène Cixous in the essay "Castration or Decapitation" writes, "I say 'masculine interrogation': as we say so-and-so was interrogated by the police. And this interrogation precisely involves the work of signification: 'What is it? Where is it?' A work of meaning, 'This means that,' the predicative distribution that always at the same time orders the constitution of meaning. And while meaning is being constituted, it only gets constituted in a movement in which one of the terms of the couple is destroyed in favor of the other."[37] As Cixous implies, part of the value of feminism is in generating or making space for critiques of injustice that are rigorous yet without the authoritarian associations of interrogation. Crime fictions like Mina's and Campbell's do not treat issues of gender politics (or, for that matter, crimes) as necessarily being neatly soluble through interrogation; moreover, particularly because they are character-driven, open-ended series, they do not require argumentative closure. Alex's and Anna's ongoing debates with themselves sustain suspense in their stories, and also characterize them as postfeminists according to the formulation articulated by Misha Kavka, who argues that "postfeminism" refers most usefully "to this self-reflexive, ethical understanding of feminism: that it continues to seek justice and make gains without [...] measuring [these] gains as advances toward a goal" or indulging in "a fantasy of ending."[38] I am not suggesting, then, that crime fiction should supplant feminist cultural analysis or any other kind of academic writing; I am arguing that novels such as Mina's and Campbell's have the capacity to complement, and not simply to furnish illustrative examples for, academic investigations of postfeminism.

Notes

1. Gill Plain, *Twentieth-Century Crime Fiction: Gender, Sexuality and the Body* (Edinburgh: Edinburgh University Press, 2001), 245.
2. Gill Plain, "Concepts of Corruption: Crime Fiction and the Scottish 'State,'" in Berthold Schoene, ed., *The Edinburgh Companion to Contemporary Scottish Literature* (Edinburgh: Edinburgh University Press, 2007), 135.
3. *Ibid.*, 137.
4. Yvonne Tasker and Diane Negra, "Introduction: Feminist Politics and Postfeminist Culture," in Tasker and Negra, eds., *Interrogating Postfeminism: Gender and the Politics of Popular Culture* (Durham: Duke University Press, 2007), 8.
5. *Ibid.*, 6.
6. Misha Kavka, "Feminism, Ethics, and History, or What Is the 'Post' in Postfeminism?," *Tulsa Studies in Women's Literature*, Spring 2002, 29, accessed 19 February 2011, http://www.jstor.org/stable/4149214.

7. "Biography," accessed 26 June 2011, http://www.denisemina.co.uk/contents/bio.htm.
8. David Robinson review of *Still Midnight* by Denise Mina, *The Scotsman*, 25 July 2009, http://living.scotsman.com/books/Book-review—Still-Midnight.5492036.jp.
9. Robert P. Winston, "'A Duty to Care': Denise Mina's *Garnethill* Series," *Clues: A Journal of Detection*, Winter 2008, 74.
10. Ibid.
11. Ibid., 73.
12. Ibid., 76, 77.
13. Denise Mina, *Garnethill* (London: Bantam, 1998), 105.
14. Plain, "Concepts of Corruption," 135.
15. Denise Mina, *The Dead Hour* (New York: Little, Brown, 2006),122. Subsequent citations will appear parenthetically in the text.
16. Denise Mina, *Resolution* (London: Bantam, 2001), 458.
17. Denise Mina, *The Last Breath* (London: Bantam, 2007), 297.
18. Denise Mina, *Still Midnight* (Toronto: McArthur, 2009), 129. Subsequent citations will appear parenthetically in the text.
19. Kate E. Brown and Howard I. Kushner, "Eruptive Voices: Coprolalia, Malediction, and the Poetics of Cursing," *New Literary History*, Summer 2001, 539, accessed 13 March 2011, http://www.jstor.org/stable/ 20057676.
20. Ibid., 550.
21. In *Swearing: A Social History of Foul Language, Oaths and Profanity in English* (Oxford: Blackwell, 1991), Geoffrey Hughes cites a "more 'liberated' attitude towards swearing" by women as an established "consequence of the feminist movement" (211). He also, however, quotes a 1985 comment by fellow language historian J. L. Dillard: "'An occasional female speaker at a scholarly conference very pointedly, aggressively, and rather self-consciously uses one of the 'four-letter' words in order to demonstrate her freedom to do so. In such a case, however, the calling attention to the usage is tantamount to an admission that it is not really commonplace for women to use such words in public'" (212). Implicit in Dillard's and Hughes's under-substantiated suggestion that swearing by women is little more than an anxious attempt at self-assertion is their own anxiety to contain the potential for postfeminist swearing to disrupt gendered conventions.
22. Relevant to Morrow's exchange with Bannerman are Ruth Wajnryb's observations in *Expletive Deleted: A Good Look at Bad Language* (New York: Free Press, 2005) on the contemporary status of *cunt*: "Women seem largely to have accepted 'their' word becoming a term used most often by males, and mostly in all-male company. This gives the term even greater provocative power on the rare occasion when it is used by a woman. In such instances, there's the sense that it's an import sourced directly from a restricted male discourse. It's as if it comes from beyond the feminine and, in so doing, breaks an additional taboo" (76).
23. Carol Craig, *The Tears that Made the Clyde* (Glendaruel: Argyll, 2010), 37–38.
24. The second Alex Morrow book, *The End of the Wasp Season* (2011), elaborates Mina's characterization of this environment and of Morrow as a maverick whose egalitarian convictions are not merely or mainly part of a self-assertive career program.
25. Karen Campbell, *The Twilight Time* (London: Hodder, 2008), 4. Subsequent citations will appear parenthetically in the text.
26. Judith Butler, *Gender Trouble: Feminism and the Subversion of Identity*, 10th anniversary ed. (New York: Routledge, 1999), 175, italics in original. Taylor & Francis e-Library, 2002, http://lib.myilibrary.com
27. Jonathan Dollimore, *Sex, Literature and Censorship* (Cambridge: Polity, 2001), 40.

28. On St Thenew, see e.g. Craig, 173.
29. See, e.g., 262.
30. Karen Campbell, *After the Fire* (London: Hodder, 2009), 38. Subsequent citations will appear parenthetically in the text.
31. See, e.g., Kavka, 35.
32. Levy succinctly evokes the simulacral shallowness of "raunch" in asking, "how is imitating a stripper or a porn star — a woman whose *job* is to imitate arousal in the first place — going to render [women] sexually liberated?" *Female Chauvinist Pigs: Women and the Rise of Raunch Culture* (New York: Free Press, 2005), 4.
33. On the "promise of justice" as enduringly central to feminism, see e.g. Kavka 38–40.
34. Karen Campbell, *Shadowplay* (London: Hodder, 2010), 134. Subsequent citations will appear parenthetically in the text.
35. As evidence of the pervasiveness of "raunch culture," Levy quotes influential and respected television executive Sheila Nevins as endorsing stripping in terms startlingly similar to those used by Campbell's character: "'The women are beautiful and the men are fools! What's the problem?'" (92).
36. See, e.g., Tasker and Negra (6–7) on links between postfeminism and postindustrial economies.
37. Hélène Cixous, "Castration or Decapitation," trans. Annette Kuhn, *Signs*, Autumn 1981, 45, accessed 17 February 2011, http://www.jstor.org/stable/3173505.
38. Kavka, 39, 40.

Works Cited

"Biography." *Denisemina.co.uk*. Accessed 26 June 2011. http://www.denisemina.co.uk/contents/bio.htm.
Brown, Kate E., and Howard I. Kushner. "Eruptive Voices: Coprolalia, Malediction, and the Poetics of Cursing." *New Literary History* 32, no. 3 (2001): 537–562. Accessed March 13, 2011. http://www.jstor.org/stable/ 20057676.
Butler, Judith. *Gender Trouble: Feminism and the Subversion of Identity*. 10th anniversary ed. New York: Routledge, 1999. http://lib.myilibrary.com.
Campbell, Karen. *After the Fire*. London: Hodder, 2009.
_____. *Shadowplay*. London: Hodder, 2010.
_____. *The Twilight Time*. London: Hodder, 2008.
Cixous, Hélène. "Castration or Decapitation." Translated by Annette Kuhn. *Signs* 7, no. 1 (1981): 41–55. Accessed February 17, 2011. http://www.jstor.org/stable/3173505
Craig, Carol. *The Tears that Made the Clyde*. Glendaruel: Argyll Publishing, 2010.
Dollimore, Jonathan. *Sex, Literature and Censorship*. Cambridge: Polity, 2001.
Hughes, Geoffrey. *Swearing: A Social History of Foul Language, Oaths and Profanity in English*. Oxford: Blackwell, 1991.
Kavka, Misha. "Feminism, Ethics, and History, or What Is the 'Post' in Postfeminism?" *Tulsa Studies in Women's Literature* 21, no. 1 (2002): 29–44. Accessed February 19, 2011. http://www.jstor.org/stable/4149214.
Levy, Ariel. *Female Chauvinist Pigs: Women and the Rise of Raunch Culture*. New York: Free Press, 2005.
Mina, Denise. *The Dead Hour*. New York: Little, Brown, 2006.
_____. *Garnethill*. London: Bantam, 1998.
_____. *The Last Breath*. London: Bantam, 2007.

_____. *Resolution*. London: Bantam, 2001.
_____. *Still Midnight*. Toronto: McArthur, 2009.
Plain, Gill. "Concepts of Corruption: Crime Fiction and the Scottish 'State.'" In *The Edinburgh Companion to Contemporary Scottish Literature*, edited by Berthold Schoene. 132–140. Edinburgh: Edinburgh University Press, 2007.
_____. *Twentieth-Century Crime Fiction: Gender, Sexuality and the Body*. Edinburgh: Edinburgh University Press, 2001.
Robinson, David. Review of *Still Midnight* by Denise Mina. *Scotsman*, July 25 2009. Accessed September 2, 2011. http://living.scotsman.com/books/Book-review—Still-Midnight.5492036.jp.
Tasker, Yvonne, and Diane Negra. "Introduction: Feminist Politics and Postfeminist Culture." In *Interrogating Postfeminism: Gender and the Politics of Popular* Culture, edited by Tasker and Negra, 1–25. Durham: Duke University Press, 2007.
Wajnryb, Ruth. *Expletive Deleted: A Good Look at Bad Language*. New York: Free Press, 2005.
Winston, Robert P. "'A Duty to Care': Denise Mina's *Garnethill* Series." *Clues: A Journal of Detection* 26, no. 2 (2008): 64–78.

(DE)CONSTRUCTED BODY AND SEXUAL PSYCHOPATHY:
SERIAL KILLING OF GENDER BINARIES

9. Beyond Gender and Sexuality
The Serial Killers of Val McDermid
NEIL MCCAW

Approximately 85 percent of all known serial killers since 1900 have been male.[1] And even in the United States, which supposedly has the largest proportion of women serial killers, "only 1.5 percent of the Death Row population is [ever] female."[2] It is thus little surprise that within the thriving "true crime" genre—within which titillating titles such as *The Serial Killer Files*,[3] *Blind, Torture, Kill*,[4] and *The A-Z Encyclopaedia of Serial Killers*[5] proliferate—the clear implication is that there is something inherent in men that makes them more likely to commit serial murder. When police "discover a corpse with its throat slit, its torso cut open, its viscera removed, and its genitals excised," we are told, they are "justified in making one basic assumption: the perpetrator was a man."[6] The supposition of such pop-criminal-profiling, "the derivation of personality characteristics from crime scene actions,"[7] is that serial killing is part of an articulation of a definable, if extreme, masculinity, a "function"[8] of "the cultural meanings, social roles, and personality traits"[9] associated with a particular gender[10] identity.

Thus, until relatively recently, most research on serial killers "has concentrated on male offenders."[11] For a long time it was taken for granted that there were no women who fit "that particular [male] model" outside "overheated Hollywood fantasies"[12] such as *Basic Instinct*,[13] with "females convicted of multicide" seen as "a rare breed."[14] In particular, the excesses of "sadistic mutilation-murder" have tended to be equated with a "grotesque distortion ... of normal *male* [my italics] sexuality,"[15] supposedly incompatible with any prevailing notion of femaleness. Within such a logic women are victims-in-waiting rather than perpetrators: "crime remains a profoundly gendered phenomenon. To put it simply, the vast majority of crimes and particularly violent crimes are committed by boys or men and not by girls or women."[16] This assumes an underlying continuum of violence at the core of male social experience that ranges from, on the one hand, mildly aggressive behaviors to, on the other, grievous assaults and sexual violations. According to James Messerschmidt, such a narrative of identity begins with puberty, during which "certain boys use sexual and assaultive violence as what might be called 'masculine practice.'"[17] This is a view that (perhaps unwittingly) chimes with the second wave feminist notion that "if the professional rapist is to be separated from the average dominant heterosexual, it may be mainly a quantitative difference."[18]

Over the last decade or so there has been a necessary corrective to such phallocentric notions of "the serial killer." A host of books have been published that focus specifically on women perpetrators,[19] and within such works the "truth" of a predominantly male/masculine form of murder has been challenged by an alternative sense of individuals "doing gender"[20] in which female serial killing is intrinsically related to notions of femininity. It is as a result no longer feasible to argue that "the female serial killer has never entered popular consciousness in the way that the male serial killer has."[21] However, this "corrective" to the phallocentrism of popular understandings of serial murder also reveals how entrenched such assumptions have become. Discussions of the motivations and *modus operandi* of women killers are regularly couched in terms that establish "boys and men as the norm,"[22] with the notion of the female serial killer fundamentally reliant on its own position as counterpoint: "unlike their male counterparts who usually kill for sexual reasons, most female serial murderers kill either for money ... or for excitement and power in institutional settings like hospitals and nursing homes."[23] There is a broad, prevailing assertion that there are essential, coherent, comprehensible meanings and relations of gender played out in serial killing, making them part of the broader canvas of what Simone de Beauvoir called the "unchangeably fixed entities that determine [the] given characteristics"[24] of men and women.

Clearly, such essentialism in theories of criminal behavior belies serial killers who confound our expectations of women (and indeed men), those who operate outside "received notions of masculinity and femininity."[25] The narrative of the life of Aileen Wuornos, dramatized in the Oscar-winning film *Monster* (2003),[26] is an example of this. Wuornos's pattern of criminality fundamentally challenges "deeply held assumptions about women and their capacity to nurture others,"[27] calling into question the effectiveness of "gender" as a central plank of the criminal profiler's logic; the same can also be said of murderers such as Myra Hindley and Rosemary West in the UK, who were both sexual sadists and predators, violators and aggressors. These women threaten the coherence of essentialist ideas of female behavior, and more particularly about female killers,[28] for within the framework of criminal profiling men are typically seen as inherently powerful and thrusting (aka masculine), qualities that male serial killers pervert into crimes of phallic violation and domination. Women are generally viewed as innately nurturing and sensitive and desirable (aka feminine), attributes travestied by female serial killers in the snuffing out of vulnerable children or defrauded husbands.[29]

This leaves women such as Wuornos, Hindley and West situated at the very margins of the margins, with generic notions of gender identity (within which the twin peaks of *masculinity* and *femininity* are viewed as observable and coherent patterns of male/female behavior) often unhelpful. *Gender* as a profiling category is increasingly ineffective as the actions and identities of women serial killers become less and less distinguishable from those of their male counterparts, inhabiting too often the territory of outmoded stereotypes of male/female-ness, wherein the paralysing contingency of masculinities and femininities becomes overwhelming. In a modern world characterized by the blurring of identities, gender becomes just one element of a wider social *performance*: "a kind of doing, an incessant activity performed ... a practice of improvisation within a scene of constraint."[30] And this detachment from considerations of biology (with the labels of *feminine* and *masculine* being applied to both men and women) undermines the viability of gender as a fruitful demarcation of male/female social and cultural identities. The debate tends towards the inevitable rehashing and recycling of traditional archetypes of the masculine and the feminine (strong vs. weak, active vs. passive, dominant vs. submissive etc.). Within the context of understanding a complex, pluralistic world in which borders between identities are continuously challenged and transgressed, such a conventional framework proves wholly inadequate.

Interestingly, within many popular-cultural representation of serial killers, such simplistic binary oppositions of masculine/feminine and male/female are deliberately explored. True, there are examples that amplify — or simply pander to — stereotypes, such as *Basic Instinct* (in which the overt and assertive female sexuality of the central character Catherine Trammell is reductively equated with a potential for serial murder), but there are a variety of other examples wherein such easy juxtapositions of identity and character are denied. The characterization of "Buffalo Bill" in Thomas Harris's *The Silence of the Lambs* (1988),[31] for instance, sees questions and anxieties about serial killers played out in a dynamic, creative exploration of what marks out the killer from the non-killer in terms of wider aspects of their identity, including, but not limited to, overlapping, nascent, and ill-defined territories of gender and sexuality.

And it is the intention in this chapter to explore another "creative" vision of serial killers, that found in the crime novels of the British writer Val McDermid featuring the heroized forensic profiler Dr. Tony Hill. These novels represent serial killers in ways that ultimately call into question the foundation of all notions of the masculine and feminine, and as such the discussion will begin by examining how the portrayal of the psychology and methodology of the male and female serial killers contrasts. This discussion, which will focus in particular on McDermid's use of gender stereotypes, will serve as the baseline for the subsequent consideration of the extent to which gender functions as a meaningful category in social and criminal profiling terms. This will feed into the examination of the ways in which the "implicit associations"[32] of gender and sexuality are ultimately deconstructed in these works, shifting away from signs of coherent identity towards a more fluid, dialectical understanding of what gender might mean and how it is constructed and played out.

One of the many interesting elements of McDermid's work is that at the basis of her radical exploration of gender identities is her depiction of apparently orthodox stereotypes of masculinity and femininity situated within a conventional relationship of power. In *The Wire in the Blood*, for instance, the serial killer is former international sportsman Jacko Vance, a man rooted in an overweening stereotype of masculine energy and endeavor (although we later find out that these energies have become twisted following a severe injury to his arm that cut short his athletic career). While incapacitated in hospital after his accident, his long-time girlfriend ends their relationship, and his gendered self-image suffers major trauma as a consequence in "a core experience that comes to constitute identity."[33] His masculinity is thus central to his evolving story: "First Vance had lost his arm and his future. Then he had lost the one person who had believed in him as a human being rather than as a throwing machine. It would take a strong man to survive them unscathed."[34] As one of the journalists who has followed his career notes, "nothing can compensate a man who thinks he's god for the discovery of his vulnerability" (379). After this trauma he marries the secretly-lesbian TV presenter Micky Morgan in an attempt to maintain the fiction of his own normative heterosexuality, a marriage that reinforces his popular persona as a good-looking, charismatic, sexually-attractive TV presenter, imbued with a powerful sense of masculine self-confidence. It is a fiction that cleverly masks his sado-masochistic deviancy, and ultimately his serial killing.

Vance kidnaps, rapes and murders a succession of young women who resemble his former girlfriend ("You're all the same aren't you?... all out for what you can get" [157]). He tortures and defiles his victims, having first seduced them with his intoxicating caricature of irresistible maleness. This quest for prey is his own deviant form of "gendered realness" (206), with his masculine image facilitating his overwhelming, violent personality disorder. His increasingly sadistic and deviant sexuality is thus an overcompensation for his physical impairment. The "materiality" of his body is in this way directly linked to "the performativity of [his] gender,"[35] with a perceived deficiency in the former the precursor of a re-imagining of the latter. Cruelty and sexual violation go hand in hand, as in the following passage describing his torture: "The breaking of her hymen went unnoticed among the splintering of the bones of her wrist and forearm and the pulverizing of her flesh between the blank metal plates" (157). His accident does not *cause* his deviancy, but it has triggered an extrapolation of previously established patterns of sexual behavior. We are told:

> There was nothing normal about Jacko's bedroom habits. Right from the start of their sex life, he had to be in control. She was supposed to be passive and adoring. He hated her touching him sexually and, on occasion, he actually slapped her for laying hands on him. He became more interested in S&M pornography and wanted her to act out fantasies from magazines and books and from his own imagination. She didn't mind being tied up, she says, and she didn't much mind the spanking or the whipping, but when he started on the hot candle wax and the nipple clamps and the outsize vibrators, she drew the line [408].

Vance represents an almost all-conquering masculine psychopathy[36] rooted in a need to dominate and to induce the sexual suffering of women: "the pain, as far as he was concerned, was not quite the only necessity but it was certainly one of them" (2).

However, there is more to this than a simple connection between (denied) gender role and (abnormal) sexual *performance*, something most shockingly revealed in Vance's killing of the policewoman Shaz Bowman. For Bowman is not sexually assaulted at all; indeed the crime has no overt sexual element. Rather her body is desecrated, and when she is discovered by Hill there is little left of her:

> dark holes where her startling eyes had last looked out at him. Gouged out, he guessed, judging by what looked like threads and strings trailing from the wounds. Blood had flowed and dried around the black orifices, making the hideous mask of her face even more grotesque. Her mouth looked like a mass of plastic in a dozen hues of purple and pink. There were no ears. Her hair stuck out in spikes above and behind where the ears should have been, held in place by the dried blood that had sprayed and flowed over them [230].

This perverse form of artistic display is not about sexuality but a performance of an exponentially-inflated sense of male selfhood and a fundamental disrespect for humanity in *all* its forms. Thus Vance's killing is rooted in a massive superiority complex, committed with "self-important righteousness" (214). During his acts of brutality, he even allows himself "the luxury of a smile ... so relaxed ... that he actually caught himself singing softly as he worked" (215). Such sadism literally and metaphorically deconstructs what it means to be human, with the human body "more like a pastiche of a Bacon painting executed by a psychopath" (229).

This *masculine* disrespect for the female body also oozes through the pores of the ultra-macho Eastern-European gangsters Tadeusz Radecki and Darko Krasic in *The Last Temptation*, for whom systematic rape is a means of punishment, and a means of maintaining physical and mental dominance over women within the context of their wider campaign of intimidation and violence. Rape is a form of crime intended to maintain the conventional power dynamic between men and women. So, for instance, "for a woman like [Detective Inspector Carol Jordan], whose sense of identity was bound up in her perception of herself as strong and ultimately inviolable, rape brought havoc to the personality,"[37] underpinned by orthodox assumptions about what it means to be masculine and feminine. The behavior of Radecki and Krasic establishes a stereotype against which the other characters of the novel can react, giving their more fluid interpretation of gender roles an informing context. And, in the case of the killer Jack Anderson in *Beneath the Bleeding*, McDermid offers such a contrast *within* the character himself. He is, on the one hand, "up for anything ... shocking with the lasses — if they wouldn't shag him, he dropped them like a hot potato. And if they did shag him, he'd get bored in a few weeks and dump them anyway ... he was into all sorts ... you name it, he'd have a crack at it."[38] But on the other, ironically, Anderson's hyper-masculinity disguises bi-sexual experimentation and the denial of the supposed fulfilment of the heterosexual ideal.

Thus gender stereotypes are established in McDermid's novels only in order to be deconstructed — when the familiar dynamic of masculine perpetrator and feminine victim begins to break down, and is ultimately rejected. DI Carol Jordan confounds convention at almost every point of her career, and even resists the role of rape victim in *The Last Temptation* by deliberately self-medicating with casual sex as a remedy for her trauma. Her attacker's claim that "I might be going to jail, but compared to you, I'm free. You'll never be free of me" (563), is ultimately rebuffed by her response. The image of woman as victim is undercut even further with the characterization of Diane Patrick in *Fever of the Bone*, which perverts an ideal of femininity as maternal and nurturing by murdering rather than caring for her husband and his supposed children. And in the case of Jacko Vance it is the masculine image that is eventually undermined, as the text repeatedly denies — through its profiler Tony Hill's perspective — the rationalization of the serial killing in terms of deficiencies in male childhood socialization and individual psychological trauma:

> There had long been a theory among psychologists that discounted the existence of evil, ascribing the worst excesses of the most sociopathic abductors,

torturers and killers to a linked series of circumstances and events in their past that culminated in one final stress-laden event that catapulted them over the edge of what civilized society would tolerate. But that had never entirely satisfied Tony [48].

Vance's later childhood may have "been scarred with oppressive discipline, any rebelliousness or frivolity stifled with force" (98), and the stifling of his masculine ambitions may have fuelled him with rage and injustice. But his nascent psychopathy predated both of these events, and the reader is shown that. The gender he performs is a *symptom* of his underlying psychopathy, and "what is being chalked up to hardwiring on closer inspection starts to look more like the sensitive tuning of the self,"[39] a rampant masculinity that is a convenience, a strategy to suit the circumstances.

In *The Last Temptation* the trajectory of McDermid's representation of masculinity, beyond her Eastern-European gangsters, travels in the opposite direction — from fluidity to stereotype rather than stereotype to fluidity. The gender and sexual identity of the tragically damaged Wilhelm Mann is barely articulated at first — part of his social image as a downtrodden victim — muted and awkwardly realized. He is the product of a distorted and disturbed upbringing, punctuated by cruel, degrading treatment (like having to "get down on all fours and eat the [dog] food without touching it with his hands" [26] or being "sent to stand in the toilet bowl ... naked and shivering" [27]). It is the resulting sense that "he was worthless" (28) that manifests itself in a violent reaction against experimental psychologists as redress for the maltreatment of his (ultimately abusive) grandfather within Nazi "experiments." For Mann, experimental psychology itself is guilty — with psychologists playing God — and the male and female psychologists he selects fully deserve having a tube forced down their throats and water poured into their lungs until they drown (76). They are then degraded further through pubic scalping (333), a perverse yet only partially-articulated sexual act of sorts, which links to the narrative of his and his grandfather's abuse implicitly rather than explicitly (144).

Ultimately, however, Mann's revenge-fuelled mission begins to play out in a confused serial killing methodology that betrays broader psycho-sexual instabilities. Pubic scalping is the first stage of this — a curious sexual manifestation of his broader disgust and rage — but this eventually gives way to rape, a more primal, instinctive and dominant form of sexuality: "he felt like a god. When he'd finished, he'd untied her and forced her on to her stomach so he could celebrate his new potency by sodomizing her too. Then he'd left, throwing her a handful of coins to demonstrate his contempt" (77). This underlying aggression consumes his rationalized killing method, with the organization and control of the earlier crimes giving way to confusion and mayhem, as we can see in the following passage: "suddenly he felt desire well up inside him, a richness in his blood that made him almost dizzy. Until now, he'd always refused to acknowledge that the surge of adrenaline-fuelled urgency that swept through him when confronted with his victims had anything to do with sex" (331). This nascent sexuality more accurately accords with the dominant stereotypes of male serial killers, meaning that although after he first commits rape-murder Mann is wracked with guilt for the way his sexual urges have taken control ("what was he thinking of? He had a plan, a mission, and he'd failed. He'd killed her, but in the wrong way. A wave of despair washed through him" [333]), he has now, as Tony Hill says, given everyone "an excuse" to treat him "like any other sexually motivated psychopath" (588). Whilst his targets were experimental psychologists *per se*, and his method of killing was a re-enactment of his grandfather's own suffering, he could maintain the fiction of his "justifiable" revenge. But once he resorts to the orthodoxy of the (hetero)sexual predator this justification is lost as he increasingly becomes "astonished to find, driving back to the boat, that he wanted a woman" (77). Consequently the reader is left doubting whether Mann's violent sexuality is a product of his abuse at all, or whether in fact these crimes simply gave him an outlet for already implicit tendencies. Therein the novel embodies the transitory, inconsistent nature of male sexual identity, by offering and simultaneously critiquing, but never satisfactorily resolving or explaining, familiar paradigms of heterosexual dominance and misogyny.

This unravelling of familiar gendered notions of serial killing and victimhood is also apparent in *Beneath the Bleeding*, wherein the serial poisoner Jack Anderson (who from the beginning of the novel confounds the criminal profiler's wisdom that poisoning is more commonly the method of female serial killers) is seen beyond his initial image as a devil-may-care playboy. Anderson's apparently stereotypical heterosexual masculinity, broadly disinterested in the feelings and sensitivities of others, is no simple rehashing of a dynamic hetero-masculine archetype; he has contracted HIV after a hedonistic sexual encounter with another *man*. And it is his outraged reaction to this that triggers darker, murderous behaviors: "And then you found out. Just one time, that's all it took. That infection in the blood, poisoning you. Killing you. It doesn't matter that these days you can take the drugs and live longer. Who wants to live longer without their dreams? What's the point in existing?" (473). Existential crisis and serial killing go hand-in-hand.

As a result, although the killer's actions are not sexually *motivated* ("that's not what you're about, is it? You're not interested in them as bodies, as objects of desire" [220]), they can be viewed as sexually *inspired*. Because of Anderson's self-gratifying quest to experience all there was to experience, he "pushed the boundaries" (472) and paid the consequences: "You're not a poof. You thought it would be OK, but you hated it. Hated it so much it made you hate yourself. That's when you stopped being Jack, wasn't it? Jack was ruined, fucked up. So you left Jack behind" (472). His murder of men who went to school with him is about his need to prevent them from enacting the stereotypical masculine desires (cars, money, jobs, women, etc.) that he himself cannot now achieve because of his illness. He is thus situated on the boundaries of conventional and transgressive sexualities, not denying "the biological aspects of sexuality" but illustrating the complex interplay of cultural forces that determine "which organs and 'orifices' become sexual, how such ... may be used or expressed, [and] their social and moral meaning."[40] Initially, he found living out the masculine heterosexual ideal wholly attractive, then it became limiting (resulting in his "experimentation"), and his exploration of his sexual identity led to his pleasure being curtailed and his self-image undermined. His life arc thus embodies first, stereotypical masculine and heterosexual identity in symbiosis, then a counteraction wherein these identities come into conflict with each other, and finally the ultimate thwarting of his conventional hetero-masculinity by an emergent, more fluid, aspect of his own sexuality.

This blurring of identities leaves profiling assumptions muddled to the point where it is difficult to ascertain the relations of male/female, masculine/feminine at all. This is also apparent in the murders of Diane Patrick in *Fever of the Bone*. At first these concur with the criminal profile of a male sexual serial killer of young women, as indicated by the following mistaken identification of a "bastard" as the perpetrator: "Bastard butchered her. I don't know that I'd call it sexual assault, as such. Sexual obliteration, more like.... Worst I've ever seen."[41] But the coherence of this profile soon disintegrates when young men start to become victims as well. This results in profound confusion in Tony Hill's understanding of method and motive: "he made it look like she'd been raped with the knife. What I need to work out is whether he did that deliberately to make us think it was sexual. Or whether he did it for another reason and the fact that it looks sexual is just by the by" (254). He is confident that despite appearances the crimes are "not about sex" (256), because if they had been sexual the killer would have kept and savored his victims for a much longer period of time. But Hill is unable to imagine beyond established wisdoms about serial killers and, in particular, to see that the killer could be a woman rather than a man.

Furthermore, the killer's actions are not underscored by a typical pattern of "extreme emotional, physical sexual abuse"[42] in childhood but instead arise directly from a performed, idealized female identity. The killer tells herself: "There's a reason for what you're doing. This is about healing your life. This is about you needing to do this so you can feel better" (1). Diane Patrick has become obsessed with having her husband's baby, and this obsession has "been so overwhelming, so deep-seated" that when it is denied she feels compelled "to obliterate him utterly" (486). That means not just murdering the husband himself but also (because he was previously a sperm donor) destroying all the children created with his "seed": "It was utterly unreasonable yet entirely comprehensible" (486). For Hill, this gives the crimes a logic, if not a justification, and this is related to a prevailing sense of womanhood as inextricably bound up with an all-encompassing sense of motherhood.

Diane Patrick's actions therefore reinforce *and* contradict conventional gender and sexual identities simultaneously: bloody killings and sexual mutilations of innocent young people by a deranged female murderer fuelled by a delusional perception of herself as wife and mother, whose "single obsession had taken control of her, obliterating everything else" (485). And, just as with the depiction of Jack Anderson, it is the initial unyielding faith in a particular notion of herself as a gendered/sexual individual, when thwarted, that precipitates her descent into serial murder. The deviation from this "norm" of a previously imagined heteronormative self — with Anderson it was his bisexual experimentation, with Patrick it is her inability to become a mother — serves as the ultimate catalyst. Serial killing manifests as a response to a mismatch between idealized, conventional gender/sex roles and the more incoherent, more complex social realities of actual human lives, a mismatch that these individuals are unable to reconcile themselves with.

In McDermid's other novels featuring the profiler Tony Hill this deconstruction of gender goes even further, with serial killing not a consequence of thwarted conventional identities but an articulation of a radical Otherness. Stereotypes of the masculine and, in particular, the feminine are not simply unpicked, but entirely rejected. *The Mermaids Singing* begins with the narrative conceit of an unidentified (in terms of gender, sex, age, ethnicity etc.) narrator detailing the horror of his/her desires. Consequently, from the first moment the pervasive criminal compulsions and motivations of the killer are the focus. We hear in the second paragraph of the novel: "Although I didn't realize it before the decision to act was forced upon me, I had been paving the way for murder well in advance."[43] It is not so much that the killer "*cannot* [my italics] be understood"[44] in terms of gender, but more that McDermid does not *allow* such a reductive interpretation of these perversions, consistently teasing out their ambiguity:

> I moved through the rooms, savouring each and every toy, from the gross spikes of the Iron Maiden to the more subtle and elegant machinery of the pears, those slender, segmented ovoids which were inserted into vagina or anus. Then, when the ratchet was turned, the segments separated and

extended till the pear had metamorphosed into a strange flower, petals fringed with razor-sharp metal teeth. Then it was removed [4].

These images of sadistic mutilation are not gendered, or tied to specific sexualities, but rather imply a context of exploration and transcendence in which assault and violation are equally likely to be carried out, and suffered, by men and women.

The extraordinary and grotesque drives of the unidentified assailant thus deny easy gender associations, highlighting behavior far outside the range of the commonplace. The narrative goes on to ponder: "how could anyone not admire the minds that examined the human body so intimately that they could engineer such exquisite and finely calibrated suffering?" (3). There is such delight at the torture and destruction of living forms that it is not only humans who are attacked but animals too (55). This cruelty is so systematic and hedonistic that it confounds the criminal-profiling brilliance of Hill, and the grand misdirection of the disembodied narrative voice confounds both reader and characters, forcing a reconsideration of preconceptions about the extent to which a comprehensible, coherent gender identity is being played out in any recognizable sense.

From the point at which it is revealed that the reader has been witnessing the serial murder of men by a male-to-female (MTF) transsexual called "Angelica" (towards the end of the novel) this questioning of assumptions takes on a more crystallized form, with the killer seen as an embodiment of a deep-seated transgression of conventional associations of gender and sexuality. Angelica's sexual expression is motivated by a drive to mutilate and destroy the materiality of her victims if they prove themselves unable to satisfy her cross-gender, cross-sexuality longings. And the flipside of her extreme desire is profound loathing she expresses for the male victims: "I had suspended Damien in midair, his limbs spread in a massive, human X, his pathetic genitals dangling in the middle like something in a butcher's shop" (340).

By the time each torture has concluded, each male body is disfigured or destroyed, an aggressive negation that leads Tony Hill's criminal profile astray as he imagines a killer driven by thwarted, stereotypically masculine energies: "he's desperate to be the best.... He just doesn't go for the easy options. His victims are all in the high-risk category. His dumping grounds aren't obscure, deserted hiding places. The bodies are cleaned of forensic clues. He's smarter than us, he thinks, and he has to keep proving it to himself" (167). Hill constructs an image of the killer he calls "Handy Andy" (230), blindsided by the fraught combination of gender and sexual pluralities in the method and predilections he witnesses. But the killer's callousness cannot be contained within unifying conceptualizations of masculine and feminine. Thus whilst it might appear that everything is about masculine manipulation and toying with each victim and the keen celebration of human suffering, the graphic horror of the killings destabilizes our understanding of the limits of depravity. The question is not "what man/woman could do this?" but rather "how could *anyone* do this?"

The overarching sense of profound incomprehension (symbolized by Tony Hill, who is even oblivious of the fact that he spends many of his evenings conducting a phone-sex relationship with Angelica herself) is magnified by the way all *rational* interpretations of events are thwarted in the novel. Angelica's rationalization of her own behavior in particular — placing serial murder within the context of her attempt to establish some kind of normality after years of abuse and neglect — is never given significant credence:

> I was having the best Christmas I'd ever had. I remembered all those years of desperate hope, praying that this would be the year my mother would buy me presents like other children got. But all she'd ever done was let me down.... I knew that for the first time in my life, I could look forward to the kind of Christmas other people have, filled with surprises, satisfaction and sex [297].

The novel's implied narrative of physical abuse by an aunt (340) attempts to pair developing alienation and neglect with a graphic, illicit sense of human sexuality: "I grew accustomed to the procession of disgusting, drunken sailors traipsing through the succession of grubby flats and bedsits where we lived.... I grew to hate the ugly, grunting copulation that I was a constant witness to" (404). But within the profiler's logic this narrative only suffices at all, as Hill reveals, if the perpetrator is male, which would allow "Handy Andy" to be viewed as a male psychopath, responding to childhood trauma through an adolescent Conduct Disorder (a recognized precursor for eventual adult psychopathy). This could then be seen to evolve into a grandiose sense of self-worth and a concomitant desire to "thrive on publicity as long as it appears to accord him the glamour and respect he craves" (274). The problem with this interpretation, of course, is that Angelica is a MTF transsexual, and thus the link between adult behavior and the narrative of childhood and adolescence is ill-formed, partial, at best fractured.

Perhaps as a consequence, Hill is blind to Angelica's transgender "discomfort with role expectations,"[45] mistaking these for a violent masculinity. By the time he realizes his mistake further murders have taken place, and he has to admit: "I should have realized you were a woman. The subtlety, the attention to detail, the care you took to clear up after yourself" (393). Ironically, even at this apparent point of realization, Hill's profiling logic is still constrained by gender stereotypes, equating female/feminine identity with domestic cleanliness and order (she was too tidy to be a man, it seems). He does not sufficiently grasp the extent to which Angelica's identity is eminently "unstable" (421), and how, as a consequence, she represents a "new sexuality" in which the determination of the body is left "open to exploration and invention."[46] She confounds profiling wisdom as a transgendered and transsexual subject who "disrupts, denaturalizes, rearticulates, and makes visible the normative linkages we generally assume to exist between the biological specificity of the sexually differentiated human body ... [and] the social roles and statuses that a particular form of body is expected to occupy."[47] Angelica is not simply what the National Health Service psychologist labels "a gay man who couldn't cope with his sexuality because of cultural and family conditioning" (439), but rather a personification of the crisis of an infinitely malleable identity — an identity that will *always* resist classification. As such, through her, the novel denies the feasibility of coherent identities, illustrating that "the distribution of hetero-, bi-, and homo- inclinations cannot be predictably mapped onto the travels of gender bending or changing."[48] *Gender* is not secure enough, simply not adequate enough, to effectively come to terms with such individuals.

This inadequacy is also apparent in terms of the central killer in *The Torment of Others*, the controlling serial-killer-mastermind who adopts the pseudonym "The Voice." This killer controls fragile and malleable men in order to carry out crimes by proxy, making each of them both victims and perpetrators simultaneously, at one moment sexual sadists ("he grips his weapon tightly. The razor blades glint sharp and savage in the lamplight"[49]) the next emasculated slaves to a hidden master ("when it came to it, when he had to stick that thing inside her again and again, he wilted. It wasn't sexy. It was bloody and terrible and frightening" [75]). Crucially, the unidentified nature of the speaking "Voice" leaves the gender of the orchestrating killer an "everywhere and nowhere phenomenon,"[50] a metaphor for gender as an identity within the novel as a whole: "we can neither essentialize ... nor dematerialize it."[51] As one of the male dupes notes: "It sounded really easy when the Voice explained it. You're pretty sure you got it right, because the Voice went over it so many times you can replay the whole spiel just by closing your eyes and mouthing the words: 'I am the Voice. I am your Voice. Whatever I tell you is for the best. I am your Voice'" (2). Control and domination are at this point disembodied, pared back to their most essential elements.

Once it is revealed that the policewoman Jan Shields is the serial-killing mastermind, the reader becomes aware of the extent of the concerted rejection and reversal of stereotypical femininity and masculinity in the text. We are told: "One of the reasons for my success is my ability to think on my feet, to adapt my plans to accommodate changing circumstances. After the time I took to train him [Carl], I'd hoped to get more use out of this monkey, but it's become clearer that sooner rather than later he's going to be fingered — and that presents a risk I'm not prepared to take" (408). Shields's craving for control and domination pushes beyond orthodox notions of male and female behavior, towards ill-defined and inexplicable facets of humanity: "It wasn't so bad after all. Nothing like as exciting as making the others do the work, but still a thrill. Having the power to take a life and having the nerve to exercise it; how could that not be close to as good as it gets?" (416). This reverses the polarities of Jean Laplanche's "displacement of the question of sexual identity onto the question of gender identity,"[52] in that ambivalent gender is displaced onto a sadistic sexual psychopathy, coupled with an over-inflated sense of self and a callous disrespect for the human form. This woman's superiority complex commands the destruction of all those defined as less worthy, whether male or female: "outrage swelled inside her and she knew she wasn't about to run. Nobody got one over on her. Nobody" (427). There is very little here that even vaguely resembles conventional gender/sex roles, with ideas of masculinity and femininity reduced to simulacra: "models of a real without origin or reality."[53]

With gender disintegrating as a knowable human characteristic, sexuality comes to the fore. An evident (if perverse) sexual identity underpins all of the killings, each "sea of gore" (90), with victims bleeding to death "as a result of injuries inflicted vaginally" (106), assaulted with "something along the lines of a latex dildo with a series of razor blades inserted quite deeply into it" (110). In criminal profiling terms this makes them masculine crimes, part of a male "perverted gratification of desire" (98). And it is this tension between the phallic dimension of the crimes and Shields's own womanhood that calls into question all assumptions about gender and sexuality. Shields's deviant sexual desires thus confront the reader with profound questions as to what female identity might consist of — or even whether it has any essence at all, and each murderous act places her further and further outside the comprehensible and the predictable, at the margins of even the most extreme forms of sexually-inspired serial killing.

The relationship between identity and sexual practice in McDermid's fictionalized worlds is, as such, anything but straightforward, never a simple matter of "where we stand in relation to reproduction."[54] Fundamental questions emerge as to the nature of the relationship between extreme violence, serial killing and individuality, breaking down the basis of the criminal profiler's assumptions and blurring the divide between what we understand by *normality* and *abnormality*. The search for coherent identity is thwarted first by an unstable sense of gender, then an (as it turns out) equally unstable conception of sexuality, metaphorized in the methods of killers who reinterpret and obliterate both the physiological and social senses of selfhood. The recasting of gender into an "ironic register" does not lead to a more lucid sense of sexuality as "the [default] space for the 'authentic,'"[55] for the depiction of sexuality is no more secure than that of gender, with "several, changing and often contradictory norms, or structural forces or discourses at play simultaneously."[56] Although there seems to be some consistency in the way in which the motivations of the serial killers imply an "interaction between the corporeal, the sensorial, and the social,"[57] this comes within the context of such an abundant variety of heterosexualities, homosexualities, bisexualities, and transsexualities in uneasy relation that the quest for meaning moves far beyond the relatively (in comparison) straightforward Foucauldian acknowledgment that "sexuality must not be thought of as a kind of natural given."[58] In McDermid's novels, such identities are not only not natural givens, they are eminently multi-layered and shifting features of human identity, in which the sexual self displays a "chameleon-like ability" to "take many guises and forms,"[59] reinforcing the sense that "a gender cannot be said to follow from a sex in any one way" and that the "radical discontinuity between sexed bodies and culturally constructed genders" leaves both as part of the "free-floating artifice"[60] of identity.

The depiction of serial killers in these novels amounts to a pronounced, multi-faceted exploration of, and ultimately dissension from, orthodoxies. Within worlds beyond the boundaries of criminal-profiling "truths," McDermid imagines the transsexual (Male-to-Female) sadistic sexual killer "Angelica" in *The Mermaids Singing*, the S&M-loving violent sadist Jacko Vance in *The Wire in the Blood*, the vengeful and deranged Wilhelm Mann in *The Last Temptation*, the torturer-cum–sexual deviant rogue policewoman Jan Shields in *The Torment of Others*, the callous and cold-blooded poisoner Jack Anderson in *Beneath the Bleeding*, and the grisly castrator Diane Patrick in *Fever of the Bone*. Each portrayal fetishises patterns of identity and behavior that cannot be easily labelled male/female, or masculine/feminine. The meaning of gender as an identifiable, coherent social category becomes deeply fractured, neither an "ontological attribute"[61] nor a lucid, consistent form of social performance. Even where characters attempt to live out specific forms of gendered lifestyles these are always in the end revealed to be compromised, flawed, or fraudulent.

These are works, as such, that acutely embody what Robert Nye has called "creative ways of thinking about [gender and] sexual categories and sexual identity."[62] Val McDermid's serial killers live lives and follow patterns of behavior that disregard/disrespect the human body through sadistic forms of obliteration. They offer not so much a "radical proliferation"[63] of these identities as a disintegration of coherent meaning, within the context of a destabilising of the "heterosexual matrix."[64] Sexual desires are not "expressions of [a particular, defined] sexuality" but more primal — irrespective of biological features—"feelings and acts that give pleasure."[65] They are part of the contingent "issues of desire, pleasure, identity, norms of sexual behaviour, and intimate arrangements."[66] All of which leaves McDermid's hero/criminal profiler, Dr. Hill, in a nebulous position, reliant on knowledge and assumptions and "scientific" truths that the world around him does its best to disavow. Reading behavior becomes infinitely complex in a world in which no one is sure what gender really means anymore.

Notes

1. James Alan Fox and Jack Levin, *Extreme Killing: Understanding Serial and Mass Murder* (London: Sage, 2005), p. 38
2. Carol Anne Davis, *Women Who Kill: Profiles for Female Serial Killers* (London: Allison & Busby, 2001), p. 396
3. Harold Schechter, *The Serial Killer Files: The Who, What, Where, How and Why of the World's Most Terrifying Murderers* (New York: Ballantine, 2003).
4. Roy Wenzl, *Blind, Torture, Kill: The Inside Story of BTK, the Serial Killer Next Door* (London: Harper Collins, 2008).
5. Harold Schechter and David Everitt, *The A-Z Encyclopaedia of Serial Killers* (London: Pocket Books, 2006).
6. Schechter, *The Serial Killer Files*, p. 30.
7. Laurence Alison, Craig Bennell and Andrea Mokros, "The Personality Paradox in Offender Profiling: A Theoretical Review of the Processes Involved in Deriving Background Characteristics from Crime Scene Actions," *Psychology, Public Policy, and Law*, 8 (1) May 2002, 115.
8. Schechter, *The Serial Killer Files*, p. 31.
9. Christine L. Williams and Arlene Stein, *Sexuality and Gender* (Oxford: Blackwell, 2002), p. 2.
10. Here the term "gender" is being utilized rather naively, as if it is unproblematic, which is entirely deliberate. Seeing gender simply as equating to the condition of being (and behaving as) a man or a woman (often defined in terms of the masculine and the feminine) is the necessary starting point of the discussion of meaning and fluidity in gender identities that is to follow.
11. Deborah Schurman-Kauflin, *The New Predator: Women Who Kill, Profiles of Female Serial Killers* (New York: Algora, 2000), p. 3. For a summary of much of the work carried out in this area up to 2006 see Andreas Freii, Birgit Völlmz, Marc Grafz, and Volker Dittman, "Female Serial Killing: Review and Case Report," *Criminal Behaviour and Mental Health*, 16 (2006), pp. 167–76.
12. Schechter, *The Serial Killer Files*, p. 30.
13. *Basic Instinct*, Paul Verhoeven, dir. (Carlco Pictures, 1992).
14. Schurman-Kauflin, *The New Predator*, p. 4.
15. Schechter, *The Serial Killer Files*, p. 31.
16. Tim Edwards, *Cultures of Masculinity* (London: Routledge, 2006), p. 11.
17. Eamonn Carrabine, Paul Iganski, Maggy Lee, Ken Plummer and Nigel South, *Criminology: A Sociological Introduction* (London: Routledge, 2004), p. 154.
18. Susan Griffin, "Rape: the All-American Crime," *Ramparts*, September (1971), p. 35.
19. See, for example, Carol Anne Davis, *Women Who Kill*, Michael D. Kelleher and

C. L. Kelleher, *Murder Most Rare: The Female Serial Killer* (London: Bantam, 2000), and Peter Vronsky *Female Serial Killers: How and Why Women Become Monsters* (London: Berkley, 2007).
20. Candace West and Don H. Zimmerman, "Doing Gender," *Gender & Society* 1 (2): 129.
21. Davis, *Women Who Kill*, p. 362.
22. Kathleen Daly, "Different Ways of Conceptualizing Sex/Gender in Feminist Theory and Their Implications for Criminology," in Eugene McLaughlin, John Muncie and Gordon Hughes, eds, *Criminological Perspectives: Essential Readings*, 2d ed. (London: Sage, 2008), p. 507.
23. C. Wade, C. Myers, Erik Gooch and J. Reid Meloy, "The Role of Psychopathy and Sexuality in a Female Serial Killer," *Journal of Forensic Sciences*, 50(3) May 2005, p. 1.
24. Simone de Beauvoir, *The Second Sex*, trans. and ed. by H. M. Parshley (Harmondsworth: Penguin, 1982), p. 14.
25. Judith Butler, *Gender Trouble: Feminism and the Subversion of Identity* (London: Routledge, 2006), p. viii.
26. *Monster*, Patty Jenkins, dir. (Newmarket Films, 2003). Charlize Theron's performance in the film was reportedly inspired by an earlier documentary on the same subject matter, Nick Broomfield's documentary *Aileen Wuornos: The Selling of a Serial Killer* (1992).
27. Elisabeth Storrs, "'Our Scapegoat': An Exploration of Media Representations of Myra Hindley and Rosemary West," *Theology and Sexuality* 11 (1) 2004, p. 12.
28. For instance, it is said that only 10 percent of female serial killers shoot their victims (as Wuornos did), as opposed to 38 percent who poison them. See (for example) Kelleher & Kelleher, *Murder Most Rare*, p. 286.
29. Kelleher and Kelleher suggest that 44 percent of individual female killers fall into the "Angel of Death" or "Black Widow" categories, wherein women murder the sick and vulnerable or else repeatedly seduce and financially exploit men before dispatching them. Only 3 percent of individual female serial killers are sexual predators (p. 285).
30. Judith Butler, *Undoing Gender* (London: Routledge, 2004), p. 1.
31. See also *The Silence of the Lambs*, Jonathan Demme, dir. (Orion Pictures, 1991).
32. Cordelia Fine, *Delusions of Gender: The Real Science Behind Sex Differences* (London: Icon, 2010), p. 5.
33. Virginia Goldner, "Ironic Gender/Authentic Sex," *Studies in Gender and Sexuality*, 4 (2) 2003, p. 115.
34. Val McDermid, *The Wire in the Blood* (1997; London: HarperCollins, 2006), p. 344. All subsequent references in parentheses within the main body of the text.
35. Judith Butler, *Bodies That Matter: On the Discursive Limits of Sex* (London: Routledge, 1993), p. 1.
36. Within this paper the term "psychopathy" is used in the clinical sense defined in the work of Robert D Hare, the complex of traits that make up this personality disorder including: a lack of guilt/conscience/remorse, superficial charm, the deliberate manipulation of others, grandiose self-worth, shallow affect, lack of empathy, pathological lying, a general lack of responsibility, impulsivity, aggression, lack of attention and realism, sexual promiscuity, juvenile delinquency and behavior problems. See (for example) *Psychopathy Checklist-Revised (PC-R)*, 2d ed. (Toronto: Multi-Health Systems, 2003).
37. Val McDermid, *The Last Temptation* (2002; London: HarperCollins, 2006), p. 538. All subsequent references in parentheses within the main body of the text.
38. Val McDermid, *Beneath the Bleeding* (2007; London: Harper, 2008), p. 396. All subsequent references in parentheses within the main body of the text.
39. Fine, *Delusions of Gender*, p. 13.

40. "Introduction" to Steven Seidman, Nancy Fischer and Chet Meeks, eds., *Introducing the New Sexuality Studies: Original Essays and Interviews* (London: Routledge, 2006), p. xiii.
41. Val McDermid, *Fever of the Bone* (London: Sphere, 2009), p. 8. All subsequent references in parentheses within the main body of the text.
42. Schurman-Kauflin, *The New Predator*, p. 4.
43. Val McDermid, *The Mermaids Singing* (1995; London: HarperCollins, 2006), p. 1. All subsequent references in parentheses within the main body of the text.
44. Rachel Alsop, Annette Fitzsimons and Kathleen Lennon, *Theorizing Gender* (Cambridge: Polity, 2002), p. 205.
45. Stephen Whittle, "Foreword" to Susan Stryker & Stephen Whittle, eds, *The Transgender Studies Reader* (London: Routledge, 2006), p. xi.
46. *Ibid.*, p. xii.
47. Susan Stryker, "(De)Subjugated Knowledges: An Introduction to Transgender Studies," in Susan Stryker and Stephen Whittle, eds, *The Transgender Studies Reader*, p. 3.
48. Butler, *Gender Trouble*, p. xiv.
49. Val McDermid, *The Torment of Others* (2004; London: HarperCollins, 2005), p. 71. All subsequent references in parentheses within the main body of the text.
50. Goldner, "Ironic Gender/Authentic Sex" p. 135.
51. *Ibid.*, p. 115.
52. Jean Laplanche, "Gender, Sex and the Sexual," trans. Susan Fairfield, *Studies in Gender and Sexuality*, 8 (2) 2007, p. 202.
53. Jean Baudrillard, *Simulations*, trans. by Paul Foss, Paul Patton and Philip Beitchman (New York: Semiotext(e), 1983), p. 2.
54. Riki Wilchins, "Gender Rights are Human Rights," in Joan Nestle, Clare Howell and Riki Wilchins, eds., *GenderQueer: Voices from Beyond the Sexual Binary* (Los Angeles: Alyson, 2002), p. 292.
55. Goldner, "Ironic Gender/Authentic Sex," p. 115.
56. "Introduction" to Lena Martinsson and Eva Reimers, eds., *Norm-Struggles: Sexualities in Contentions* (Cambridge: Cambridge Scholars Publishing, 2010), p. 3.
57. Jennifer Germon, *Gender: A Genealogy of An Idea* (Basingstoke: Palgrave, 2009), p. 16.
58. Michel Foucault, *The History of Sexuality Volume 1: An Introduction*, translated by Robert Hurley (London: Allen Lane, 1979), p. 105.
59. Jeffrey Weeks, *Sexuality* (London: Routledge, 1986), p. 11.
60. Judith Butler, *Gender Trouble: Feminism and the Subversion of Identity* (New York: Routledge, 1990), p. 6.
61. Germon, *Gender*, p. 14
62. Robert A Nye, ed., "Introduction" to *Sexuality* (Oxford: Oxford University Press, 1999), p. 7.
63. Butler, *Gender Trouble*, p. 148.
64. *Ibid.*, p. 35.
65. Steven Seidman, "Theoretical Perspectives," in Steven Seidman, Nancy Fischer and Chet Meeks, eds. *Introducing the New Sexuality Studies* (London: Routledge, 2006) p. 11.
66. Seidman, Fischer and Meeks, eds., "Introduction," p. xi.

Works Cited

Alison, Laurence, Craig Bennell, and Andrea Mokros. "The Personality Paradox in Offender Profiling: A Theoretical Review of the Processes Involved in Deriving

Background Characteristics from Crime Scene Actions." *Psychology, Public Policy, and Law*, 8(1) May 2002, 115–35.
Alsop, Rachel, Annette Fitzsimons, and Kathleen Lennon. *Theorizing Gender*. Cambridge: Polity, 2002.
Baudrillard, Jean. *Simulations*. Trans. Paul Foss, Paul Patton and Philip Beitchman. New York: Semiotext(e), 1983.
Beauvoir, Simone de. *The Second Sex*. Trans. and ed. H M Parshley. Harmondsworth: Penguin, 1982.
Bristow, Joseph. *Sexuality*. London: Routledge, 1997.
Butler, Judith. *Bodies That Matter: On the Discursive Limits of Sex*. London: Routledge, 1993.
_____. *Gender Trouble: Feminism and the Subversion of Identity*. New York: Routledge, 1990.
_____. *Undoing Gender*. London: Routledge, 2004.
Carrabine, Eamonn, Paul Iganski, Maggy Lee, Ken Plummer, and Nigel South. *Criminology: A Sociological Introduction*. London: Routledge, 2004.
Davis, Carol Anne. *Women Who Kill: Profiles for Female Serial Killers*. London: Allison & Busby, 2001.
Edwards, Tim. *Cultures of Masculinity*. London: Routledge, 2006.
Fine, Cordelia. *Delusions of Gender: The Real Science Behind Sex Differences*. London: Icon, 2010.
Foucault, Michel. *The History of Sexuality Volume 1: An Introduction*. Trans. Robert Hurley. London: Allen Lane, 1979.
Fox, James Alan and Jack Levin. *Extreme Killing: Understanding Serial and Mass Murder*. London: Sage, 2005.
Freii, Andreas, Birgit Völlmz, Marc Grafz, and Volker Dittman. "Female Serial Killing: Review and Case Report." *Criminal Behaviour and Mental Health*, 16(2006), pp. 167–76.
Germon, Jennifer. *Gender: A Genealogy of An Idea*. Basingstoke: Palgrave, 2009.
Goldner, Virginia. "Ironic Gender/Authentic Sex." *Studies in Gender and Sexuality*, 4(2) 2003, pp. 113–39.
Griffin, Susan. "Rape: The All-American Crime." *Ramparts*, September (1971), pp. 26–35.
Harris, Thomas. *The Silence of the Lambs*. New York: St Martin's, 1988.
Kelleher, Michael D. and C.L. Kelleher. *Murder Most Rare: The Female Serial Killer*. New York: Dell, 1998.
Laplanche, Jean. "Gender, Sex and the Sexual." trans. Susan Fairfield. *Studies in Gender and Sexuality*, 8(2) 2007, pp. 201–219.
Martinsson, Lena, and Eva Reimers, eds. *Norm-Struggles: Sexualities in Contentions*. Cambridge: Cambridge Scholars, 2010.
McDermid, Val. *Beneath the Bleeding*. 2007; London: Harper, 2008.
_____. *Fever of the Bone*. 2009; London: Sphere, 2009.
_____. *The Last Temptation*. 2002; London: HarperCollins, 2006.
_____. *The Mermaids Singing*. 1995; London: HarperCollins, 2006.
_____. *The Torment of Others*. 2004 London: HarperCollins, 2005.
_____. *The Wire in the Blood*. 1997; London: HarperCollins, 2006.
McLaughlin, Eugene, John Muncie, and Gordon Hughes, eds. *Criminological Perspectives: Essential Readings*, 2d ed. London: Sage, 2008.
Messerschmidt, James W. *Nine Lives: Adolescent Masculinities, The Body and Violence* Boulder: Westview, 2000.
Nestle, Joan, Clare Howell, and Riki Wilchins, eds. *GenderQueer: Voices from Beyond the Sexual Binary*. Los Angeles: Alyson, 2002.

Nye, Robert A. ed. *Sexuality*. Oxford: Oxford University Press, 1999.
Schechter, Harold. *The Serial Killer Files: The Who, What, Where, How and Why of the World's Most Terrifying Murderers*. New York: Ballantine, 2003.
Schurman-Kauflin, Deborah. *The New Predator: Women Who Kill, Profiles of Female Serial Killers*. NewYork: Algora, 2000.
Seidman, Steven, Nancy Fischer, and Chet Meeks, eds. *Introducing the New Sexuality Studies: Original Essays and Interviews*. London: Routledge, 2006.
Storrs, Elisabeth. "'Our Scapegoat': An Exploration of Media Representations of Myra Hindley and Rosemary West." *Theology and Sexuality* 11(1) 2004, pp. 9–28.
Stryker, Susan, and Stephen Whittle, eds. *The Transgender Studies Reader*, London: Routledge, 2006.
Wade, C, C. Myers, Erik Gooch, and Reid Meloy, J. "The Role of Psychopathy and Sexuality in a Female Serial Killer." *Journal of Forensic Sciences*, 50(3) May 2005, pp. 1–6.
Weeks, Jeffrey. *Sexuality*. London: Routledge, 1986.
West, Candace, and Don H Zimmerman. "Doing Gender." *Gender & Society* 1(2): 125–51.
Williams, Christine L. and Arlene Stein. *Sexuality and Gender*. Oxford: Blackwell, 2002.

10. Neither Victim nor Vixen
Reading the Female Detective's Receding Body and Textual Violence

WINTER S. ELLIOTT

According to Val McDermid, Raymond Chandler has a lot to answer for. "He had a problem with women," she says bluntly, commenting on a misogynist anxiety that manifests itself in the limited number of roles he crafted for female characters, which McDermid describes as "Vamps, victims, and vixens."[1] In fact, McDermid blames the "perennial popularity"[2] of Chandler's fiction for ensuring that this understanding of femininity and female roles continue to underlie the *noir* genre. But that awareness of gendered limitations could also be said to motivate a good deal of crime fiction, not only the *noir* novels featuring primarily male detectives but also to the more recent and diverse works written by, for, and about women. In fact, established gender roles pervade both early and late crime fiction. Modern crime fiction by women, like that by Marcia Muller, Val McDermid, and even Chelsea Cain, naturally reflects altered social concepts of femininity and masculinity. Received largely by a female audience, these works also present an important contrast between the body of the female detective and that of the female—or male—victim. As the female detective's body ceases to be a focal point, the victim's body has increasingly become a target of graphic, and sexual, violence. Just as gendered identity in early crime fiction derived definition from allocations of power, so too does this shift in modern crime fiction depend upon the female reader's understanding of social hierarchy.

It used to be easy to identify, and define, the detective in a crime novel. *He* was easy to spot, after all, marked by his gender, race, and, if not class, as least social position. Megan Abbott, for example, describes the hardboiled hero as "a white male loner traversing a modern urban city, crippled by threats to his whiteness, his gender, his sexuality, and, simultaneously, tantalized by those threats."[3] For Abbot, the detective's identity is precarious, both defined and limited by his relationship to society. Despite the potentially fragile nature of his masculinity, the detective has clung to maleness, even as he has become a *she*; Kathleen Klein, for example, has argued that the detective always occupies a symbolically male position, while the victim also occupies a female one, both regardless of actual physical gender.[4] Maureen Reddy agrees, pointing out that the isolation so typical of the male hard-boiled hero does not present an acceptable role for a woman, who would be "assigned to the domestic sphere and defined by [her] relationships to others, particularly to family members."[5] If the detective was, by default, male, that left open a very different function for women, who often supplied the victims of the crimes investigated by the detective. Of late, however, that linear understanding of gender has begun to change. In discussing victimology, Sandra Walklate seeks an alternative to "an underpinning world-view that constitutes the potential victim as being powerless, and, in many instances, female. Thus women's victimisation is made visible and men's invisible."[6] Some recent crime novels, either ostensibly featuring female detectives or female villains, also struggle with this issue, visibly portraying male victimization. Because these novels also often partake of a recent tendency to de-emphasize the role of the otherwise central female detective, they enable the reader to act as that detective, voyeuristically uncovering the mystery—and, more importantly, scrutinizing the violated bodies of the victims. The reader's gaze, focused on those bodies, perceives more than gender roles turned topsy-turvy. It also uncovers a connection between power and sexual violence that pervades social structure and now operates, not equally but randomly, upon both women and men.

Indeed, because crime novels, like Muller's *Locked In*, can structure the reading experience as a simulation of the investigation itself, the reader explores not just a mystery or the puzzling identity of a serial killer but also the nature of power structures inherent in the genre itself. Pamela Bedore, for example, terms detective fiction "a highly gendered form in which dominant structures of power are reified through the ritual of the narrative: a disruption to social order labeled as crime is followed by the restoration of that order by the figure of the detective."[7] Generally speaking, most crime fiction has substantiated, rather than undermined, those same "dominant structures of power," those same *gendered* power structures. However, crime fiction in which the reader's experience simulates the act of investigation undermines that dichotomy and forces a reconsideration of the nature of power. In these texts, the reader explores not just the mystery driving the narrative, but also the underlying social structure that has permitted the crime to occur.

In fact, a particular kind of reader chooses crime fiction by women as her—and the proper pronoun is, perhaps surprisingly, "her"—genre of choice. As Pamela Caughie remarks, "Our theories of reading are based on the hypothesis of a male reader,"[8] but the consumer of popular fiction is increasingly, and overwhelmingly, female. In terms of true crime fiction, "from two-thirds to three-quarters of the readers of these grisly nonfiction accounts are women."[9] So too are the authors they choose to read. For one thing, "60 percent of English novels are written by women,"[10] a figure that implies a proportionate total for crime fiction in general and detective novels specifically. Consequently, the relationship that Klein describes as a "woman-oriented trio of writer, detective/text, and reader"[11] can be assumed to be at work both in the author's choice of content in the texts themselves and in the reader's choice to buy those same texts.

It's not a huge leap, then, to note that the woman reader must find some kind of special interest in crime fiction. Laura Browder posits that true crime readers "read true crime to help themselves cope with the patriarchal violence they have encountered in the past, and fear in the present,"[12] adding that "true crime books provide a secret map of the world, a how-to guide for personal survival — and a means for expressing the violent feelings that must be masked by femininity."[13] Bethe Schoenfeld describes the experience of a woman reading crime fiction more positively, but still with overtones of a transformative encounter with the text, as an "empowerment" occasioned by "the large quantities of crime fiction books by women authors about women investigators that are bought by women readers. Secondly, a woman reads the text written by a woman as a woman confirming her status as woman and allowing her to connect to the greater community of women."[14] Both Browder and Schoenfeld imply that works dealing with crime, whether non-fiction or fiction, provide an outlet for women's discomfort with "true life" social conditions. In particular, women seem to read crime novels in order to deal with the disparities of power in place in still-patriarchal societies—disparities that are often manifested as sexual violence. As Michel Foucault points out, the body and its sexuality is often a receptacle for social power. Indeed, Lois McNay describes Foucault's understanding of sexuality as "the result of a productive 'biopower' which focuses on human bodies."[15] Sexual abuse is an ultimate, and one of the worst, demonstrations of that power, deriving not from desire but from an unequal application of agency and individual authority. Its depiction in fiction, therefore, is an unpleasant representation of social realities, the victim acting as a stand-in for a powerless social Other.

In contrast, the reader of a crime novel enjoys a privileged position, one of power and, to some extent, authority. At the very least, this reader acts as a spectator, observing the crime itself. Moreover, in detective fiction, that reader becomes an active, rather than passive, participant, something dramatized clearly in William Faulkner's classic short story "A Rose for Emily,"[16] which Lawrence Rodgers labels "an interestingly conventional detective tale."[17] In this story, the pieces of Emily's life, a dead body, and the Southern Gothic background of the text all provide clues to the detective, voiced as a global "we" that encompasses the reader. In crime fiction by and for women, the reader's role is all the more important — and controversial, as such novels often feature violence enacted upon female bodies. Christiana Gregoriou suggests that the critical idea of carnival might be useful in understanding readers' motivations for consuming graphic and often distasteful depictions of violence or social deviance. She explains:

> Devoted readers of the genre, often accused of enjoying the crimes described in such novels in a way that isn't socially acceptable ... are in fact 'allowed' to be socially *deviant* themselves for the duration of the reading, just like carnival participants were in the course of Renaissance carnivalesque festivals. If readers of crime novels are thought of as the *spectators* of carnivals, they are enabled to consume and enjoy pain, violence, cruelty and crime in the privacy of their own homes, while in a sense 'letting others do their crimes for them' ... readers of crime novels could be thought of as *participants* in the violence of the novels they read, while not advocating that such violence is, in the course of everyday life, acceptable.[18]

The act of reading a crime novel, in this framework, serves a voyeuristic purpose that is doubled if for a female reader of a crime novel.

At its heart, crime fiction deals with the structure of society; by its very nature, it must contain an action that upsets social balance. Crime fiction is also often "fundamentally conservative,"[19] forcing the reestablishment of social norms through the resolution of the crime at the end of the novel. Because it so clearly reflects social structure, crime fiction also replicates social anxieties about gender. Specifically, hardboiled detective fiction features "the configuration of gender through binary structures — in particular binaries produced in the service of constituting a fearless and potent maleness."[20] Recent crime fiction, however, is less concerned with the masculinity of the detective than the distribution of power throughout society. Thus, the gender of bodies in crime fiction is less important than what happens to those bodies. Indeed, recent texts elide the detective's body entirely, opening a space for the reader to participate in the text. As the reader takes over the space vacated by the detective, she explores the crime; but, given that the perpetrator of the crime is frequently either known or obvious, the real mystery for the reader involves investigating the social structure that permitted the crime to occur.

As one of the earliest female detectives in the hard-boiled fashion, Marcia Muller's Sharon McCone offers an easy standard by which to evaluate contemporary treatment of the detective's own body. In a recent novel, Marcia Muller portrays Sharon McCone as literally "locked in" her body, unable to move, for the duration of the book. Beyond the fact of its disability, McCone's body — and certainly its gender — is almost irrelevant to the detection in the novel, which showcases a kind of committee-solving of the crime. Similarly, McDermid's character Carol Jordan seems frozen and admits to an inability to pursue a sexual relationship with her friend and partner-in-detection, Tony Hill. Like Sharon McCone, Carol Jordan's gender is less important than her status as a police detective, and thus part of an official, state-sanctioned group. In contrast to the receding body of the female detective, the victim's body is diverse and displayed. McDermid's victims are often young, female, and vulnerable; they are also frequently male, older, or established in society. Chelsea Cain's psychopathic killer Gretchen Lowell, the star — in more ways than one — of her series, also targets a man, the police detective Archie Sheridan. Works like McDermid's *The Mermaids Singing* and Chelsea Cain's *Heartsick* feature violence inflicted upon male bodies, bodies open and exhibited to the reader. In viewing violence enacted upon bodies throughout society, the reader sees an ultimate and extreme application of power. As McNay points out, for Foucault, "the sexed body is to be understood not only as the primary target of the techniques of disciplinary power, but also as the point where these techniques are resisted and thwarted."[21] The graphic and often sexual nature of the crimes committed in McDermid's and Cain's works illustrate a power structure readily recognizable to a female reader. It's patriarchal, not so much because the power derives from a centrally located *male* figure, but because of the unequal and potentially abusive distribution of authority. In these works, however, the rigidly hierarchical social net created through patriarchy has entrapped more victims than just women.

Sharon McCone, the female private investigator featured in the long-running series by Marcia Muller, has come a long way since the series began: she's grown up, gone out on her own, and gotten married over the course of more than twenty books. This character plainly reveals the growing, participatory space open to the reader. The 2009 *Locked In* forces McCone into frozen inertia — literally, as the detective, suffering from a gunshot wound to the head, experiences the medical condition described in the title. Unable to move or to communicate beyond blinking her eyes — once for yes, twice for no — McCone can only "lie here. Silent. Motionless. Afraid."[22] Of course, the detective drags herself out of most of her depression, though she never quite shakes the realistic and understandable terror her condition evokes; she even manages to assist in the investigation that tracks her assailant. But "assist" is the operative word. McCone *doesn't* go out on the streets, interview suspects, or track down clues. Instead, a small army of angry and devoted friends, family, and employees forms "a tribal war council" in order to "find out who shot her" and "nail this person" (20). With McCone very occasionally making suggestions via blinks — her ability to squawk out "*ack*" marks a turning point in her communicative ability late in the novel — the efforts of her entire detective agency, husband Hy Ripinsky, and family finally succeed, and the perpetrator is dragged into her hospital room to face her.

In a way, Sharon McCone doesn't detect anything in the novel, though she's certainly its heart. In fact, her position at the background, rather than the foreground, of the novel, suggests a new and alternative role for the female detective in recent crime fiction by women. McCone's body, subject as it is to various tubes and surgeries throughout the book, *is* important, but its femininity is not. In fact, McCone's status as a female detective in general is elided by her medical condition and her silence throughout the book, a speechlessness that she describes, at one point, as a "voiceless scream" (27). The actual detection in the book is diffused; the investigation is pushed forward through a series of short chapters, each dedicated to an individual member of McCone's "war council." Typically, Muller organizes the book by days; the section occurring on Sunday, July 20, for example, consists of fifteen individual sections, with Mick Savage, Julia Rafael, Rae Kelleher, Hy Ripinsky, and Sharon McCone herself each the focus of one or more of the sections. This diffusive detection removes the focus from the female detective and radiates it outward, replacing a central main character with a very different kind of investigative experience — that of the reader.

Like Muller, Val McDermid invites her readers into the text, offering them a rather more privileged position than does Muller. Sharon McCone may be silent and in distress for much of *Locked In*, but, thanks to the mystical pronouncements of her Native American father and her own iconic status, the reader is never in doubt that the detective will pull through — or push out of the silenced shell of her body. McDermid does not so kindly dispose of her own detectives. Several of her lead characters die, often brutally and in agony, over the course of the series. In contrast, the reader usually suffers no worse treatment than a queasy stomach or passing doubts about the nature of humanity — or human monsters. In *The Wire in the Blood*, the psychologist Tony Hill, who suffered his own traumatic experience at the end of the first book in the series, *The Mermaids Singing*, has recruited and is training a novice group of psychological profilers. Privy to that same education is the hapless reader, who learns, as does the motley group of infant profilers, the terms and definitions of serial killers and their accoutrements. In teaching the profilers, Tony Hill also instructs the reader, who learns, for example, what defines a serial killer's signature:

> it's all the bits of behaviour that exceed what is actually necessary to commit the crime. The ritual of the offence.... Examples of signature in a killer might be things like: does he strip the victim? Does he make a neat pile of the victim's clothes? Does he use cosmetics on the victim after death? Is he having sex with the victim postmortem?...[23]

Significantly, for a good bit of the story, the reader is positioned to invisibly peer over the shoulder of one of those trainee profilers, haunting her from the beginning of the story to her (untimely) demise slightly before the midpoint of the book. Even more so than this young and ill-fated profiler, the reader learns Tony Hill's lessons. Through this participatory exercise, the reader becomes a profiler herself for the duration of the book, vicariously engaged in the investigation. It's the reader who receives Tony Hill's knowledge, becomes educated with his instruction, and ultimately perceives more than the fictional profilers themselves.

McDermid uses a young, female profiler almost to taunt the reader, questioning the suitability of her interests in profiling and detection and warning of the risks. This detective, Shaz Bowman, is introduced with the ironic observation that she "understood perfectly why people commit murder" (13). Her positioning at the front — and center — of the book is, no doubt, intentional; she is the third character noted, following the killer himself, who really *does* understand "why people commit murder," and Tony Hill, who also must have a pretty good idea after his experiences in the first book in the series. Shaz Bowman, however, has only a limited understanding of killers and killing; in that, she's like the reader, and both must question their participation in the events narrated in the book. Shaz Bowman tries to prove herself, to quell lingering doubts about her detective status, to conclusively answer the nagging question "After all, she was a detective, wasn't she?" (43). To put it bluntly — or perhaps mildly — Shaz Bowman ends up dead as a result of her intrepid enquiries ... and she does not die peacefully. Instead, she's both aware that she's going to die and cognizant of her inability to save herself. For Shaz Bowman, there is no knight in shining armor, or fellow policeman, or even good Samaritan who drops in at the nick of time to save her, and, lacking that *deus ex machina* assistance, Shaz dies in agony.

Up until the point of her death, Shaz Bowman has been the primary instigator behind the investigation into a supposed cluster of killings. Her death opens a kind of lacuna in the text, an empty space that the other characters do step forward to fill. Less obviously, though, that space is already occupied, by a different kind of detective, the reader herself. While McDermid has designed Shaz's death to be shocking and surprising — and she certainly succeeds — there's probably one small part of the reader that remains unsurprised. As McDermid herself has pointed out, women, "after all, are overwhelmingly the victims of sexually motivated brutality and homicide."[24] Similarly, "[t]he voyeuristic gaze of traditional hard-boiled fiction is thus often intimately associated with sadistic violence against women."[25] Both social norms and conventions of the crime genre, then, dictate that sexualized violence focused on women lacks surprise. Shaz's death seems to reiterate that assumed relationship between victimization and femininity. After all, Shaz Bowman is young, inexperienced, somewhat foolish, and female — typical qualities of a victim. But, in actuality, her death merely indicates that there is no longer any safe, inviolable social space. While the male detective may once have operated from a privileged and unflinching position, his authority is now in question. Power in McDermid's books has the ability to target young women like Shaz as well as more experienced and aware female — and male — detectives.

Thus, not even the series' main character is inviolate; in the third book of the series, *The Last Temptation*, Carol Jordan is viciously raped by the criminal she has attempted to trap and capture over the course of the book. While the rape itself happens behind the scenes, its consequences are displayed for the reader; Jordan's "raped, sodomized, and battered body"[26] is described in detail reminiscent of that applied to murder victims:

> Carol lay in a crumpled heap, wrists and ankles bound behind her back with leather belts. Her face was a streaked mess of blood, saliva, mucus and tears. Her nose was swollen and angled improbably. Her eyes were invisible in the puffy purpling of bruised flesh. Smudged trails of blood and shit were visible on her thighs. There was no room for doubt about what had happened here [441].

Given that the rape has already been stated as a given, that last observation seems redundant, notwithstanding the fact that it somewhat conveys the reaction of the woman who finds Jordan. If not unnecessary, then, the detailed physical description of Jordan's body must serve a purpose — and it does. It underscores the reader's active gaze.

First introduced by Laura Mulvey in her essay "Visual Pleasure and Narrative Cinema," and applied by her to film, the concept "male gaze" has been co-opted by feminism and developed beyond the parameters of that original essay. Mulvey originally observed that, "In a world ordered by sexual imbalance, pleasure in looking has been split between active/male and passive/female. The determining male gaze projects its fantasy onto the female figure, which is styled accordingly."[27] As Priscilla Walton and Manina Jones point out, though, "Mulvey's theories of the male gaze as orienting filmic spectatorship have been contested — or at least complicated — in recent years by theorists (including Mulvey herself) who have envisioned an active and resistant female spectatorship of popular culture and by advocates of women's participation in popular culture production."[28] In the treatment of Carol Jordan's victimized body, half of Mulvey's scenario would seem to be met — the graphically displayed female body is objectified for the reader's gaze. Yet, here, that gaze seems split, between a *female* viewer and an unseen social eye. It is, of course, a woman that Jordan calls for rescue, and a woman who finds her, and another woman who helps her clothe and hide her vulnerable and violated body; similarly, the book's largely female readership views both Jordan's exhibited body and her reclamation of it — though not the rape itself. In viewing Jordan's raped body, the other characters necessarily draw the reader's attention beyond the body and onto the act of rape and its symbolic positioning within society.

Notably, Jordan's rape takes place within both her police and social systems — and it occurs because of the norms of both systems. As usual, Tony Hill offers a kind of psychological interpretation of the situation, pointing out that Carol Jordan has been "set up by her own side" (439). Hill's observation points to the use to which Jordan has been put in the book; she has been deployed by her superiors as bait to lure in a criminal. While Jordan rejects the overt sexuality of the situation, her usefulness derives from her physical similarities to the criminal's dead lover. Although it can't be, and shouldn't be, argued that Jordan's male superiors intended her to get raped, it's undeniable that she has intentionally been positioned in a kind of sexual economy — of which rape is the ultimate outcome.

Additionally, Hill reiterates the pervasive social response to rape, believing it equivalent to a destruction of the woman's self rather than just an attack on her body. He has never accepted "the arguments about rape not being the worst thing that could happen to a woman" and believes that "rape brought havoc to the personality" (438). Hill's statement implies that rape, not death, *is* "the worst thing that could happen to a woman" apparently because it destroys her sense of self. He adds that rape "left her with nothing but fragments of the life she thought she had owned. It undermined everything she thought she knew about herself" (438). To some extent, Tony Hill's masculine assessment of the situation evokes centuries of equivalence between a woman's sexual value and her personhood. If a woman's sexuality is breached, Hill's comments suggest, so too is her personality. Thus, like the traditional misogynists that the character would criticize, Hill defines a woman's identity as sexual, and therefore subject to both social control and social censure. But Hill's comments also suggest that sexuality, and anything that disrupts it, has the potential to destabilize social structures.

In Jordan's case, the rape serves as a catalyst that reveals the corruption of the law enforcement system in which she serves. Ultimately, Jordan's rape positions her to define her own future within the police system; she chooses to remain in law enforcement, but has gained the ability to "decide where I want to go" (481). Moreover, Jordan ultimately rejects Tony Hill's equation of a woman's self with her body, arguing that her rapist "never got inside me. Only my body. And that doesn't count. Not really. He's the one who's never going to be free. Because I did get inside him" (480–1). Consequently, while not denying the lasting effects of her experience (which she exhibits clearly in later books), Jordan defines rape as primarily an act of physical violence rather than an emotional assault on selfhood.

Disengaging rape from an assault on selfhood and locating it more tangibly as physical, rather than primarily sexual, violence ultimately changes the gendered nature of the act. Notably, a group of women — Jordan and two other female police officers from different nations — form a community that counters the corrupt and primarily male police force that has so used Carol Jordan. Their small coalition stands in contrast to that less effective male force and undermines both its social structure and accompanying axioms about gender. Essentially, Jordan's superiors have traded upon her sexuality, equating her to a useful good because of physical similarity to another woman. Traditionally, patriarchy accepts both that kind of objectification and its most extreme manifestation, rape, whereas the transgressive female society in which Jordan participates undermines that positioning of women. Thus, that female community must reject patriarchal assumptions about women, gender, and rape. By extension, the reader, herself a potential member of that female community, is invited to also consider and evaluate the connections between patriarchal society and sexualized violence.

In fact, the second of the book's dueling plotlines, which deals not with Jordan's criminal pursuit but with a serial killer pursued by Tony Hill and two other female police detectives, acknowledges the equal opportunity nature of sexual violence. The practical Dutch detective Marijke — who, in an ironic and tongue-in-cheek allusion to *The Silence of the Lambs*, is described as having grown up on a farm and "really didn't care how much noise the lambs made" (51) — realizes that her victim's pubic hair has been scalped. This quasi-sexual element of the murder further problematizes the association of sexual assault with female victimization due to the killer's interest in male and female victims alike. What's up for debate is a binary association between femininity and victimization and masculinity and power. The victim's role, in this situation, is not a symbolically female one, because the text proposes that anyone, regardless of gender, may fall prey to abusive power. In the Tony Hill/Carol Jordan series, the usual understanding of the powerful — and therefore masculine — detective hero and the utterly vulnerable — and therefore feminine — rape or murder victim is dissolved.

Indeed, the only safe space in this series is occupied by the reader, not the detective, whether male or female. As Margaret Kinsman observes in her discussion of Paretsky's V.I. Warshawsky, "[d]etective novels traditionally emphasize the safety of such stable boundaries as geography, class, race, and gender."[29] If Paretsky "disrupt[s] the stability of this legacy by moving the boundaries,"[30] then McDermid does so by disrupting the lines demarcating detective and victim. In Shaz Bowman's death and Carol Jordan's rape, the reader is left without a strong, inviolate detective character with which to empathize. Nor can the reader rest certain of male power in this series. In fact, the series opens by emphasizing male vulnerability to sexualized violence in the novel *The Mermaids Singing,* in which Tony Hill's position as both privileged psychologist/detective *and* final victim in the work further challenges the position of the male detective as invincible and powerful. As Klein points out, the traditional "fictional male detective is a superior, solitary figure" who "is the novel's hero not only in structural terms but also in the content, tone, and impact of the story."[31] Acknowledging a difference in the approach taken by the "modern police-procedural novel" which "attempts to establish a team approach to detection," Klein still notes that "even here, there are varying degrees of participation and certain characters clearly lack star status."[32] Consequently, in following the trend of diffused, wide-spread investigation seen in Marcia Muller's *Locked In* and her own later *The Last Temptation,* McDermid undercuts the social positioning of the traditional male detective.

Besides the figure of the serial killer, who opens the book with a description of her proclivities and "first time" to kill,[33] Tony Hill is the first character mentioned in the book, and the first to consciously acknowledge that "they"— the police, society in general— actually *have* a serial killer at work. His specialized and private knowledge of the situation would seem to place him in a position of authority, but Tony Hill works within the system, partnering with Carol Jordan, a police detective, to hunt down the killer. Whatever authority and power his specialized knowledge would have given him vanishes abruptly at the end of the book, as his link to the police investigation makes him an especially attractive target for the killer. "Every hour I'd suffered would be an hour added on to the agonies of Dr. Tony Hill ... the stupid man who hadn't even recognized that all my crimes belonged to me," vows the killer (314). As a result, Tony Hill finds himself doubly exposed—first, before the reader's eye, and, secondly, before the "blind eye of a camcorder on a tripod, a red light on the side indicating that his scrutiny was not going unrecorded" (315). What follows is very much a gruesome rape—if not a "traditional" one.

The serial killer, a probably gay man who has undergone sex change surgery and now kills as a woman named Angelica, repeatedly targets Tony's sexuality. In an attempt to preserve his life, Tony Hill deploys his psychologist's weapon — talking — and penetrates Angelica's weakness, an apparent desire to be loved by a man. "I love you, Angelica," Tony Hill pleads at one point, repeating "I love you" (340). Emotionally, Angelica may be tempted to believe her victim; intellectually, she doubts the evidence before her eyes:

> Her lower lip thrust out, bringing an expression of calculating petulance to her face. She nodded in the direction of his groin, where his penis hung limp. "So if you find me that attractive, how come it doesn't show?"
> It was the one question to which Tony had no answer at all [346].

Angelica has proven, with her other victims, thoroughly creative in her exploration of exactly what sexual violence against a male might entail. But, with Tony Hill, she's intrigued by the possibility of his complicity in his own violation. From a man, that complicity requires evidence of arousal — and, not insignificantly, Tony has exhibited difficulty in that area throughout the book, blaming his sexual issues on his own traumatic childhood, a scarring upbringing that a serial killer, actually, would not find all that foreign. But Tony's sexual difficulties do not call his masculinity into question in the novel. For one thing, Angelica, the killer, has targeted potent males throughout the book, and she shows no hesitation to include Tony Hill in that category. It might be argued that Angelica, with her own gender issues, is in no position to judge, but other females have similarly exhibited an interest in the psychologist — most notably, Carol Jordan, the principal female protagonist, finds herself half in love, and thoroughly attracted to, Tony Hill. So, in the book's eyes at least, Tony's difficulty in exhibiting physical desire does not make him any less male.

Nor does his victimization at the hands of Angelica rob him of all agency. Like Carol Jordan later in the series, Tony Hill endures a sexual assault and concludes that "there were worse things in the world, and this woman had made her previous victims endure some of them" (354). Willing to compromise himself emotionally in order to save his body physical pain and torture, the psychologist promises to make love to the killer and guides her abuse of his body. "Give me head," he tells her bluntly, and she quickly complies:

> Almost before he'd finished speaking, she was on her knees, hands flickering over his balls. Tenderly, she lifted his flaccid penis and slipped it into her mouth, not taking her eyes from his face. Tony reached out and began to stroke her hair. Then, with what felt like infinite slowness, he pulled her head forward on to him, forcing her head down, her eyes away from him [352–3].

Naturally, Tony Hill uses the killer's distraction to his advantage, hitting her, struggling free, and eventually killing her. His police companions arrive one moment past the nick of time, an anticlimactic charge to the rescue that follows the psychologist's act of self-defense.

It might be tempting to read Tony Hill's abduction and molestation as part of a "kind of revenge fantasy against threatening or patriarchal figures," as Walton and Jones suggest frequently happens in an interpretation of "women's recasting of hard-boiled violence."[34] But Tony Hill's unfortunate encounter with a serial killer actually says more about his position as victim than her position as murderer. Although Tony Hill has been a part of the police system, he has never been its lead; nor has he been the star of the book. Instead, the book shows him as ultimately vulnerable to the same system that placed Carol Jordan in harm's way in *The Last Temptation* discussed earlier in this essay. Whereas traditional detective/crime works feature women in jeopardy as part of a substantiation of traditional gender structures, power holds the same threat for men *and* women. As a result, these works do not challenge the sexual abuse of women as part of a patriarchal system of power; rather, they extend that danger to men as well, implying that the prurient interest that drives the objectification of women's bodies holds true for men's bodies as well. If the history of the detective story is one in which "male sexuality [has functioned as] power, knowledge, entitlement; the female body as the site of seduction and death,"[35] then the erasure of a strong, inviolate detective and his/her replacement with the ever-present potential for victimization has redefined this gendered code — but not necessarily for the better.

A final work, Chelsea Cain's thriller *Heartsick*, drives this point home exceedingly well. Portraying the twisted relationship between a female serial killer and the male victim that she has — for her own apparent amusement — simply *let go*, alive, the book shows the victim, Detective Archie Sheridan, attempting to survive both the serial killer's lingering damage and a new investigation. The book opens with a flashback scene of Archie Sheridan's kidnapping by Gretchen Lowell; from the start, there is no mystery about *her* identity as a serial killer. Instead, the book *begins* with Archie's awareness, apparently finally, that "Gretchen Lowell is the killer"[36]; "Archie doesn't know for sure that it's her until that moment. There is a dull bloom of warmth in his spine, his vision blurs, and then he knows..." (1), the text begins. He attempts to go for his gun, but he's too drugged; she "takes it and smiles, kissing him gently on the forehead" (1). So, in a few brief bursts of information, the book actually verifies several important facts: Archie hasn't solved a mystery, but has (rather forcibly) had it solved for him; he is a cop, but a vulnerable one whose weapon has just been taken from him; and there's something deeply sexual — and twisted, of course — about Gretchen Lowell's intentions towards him.

In fact, Gretchen Lowell is a kind of red herring throughout the book, drawing attention away from Archie Sheridan's transgressive status as victim and assigning it falsely to herself. At various times, Gretchen seems either feminist or misogynist — feminist because she pursues a kind of serial killer equality, and misogynist because she is, after all, composed of a collection of tired sexist — and improbably sexy — stereotypes. For example, Susan, a reporter meeting the incarcerated Gretchen for the first time, feels intimidated by her and remembers that pictures of the woman had been popular in the media "because she was beautiful. And a serial killer. A perfect combination. And aren't all stunning women capable of murder? the pictures seemed to ask" (192). In some ways, Gretchen would actually be more interesting as a female serial killer if she *weren't* beautiful, if it wasn't her physical attractiveness at least as much as her killing that marked her as different, as Other.

Unfortunately, the character of Gretchen isn't really novel as far as serial killers go. She seems to be almost a female version of the (in)famous Hannibal Lecter who pursued the novice FBI agent Clarice Starling. In the film version of Thomas Harris's *The Silence of the Lambs*, "Lecter is clearly Clarice's superior in education, intellect, and imagination"[37] and, importantly, a love interest for her, a figure of strange sexual allure that both the novel and film depiction of the sequel, *Hannibal*, develop further, though in different ways. As Linda Mizejewski comments, "The sexy question bonding Lecter and Starling to each other and to us, the hungry consumers and audiences, is how dangerous our tastes might be."[38] Mizejewski suggests that our interest in Hannibal derives from his transgressive allure and his status as "postmodern commodity — consumer and consumed,"[39] who reflects our own interests and desires back at us. Like Hannibal, Gretchen possesses a kind of superiority over the other characters in the book; she catches the cop, not the other way around, and toys with him for the entirety of the book, just as Hannibal does with Clarice. Like Hannibal, too, Gretchen is a figure of sexual interest for the main character, Archie Sheridan, despite the torture he has suffered at her hands. Her excessive beauty seems to recall tired tropes of female power; if Hannibal has brains, Gretchen has both brains *and* beauty.

So, Gretchen does not really break new territory as a female version of the potent and alluring — and *dangerous*— Hannibal Lecter. She does provide a draw for the reader's gaze. Just as Hannibal lures Clarice, Gretchen entices the reader's eye, providing a focus in an episodic book that begins with a flashback and depends on other flashbacks to develop its back story — the relationship between Archie Sheridan, police detective and victim, and Gretchen Lowell, serial killer. In her lurid interest in either Hannibal Lecter or Gretchen Lowell, the reader (or, in the case of the film versions of Harris's books, the viewer) gives these characters tacit approval, sanction for their sins, of which there are many.

For Gretchen Lowell, the most significant of those transgressions is her prolonged, patient, and almost pornographically described torture of Archie Sheridan. Notably, Archie's interest in Gretchen is purely heterosexual, as later books in the series reveal; his heterosexuality is never in question, and neither is his masculinity. Indeed, Gretchen at one point carves a heart into his chest, capturing their mutual attraction to each other. However, the book begins with a complete rejection of Archie's agency. In Gretchen's hands, he has no power, and every scene in the book that describes his treatment by Gretchen underscores that vulnerability. In fact, Gretchen blatantly tells Archie, "You don't get to choose, though, do you? I get to make all the decisions. I get to be the one in charge. All you have to do is go along" (310). In graphic detail, the book depicts Archie "going along" with Gretchen's torture; he becomes increasingly passive, less resistant, in mind, speech, and action as the days of his captivity progress. Even when Gretchen finally asks, "Do you want me to stop?" Archie replies, "No ... I'm hoping you'll nick an artery" (310–1). In surrendering his agency, Archie accepts his place in the system Gretchen has created.

Ultimately, that system will resonate with a female reader. Patriarchy depends upon a hierarchical exercise of power. In McDermid's *The Last Temptation*, that power manifested itself as a system in which the main female character, Carol Jordan, was exploited sexually, first for her appearance, and then, more graphically, in an act of rape. This social structure operates outside of the characters' interests or intentions, and it depends upon the interplay between the powerful and the disempowered. Although it may be apparent in a social structure like a police organization, it actually permeates all social interaction. Interest in the fictional serial killer derives from this character's ability to manipulate those boundaries; serial killers, through their transgressive actions, seem to operate outside of normal social boundaries, free of the rules through which the rest of society operates. In reality, however, a fictional serial killer merely takes the mechanisms of power through which society operates to its logical conclusion — control over another human's body and life.

These detective/crime novels by Marcia Muller, Val McDermid, and Chelsea Cain vary widely in terms of subject, quality, and emphasis; there is no graphic depiction of a tortured body in pain in Muller's works, for example. However, these authors do share similarities in their treatment of the detective, and McDermid and Cain suggest a similar understanding of the significance of the male body in pain. All of these works diffuse the role of the female detective, spreading it throughout several characters rather than one. Consequently, these works lack a typically strong, solitary, and moral detective-hero with which the reader can identify and empathize. Instead, the reader operates voyeuristically, seeing the action within the novel from the viewpoint of an all-seeing observer. In a way, the reader's position reminds one of Foucault's idea of the panopticon, whereby prisoners internalize the power of the prison system and submit, rather than resist, to an unseen authority figure. In these books, the reader sees a system of power at work and observes its deployment upon the characters within the text. Although the reader doesn't function as an authority within the text that acts upon the characters/prisoners, as she explores the power structures within the text, she is nonetheless complicit in their continuance. In fact, the reader's voyeuristic eye reifies, rather than challenges, the exertion of power upon bodies exhibited in McDermid's and Cain's works.

None of these works challenges the hierarchical disposition of power and authority. Rather, they modify the application of that power. Under this system, women can certainly be victims—and frequently are. That much a female reader would find unsurprising. But positing a female reader, and a female gaze, also conveys power and authority to that reader. Consequently, the role of victim, and the body in pain, becomes available to female *and* male characters. As Sally Munt points out, "critics have drawn attention to the way feminism's original activism has been rechanneled into the self, rather than being directed at the state."[40] Indeed, these works do not challenge the state, nor the hierarchical disposition of power that it requires. Instead, they attempt to divorce gender from power. That in itself is a radical move, for historically power has partially defined itself along gendered lines, typically equating masculinity with empowerment, for example. However, these works suggest that gender, at least in the simplistic division into masculinity and femininity, operates separately from the exercise of power—which is not to say that gender can't, or isn't, shaped by power, a different subject entirely.

Essentially, power depends upon the control of another's body, and that control most radically manifests itself as the destruction, either through excessive containment, torture, or murder, of that body. In books like *The Mermaids Singing* and *Heartsick*, the body contained, controlled, and, in a way, consumed, is male. Displayed before the female gaze, that body is robbed of its innate—and, some might say, innately masculine—agency. While these works, therefore, assume that power is accessible to that female reader, are they really feminist? Klein comments that "[k]nowing the truth does not lead to justice or action; and radical feminism cannot work within the system," adding that "[s]imilarly, radical feminism cannot work within even the broadest boundaries of the detective genre."[41] Ultimately, these works "trouble"— to borrow Judith Butler's apropos word choice—the system, but they do not undermine it. Instead, they accept a view of power in which anyone, regardless of gender or economic position, may suddenly end up flat on his (or her) back at the bottom of the ladder—and on the serial killer's table. While Muller's work demonstrates the extent to which a female detective's body *doesn't* matter, Cain and McDermid reveal the importance of the victim's body. In fact, to greater or lesser degrees—Cain and McDermid, respectively—these works also recognize the act of killing as an extension of the political state's authority, problematic only because it is not condoned by the state, rather than because of something inherently wrong in the act of killing. Indeed, these graphic depictions of violence against the human body invite the reader into a kind of conspiracy, an observation if not a participation, in this exercise of power.

Notes

1. Val McDermid, Foreword, *A Hell of a Woman: An Anthology of Female Noir*, ed. Megan Abbott (Houston: Busted Flush Press, 2007), 1.
2. Ibid.
3. Megan E. Abbott, *The Street Was Mine: White Masculinity in Hardboiled Fiction and Film Noir* (New York: Palgrave Macmillan, 2002), 11.
4. Kathleen Klein, "*Habeas Corpus*: Feminism and Detective Fiction" in *Feminism in Women's Detective Fiction*, ed. Glenwood Irons (Toronto: University of Toronto Press, 1995), 173.
5. Maureen T. Reddy, *Sisters in Crime: Feminism and the Crime Novel* (New York: Continuum, 1988), 103.
6. Sandra Walklate, "Can there be a Feminist Victimology?" in *Victimization: Theory, Research, and Policy*, eds. Pamela Davies, et al. (Basindstoke: Palgrave Macmillan, 2003), 33.
7. Pamela Bedore, "Queer Investigations: Foxy Ladies and Dandy Detectives in American Dime Novels," *Studies in Popular Culture* 31.1 (2008): 21.
8. Pamela L. Caughie, "Women Reading/Reading Women: A Review of Some Recent Books on Gender and Reading," *Papers on Language and Literature* 24.3 (1988): 318.
9. Laura Browder, "Dystopian Romance: True Crime and the Female Reader," *Journal of Popular Culture* 39.6 (2006): 929.
10. Britta Zangen, "Women as Readers, Writers, and Judges: The Controversy about the Orange Prize for Fiction," *Women's Studies* 32.3 (2003): 283.
11. Kathleen Klein, "Women Times Women Times Women," in *Women Times Three: Writers, Detectives, Readers*, ed. Kathlein Klein. (Bowling Green, OH: Bowling Green State University Popular Press, 1995), 13.
12. Browder, "Dystopian Romance," 928.
13. Ibid., 929.
14. Bethe Schoenfeld, "Women Writers Writing about Women Detectives in Twenty-First Century America," *The Journal of Popular Culture* 41.5 (2008): 847–48.
15. Lois McNay, *Foucault and Feminism: Power, Gender, and the Self* (Boston: Northeastern University Press, 1992), 29.
16. William Faulkner, "A Rose for Emily," in *Selected Short Stories of William Faulkner* (New York: Modern Library, 1993), 47–49.
17. Lawrence R. Rodgers, "'We All Said, 'She Will Kill Herself': The Narrator/Detective in William Faulkner's 'A Rose for Emily,'" *Clues* 16.1 (1995): 120.
18. Christiana Gregoriou, *Deviance in Contemporary Crime Fiction* (New York: Palgrave Macmillan, 2007), 101–102.
19. Reddy, *Sisters in Crime*, 16.
20. Abbott, *The Street Was Mine*, 7.
21. McNay, *Foucault and Feminism*, 39.
22. Marcia Muller, *Locked In* (New York: Grand Central, 2009), 91. Hereafter, references to this work will appear in text.
23. Val McDermid, *The Wire in the Blood* (New York: Minotaur, 2002), 55–56. Hereafter, references to this work will appear in text.

24. Val McDermid, "Complaints about Women Writing Misogynist Crime Fiction Are a Red Herring," BooksBlog, *The Guardian* (29 October 2009), http://www.guardian.co.uk/books/booksblog/2009/oct/29/misogynist-crime-fiction-val-mcdermid (accessed March 28, 2011).
25. Priscilla L. Walton and Manina Jones, *Detective Agency: Women Rewriting the Hard-Boiled Tradition* (Berkeley: University of California Press, 1999), 158.
26. Val McDermid, *The Last Temptation* (New York: St. Martin's, 2003), 435. Hereafter, references to this work will appear in text.
27. Laura Mulvey, "Visual Pleasure and Narrative Cinema," in *Visual and Other Pleasures* 2d ed. (New York: Palgrave Macmillan, 2009), 19.
28. Walton and Jones, *Detective Agency*, 158.
29. Margaret Kinsman, "A Question of Visibility: Paretsky and Chicago," in *Women Times Three: Writers, Detectives, Readers*, ed. Kathleen Klein (Bowling Green, OH: Bowling Green State University Popular Press, 1995), 25.
30. *Ibid.*
31. Kathleen Klein, *The Woman Detective: Gender and Genre* (Urbana: University of Illinois Press, 1988), 185.
32. *Ibid.*
33. Val McDermid, *The Mermaids Singing* (New York: St. Martin's, 1995), 1. Hereafter, references to this work will appear in text.
34. Walton and Jones, *Detective Agency*, 176.
35. Linda Mizejewski, *Hardboiled and High Heeled: The Woman Detective in Popular Culture* (New York: Routledge, 2004), 17.
36. Chelsea Cain, *Heartsick* (New York: Minotaur, 2007), 1. Hereafter, references to this work will appear in text.
37. Mizejewski, *Hardboiled and High-Heeled*, 185.
38. *Ibid.*, 187.
39. *Ibid.*
40. Sally Munt, *Murder by the Book? Feminism and the Crime Novel* (London: Routledge, 1994), 150.
41. Klein, *The Woman Detective*, 220.

Works Cited

Abbott, Megan E. *The Street Was Mine: White Masculinity in Hardboiled Fiction and Film Noir.* New York: Palgrave Macmillan, 2002.
Bedore, Pamela. "Queer Investigations: Foxy Ladies and Dandy Detectives in American Dime Novels." *Studies in Popular Culture* 31.1 (2008): 19–38.
Browder, Laura. "Dystopian Romance: True Crime and the Female Reader." *Journal of Popular Culture* 39.6 (2006): 928–53.
Cain, Chelsea. *Heartsick.* New York: Minotaur, 2007.
Caughie, Pamela L. "Women Reading/Reading Women: A Review of Some Recent Books on Gender and Reading." *Papers on Language and Literature* 24.3 (1988): 317–335.
Gregoriou, Christiana. *Deviance in Contemporary Crime Fiction.* New York: Palgrave Macmillan, 2007.
Kinsman, Margaret. "A Question of Visibility: Paretsky and Chicago." *Women Times Three.* Ed. Kathleen Klein. Bowling Green, OH: Bowling Green State University Popular Press. 15–27.
Klein, Kathleen. "*Habeas Corpus*: Feminism and Detective Fiction." *Feminism in*

Women's Detective Fiction. Ed. Glenwood Irons. Toronto: University of Toronto Press, 1995. 171–89.

_____. *The Woman Detective: Gender and Genre.* Urbana: University of Illinois Press, 1988.

_____. "Women Times Women Times Women." *Women Times Three.* Ed. Kathleen Klein. Bowling Green, OH: Bowling Green State University Popular Press. 3–13.

Klein, Kathleen, ed. *Women Times Three: Writers, Detectives, Readers.* Bowling Green, OH: Bowling Green State University Popular Press, 1995.

McDermid, Val. *Beneath the Bleeding.* New York: Harper, 2009.

_____. "Complaints about Women Writing Misogynist Crime Fiction Are a Red Herring." BooksBlog. *The Guardian.* 29 October 2009. http://www.guardian.co.uk/books/bookblog/2009/oct/29/misogynist-crime-fiction-val-mcdermid (accessed March 28, 2011), 29 October 2009. Web.

_____. Foreword, *A Hell of a Woman: An Anthology of Female Noir.* Ed. Megan Abbott. Houston: Busted Flush Press, 2007.

_____. *The Last Temptation.* New York: St. Martin's, 2003.

_____. *The Mermaids Singing.* New York: St. Martin's, 1995.

_____. *The Wire in the Blood.* New York: Minotaur, 2002.

McNay, Lois. *Foucault and Feminism: Power, Gender, and the Self.* Boston: Northeastern University Press, 1992.

Mizejewski, Linda. *Hardboiled and High Heeled: The Woman Detective in Popular Culture.* New York: Routledge, 2004.

Muller, Marcia. *Locked In.* New York: Grand Central, 2009.

Mulvey, Laura. "Visual Pleasure and Narrative Cinema." *Visual and Other Pleasures.* 2d ed. New York: Palgrave Macmillian, 2009.

Munt, Sally. *Murder by the Book? Feminism and the Crime Novel.* London: Routledge, 1994.

Reddy, Maureen T. *Sisters in Crime: Feminism and the Crime Novel.* New York: Continuum, 1988.

Rodgers, Lawrence R. "'We All Said, 'She Will Kill Herself'": The Narrator/Detective in William Faulkner's 'A Rose for Emily,'" *Clues* 16.1 (1995): 117–129.

Schoenfeld, Bethe. "Women Writers Writing about Women Detectives in Twenty-First Century America." *The Journal of Popular Culture* 41.5 (2008): 836–853.

Walklate, Sandra. "Can there be a Feminist Victimology?" *Victimisation: Theory, Research, and Policy,* Eds. Pamela Davies et. al. New York: Palgrave MacMillan, 2003. 28–45.

Walton, Priscilla L., and Manina Jones. *Detective Agency: Women Rewriting the Hard-Boiled Tradition.* Berkeley: University of California Press, 1999.

Zangen, Britta. "Women as Readers, Writers, and Judges: The Controversy about the Orange Prize for Fiction." *Women's Studies* 32.3 (2003): 281–99.

About the Contributors

Peter Clandfield teaches in the Department of English Studies at Nipissing University in North Bay, Ontario. His main research interests include contemporary Scottish literature as well as theories and practices of censorship. He has published essays on television and detective fiction, and is working on an extended project about representations of urban development and redevelopment in fiction — including crime fiction — and film.

Michael G. Cornelius is the chair of the English Department of Wilson College in Chambersburg, Pennsylvania, and the author or editor of 11 books for various publishers including McFarland; his shorter writings have been published by or appeared in numerous works, published by the University of South Carolina Press among others. He has published extensively on girl and boy sleuths in such journals as *Clues: A Journal of Detection*, *Dime Novel Round-Up*, and *The EAPSU Journal*.

Heath A. Diehl is a faculty member in the University Honors Program at Bowling Green State University (Ohio) where he teaches critical thinking, great ideas, academic writing, and seminars on literature and popular culture. His work has appeared in *M/C: A Journal of Media and Culture*, *SLI: Studies in the Literary Imagination*, *Approaches to Teaching the Works of Oscar Wilde*, and *The Problem Body: Projecting Disability on Film*. He is the author of *Stages of Sexuality: Performance, Gay Male Identity, and Public Space(s)*.

Winter S. Elliott is an associate professor of English at Brenau University, Gainesville, Georgia. She teaches first-year writing as well as literature classes, and is the director of Brenau's Honors Program. Interested in murder and mayhem from an early age, she is drawn to detective and speculative fiction. She enjoys investigating the relationship between writer, work, and reader.

Megan Hoffman is a Ph.D. candidate and teaching assistant in the School of English, University of St. Andrews. She has previously published and presented work on contemporary women's crime fiction as well as 19th and 20th century British and American crime fiction. Her dissertation research focuses on representations of femininity in the novels of British women "golden age" crime writers.

Julie H. Kim is a professor of English and women's studies at Northeastern Illinois University in Chicago. Her primary fields of research include early modern British literature and detective fiction. She has published on Milton, British culture, and film and is the editor of *Race and Religion in the Postcolonial British Detective Story* (McFarland, 2005).

Neil McCaw is a reader in literature and culture at the University of Winchester (UK). His previous publications include *George Eliot and Victorian Historiography* (2000), *Writing Irishness in Nineteenth-Century British Culture* (2004), *How to Read Texts* (2008), and *Adapting Detective Fiction: Crime, Englishness and the TV Detectives* (2010), in addition to numerous articles and chapters on 19th and 20th century culture.

Jennifer Mitchell is a doctoral candidate in English literature at the City University of New York Graduate Center. At Hunter College, she teaches children's literature and Victorian literature. She has published pieces about sadomasochism, sexuality and reading practices, bisexuality and queer theory. She serves on the Executive Board of the Center for Lesbian and Gay Studies, an organization that promotes scholarship, activism and discourse about LGBTQ issues.

Andrew Hock Soon Ng is a senior lecturer at Monash University, Malaysia. He has taught theories of authorship, film studies, postcolonial writings, and contemporary literature. He is the author of *Dimensions of Monstrosity in Contemporary Narratives* (2004), *Interrogating Interstices* (2007) and *Intimating the Sacred* (2011), and he is the editor of *Asian Gothic* (McFarland, 2008). He has also published several articles in peer-reviewed journals.

Kelley Wezner is an Assistant Professor in the Department of English and Philosophy at Murray State University, Murray, Kentucky, where she also directs institutional assessment. She earned her Ph.D. in English literature from Northern Illinois University. Her research interests include intersections of power and gender, as well as textual claims for authority. Her work related to gender and power has appeared in *The CEA Critic*.

Betsy Young is an M.A.T. candidate in secondary education and English at Rhode Island College. A 1988 graduate of the University of Pennsylvania in English and communications, she had a career in book publishing prior to entering the education field. At RIC, Betsy has served as a teaching assistant in the English department and as a tutor in the Writing Center.

Index

Abbott, Megan 211, 227, 228, 229
African 110
African American 8, 9, 101, 103–5, 107, 109, 112, 115, 117–9
Alison, Laurence 206, 208
Alsop, Rachel 208, 209
Auden, W.H. 63, 79

Bakhtin, Mikhail 161, 165
Basler, Robert 26, 33, 34
Baudrillard, Jean 208, 209
Beauvoir, Simone de 192, 207, 209
Bedore, Pamela 212, 227, 228
Beitchman, Philip 208, 209
Belsey, Catherine 122, 138, 141
Benjamin, Jessica 18, 32, 34, 146, 156, 157, 164, 165
Bennell, Craig 206, 208
Bernheimer, Kate 32, 35
Berran, Bob 34
Betz, Phyllis M. 79
Billman, Carol 57, 59
Bisexuality 2, 3, 5, 57, 60, 200, 205, 232
Bollas, Christopher 157, 164, 165
Bolton, Judy 14, 15, 23, 24, 33, 35
Borossa, Julia 165
Bowen, Rhys 5, 8, 61–80
Brault, Pascale-Anne 165
Bristow, Joseph 209
Broomfield, Nick 207
Browder, Laura 213, 227, 228
Brown, Ellen 50, 59
Brown, Kate E. 175, 188, 189
Brownmiller, Susan 43
Burwell, Hope E. 33, 34
Butch 7, 44, 46, 58
Butler, Judith 5, 12, 81, 93, 99, 100, 152, 164, 165, 182, 188, 189, 207–9, 226

Cain, Chelsea 11, 211, 215, 223, 225, 226, 228
Campbell, Karen 10, 167–9, 175, 178–90

Cannon, Katie 104, 117
Caprio, Betsy 14, 19, 22, 24, 25, 31–3
Carrabine, Eamonn 206, 209
Carter, Eric 165, 166
Casteras, Susan P 49, 59
Caughie, Pamela 212, 228, 228
Cawelti, John G. 63, 79, 80
Chadwick, Carol 33, 34
Chamberlain, Kathleen 37, 43, 57, 58, 59
Chandler, Raymond 123, 211
Chesney-Lind, Meda 163, 164
Christianson, Scott 122, 123, 139, 141
Christie, Agatha 1, 2, 11, 12, 104, 144
Cixous, Hélène 31, 34, 187, 189
Clandfield, Peter 5, 10, 167–90, 231
Clément, Catherine 34
Coale, Samuel 63, 67, 78–80
Cole, Cathy 137, 141
Collins, Patricia Hill 107, 117, 118
Collins, Wilkie 2
Conan Doyle, Sir Arthur 2, 8, 81–3, 85, 94, 96–100
Cornelius, Michael G. 7, 13–35, 37, 57, 59, 231
Corpi, Lucha 79
Cozy 104, 105
Craig, Carol 188, 189
Crocker, Liz 41, 57–9
Cross-Dress 81–6, 91–7, 99, 100, 182

Daly, Kathleen 207
Davis, Carol Anne 206, 207, 209
Davis, Pamela 212, 227, 228
Décuré, Nicole 111, 117, 118
Demme, Jonathan 207
Derrida, Jacques 147, 163, 165
Diehl, Heath A. 9, 120–41, 231
Dillard, J.L. 188
Dilley, Kimberly J. 11, 12, 79, 126, 135, 139–41
Dittman, Volker 206, 209
Dolan, Jill 122, 136, 138–41

233

Dollimore, Jonathan 182, 188, 189
Double Consciousnes 102, 107, 109
Drag 81–3, 87, 94–6, 98, 99, 180–3, 215
Drew, Nancy 13–45, 48–51, 53–60
Du Bois, W.E.B. 107, 108
Dupin, C. Auguste 144
Dyer, Stewart 33, 34

Edwards, Tim 206, 209
Elliott, Winter 3, 11, 211–29, 231
Everitt, David 206

Fairfield, Susan 208, 209
Faulkner, William 213, 229, 229
Femininity 8, 16, 24, 31, 48, 62, 63, 60, 71, 74, 77, 78, 89, 96, 112, 192–4, 196, 203, 204, 211, 213, 216, 218, 220, 226, 231
Femme 44, 46, 57, 59
Ferenczi, Sandor 158, 159, 165
Fessenden, Tracy 59
Fielding, Ruth 14, 15
Fine, Cordelia 207, 209
Fischer, Nancy 208, 210
Fischer-Hornung, Dorothea 103, 116–8
Fitzsimons, Annette 208, 209
Flys-Junquera, Carmen 109, 111, 116–8
Foote, Stephanie 44, 45, 50, 58, 59
Foss, Paul 208, 209
Foucauldian 123, 205
Foucault, Michel 21, 32, 34, 139, 141, 208, 209, 213, 215, 225, 227, 229
Fox, James Alan 206, 209
Freii, Andreas 206, 209
Freud, Sigmund 145, 151, 163, 165, 177
Friedan, Betty 2
Furst, Lillian 162, 165
Furtak, JoAnne 33, 34

Garber, Marjorie 84, 85, 92, 98–100
Garland, Carina 58, 59
Garrido, Hector 29, 34
Gay 3, 5, 50, 57, 60, 203, 221, 231, 232
Germon, Jennifer 208, 209
Gill, C.M. 13, 31, 34
Goeller, Alison D 117, 118
Golden Age 1–4, 10, 144, 231
Goldner, Virginia 207–9
Gooch, Erik 207, 210
Gordon, Colin 139, 141
Gosselin, Adrienne Johnson 78–80, 102, 116, 118
Grafton, Sue 2, 9, 102, 120–41
Grafz, Marc 206, 209
Green, Richard L 99, 100

Gregg, Melanie 32, 34, 57, 59
Gregoriou, Christiana 220, 228
Griffin, Susan 206, 209

Hallet, Martin 57, 59
Hammett, Dashiell 1, 123
Hardboiled (or hard-boiled) 1–3, 6, 7, 9, 11, 12, 78–80, 101–5, 117, 119–23, 126, 136, 139, 140, 144, 167, 168, 212, 214, 222, 227–9
Hare, Robert D. 207
Harris, Laura 41, 57–9
Harris, Thomas 193, 209, 224
Harris, Trudier 107, 112, 113, 115, 117, 118
Hartman, Mary S 164, 165
Heilbrun, Carolyn 24, 33, 35
Hempen, Daniela 19, 32, 35
Herbert, Rosemary 116, 118
Heteronormative 6, 200
Heterosexuality 3, 5, 11, 37, 44, 45, 48, 52, 54, 56, 182, 183, 192, 194, 196, 198, 199, 205, 224
Hindley, Myra 192, 193, 207, 210
Hoffman, Megan 8, 81–100, 231
Homoeroticism 44, 49, 145, 148, 152, 153, 154, 160, 161
Homosexuality 44, 76, 114, 154, 160, 165, 205
Hoodoo (or hoo doo) 9, 108–11, 117, 118
Horsley, Katherine 166
Horsley, Lee 12, 97, 100, 148, 152, 163, 166
Howell, Clare 208, 209
Hughes, Geoffrey 188, 189
Hughes, Gordon 207, 209
Humm, Maggie 89, 99, 100
Hurley, Robert 208, 209
Hutchings, Peter 163, 166

Iganski, Paul 206, 209
Innes, Sherrie A. 31, 33, 35, 37, 43, 44, 48, 51, 56–60
Irons, Glenwood 11, 12, 79, 80, 139, 141, 227, 229

James, Dean 121, 122, 138, 141
James, P.D. 2, 3
Jameson, Anna 49
Jann, Rosemary 83, 84, 94, 99, 100
Jardine, Alice 18, 19, 32, 35
Jenkins, Patty 207
Jenks, Aleta 34
Johnsen, Rosemary 90, 99, 100
Johnson, Patricia E. 122, 139, 141

Index

Jones, Manina 11, 12, 61, 78-80, 117, 119, 135, 140, 141, 218, 228, 229

Karesek, Barbara 57, 59
Kavka, Misha 168, 187, 189
Keehnen, Owen 43, 57, 58, 60
Keeline, James D. 32, 35
Keene, Carolyn 6, 7, 31, 33, 35, 38, 41, 44, 57, 58, 60
Kelleher, C.L. 207, 209
Kelleher, Michael D. 206, 207, 209
Kestner, Joseph A. 83, 85, 94, 95, 99, 100
Kim, Julie H. 1-12, 231
King, Katie 138, 141
King, Laurie R. 5, 8, 81-100
King, Nicola 148, 154, 163, 164, 166
Kinsman, Margaret 220, 228
Klein, Kathleen Gregory 3, 4, 9, 11, 12, 61, 78-80, 102, 116, 118, 121, 138, 141, 212, 213, 221, 226-9
Klein, Melanie 145, 150-4, 163, 165, 166
Kofman, Sarah 158, 165, 166
Krafft-Ebing, Richard von 43
Kuhn, Annette 189
Kushner, Howard I. 175, 188, 189

Lacan, Jacques 147, 160, 165, 166
Laplanche, Jean 163, 204, 208, 209
Lauretis, Teresa de 18, 32, 34
Lawrence, James 31, 32, 34
Lee, Maggie 206, 209
Lennon, Kathleen 208, 209
Lesbianism 3, 5-7, 37, 43, 44, 46, 48, 49, 51, 53, 54, 57, 59, 60, 113, 139, 194, 232
Levin, Jack 206, 209
Levy, Ariel 184, 189
Linton, Patricia 62, 79, 80

MacLeod, Ann Scott 22, 32, 35
Maney, Mabel 7, 8, 36-60
Marsh, Ngaio 1, 2, 144
Marshall, Elizabeth 47, 48, 56, 58-60
Martinsson, Lena 208, 209
Masculinity 10, 26, 27, 42, 66-9, 75-8, 81, 85, 90, 95, 96, 99, 100, 167, 170, 179, 191-4, 196-9, 202-4, 206, 209, 211, 212, 214, 222, 224, 226-8
Mason, Bobbie Ann 24, 33
Massey, Doreen 20, 30, 32, 35
Massey, Sujata 99
McCaw, Neil 10, 11, 191-210, 232
McDermid, Val 3, 10, 11, 191-211, 215-8, 220, 221, 225-9
McGrath, Anne 32, 35

McLaughlin, Eugene 207, 209
McNay, Lois 213, 215, 227, 229
Meeks, Chet 208, 210
Melancholia 143, 145, 147, 149, 151-4, 160, 161, 163, 165
Meloy, Reid 207, 210
Messerschmidt, James 192, 209
Mickenberg, Julia 58, 59
Millet, Lydia 32, 35
Mina, Denise 10, 167-79, 182, 184-90
Mitchell, Jennifer 7, 36-60, 232
Mitchell, Juliet 153, 163, 164, 166
Mizejewski, Linda 224, 228, 229
Mokros, Andrea 206, 208
Morris, Pam 165
Mueller, Monika 103, 113, 116-8
Mullan, John 79, 80
Muller, Marcia 2, 11, 120, 211, 212, 214-6, 221, 225-7, 229
Mulvey, Laura 29, 34, 35, 218, 228, 229
Muncie, John 207, 209
Munt, Sally R. 3, 4, 12, 78-80, 92, 100, 121, 122, 138, 139, 141, 145, 163, 166, 226, 228, 229
Myers, C. 207, 210

Naas, Michael 165
Nash, Ilana 23, 33, 35, 36, 38, 40, 43, 44, 57, 58, 60
Near, Michael 29, 34, 35
Neely, Barbara 5, 8, 9, 99, 101-19
Negra, Diane 163, 183, 187, 189, 190
Nelson, Nancy Owen 33, 34
Nestle, Joan 208, 209
Ng, Andrew 9, 10, 143-66, 232
Nickerson, Catherine Ross 78-80
Nye, Robert A. 205, 208, 210

Oedipal 151, 153

Paretsky, Sara 2, 12, 102, 120, 122, 139, 141, 220, 228
Parry, Sally 23, 24, 33, 35
Parshley, H.M. 207, 209
Patton, Paul 208, 209
Pepper, Andrew 101, 104, 116, 117, 119
Perform (gender) 197, 199
Performance (gender as) 81, 87, 93, 139, 141, 174, 180, 181, 182, 184-6, 193, 195, 205, 131
Performativity (of gender) 84, 98, 195
Perrault, Charles 15-22, 27, 29-33, 35
Phillips, John 164, 165
Phillips, Kathy 104, 113, 117-9

Plain, Gill 1, 10, 11, 12, 144, 162, 166, 167, 187, 190
Plummer, Ken 206, 209
Plunkett-Powell, Karen 15, 31, 32, 35
Postfeminism 3, 6, 7, 10, 167–9, 172, 174, 179, 181–90
Postmodernism 123, 143, 224
Priestman, Martin 116, 119
Psychoanalysis 7, 10, 32, 143, 145, 149, 150, 158, 160, 163, 165

Queerness 43, 50–4
Quin-Harkin, Janet 79

Rankin, Ian 167, 168, 180
Reddy, Maureen T. 9, 11, 12, 63, 64, 69, 75, 79, 80, 102, 103, 107, 108, 111, 115–9, 121, 123, 138, 139, 141, 212, 227, 229
Rehak, Melanie 33
Reimers, Eva 208, 209
Rendell, Ruth 2, 9, 145
Reynolds, Diane 24, 33, 35
Reynolds, Nedra 28, 30, 34, 35
Richetti, John 79, 80
Riviere, Joan 163, 165
Robinson, David 188, 190
Rodgers, Lawrence 213, 227, 229
Rogers, Katherine M. 49, 59, 60
Romalov, Nancy Tillman 33, 35

Salvaggio, Ruth 18, 32, 35
Sayers, Dorothy 1, 2, 144
Scaggs, John 162, 165
Schechter, Harold 206, 210
Schoene, Berthold 187, 190
Schoenfeld, Bethe 135, 138, 140, 141, 213, 227, 229
Schurman-Kauflin, Deborah 206, 208, 210
Second wave (feminism) 2, 121, 122, 138, 141
Seidman, Stephen 208, 210
Siegel, Deborah 31, 35
Simon and Schuster 15, 31, 58, 60
Smith, Andrew 84, 99, 100
Smith, Barbara 114, 118
Smith, Johanna M. 79
Soitos, Stephen 107, 109, 111, 117, 119
South, Nigel 206, 209
Stein, Arlene 206, 210

Stonebridge, Lyndsey 164, 165
Storrs, Elizabeth 207, 210
Strachey, James 163, 165
Stratemeyer Syndicate 31, 38, 44, 57, 59
Stryker, Susan 208, 210
Suttie, Jane Isabel 165
Sutton, Margaret 33, 35

Tasker, Yvonne 168, 183, 187, 189, 190
Tatar, Maria 16, 17, 19, 27, 32, 33, 35
Taylor, Bruce 140, 141
Tey, Josephine 144
Theweleit, Klaus 160, 165, 166
Tickamyer, Ann R. 22, 32, 35
Tomc, Sandra 76, 79, 80
Transgender 3, 5, 57, 60, 202, 203, 208, 210
Transsexuality 201–3, 205
Transvestism 98
Turner, Chris 165, 166

Verhoeven, Paul 206
Vine, Barbara 2, 9, 143–66
Vronsky, Peter 207

Wade, C. 207, 210
Wajnryb, Ruth 188, 190
Walklate, Sandra 212, 227, 229
Walton, Priscilla 11, 12, 61, 78–80, 117, 119, 135, 140, 141, 218, 222, 228, 229
Weeks, Jeffrey 208, 210
Wenzl, Roy 206
West, Candace 207, 210
West, Rosemary 192, 193, 207, 210
Wezner, Kelley 8, 61–80, 232
Whittle, Stephen 208, 210
Wilchins, Riki 208, 209
Williams, Christine 206, 210
Wing, Betty 34
Winks, Robin 79
Winston, Robert P. 170, 188, 190
Woodman, Marion 19, 32, 35
Woolston, Jennifer 36, 39, 48, 57, 58, 60
Wuornos, Aileen 193, 193, 207

Young, Betsy 8, 9, 101–19, 232
Younger, Beth 47, 48, 58, 60

Zangan, Britta 227, 229
Zimmerman, Don H. 207, 210

www.ingramcontent.com/pod-product-compliance
Lightning Source LLC
Chambersburg PA
CBHW051219300426
44116CB00006B/644